URBAN TRANSIT

URBAN TRANSIT
The Private Challenge to Public Transportation

Edited by
CHARLES A. LAVE

Foreword by
JOHN MEYER

Pacific Studies in Public Policy

PACIFIC INSTITUTE FOR PUBLIC POLICY RESEARCH
San Francisco, California

International Standard Book Number: 0–88410–969–0 (CL)
0–88410–970–4 (PB)

Library of Congress Catalog Card Number: 84–21529

Printed in the United States of America

Library of Congress Cataloging in Publication Data

Main entry under title:

Urban transit.

  (Pacific studies in public policy)
  Bibliography: p.
  Includes index.
    1. Local transit—United States—Addresses, essays, lectures.
  2. Paratransit services—United States—Addresses, essays, lectures.
  I. Lave, Charles A. II. Series.
  HE4441.U735 1984   388.4′0973   84–21529
  ISBN 0–88410–969–0
  ISBN 0–88410–970–4 (pbk.)

PACIFIC INSTITUTE
FOR PUBLIC POLICY RESEARCH

The Pacific Institute for Public Policy Research is an independent, tax-exempt research and educational organization. The Institute's program is designed to broaden public understanding of the nature and effects of market processes and government policy.

With the bureaucratization and politicization of modern society, scholars, business and civic leaders, the media, policymakers, and the general public have too often been isolated from meaningful solutions to critical public issues. To facilitate a more active and enlightened discussion of such issues, the Pacific Institute sponsors in-depth studies into the nature of and possible solutions to major social, economic, and environmental problems. Undertaken regardless of the sanctity of any particular government program, or the customs, prejudices, or temper of the times, the Institute's studies aim to ensure that alternative approaches to currently problematic policy areas are fully evaluated, the best remedies discovered, and these findings made widely available. The results of this work are published as books and monographs, and form the basis for numerous conference and media programs.

Through this program of research and commentary, the Institute seeks to evaluate the premises and consequences of government policy, and provide the foundations necessary for constructive policy reform.

PACIFIC STUDIES IN PUBLIC POLICY

Forestlands
Public and Private
Edited by Robert T. Deacon and M. Bruce Johnson
Foreword by B. Delworth Gardner

Urban Transit
The Private Challenge to Public Transportation
Edited by Charles A. Lave
Foreword by John Meyer

Politics, Prices, and Petroleum
The Political Economy of Energy
By David Glasner
Foreword by Paul W. MacAvoy

Rights and Regulation
Ethical, Political, and Economic Issues
Edited by Tibor M. Machan and M. Bruce Johnson
Foreword by Aaron Wildavsky

Fugitive Industry
The Economics and Politics of Deindustrialization
By Richard B. McKenzie
Foreword by Finis Welch

Money in Crisis
The Federal Reserve, the Economy, and Monetary Reform
Edited by Barry N. Siegel
Foreword by Leland B. Yeager

Natural Resources
Bureaucratic Myths and Environmental Management
By Richard Stroup and John Baden
Foreword by William Niskanen

Firearms and Violence
Issues of Public Policy
Edited by Don B. Kates, Jr.
Foreword by John Kaplan

Water Rights
Scarce Resource Allocation, Bureaucracy,
and the Environment
Edited by Terry L. Anderson
Foreword by Jack Hirshleifer

Locking Up the Range
Federal Land Controls and Grazing
By Gary D. Libecap
Foreword by Jonathan R. T. Hughes

The Public School Monopoly
A Critical Analysis of Education and the State
in American Society
Edited by Robert B. Everhart
Foreword by Clarence J. Karier

Resolving the Housing Crisis
Government Policy, Decontrol, and the Public Interest
Edited with an Introduction by M. Bruce Johnson

Offshore Lands
Oil and Gas Leasing and the Environment on the Outer Continental Shelf
By Walter J. Mead, et al.
Foreword by Stephen L. McDonald

Electric Power
Deregulation and the Public Interest
Edited by John C. Moorhouse
Foreword by Harold Demsetz

Taxation and the Deficit Economy
Fiscal Policy and Capital Formation in the United States
Edited by Dwight R. Lee
Foreword by Michael J. Boskin

The American Family and the State
Edited by Joseph R. Peden and Fred R. Glahe

Dealing With Drugs
Problems of Government Control
Edited by Ronald L. Hamowy

Crisis and Leviathan
Critical Episodes in the Growth of American Government
By Robert Higgs
Foreword by Arthur A. Ekirch, Jr.

FORTHCOMING

The New China
Comparative Economic Development in Hong Kong, Taiwan, and Mainland China

Political Business Cycles
The Economics and Politics of Stagflation

Rationing Health Care
Medical Licensing in the United States

Crime, Police, and the Courts

Myth and Reality in Social Welfare

Health Care Delivery Institutions

Rent Control in Santa Monica

Health Insurance: Public and Private

Unemployment and the State

For further information on the Pacific Institute's program and a catalog of publications, please contact:

PACIFIC INSTITUTE FOR PUBLIC POLICY RESEARCH
177 Post Street
San Francisco, California 94108

CONTENTS

List of Figures xv

List of Tables xvii

Foreword
—John Meyer xix

Chapter 1
The Private Challenge to Public Transportation—
An Overview
— Charles Lave 1

Introduction 1
History of the Problem: How We Got Here 3
Solutions to the Problem: Redesigning Service to Cut Costs and
 Increase Patronage 12
Implementation: How Will We Get There From Here? 25
Summary 28

Chapter 2
The Rise and Fall of Monopolized Transit
— George W. Hilton 31

Urban Transit Innovation 32
The Electric Streetcar and Monopoly 34

Transit Industry Problems   38
The Emergence of Motor Carriers   40
Changes in Urban Patterns of Transit   43
The Decline of the Transit Industry   46

Chapter 3
Toward Fragmentation: The Evolution of Public
Transportation in Chicago
— Christine M. Johnson and Milton Pikarsky   49

Preface   49
Introduction   50
From Fragmentation to Monopoly: The Birth of CTA   54
RTA: A New Approach in Public-Private Partnership   58
Traditional Taxi Firms' Financial Problems   65
Solutions for the Future   65
Lessons from the Past and Speculation for the Future   72

Chapter 4
Use of Private Companies to Provide Public
Transportation Services in Tidewater Virginia
—James C. Echols   79

The Impetus for Private Contracting   79
Commuter Services   83
Purchase of Services   84
Elderly and Handicapped Services   85
Shared-Ride Taxi Services   87
Contracting for Services   90
Monitoring Contracted Services   92
Issues Concerning the Use of Private Operators   95
Observations   97
Appendix: Maxi-Ride Services' Request for Bids   99

Chapter 5
Private Commuter Vans in New York
—Jay H. Walder   101

Introduction   101
Mass Transit and Commuter Vans   102

Costs and Revenues of the Existing NYCTA Express Service   107
Passenger Safety and Traffic Congestion   114
Conclusion   118

Chapter 6
Recent Experience with Successful Private
Transit in Large U.S. Cities
— *Edward K. Morlok and Philip A. Viton*   121

Introduction   121
Description of the Case Study Services   123
The Issue of Profitability   132
Service Characteristics   133
Costs   143
The Cream-Skimming Issue   147
Conclusions   148

Chapter 7
Privately Provided Commuter Bus Services:
Experiences, Problems, and Prospects
— *Genevieve Giuliano and Roger F. Teal*   151

Introduction   151
Types of Privately Provided Commuter Bus Services   152
Sources of Subsidies for Private Bus Services   155
Experiences with Privately Provided Commuter Bus Services   156
Economic Issues in the Provision of Private Commuter Bus
   Services   170
Institutional Issues Affecting Privately Provided Commuter
   Bus Services   176
Conclusions   178

Chapter 8
The Taxi in the Urban Transport System
— *Sandra Rosenbloom*   181

Introduction   181
Regulatory Reform of the Taxi Industry   183
The Taxi-Transit Partnership: Contracting for Public Service   193
Conclusions   212

Chapter 9
The Overseas Experience
  — Gabriel Roth   215

Introduction   215
Examples   216
Factors Associated with Successful Systems   220
Conclusion   231

Chapter 10
The Comparative Costs of Public and Private
Providers of Mass Transit
  — Edward K. Morlok and Philip A. Viton   233

Introduction   233
Background   234
Private Versus Public Costs: The Evidence   235
Competition   240
Labor Cost Differences   241
Factor Substitution and Efficiency   244
Scale Economies   245
Peak-Period Costs   247
Concluding Remarks: Forms of Private-Sector Involvement   250

Chapter 11
Redesigning Local Transportation Service
  — C. Kenneth Orski   255

Introduction   255
Sources of Current Problems   256
Options for the Future   261
Service Redesign   262
Making Better Use of Private Providers   265
Expanded Use of Unsubsidized Private Carriers   267
Private Sector Support of Parallel Transportation   268
Separation of Policymaking and Operating Functions   272
Rethinking Transit   274

Chapter 12
Government Policies Affecting Competition
in Public Transportation
—*Michael A. Kemp and Ronald F. Kirby* 277

Background 277
Evolving Problems and Policy Responses 280
The Prospects for More Competitive Urban Public
   Transportation Services 284
Some Broad Directions for Federal Policy 293
Conclusion 297

Chapter 13
Implications of Efficiency Incentives
on Use of Private Sector Contracting
by the Public Transit Industry
—*Anthony U. Simpson* 299

Introduction and Summary 299
Change of Emphasis from Effectiveness to Efficiency 300
Management Objectives and Rewards 302
Public Transit Management's Private Contracting Option 306
Public Transit's Control of the Private Contractor 306
Conclusions and Recommendations 309

Chapter 14
The Private Challenge to Public Transportation
—*C. Kenneth Orski* 311

Introduction 311
Forms of Private Sector Involvement 312
Motivation for Private Sector Involvement 330

Selected Bibliography 333

Index 341

About the Editor 363

About the Authors 365

LIST OF FIGURES

4-1 Tidewater Transportation District Commission, Virginia   81
4-2 TTDC Transit Expenses, Revenues, and Deficit   82

5-1 Map of Staten Island, New York, and New Jersey   103

6-1 Range of Profitability   131
6-2 Average Fare Versus Average Trip Length for Various
U.S. Bus Transit Systems   137
6-3 Average Fare Versus Average Trip Length for Various
U.S. Commuter Rail Systems   139

9-1 Australia: Average Operating Costs per Kilometer for
Public and Private Bus Operators   223

10-1 Typical Patterns of Peaking   248

LIST OF TABLES

4-1 TTDC Characteristics   80
4-2 Provision of Door-to-Door Elderly and Handicapped
     Services by Private Taxi Companies   86
4-3 Alternatives Analysis for Deep Creek, Month of
     July 1979   88
4-4 Comparison of Average Cost Per Vehicle Mile   92
4-5 Monthly Evaluation of Deep Creek Service Change
     to Private Operator   93
4-6 Monthly Evaluation of Ocean View Service After
     Change to Private Operator   94

5-1 Former Mode of Transit for Current Van Passengers   106
5-2 Express Buses at Staten Island Depots   108
5-3 Effect of Closing All Staten Island Express Service   109
5-4 NYCTA Staten Island Express Service Net Revenue   110
5-5 Savings Estimates from Eliminating Staten Island
     Express Routes   111
5-6 NYCTA Staten Island Express Service Marginal
     Revenue Loss   112
5-7 NYCTA Annual Net Revenue by Route   113
5-8 Van Versus Vehicle Trips   116

6-1 Financial Picture   125
6-2 Example of Profitability Analysis   130

6-3 Primary Service Characteristics of Public Transport
     Systems   134
6-4 Selected Level of Service Characterization of U.S. Bus
     Systems   135
6-5 Selected Level of Service Characteristics of U.S. Com-
     muter Rail Systems in 1972   138
6-6 Comparison of Time and Cost of Self-Supporting
     System and Alternative Travel Paths for Selected
     CBD-Oriented Trips   140
6-7 Chicago and North Western Fare Increases, Traffic,
     and the Consumer Price Index, 1969–1974   142
6-8 Bus Cost Comparison   145
6-9 Commuter Rail Cost Comparison   146

7-1 Survey of Private Commuter Bus Service in Seven U.S.
     Metropolitan Areas   154
7-2 MTA Private Operator Contract Revenue   164
7-3 Unit Costs of Regular-Route Express Service   172
7-4 Unit Cost of Subscription, Buspool, and Vanpool
     Service   172

8-1 Taxis per Capita, Selected American Cities   185
8-2 Taxis per Selected Indices of Economic and Tourist
     Activity   187

9-1 Australia: Typical Public and Private Operating Costs   225

10-1 Trends in Transit Costs, 1950–1980   234
10-2 Comparison of Average Costs per Vehicle Mile on
      Private and Publicly Owned Transit Services in
      Various Nations   236
10-3 Examples of Cost or Deficit Reduction from
      Contracting   237
10-4 Driver Costs as a Function of Firm Size and Vehicle
      Size   242

11-1 Workers Using Public Transportation, 1970 and 1980   258

FOREWORD

Cities are constantly undergoing change. Changes in workplace locations are caused by, among other considerations, ever-changing manufacturing, information processing, transportation, and telecommunication technologies. Residential choices are altered not only by workplace changes, but by demographic and income movements as well. All these changes result in constantly shifting transportation patterns. It is, therefore, imperative to understand economic, demographic, and technological forces when planning urban transportation systems. Equally important, it behooves those planning and managing urban transportation systems to retain as many options as possible—since no mortal can really predict the future with all that much assurance.

Of course, some of the broad outlines of what is to come can be foreseen. Specifically, as a city grows in population and income it typically develops from a centralized, high density, compact urban area into a more decentralized, lower density, and larger urban area. As more population is integrated into the city's commercial base and incomes rise, economic pressure is brought to bear on the scarce land available in central areas for commercial and residential uses. The scarcity and higher value of centrally located land induces businesses and residents, in turn, to look outside the established city for available and cheaper land.

One consequence of economic development, then, is that virtually all cities will decentralize. The pace may vary, depending on the city's mix of economic activities, but the trend is otherwise inexorable. As a city decentralizes, with employment and residential population moving away from the city center, the pattern of trips, including commuter trips, will also change dramatically; specifically, the change will usually be from a radial pattern serving a centralized city to a mix of radial, circumferential, and cross-city patterns serving a decentralized city. Instead of having only a radial pattern of trips to be served, a demand will arise for circumferential trips to meet the needs of people living and working outside the central urban area.

Good transport policy thus requires not only flexibility to meet the unexpected, but retention of some modal alternatives that can operate efficiently in relatively small units or at a limited scale. This book is essentially concerned with just these possibilities and, in particular, how these goals can best be achieved by retaining, or promoting, private alternatives to the public transit conventionally found in American cities today.

A more "private" public transit system is, furthermore, very much in accordance with fundamental trends generally shaping urban transportation in cities. To a rough approximation, a city typically progresses through three stages of transport development, which can be characterized as those of (1) animal power; (2) public transportation; and (3) private transportation (with both of the latter two being mechanized). The transitions between these stages are driven by changes in the (1) relative costs of incremental investment in the current dominant or incumbent modes compared to alternative modes; (2) income levels; (3) quality and type of transportation demanded; and (4) the stage of a city's economic development.

The public to private transition has, of course, been completed in most developed countries—and most assuredly in the United States—and is in process in many developing countries as well. While people tend to switch from public to private transport as soon as they can afford the freedom, convenience, and comfort provided by the private car, another force driving this substitution of private for public transport is rising labor costs. Again, as in the case of the transition from animal to mechanized power, the transition from public to private transport substitutes capital for labor and in particular reduces the need for *hired* labor. This can make the automobile a relatively cost-efficient mode of transportation, especially in providing the higher quality of transportation that people tend to seek as their incomes rise. It is almost impossible for conventional public transportation at any cost to match the schedule convenience, flexibility (e.g., combining shopping or personal trips with commuting), privacy, and comfort of the automobile. In particular, noncommuter trips are often most easily (and even sometimes most efficiently) accommodated by use of the private automobile. Once purchased, the incremental cost (especially from a strictly private view) of using the automobile for commutation can be relatively low. In fact, by using the automobile whenever possible, the initial capital or sunk cost in the automobile can be distributed among more trips, thus lowering the total average cost per trip.

The same economic forces that with economic development undermine the role of the domestic servant or household repairman can thus also undermine the economics of public transport. In a modern society, it may simply be cheaper and easier to perform many functions using one's own labor along with methods that either employ more consumer capital or make wholesale substitutions of new machines for old. In domestic service, the consumer capital takes such forms as washing machines, dryers, dishwashers, and so forth. In urban transportation, it takes the form of automobiles. Consequently, unless means are found to improve the relatively poor productivity trends in public transport, the industry's workforce can become an endangered species, much like the household domestic. As an economy develops and incomes rise, the economic system squeezes out the jobs with low marginal productivity in favor of jobs with marginally higher productivity.

In short, increased incomes induce an increase in demand for higher quality transport modes—and therefore in the demand for car ownership. At the same time, the decentralization of the city makes the ownership of a car more attractive and in some cases a necessity (as when public transportation systems fail to provide service). As more and more individuals make the personal investment in an automobile, transportation expectations (comfort, speed, privacy, etc.) change and it becomes increasingly difficult to win automobile users back to public transport. Furthermore, it may often represent a quite inefficient use of resources to even make the attempt.

Unfortunately, a society will never really know whether there are efficient public transit alternatives to the automobile if creative entrepreneurship in transit is largely prohibited—as it is in the United

States today. Most transit in the United States is performed by publicly owned and managed monopolies that have displayed little taste for trying new options, exploring new markets, or otherwise deviating from established ways. Private entrepreneurs in public transit might do little better in meeting the private automobile challenge than the existing public managements of public transit, but it would seem worth the effort to find out. Furthermore, several chapters in this book make a strong argument to the contrary—that private operators would be more efficient and creative. "Privatized" public transit would thus seem to be one more of those many public-private partnerships at least worthy of further exploration, if for no other reason than the existing trends and status quo are so bleak and unpromising.

John R. Meyer
John F. Kennedy School of Government
Harvard University

Chapter 1

THE PRIVATE CHALLENGE TO PUBLIC TRANSPORTATION— AN OVERVIEW

Charles A. Lave

INTRODUCTION

It is no exaggeration to say that public transit's financial problems have reached the crisis stage: Boston, Chicago, New York, Philadelphia, and many other cities have actually threatened to close down transit operations because their deficits are so large. Our transit systems are in need of radical change.

Although transit's financial health has been declining since the early part of the century, the patient seemed viable only fifteen years ago; there was some degree of government capital-assistance, but passenger revenues were sufficient to cover operating costs for the U.S. transit system as a whole. It is the period since then that has seen the precipitous decline in financial health. By 1980, revenues covered only 41 percent of operating costs, and the total deficit was $7.8 billion.

In retrospect, it is clear that misplaced idealism financed by federal subsidies has been a major cause of the problem. Cities were encouraged to take over privately-owned transit systems, with the goal of rationalizing competing services and expanding patronage. Transit managers were encouraged to extend service into areas that were inherently unsuitable for transit. Government funds were used to keep transit fares low for *everyone*, in order to assure access for a few—the poor. And the easy availability of these subsidies encouraged labor unions to ask for high wages and generous working conditions.

Thus we now find ourselves in a situation where transit service is spread into too many low-usage areas, supply costs are too high, and fares are unrealistically low. Two decades of well-intentioned federal subsidies have insulated management from the discipline of the farebox and encouraged the growth of inefficient service. It is no surprise that a number of observers are now proposing a return to various forms of private operation to remedy these problems.

This "privatization" movement is, so far, an uncoordinated and diffuse response to the problem. Even so, transit agencies have taken such uncharacteristic actions as these:

- Faced with the fact that peak-hour service is often the greatest money-loser of the day, some transit agencies have taken action to "shed" peak-hour passengers by promoting carpools, vanpools, and private subscription buses. They have discovered that providers of such alternative services are not competitors who "skim the cream" off their business, but rather they are friends who actually skim the deficit.

- Realizing that public responsibility for a service does not necessarily imply public operation of that service, some transit agencies are contracting out their low-density services to private companies. In addition to providing substantial cost savings for the agencies, these new transit providers perform an even more important role: by increasing the variety and quality of service available, they can attract more commuters out of their cars and into mass transit.

- The most transit-dependent city in the United States, New York, now allows private firms to operate express bus services. These firms not only provide a higher quality of service than the city-operated vehicles, but do so at a profit, and without government subsidy. Even those areas of New York well served by subways are asking to add the new private express bus service as well.

- Some transit agencies have discovered that the special services they operate—transportation for the elderly and handicapped, dial-a-ride, and so forth—actually cost more than conventional taxi fares. So they have begun to contract out such services to private companies, thus producing more service per public dollar.

- Some transit agencies have found that they can save considerable amounts of money by contracting out maintenance of engines, transmissions, brakes, and tires.

We can see from these examples that privatization has a variety of meanings, but that none imply an end to public responsibility. Rather, they suggest new ways of implementing this responsibility. The point is that government can ensure the existence of a service without actually operating it.

HISTORY OF THE PROBLEM: HOW WE GOT HERE

Public transit has been a declining industry for at least fifty years (see Hilton, Chapter 2), in the sense that it has carried a smaller and smaller proportion of urban travelers. However, this long-term decline in patronage did not, in itself, cause operating deficits. Transit districts simply reduced their capacity in step with their patronage, and the industry actually covered its operating expenses until 1968.

The villain responsible for the long-term decline in transit patronage is easy to identify: the increase in per capita income. Higher incomes gave people more freedom of choice and greater ability to do the things they wanted to do. Unfortunately, the things they chose were inimical to mass transit. Higher incomes permitted people to implement their strong desire to get out of cities and live in single-family, detached homes, resulting in the suburbanization of America. Higher incomes permitted people to implement their taste for higher quality transportation and buy automobiles.

The urban society that evolved as a result of increased incomes is inherently difficult for public transit to serve: It is a world of low-density housing and dispersed trip patterns, a world whose inhabitants have little desire for the kind of lowest-common-denominator transportation provided by most transit systems. It has provoked the long-term decline in transit patronage and the shrinkage of our transit systems. And, as in any declining industry, capital equipment was not replaced in a timely manner, maintenance was often deferred, and operations became increasingly unreliable. The financial health of the industry was certainly questionable by the early 1960s, but we did not see the kind of massive deficits that have become commonplace today. It took the well-intentioned intervention of the government to accomplish that.

Societal Goals

In 1964 Congress passed a major program that created the Urban Mass Transportation Administration (UMTA), to revitalize the transit industry. Congress hoped that an infusion of capital funding would restore the physical plant and return the transit systems to healthy operation. But once they were spending money on transit, politicians were tempted to use transit policy as a lever for dealing with a variety of societal problems. Today, the size and range of these tasks is impressive: Transit has been asked to solve congestion and pollution problems by running more service during peak hours, hoping to attract commuters out of cars; it has been asked to ease the mobility problems of the transit dependent by servicing low-density, suburban neighborhoods; and it has even been asked to alleviate poverty by subsidizing the fares of the poor and of senior citizens.

These new social policies created a situation where transit revenue could not keep pace with costs. The artificially *low fares* resulted from two goals: first, to lure commuters out of their cars—which did not work because rising incomes made commuters more sensitive to transit quality than to transit cost; second, to provide low cost transportation for the poor—though it would have been far less costly to subsidize them directly, rather than erecting a low-fare structure to be used by rich and poor alike. The *expanded service* stemmed from government's desire to make transit universally available, even in low-density neighborhoods, where it could not possibly attract enough patronage to cover costs. Perhaps an inherent problem of any publicly run project is the political danger of being asked to solve everyone's pet problem, rather than being allowed to simply function in an efficient manner.

Government Regulation

Government intervention did not begin in 1964, of course. There had always been extensive government involvement with the transit industry, principally concerned with regulation of fares, cross-subsidization of weak routes by strong ones, and control over entry in order to protect the monopoly transit franchise. Nor is such intervention limited to the United States: Writing of the British experience, Martin Wassell notes,

Irrespective of party, politicians have apparently derived an irresistible fascination from meddling in the industry. The escalation of administration regulation, purportedly to correct market 'failure,' has thoroughly politicised a major sector of commercial activity, grossly misallocating scarce and costly resources—not the least being the distraction of management from its proper function.[1]

This kind of government intervention, however, could not produce deficits for the industry as a whole, because it had to allow the private firms to make enough money to survive. If the government dictated that some uneconomic service was to be provided in one part of a system, then it had to allow the resultant deficit to be covered by a larger profit in some other part of the system. The necessity for total revenue to cover total costs ultimately provided some discipline over the kinds of things transit could be asked to do.

There were three major rationales for government regulation. They are worth examining, for they are still used today to justify the regulation of urban transit activities: (1) cross-subsidization of worthy activities; (2) preservation of economies of scale; and (3) coordination of service.

Not one of these rationales stands up under examination. Economists object, on grounds of efficiency, to having strong routes *cross-subsidize* weak ones. Such actions discourage the fullest development of the routes that produce the surplus: these popular routes should be expanded to attract more riders and provide them a higher quality of service. To the extent that the existing fares are high for the sake of cross-subsidization, then these popular routes will be used less than is desirable from society's viewpoint. Furthermore, making the subsidy implicit hides the weak routes and prevents consideration of alternative means of serving these same people, means that might be far more economic, such as "user-side" subsidies.[2]

The economies of scale rationale seems peculiar on both theoretical and empirical grounds. The received theoretical justification goes like this: Transit monopolies are good because there are substantial economies of scale in the industry (that is, big companies are more

1. John Hibbs, *Transit Without Politics* (London: Institute of Economic Affairs, 1982), p. 8.
2. Gabriel Roth and George G. Wynne, *Free Enterprise Urban Transportation* (London: Transaction Books, 1982), pp. 57–58.

efficient and can provide cheaper service for the public), hence government regulation is justified to prevent excess competition and preserve the monopoly operating rights of the existing transit system. One might wonder why a low-cost monopolist needs to be protected against competition from a high-cost interloper. Logic aside, the rationale is fatally flawed by the fact that large transit systems are not more efficient: Most of the empirical studies find that larger firms actually have higher operating costs per vehicle-hour of service.[3]

The coordination rationale stems from the belief that competing private operators would be unable to cooperate enough to form a coherent, citywide transportation network, hence a single regulated monopoly is necessary to assure coordination of service and transfers. Roth (Chapter 9) and Johnson and Pikarsky (Chapter 3) provide counterexamples to this argument. Still, the concern over service coordination persists, probably because it is one of those abstract ideals whose execution is necessarily imperfect compared to our vision of it. Certainly the regulated monopolies do not fulfill it.[4]

In any event it is clear that in the name of providing coordination of services we have often suppressed all forms of competition and innovation. Most cities now have only a single transit provider, producing a single kind of lowest-common-denominator transit service that is not acceptable to very many people, judging by the way they have been voting with their seats (moving on to other forms of transportation). The U.S. transit system, which began in diversity and innovation, has ended in coordinated stagnation.

The Incredible Growth of Transit Subsidies

From its beginning in the nineteenth century until 1968, the transit industry was self-supporting. (There were some city-owned, subsidized transit systems, but most systems were privately operated and

3. See Roth, Chapter 9; Morlok and Viton, Chapter 10; Hibbs, *Transit Without Politics*, p. 41; John Pucher, Anders Markstedt, and Ira Hirschman, "Impacts of Subsidies on the Costs of Urban Public Transport," *Journal of Transport Economics and Policy* 17, no. 2 (May 1983): 173.

4. Michael A. Kemp and Carol T. Everett, "Toward Greater Competition in Urban Public Transportation," Project Report #3025-2 (Washington, D.C.: Urban Institute, 1982), p. 27.

made small profits. Overall, the industry covered its costs.) The incredible growth of the deficit has been a recent phenomenon: In 1968 the overall deficit was only $90 million; by 1980 it had grown to over $7.8 billion. The average transit system was, by then, covering only 41 percent of its operating expenses and essentially none of its capital expenses.[5] It is not easy to make so great a change in so short a time, and most research has pointed to government intervention as the responsible agent: government operating subsidies and the new social policies that accompanied them. This combination initiated a vicious circle of ever-increasing costs and ever-decreasing real fare revenues.[6]

The dynamic set in motion by government involvement has affected transit finances in two major ways. First, it has increased the cost of production: The dollar cost of putting one bus-hour of service on the road has increased far more rapidly than the rate of inflation; transit has become significantly less efficient. Second, it has decreased the revenue from supplying these transit services; the fare revenue collected from a typical bus-hour of service has actually declined, in constant dollar terms. Either of these two major trends—increasing production cost, decreasing income—would have been sufficient by itself to cause major financial problems. Worse than that, they occurred simultaneously. The next sections explore why this happened.

The Rise in Transit Production Costs. Since the UMTA programs began, the average cost of providing a vehicle-mile of service has more than doubled, even after taking out inflationary effects.[7] An easier statistic to grasp is that many of our major transit systems now spend $50 to $60 to put a bus on the road for one hour of useful service;[8] this is just the operating cost, no capital charges are in-

5. Pucher et al., "Impacts of Subsidies on the Costs of Urban Public Transport," p. 156.

6. F. V. Webster, "The Importance of Cost Minimisation in Public Transport Operations," TRRL Supplementary Report 766 (Crowthorne, England: Transport and Road Research Laboratory, 1983); Pucher et al., "Impacts of Subsidies on the Costs of Urban Public Transport"; and Shirley Anderson, "The Effect of Operating Subsidy and Transit Tax Financing on Performance in the Bus Transit Industry, 1975-81," *Proceedings of the Transportation Research Forum, 1983* 24 (in press).

7. Pucher et al., "Impacts of Subsidies on the Costs of Urban Public Transport," p. 158.

8. Urban Mass Transportation Administration. *National Urban Mass Transportation Statistics: 1981 Section 15 Report.* Report #UMTA-MA-06-0107-83-1. Washington, D.C., November 1982.

cluded. The rapid rise in operating costs is attributable to three major causes: (1) the cost of transit's factors of production, especially labor, has risen much faster than the rate of inflation; (2) management has been asked to concentrate on expanding service rather than worrying about ways to keep the operation economically efficient; and (3) the new kinds of services that transit has begun are inherently expensive to operate.

The Increasing Cost of Transit's Factors of Production. Roughly 80 percent of transit's operating cost is wages and salaries, and for much of the recent past, they have been rising faster than labor costs in comparable occupations and faster than other public sector jobs. They have certainly outpaced any change in labor productivity.[9] The evidence shows that these disproportionate wage gains occurred as a result of the government subsidies and that a significant fraction of the government's operating subsidy money has leaked out into higher wages for transit labor and management.[10] Perhaps labor felt able to ask for more, so long as the government was footing the bill, and management felt less reluctant to fight about it.

Federal intervention has also increased the price of transit vehicles over this period. Frequent redesigns, addition of extra features, reduction of management's freedom to select the most economical vehicle, and the resultant decrease in supplier competition have all acted to increase vehicle prices. This process hit a peak with the UMTA-designed "Transbus," which was so complicated that manufacturers refused to bid for the right to produce it.

The Change in Management Incentives. Government subsidies (local, state, and federal) have had three negative effects. First, they tend to reduce concern over providing the most efficient possible operation: Once freed of the customary business standard—"cover your costs"—it is hard to know what cost objectives should be at-

9. Kemp and Everett, "Toward Greater Competition in Urban Public Transportation," p. 12; Charles A. Lave, "Dealing with the Transit Deficit," *Journal of Contemporary Studies* 4, no. 2 (Spring 1981).

10. Anderson, "The Effect of Operating Subsidy and Transit Tax Financing"; Pucher et al., "Impacts of Subsidies on the Costs of Urban Public Transport"; Webster, "The Importance of Cost Minimisation"; and Don H. Pickerell, "The Causes of Rising Transit Operating Deficits." Urban Mass Transportation Administration, Report MA-11-0037. July 1983. (Unpublished.)

tended to. Second, the whole range of new societal goals that government has imposed on transit has led management to a primary concern with the maximization of total service, rather than the efficiency with which that service is provided. The implicit compact between government and transit is something like "Don't quibble about the cost of doing all these things, we'll cover the deficit; just get those buses out there and help solve society's problems." Third, the dependence on growing subsidies leads management to maximize the willingness of the region's voters to spend tax monies on transit subsidies. This translates into attempts to maximize riders—potential voters for subsidies—even to the extent of giving rides away (as to senior citizens during mid-day hours). It further leads to opposing efforts to expand other forms of transport that may be very desirable socially, but which might draw some riders from transit (for example, van-pools and subscription buses).

The Introduction of New, Expensive Kinds of Service. There are a whole host of changes that could be cited here, but the two most important ones were the expansion of bus routes into low-density suburbs and the increased attention to peak-hour commuters. Suburban service is inherently more expensive per hour of effective operation: The initial "deadhead" run from the storage garage out to the start of the line is much longer; furthermore, the flow of passengers tends to be very strongly one-directional during peak commute hours, hence half of each run is inherently unproductive time.

The growth and expense of peak-hour service. Our current system of radially-oriented transit routes really is suited only to one kind of passenger, the commuter traveling to a downtown job. Thus it is no surprise 'hat, over time, such passengers have become an increasing proportion of the total. Transit managers think of the peak as the "cream" of their operation, and they operate two to four times as many buses during the peak hour as they do at midday. But it is this high peak/base ratio that causes one of transit's most interesting paradoxes: The peak hour is certainly the time when buses and labor are being fully utilized and are collecting the most revenue, but it is also the time when operating costs are disproportionately high.

Imagine you are a transit manager, planning to expand peak-hour service. First, you have to buy another bus, which you will only use four to five hours per day. Second, you must hire an extra driver, who will only be utilized four to five hours per day. But standard union work rules not only guarantee the driver eight hours of pay, they also require you to pay him extra for the inconvenience of driving a split shift. Your extra commuter run is going to cost nine hours of pay for four to five hours of actual bus service. Thus is born the major characteristic of modern transit systems: most resources are underutilized most of the time. When the unusually high operating costs of the peak are taken into account, it turns out that peak-hour service is actually a substantial money loser. (Morlok and Viton, Chapter 10, discuss this further.)

"Skimming the cream." Since transit managers have believed that peak-hour service is their best moneymaker, they have strongly opposed any form of private transit that might take away their peak passengers, claiming this would skim the cream off their operations. The fact is, however, that rather than skimming the cream, private transit would be stealing the deficit. Public transit could cut back on its money-losing, peak-hour runs if some current passengers would switch to private transit. (Although reducing peak service is easy to do on normal routes, it may be difficult to make cutbacks on lightly traveled routes with long headways.) Put in different words, since peak-hour passenger fares do not cover the cost of service, government's promotion of additional peak-hour service (or its reluctance to shed some of its peak load to private providers) is rather like the joke about the retailer who lost money on every sale, but made it up on volume.

The Decline in Transit Revenue. There has been a substantial decline in transit revenue caused by two factors: the expansion of transit service into markets with few potential passengers, and the reluctance to raise transit fares in line with inflation. That is, both passengers-per-bus and revenue-per-passenger have declined.

Transit's Expansion into the Wrong Markets. In the late 1960s, there was a general feeling that transit ought to be expanded and given a chance to show what it could do in areas that had never had service before. There was also a desire to give suburban dwellers some return on their tax dollars and to encourage transit's political constituency. New transit districts were created, and old ones were expanded out into the suburbs. Unfortunately these new districts and new routes failed, in the sense that they attracted comparatively few riders. While the intentions behind the expansion were noble, its failure was not a surprise and could have been predicted from a simple look at the transit market. Before embarking on major transit expansion ventures, we need to recall that transit was once a profitable business, with entrepreneurs competing fiercely to establish transit lines in any area where there was even the hint of enough patronage to generate a profit; the areas they ignored—small, diffuse cities and suburbs—were areas whose low density and chaotic trip patterns were inherently unsuitable for transit. Thus it required no special crystal ball to predict that the attempt to put new transit systems into these areas would fail, and that passenger load factors would be unusually low.

The Decline in Transit Fares. In 1967 the average bus fare was 22.4 cents; by 1980 this had risen to 37.5 cents, a 67 percent increase.[11] During this same period the consumer price index rose by 147 percent, more than twice as fast as fares. (By comparison, transit operating expenses rose by 319 percent over this period, roughly five times faster than fares.) We know from the enormous current deficit that fares did not keep up with expenses, but what is surprising is that they did not even come close to keeping up with inflation; in real dollar terms, fares were about a third lower in 1980 than they were in 1967.

The reluctance to raise fares stems from two main causes. First, since most transit directors are elected officials or are responsible to elected officials, they are particularly sensitive to the political outcry that occurs whenever fare increases are discussed. Second, there is an idealistic reluctance to raise fares, which stems from a confusion about the new societal goals discussed earlier. Fares were kept low for everyone to assure that the poor could afford public transit; thus subsidizing rich and poor alike. Imagine that the Great Society programs had been concerned with the rising price of food over this same period and had decided to subsidize food prices for everyone in order to assure that the poor could afford a wide range of food. Such an indiscriminate food-subsidy program is obviously nonsense, but no one thinks it strange that we do this in the transit industry. A better solution is to target transit subsidies to the needy, in the manner of food stamps. There are some transit agencies now that follow this user-side subsidy approach (see Kemp and Kirby, Chapter 12).

11. APTA, *Transit Fact Book.*

Relative Contribution to the Deficit
from the Different Sources

We have discussed a variety of causes of the transit deficit, and it is important to have some sense of their relative significance. A recent analysis by Pickerell for the period 1970–1982 provides the following breakdowns: The trend toward increasing production cost produced 68 percent of the growth in deficits; and the trend toward decreasing fare revenue produced 28 percent of the growth—16 percent from service expansions that could not pay their own way, and 12 percent from declining real fare levels.[12] (The remaining 4 percent comes from declining demand for transit service.)

Privatization can provide a strong counterforce against these trends. Transit agencies can reduce operating costs by contracting out service on lightly used lines, or by contracting for supplemental service during peak periods to permit reduction in their own peak/ base ratio. Opening up entry to allow self-supporting private firms into the transit market would also be a step toward these two goals and would have the added benefit of increasing the variety of services available to commuters, hence increasing the overall size of the transit market. These solutions are discussed at greater length in the next section.

SOLUTIONS TO THE PROBLEM—REDESIGNING SERVICE TO CUT COSTS AND INCREASE PATRONAGE

Most public discussion of transit's fiscal crises has focused on the two most obvious solutions: raising fares and cutting back low-volume service. Such solutions are simple to advocate, but nearly impossible to implement. There are always an impressive number of people who will show up at transit board meetings to protest the cutback of their route ("How will I be able to travel?") or to protest the increase in fares ("How can I afford such prices?"). These protests make provocative human-interest news and tend to receive broad media coverage, complete with sympathetic pictures of senior citizens, and sad

---

12. Pickerell, "The Causes of Rising Transit Operating Deficits."

quotations about the expected hardships that will occur when the new policy is implemented. It is no surprise that most such protests succeed, and that the proposed fare and service changes are quietly forgotten.

It is much easier for all the actors directly concerned to agree instead that what is needed is more money to bail out the system, and so they assume that public transportation needs ever-increasing subsidies to survive. But, as pointed out by the International City Management Association (ICMA), this "assumption is true only if policymakers continue to hold transit hostage to traditional, rigid notions of what public transit service is and how it should be provided." [13] ICMA advocates an alternative solution: supply transportation services in a more efficient manner by making much greater use of the private sector and by ending the public transit monopoly. The increased private participation can take two general forms: (1) expand contract services by having the public system hire a private operator to take over some service that it used to provide; (2) allow the growth of self-supporting private services that can develop new markets or supplement existing ones. What is needed is not new funds, but better use of existing ones; and, above all else, more flexible policies toward private sector participation.

One of the principal theoreticians of the service redesign movement (that is, providing more service with less money through increased use of private producers) is Ted Kolderie of the University of Minnesota. He points out the major distinction between government as the *provider* of services versus government as the *producer* of services. The former role involves such traditional government functions as deciding what is necessary for the common good and collecting taxes to pay for it; the latter role involves the actual production of the services. There is no inherent reason why the government must perform both roles, and Kolderie focuses on the ways in which private firms can be utilized to take over service-production, hence engaging the force of competition to keep down costs and increase efficiency. [14]

He also notes the striking parallel between public debate over today's transit crises and the energy crises of 1973: Following the

13. Paula Valente, "Final Report" (Washington, D.C.: Internation City Management Association, 1983). (Unpublished.)

14. Ted Kolderie, "Rethinking Public Service Delivery," *Public Management* 64 (October 1982).

large increase in oil prices, the problem was characterized as "Should we spend more money on energy, to maintain current standards of consumption, or should we cut back on the amount of energy provided?" The same two narrow alternatives, increasing subsidy versus cutting service, are suggested in most discussions of the transit problem. The third alternative, increasing efficiency to do more with what is available, is ignored by public policy debates, both then and now. Just as promoting energy efficiency turned out to be the best solution then—increasing auto MPG, insulating homes, turning to more efficient industrial processes—so we ought to concentrate on ways to increase transit efficiency now.

The next section focuses on the potential use of private contractors to take over existing services, and cut costs. The following section will focus on increasing the diversity of transit services available so as to expand the total transit market and attract more commuters away from cars.

Privatization to Increase Efficiency— Contracting-Out Existing Services

Some public transit agencies have wholeheartedly embraced the concept of cost savings through private contracting. Tidewater Transit in Virginia is an outstanding example (see Echols, Chapter 4), as well as the examples that follow. Although these transit agencies have encountered some implementation problems, as with any innovation, they have achieved very substantial cost savings.

The City of Phoenix has a conventional, fixed-route, fixed-schedule bus system (Phoenix Transit). But it supplements this system in a variety of innovative ways through the use of contracts with a private taxi company. In some low-density areas, it employs taxis as a dial-a-ride feeder service to its regular bus routes—the taxis cost the city $16.69 per vehicle-hour, while using its own buses for this service would have cost $36.85 per vehicle-hour. In other low-density areas, the city has the taxi company operate minibuses on a regular fixed-route basis—the contracted minibus service costs it $1.22 per vehicle-mile (operating cost only), compared to $2.86 for its own Phoenix Transit vehicles. Because of very low potential patronage, Phoenix Transit does not operate on Sundays, though there has been recent public demand to begin such service. Management estimated that it would cost about $900,000 a year to add Sunday service. Instead it contracted with a taxi company to provide a subsidized dial-a-ride service on Sundays, at a cost to Phoenix of only $100,000 a year, hence saving $800,000.[15]

The Peninsula Transit District Commission (PenTran) in Virginia provides another example of the use of public-private partnerships. To give some idea of its flexible attitude in providing transportation services, PenTran even encouraged private operators to begin bus and van service on some of its own routes and helped them undertake route expansions demanded by the public.

PenTran's major effort focuses on employer-based ridesharing. It surveys employment sites, compiles detailed information on the commuting needs of individual workers, and then uses computer matching to find groups with similar characteristics. Employees at these sites are given a list of people who live near them and have the same work hours. PenTran also fully surveys transportation options at each work site: car-, van-, and buspools; rescheduled and extended PenTran bus lines; and even recommendations for flextime, park-n-ride lots, priority parking, and ridesharing incentive programs. PenTran provides the vanpool vehicles, insurance coverage, and maintenance, if that is desired. (PenTran leases these vans from Tidewater Transit, its innovative neighbor; see Echols, Chapter 4.)

The results of this effort have been excellent: Ridesharing has grown from 25 percent to 33 percent of work trips in two years (going against a nationwide trend in the other direction); transportation accessibility has risen substantially; and PenTran's own peak/base ratio has fallen, thus increasing the efficiency of its conventional bus service. PenTran's workforce is now smaller, but this is only through attrition; No workers were laid off.[16]

The Southeastern Michigan Transportation Authority (SEMTA) in Detroit finances and operates a number of transit services: It is the funding agency for the conventional bus system in Detroit; it operates an extensive line-haul bus network from Detroit's suburbs to

15. Interview with Ed Colby, Phoenix Public Transit Administrator, June 1983. Colby is now General Manager of the Denver Regional Transit District.

16. ICMA (1983), pp. 43–48.

downtown and an extensive minibus network within the suburbs; it contracts out a variety of services to private transit operators; and it even operates a user-side subsidy program in one small city. SEMTA makes extensive use of contracting in its nontransit operations: 96 percent of the money spent on facilities maintenance — towing, snow plowing, building maintenance, and so on—goes to outside contractors. It also contracts out major portions of its vehicle maintenance: brake work, body panel repairs, tire maintenance, and major retrofits and repairs. SEMTA's Rachel Shrauner notes, "If a job is of the kind where you can assure quality control from an outside firm, then it's worth sending out."[17] This last point merits further attention, and we turn now to a discussion of implementation problems.

Contracting Is Not Simple

Although the political decision to begin contract service is the major problem, it is not the only problem. Actual implementation of the contracts requires considerable thought. Three main kinds of problems can arise: First, there may be relatively few firms willing to bid; second, the contract must have a reasonable balance between monitoring by the transit district and freedom of action for the contractor; and third, the contractors may require some guidance and advice in the early stages. Obviously, such problems can be overcome, as illustrated by the examples in this book.

Seeking private contractors for transportation services is not like asking for bids on typewriters. The private transportation market has been suppressed for so long that there are comparatively few potential suppliers. Moreover, until these suppliers have gained some experience in dealing with public agencies, they will need to be encouraged to bid: Contracts have to be explained to them, and specifications need to be stated in ordinary language. Most of the potential bidders are, after all, small operators who are likely to be frightened away by the typical fifty- to one-hundred-page document that transit agencies use in dealing with major suppliers. And most of these small bidders have little administrative experience: They run tiny operations, with relatively informal bookkeeping and controls. They may require some administrative guidance in the early stages of the

17. Interview with Rachel Shrauner, Director of Operations, November 1983.

contract service. (Echols, Johnson and Pikarsky, and Rosenbloom discuss such situations in their respective chapters.)

SEMTA's Michael Dewey notes, "Hiring a private company to do what it already knows how to do will be cheaper, but asking it to undertake new service may not be. What works well on a small scale may fall apart when expanded. At some point it takes more than just hard work—administrative skills are also needed."[18] That is, the transit agency may have to make a small investment in nurturing the development of the private transit infrastructure, but it is an investment that should pay handsome returns. Johnson and Pikarsky, discussing the role of the Regional Transit Association (RTA), in Chapter 3, put it this way, "We believe that an RTA-type institution can play an invaluable facilitating role. In this role the RTA would be accountable for conserving our mobility resources and developing new ones. It would be charged with the Solomon-like balance between regulatory market protection and the introduction of innovation."

Private Does Not Necessarily Mean Efficient

As a final point here, it is important to note that the relevant factor for producing cost savings is not private versus public, but rather competitive versus noncompetitive. A privately operated firm can be both inefficient in economic terms and unresponsive to public demand in quality terms. The monopoly private transit firms in most cities thirty years ago are an obvious example: They may have complained about the public regulatory commissions, but they welcomed the monopoly status that the regulations conferred—protected markets and insulation from the threat of competition. As economist John Hibbs comments, ". . . private businesses are not immune from the desire for a quiet life."[19] It is competitive pressure that forces them to be efficient and responsive, and the promotion of competition should be our goal.

---

18. Interview with Michael Dewey, Manager of Small Business and Paratransit Operations, November 1983.
19. Hibbs, *Transit Without Politics*, p. 69.

Privatization to Increase Patronage – Improving
the Variety of Transit Services

Thus far the focus has been on increased efficiency, achieved through contract service *controlled by the existing public transit agency.* We now examine the issues associated with opening up entry in the transit market to allow *independent* services. To the extent that these new services take passengers from the existing conventional system, they can save public money because the conventional system can reduce its (money-losing) service. Moreover, in addition to reducing the transit deficit these new transit providers can perform an even more important role: They can increase the variety and quality of transit available, and hence attract more people out of their cars.

It is important to remember that transit did not lose passengers because of its deficits; it lost passengers because it did not provide the kind of service they desired. Few other sectors of our economy offer consumers such a uniform, mediocre product. By allowing alternative transit services, we can increase the choices available to the public, offering new combinations of price and quality, to lure them out of single-person automobiles. (Frank Davis discusses the practical problems involved in producing alternative transit services. See Selected Bibliography.)

The idea of competing, self-supporting transit systems is not a utopian vision. It is a description of the way public transportation used to function. For example, Chicago once had thirty private mass-transportation companies, ten railroads, plus an assortment of taxi, jitney, and livery companies.

When we look out upon the everyday world of consumer products, there is an appearance of diverse, seemingly disorganized activity. For instance, within fifteen miles of this typewriter I can find thirty-seven different stores that sell washing machines, peddling forty-three different models over a wide range of prices. How should I react to this? Should I be appalled at the seeming chaos, and suggest that the whole thing could use a good dose of coordination? Or should I rejoice in the variety of goods available to me, and marvel at the process that got so many useful things manufactured and delivered correctly, in anticipation of my possible purchase?

These questions can serve as a kind of inkblot test to reveal the predilections of the old-fashioned transit planner – someone who perceives diversity as waste, rather than as opportunity. The rationale of coordination has been used to justify the consolidation of many diverse, private transportation providers into a single, consolidated system owned and operated by the government.

Johnson and Pikarsky (Chapter 3) show how the single-minded pursuit of coordination has affected Chicago's transportation history. Its public transport was once fragmented, diverse, and highly innovative. The formation of the Chicago Transit Authority consolidated all these diverse companies into one rigid system. This coordinated monolith has lost its vitality, its control over costs, and even its ability to adapt to external changes: A majority of the routes have not changed since the 1920–1930 period despite major shifts in population. Finally, unification gave the transit unions a high degree of monopoly power, enabling them to shut down the *whole* system during disputes, and the rise in wages and the fall in productivity can be traced partly to this.

The current organization of U.S. mass transportation is only an accident; it is not the result of some inevitable historic process. There are many other ways transit could have evolved, and we can see examples of these alternatives throughout the rest of the world, or by examining our own past.

- Transit need not be publicly owned. Private ownership and operation was the rule in the United States until twenty years ago.

- Transit need not be organized on a monopoly basis, with a single provider for an entire region. Many U.S. cities grew up with multiple providers, and these different companies competed strongly for business. Other sectors of the economy accept competition as an essential ingredient in a market—even other sectors within transportation.

- Transit need not be limited to conventional buses and rail cars. The largest source of public transit rides in the United States is the ordinary taxi cab. Taxis not only carry more total passengers than standard buses or trains, they even carry more poor passengers.[20]

- Transit need not be a uniform homogenous product—a ride on a standard bus. Just as we have different combinations of fares and

20. See Rosenbloom, Chapter 8 in this volume.

amenities in air travel and intercity trains, we can do so in public transit as well. This does not necessarily mean multiple-class operation in each bus. It merely means that we allow multiple classes of transit to operate in the same city.

Competition and diversity can be powerful forces for improving transit. Because private companies showed the way (see Chapters 5 and 6), New York City now offers a choice of expensive/high-quality express bus rides or cheap/low-service subway rides. In doing so it is increasing the size of the transit market by attracting new users. Obviously, there is room for other similar services, each tailored to the requirements of a particular market niche, each adapting to provide the kind of service and fares its customers desire.

The problem with such self-supporting systems is that they are small, and hence many of them are required. From the viewpoint of the transit planner, it seems easier to start one new consolidated service than to rely on hundreds of vanpool operators or jitney drivers. It is hard to believe that a complex task can be accomplished via hundreds of small decisions, though this is exactly the way the energy crises were solved. In the midst of the grand government debate over which large-scale public policy actions might produce the desired result, most individuals simply got busy: They insulated their houses, bought more fuel-efficient cars and appliances, and so forth. Ultimately, it was the sum of these individual actions that alleviated the energy crises, a totally unexpected result from the standpoint of the government policy planners.

There are other general lessons to be learned from the history of the energy problem, lessons that tell us how we might facilitate a solution to the transit problem. As Kolderie notes, energy efficiency solutions were created in an environment that was " . . . largely private; very diverse, with many points of decision; driven by incentives rather than by command; partly professional and partly non-professional work; lots of opportunity for individuals to make different tradeoffs between costs and service; not a lot of decision-making through the political process."[21]

---

21. Ted Kolderie, "Many Providers, Many Producers," Hubert H. Humphrey Institute of the University of Minnesota, 1982. (Unpublished.)

The Municipal Bread Company:
A Fable For Our Times

We have lived with the monopoly transit system for so long that it seems to be the only possible way transit services can be provided. We now regard as natural a system where a single company provides all the transit service in a given area, and any competition from rival forms of public transportation is forbidden; where a single kind of transit service—large vehicles operating with fixed routes and fixed schedules—is supplied, where an identical, uniform, mediocre product is the only option.

Imagine a world that provides bread the way we provide public transit. First, the government of each city buys up all the private bread companies and establishes a monopoly provider, the Municipal Bread Company:

> We did it for the public good. We can provide cheaper bread because we will have a single, coordinated bakery and delivery system, thus eliminating duplication of services. We can also control quality standards directly to assure that the public gets what it is paying for, and to assure that there will always be bread available when people want it.

Next, the government selects a single, standard type of bread:

> We have concentrated on the kind of bread that is the most acceptable to the most people (fluffy white bread) and eliminated the wasteful redundant products; we will even sell it in a single size, the giant economy version.

They price the bread inexpensively:

> Since good bread is necessary for everyone, we want to make it cheap enough so that the poor can afford it.

Of course, some malcontents begin complaining that they don't like the one kind of bread produced by the Municipal Bread Company, and soon total sales start to fall off. Then some gypsy bakers begin providing their own black-market bread, and sales of Municipal Bread fall even more. There is now a financial deficit:

> We cannot raise prices since that would hurt the poor; what we will do instead is cut quality a little bit. We will also begin selling advertising rights— "Put your message on the side of our Bread, millions see it daily." Perhaps we will try some technological innovations as well: If we had automatic slice-

counters in each home's breadbox, radioing the information to our central computer, we would always know how much Municipal Bread was in service and could adjust production to match use better."

Such a situation is, of course, ridiculous. We don't have government regulations holding down the price of bread in order to protect the poor, rather we subsidize them directly. Keeping the price low for an entire society in order to protect a small part of it is truly having the tail wag a dog. Likewise, we know that different people like different kinds of bread, so we allow many combinations of price and quality. We don't get upset if someone tries to market a higher quality of bread at a higher price, and no one accuses the new company of trying to "skim the cream" off of society's basic bread service.

Yet we think it reasonable to do all these strange things in the transit industry. We insist on a single, monopoly provider, with a single, uniform standard of service that is pegged to someone's notion of what the majority will accept. Why should it be surprising, then, that people choose to desert such a lowest common denominator product?

Open Entry: Implementation Issues

Supposing that we do liberalize entry restrictions, there are two basic questions to be examined: Will the private sector respond to the opportunities, and how will the publicly operated systems respond to the new entrants?

Private Sector Response. Advocates of open entry point to the favorable experience of other countries with liberalization. Of the various possible examples, the experience of the United Kingdom is perhaps the most relevant to our situation. The Transport Act of 1980 substantially liberalized entry controls throughout Britain: For long-distance express coach service, the act abolished essentially all regulations except for those concerning safety; for local services, the act liberalized entry restrictions on subscription buses and other forms of commercial ridesharing arrangements. The private sector responded well to the new opportunities: " . . . roughly 200 new long-distance express coach services were in operation or planned within four months of the passage of the Act. . . . Roughly a dozen firms were providing subscription commuter services into London, and there was evidence of a growing number of small new firms providing services in the provinces.[22] (An interesting side effect here was the change in the National Bus Company, itself. It responded to the private challenge by improving and dramatically increasing its own long distance services, and is doing well despite the private competition. Once again, we see that the issue is not public versus private, but rather the responsiveness of competition versus the inertia of monopoly.)

Judging by the data from the other chapters of this book, such positive responses are not unusual, but there will also be situations where the response of the private sector will be relatively minimal, especially in smaller urban areas—the private transportation infrastructure may simply have atrophied. And even when the private capacity is present, it may be reluctant to enter the transportation market in competition with a hostile and subsidized public agency.[23]

Public Sector Response.   The recent history of Express Transit District (ETD), a private company in Los Angeles, provides an example of how things can go wrong. ETD applied for permission to start a jitney service in Central Los Angeles, which is in the main service area of the Southern California Rapid Transit District (SCRTD). The SCRTD fare was 85 cents and was expected to rise to $1.25 because of its financial problems. ETD planned a $1.00 fare.

During the course of the long approval process, there was a fresh influx of subsidy money into SCRTD, and it lowered its fare to 50 cents in order to increase patronage. ETD was forced to match this lower fare and so, instead of becoming a financially healthy firm at $1.00 per ride, it became a financially shaky firm at 50 cents per ride. SCRTD receives a subsidy of 69.1 cents per passenger on top of its 50-cent fare; ETD received no subsidy whatsoever and was therefore in an inherently difficult position.

It is clear that SCRTD had little appreciation of how it might be helped by ETD: Given SCRTD's 69.1-cent subsidy per passenger, any diversion of passengers to ETD would actually have helped reduce SCRTD's deficit—assuming, of course, that SCRTD would

22. Kemp and Everett, "Toward Greater Competition in Urban Public Transportation," p. 25.

23. Roger Teal, Mary Berglund, and Terry Nemer. "Urban Transportation Deregulation in Arizona," *Transportation Research Record* (in press).

have cut back its own service as ETD took up more of the peak load. SCRTD's misunderstanding is clear in an interview with its planning director, who was explaining his opposition to ETD: "Instead of attempting to tap new riders, they appear to be vying for our market."[24]

At the height of its operation, ETD carried 6,500 passengers per day, but it could not survive against SCRTD's subsidized 50-cent fare and eventually went out of business. Commuters lost their opportunity to use the new system, taxpayers lost their chance to reduce the amount of money being spent on transit subsidies, and the public lost a chance to reduce traffic congestion (ETD's fast, high-quality service could eventually have attracted a substantial number of auto-users).

Obviously none of these results were intended; the public's decision to subsidize transit was only an attempt to make it more attractive to potential riders. But the resultant low fare has created a situation where self-supporting alternative services cannot survive, despite being more cost efficient than the public operator. The public subsidy serves as a deterrent to competition and prevents the development of the kind of alternative-service providers who might be genuinely effective at luring people out of cars.

The implication of the story is not that we should forbid government subsidies, but rather that we should consider subsidizing an industry rather than a *single* operator; for example, pay *any* transit provider 30 cents per passenger, thus permitting a competitive supply situation. Given some innovative approaches to subsidy setting and disbursement, the question of subsidization is completely separable from the question of competitive provision of services.[25]

Evaluation. The effort to preserve public transit has concentrated on a single feature—its price—but we have carried this policy as far as it can go. It is time to think about the other determinant of consumer demand—product quality. New kinds of transportation need to be provided, with a variety of price and quality levels. The case studies in this book show that some of these new services would be of higher quality than is available now; but some would also be of

24. *Los Angeles Times*, 27 December 1982, Part II, p. 3.

25. Michael A. Kemp, Carol T. Everett, and Frank Spielberg, "The Prospects for Public Transportation in U.S. Cities," Project Report #3025-1 (Washington, D.C.: Urban Institute, 1982), p. 59 ff.

lower quality with lower prices. If we want to expand the market for transit services, we must expand the variety of services available. There is evidence that potential users will be quite responsive to such changes.

It is possible that some of these new transit services can be invented by the existing public operators but, given their protected monopoly status, they have little incentive to do so. The handful of innovative operators discussed in this book stand out as the exception rather than the norm; it seems optimistic to believe that we can get others to follow their good example. It is far more likely that significant development of innovative services will require more than the addition of new, private companies. The diversity of ideas inherent in a system of multiple providers and multiple managements is likely to be a far more powerful creative force.

IMPLEMENTATION: HOW WILL WE GET THERE FROM HERE?

The Goals

This book discusses two distinctly different goals for our transit systems:

1. Increase efficiency to reduce deficits, by contracting out some services;
2. Increase variety to attract more patronage, by relaxing some entry controls.

The first goal concentrates on saving money: Subsidies will be reduced because contract service costs less than the publicly operated service that it replaces. The second goal concentrates on increasing the *total* number of people who use some form of public transportation: Patronage on conventional systems may decline, but overall transit patronage will increase as the new kinds of transit providers attract new people away from single-person auto travel. This will reduce transit deficits as well, since the conventional system will be able to cut back on its money-losing services as the new providers increasingly take up more of the overall burden.

What these two goals have in common is the principle of increasing the degree of competition in the transit industry. Increased competition, in the form of bidding for contracts, provides an incentive to increase cost efficiency; and increased competition, in the form of multiple providers of transit services, provides an incentive to discover the kinds of services that might lure people out of cars. Both goals also share a concern about preserving public transportation to assure the continued viability of our cities: Either contracting or liberalized entry restrictions will reduce the deficit of existing transit services, hence reducing city taxes; and liberalized entry should enhance the creative responses of transit producers, and give us the kind of diverse new transit services that can expand the total transit market.

What Will Bring about the Transition

How do we implement these goals? The principal agents for change can be the Regional Transit Commissions (RTCs) in those areas that have them. Secondarily, change may be initiated by the transit managers themselves, if we can alter the way they are paid so as to tie their salaries to productivity improvements.

Regional Transit Commissions as Agents of Change. It is no coincidence that the innovators mentioned in this book are (with only one exception) all RTCs: SEMTA, PenTran, Tidewater, Chicago, and so on. This does not mean that all RTCs will be innovative, only that an RTC is likely to have some sense of the possible variety of transportation systems. Since it is the funding agency for the region—RTCs are the direct recipient of all regional transportation funds from the various government sources—it is constantly confronted by the challenge of allocating money among alternative transportation systems. Thus it is somewhat natural for an RTC to consider the idea of contracting out some services to save money, or the idea of allowing some kinds of new entrants into the region, especially if they are self-supporting. By contrast, in those cities where subsidy funds flow directly to the operating transit agency, a decision by the agency to fund alternative providers is a decision to decrease its own budget and its own relative political importance.

Some RTCs have two functions—they distribute funds and operate their own transit systems—while other RTCs only act as funds-distribution agencies. We would expect that the pure funds-distribution RTCs will be the ones most amenable to innovation: They have no power or function to lose if they embrace contracting or open-entry; the potential cost savings are a totally unmixed blessing. Of course, none of this is meant to contradict the idea that a strong board of directors, or an innovative general manager, may decide to do these things regardless of the organizational structure of the local transit agency.

Transit Managers as Agents of Change.   Simpson (Chapter 13) points out that under current arrangements, transit managers actually have a set of perverse incentives to avoid increasing efficiency. Their importance in the community is a function of the size of their own vehicle fleet; and their salaries tend to reflect fleet size as well. In other words, we perceive that managers of big, complex systems are performing a more difficult and more important job, hence we give them higher rewards. Add these kinds of incentives to the manager's natural feeling that he or she knows how to do a job better than anyone else, and it is not surprising that such innovations as contracting-out, load-shedding, or encouraging alternative transit providers are rarely taken seriously. Furthermore, the importance of efficiency is a new idea: For the last two decades, transit managers have been told that maximization of service and ridership was the overall goal. Managers trained by that environment are obviously having a hard time responding to the new one.

Simpson proposes that the transit system's board of directors should add a performance incentive to the manager's contract: set a mutually agreed-upon budget based on current financial performance and expected improvements; then, if the transit system can better these goals, the board would award, say, 5 percent of the savings as bonuses to be split among the top-echelon management of the transit system. Obviously, contract services introduced by the transit manager, in a cooperative manner, will function more smoothly than contract services imposed upon the manager from above.

Could such a system work? Well, the one example we have of financial innovation outside the RTC framework is in Phoenix, where the entire city government makes extensive use of goals and objectives in evaluating the performance of executives and middle managers: Salaries are adjusted in response to these evaluations, and a "distinguished" rating results in a very substantial increase.

A Feasible Sequence Of Actions

Of the two goals – increased efficiency via contracting and increased variety via open entry – it seems clear the former will be less troublesome to implement. The concept of contract service is easier to understand and more acceptable to the transit operators: To some extent, it is only an extension of what they are already doing, and they still maintain a modicum of control over what takes place. The concept of open entry seems threatening to transit operators, and it is incomprehensible to everyone else. The public and the government planners ask questions like "How do I know there will be a vehicle there when I need it?" or "How do I know there will be service to all areas that should have it?" It requires the faith of an economist to trust markets and believe that the public will be supplied with what it wants. The advantage of a centralized system, like monopoly transit, is the presumption of assured service. It takes time and experience to learn that decentralized private providers, such as taxi operators, can do a reliable job.

So the logical place to begin is with greatly increased use of contract services. This gives everyone the necessary experience with the reliability of private operators, and more importantly, it helps develop the private infrastructure. Contracting will eventually create a number of private firms, and give their management a chance to develop administrative skills. Once these private firms are created, it will be natural for them to lobby for permission to compete independently on certain routes; and once everyone has acquired some experience with the capabilities of these firms, it will seem logical to support such a request.

SUMMARY

Transit's financial problems have brought forth two conventional solutions: raise fares or cut service. This book presents a better alternative, the concept of Service Redesign: doing more with what is available by restructuring the way transit services are organized, managed, and delivered; utilizing the force of competition to increase efficiency; and utilizing the marketing creativity of multiple providers to lure new riders by presenting them with more choices. Our current form of transit—large monopoly providers—has not changed in fifty years, though the world has, and so it is no longer capable of effective service. Transit system planners must learn a market-oriented, user-sensitive approach to service delivery so they can adapt to the changed pattern of demand. Rather than a single kind of service—large buses or rail cars on fixed routes—there must be a multitude of services providing different combinations of cost and service quality. Today's transportation market is highly segmented, and the transit system must be ready to provide a variety of services to accommodate these different segments.

Most importantly, transit systems must give up their status as the monopoly supplier of services. This means contracting out service to private providers in low-density areas; encouraging van pools and jitneys to "steal" some of transit's peak-hour load; encouraging the development of private competitors to provide high-quality/high-fare express bus service for those people who want it, and low-quality/low-fare service for others who want that. It means encouraging the vast number of actions possible via shared-ride taxi services.

Transit districts must move toward being the central coordinator and facilitator of transit service, rather than the sole supplier of it. The transit district needs to "involve a more diverse group of providers, to open up the system to private operators, and to stimulate greater competition in service provision" (Orski, Chapter 11). Such a set of actions might cut costs per passenger-trip by as much as 50 percent, while drawing far more people out of single-user automobiles because the service choices provided are more closely attuned to today's diverse needs. The way to expand the total size of the transit market is to discard our preoccupations with fare policy and conventional modes, and to concentrate on providing a greater variety of transit services.

Chapter 2

THE RISE AND FALL OF MONOPOLIZED TRANSIT

George W. Hilton

Americans are accustomed to thinking of an urban transit system as a regional monopoly under public ownership, providing service with large buses operating on specified schedules with fixed fares and city-wide transfer privileges. Currently, this system is subject to widespread academic criticism as expensive to operate, inflexible with respect to change in urban transit demands, and perverse with respect to the demands of the public for quality service. Even though the historical roots of present-day transit systems — the electric streetcar and the technology it embodied — have been almost entirely replaced with new technology, the monopolistic economic organization has survived because governments from the municipal to the federal level have sought to maintain the monopoly. The problem is of more than historical interest, for there is reason to believe that governments are nearing the end of their ability and willingness to further perpetuate this type of system.

At their peak on the eve of World War I, America's street railways constituted an industry of about a fourth of the investment of the mainline steam railroads. It is most useful to consider the history of U.S. urban transit parallel to the history of the railroads since both arose in response to the demands of an urbanizing, industrializing nation and both represented adaptations of the technology made possible by James Watt's perfection of the stationary steam engine in the mid-eighteenth century.

URBAN TRANSIT INNOVATION

The public transit industry in the United States is usually dated from Abraham Brower's establishment of horsedrawn omnibuses in New York in 1827.[1] Previous to this, home-to-work trips, shopping trips, and the like had been made virtually entirely on foot by the great majority of the population. New York was the obvious place for the omnibus and, indeed, many of the later advances in urban public transportation to take place. Following completion of the Erie Canal, the city had replaced Philadelphia as the metropolis of the nation. New York's comprehensive water barriers channeled the demand for transportation onto north-south movements along Manhattan Island. The unpaved character of most streets, however, had proved an impediment to omnibus operation, especially in rainy weather. Not surprisingly, the horse car was also innovated in New York: In 1832 the New York and Harlem Railroad established the first American horsecar line in Manhattan. When the municipal government proved unwilling to allow the railroad to engage in steam operations south of Forty-second Street, which would have connected the site of Grand Central Terminal with the downtown business area, the company built a horsecar line on the streets. In 1835 a horsecar line was built on St. Charles Avenue in New Orleans.

As simple as was the technology of the horsecar, the innovation did not spread beyond the New York and New Orleans installations for another two decades. With the advance in urbanization during the long prosperity of the 1850s, demand for urban transportation increased sufficiently to bring forth horsecar lines in Boston in 1855, in Philadelphia in 1858, in Chicago in 1859, and then in various cities during the immediate pre–Civil War period. In the years immediately following the Civil War, the use of horsecars spread widely. By the early 1870s they were ubiquitous in large cities and fairly common even in medium-sized communities.

The spread of the horsecar technology was not accompanied by much enthusiasm from either passengers or operators. The service was provided at only about 4 miles per hour, about the speed of walking. Much of the investment was necessarily embodied in the

---

1. On the basic history of the industry, see John Anderson Miller, *Fares Please!* (New York: D. Appleton Century, 1941).

horses, which had relatively short working-life expectancies and were likely to be decimated by disease. Steam locomotives, which had been available for mainline railroad use from about 1830, were the most obvious alternative, but they were considered unsuitable for urban transportation. Their exhausts were loud and dirty, they frightened horses, and, owing to the economies of scale in steam boilers, a locomotive small enough for street railway use was relatively inefficient. As a consequence steam dummies, as such locomotives were called, were mainly relegated to service on suburban routes.

The first extensive effort to apply the stationary steam engine to urban transportation was the cable car.[2] In this technology a stationary steam engine reeled in and payed out one or more endless cables that the cars gripped and ungripped. The technology was basically simple, requiring only the steam engine, a cable, a geared mechanism for reeling the cable in and paying it out, plus some method of maintaining constant tension on the cable. This technology is usually said to have been invented in San Francisco in the early 1870s, though there were antecedents in London in the 1840s, New York in the 1860s, and elsewhere. Because of the superiority of the stationary steam engine to the horse as a prime mover, the cable car was an advance over the horsecar on major routes or for installations that entailed steep gradients or continuous undulation. The majority of cable installations were replacements of major horsecar lines on radial routes out of central business districts. Typically, a cable line had a powerhouse approximately two and a half miles from the central business district. Such a powerhouse could pay out a rope totaling 5 miles into the central business district and another of the same length in the opposite direction, and thus power a double track line approximately 5 miles long. St. Louis had six such powerhouses operating the lines of five companies, each of which operated in and out of the central business district on a single street.[3] Two other major companies operated in and out of the same area with horsecars.

St. Louis's arrangement was typical, though not universal, among American cities. Neither the horsecar nor the cable car had apparent economies of scale such that proliferating lines under a single man-

2. George W. Hilton, *The Cable Car in America* (Berkeley: Howell-North Books, 1971).
3. Ibid., p. 340. See map.

agement lowered cost. Consolidating cable lines at a single power-house with a radial pattern entailed a compensating diseconomy of locating the powerhouse in the central business district, where land was expensive. Both cable operators in Denver did this, but the usual pattern was that of St. Louis. Cities that had unified street railway systems in the days of the horsecar, such as Grand Rapids and Providence, typically did so for entirely political reasons. That is, the transit operator was powerful enough politically to get a citywide franchise from the municipal government. The situation was to change drastically with the introduction of the electric streetcar.

THE ELECTRIC STREETCAR AND MONOPOLY

Various inventors had been endeavoring to electrify street railways since the 1870s, but the electric streetcar was in fact made practical by Frank J. Sprague in installations in St. Joseph, Missouri, late in 1887 and in Richmond, Virginia, early in 1888. The cost advantage of the electric streetcar over both of its rivals was so great that the innovation was quickly disseminated, replacing the alternatives (with trivial exceptions) by the end of 1906. The typical organization of the electric streetcar was a citywide monopoly. The technology was free of the inflexible relation between the powerhouse and the line that had characterized the cable car. After 1907, the optimal arrangement was to have a single powerhouse generating alternating current and sending it about the city for conversion to direct current at sub-stations. The powerhouse was typically placed for accessibility for rail deliveries of coal. Portable substations gave a degree of flexibility in responding to demands for direct current.

With this technology the optimal number of street railway systems in a city was one. New York, Washington, D.C., and a limited number of other cities had rival street railways because of franchise problems. Citywide monopoly was virtually universal elsewhere. The innovation did not result in a reduction of the fare, which had previously been 5 cents per ride. Rather, municipal governments required city-wide transfer privileges as quid pro quo for issuance of the franchise. This amounted to a discriminatory fare structure, since passengers who traveled short distances of up to 2.5 miles cross-subsidized passengers who traveled longer distances. In large cities such as Chicago, it was possible to travel over 30 miles for a nickel fare.

The fare structure was regulated at the outset frequently by writing the five-cent fare into the franchise of the company. Later the fare was set through a typical regulatory process. The street railways were customarily regulated firms subject to the procedures of *Smyth* v. *Ames* of 1898.[4] This process was intended to simulate a competitive rate of return in a noncompetitive industry through a procedure of valuation of the property, determination of a fair rate of return on that valuation, and establishment of a fare structure.

The situation was a standard one for the regulated industries. The railroads had been regulated on the basic presumption that the irrecoverability of the investment in their rights-of-way and their high level of fixed cost relative to variable cost rendered them incapable of competitive economic organization. Both electric power generation and the telephone industry arose in the same period as the electric street railways. They entailed city-wide distribution facilities for electricity such that the optimal number relative to a city was also thought to be one. All came to be among the regulated industries of the nation.

The regulatory framework of *Smyth* v. *Ames* is open to a variety of objections, but most notably it presumes that the noncompetitive character of the regulated industry can endure indefinitely.[5] The nature of the discriminatory fare structures of these industries, in effect, assured the eventual decline of their monopoly situations. The railroads and street railways simultaneously demonstrated this proposition approximately around the opening of World War I. Railroad tariffs discriminated against goods that were high in value relative to weight and against shipments that were not competitive with steamboats. Such tariffs gave the economy the incentive to develop a device which could go anywhere, which offered a comparative advantage for goods high in value relative to weight, which was free of the coupler slack in railroad technology, and which could provide faster service or at least service with more predictable arrival times than the railroads managed to provide. Such a device arose in the form of the truck, which became a comprehensive rival to the railroads beginning about 1914.

4. Smyth v. Ames, 169 U.S. 466 (1898).
5. Ed. Renshaw, "Utility Regulation: A Re-Examination," *Journal of Business* 21 (1958): 335–43.

The urban bus arose in response to a similar incentive in the economic organization of the street railways. The cross-subsidy of long-distance passengers by short-distance passengers gave the economy an incentive to develop a device with a comparative advantage for short-distance movements, capable of higher speeds and greater comfort than the streetcar, and able to deviate from fixed routes to take passengers to their doors or to avoid obstructions. Such a device arose in the form of the jitney bus, developed in 1914 in Los Angeles, a city which had already developed a reputation for automobile-dependence. On July 1, 1914, L. P. Draper ascertained that he might legally use his Model T Ford touring car as a common carrier if he secured a chauffeur's license. He did so, picked up a passenger at a streetcar stop on Broadway, and charged him a nickel, a sum for which the current slang term was a "jitney." This superficially trivial episode sparked a movement for the use of private automobiles as common carriers, which is thought to have peaked about the second quarter of 1915 with some 62,000 vehicles in the trade nationally.[6]

Operation of a jitney was a casual activity pursued by people who were temporarily or permanently without highly satisfactory alternative employment. It was common to drive a jitney during periods of unemployment, for example. The most common form of jitney operation was to use private automobiles as common carriers during the morning and evening rush hours. Some people drove for an hour or two before work and again after work. A more frequent practice was simply posting the place of work as the destination on the morning trip with one's home as the destination on the evening trip and picking up anyone whose trip was consistent with such destinations. This type of jitney operation caused cities to be criss-crossed with an infinity of common-carrier trips between various points during each rush hour. Accordingly, the jitneys were a highly demand-responsive form of transportation, in contrast to the street railways, which ran on fixed routes and fixed schedules. In San Francisco, where the demand for transportation was highly concentrated around the Ferry Building, jitney drivers would begin their trips without a destination in mind, head for the destination desired by the first passenger, and pick up any further passengers going in the same direction. It was common for jitney drivers to deviate from routes to take passengers

---

6. Ross D. Eckert and George W. Hilton, "The Jitneys," *Journal of Law and Economics* 15 (1972): 293–325.

to their doors, most commonly at fares of two passengers for 25 cents. Jitney fares were customarily at the street railways' level of 5 cents but temporarily rose during street railway strikes or during storms and other circumstances that increased the disutility of driving. Nighttime rates were usually higher than daytime rates.

In short, an ordinary competitive market comprised of jitneys emerged in urban transportation. Municipal governments proved to be unanimously hostile to this development. They were directly dependent on the street railways for tax revenues, and they achieved some implicit benefits from the monopolistic status of the street railways such as free movement of members of the police and fire departments, paving of the centers of streets, street lighting, and the like. It would have been very difficult to secure similar advantages from a competitive industry such as the jitneys. More basically, the electric streetcar had produced an urban pattern that most municipal governments liked. The electric streetcar, which could provide service at 8 to 10 miles per hour overall, approximately doubled the feasible home-to-work distance relative to the horsecar. The noise of the electric streetcar and the visual impact of its overhead electric wires, however, caused the streets on which it operated to be relatively unattractive for residents. Such streets usually became strip shopping streets in which the stores sold groceries, basic clothing, and other things, the supply of which had to be replenished frequently. The central business districts provided shopping of more specialized sorts and also provided the central-office function and the restaurant-amusement complex of the cities.[7] Such a pattern generated considerable tax revenues from the central business districts.

Consequently, every municipality in the United States put down the jitneys as a comprehensive competitive market in urban transportation. Jitneys were allowed to operate on only three streets in the country—Mission Street in San Francisco, Martin Luther King Drive in Chicago, and Pacific Avenue in Atlantic City—but they were restricted to a linear function, so that their operations were not greatly differentiated from those of the street railways. By 1915 the jitneys had given every impression of being a viable industry; in some cities that had been slow about their suppression jitneys still operated into the early 1920s. Jitneys resulted in the abandonment of

7. George M. Smerk, "The Streetcar: Shaper of American Cities," *Traffic Quarterly* 21 (1967): 569.

three streetcar systems in small- or medium-sized cities: Everett, Washington; Bay City, Michigan; and Newburg, New York. In none of the three, however, were jitneys allowed to survive as a competitive industry. Buses within the typical monopolized, linear framework of the street railways continued to operate in these three cities and elsewhere, but it remained the view of the urban transit industry that buses were not cost-competitive with electric streetcars except in small communities or on peripheral routes of larger systems.

TRANSIT INDUSTRY PROBLEMS

The jitneys were eradicated in most cities between mid-1915 and America's entry into World War I in 1917. Leaders of the transit industry, as might be expected, were of the opinion that the suppression of the jitneys would return the industry to such prosperity as it had attained previously. Actually, the industry had never been characterized by high rates of return. A representative of the American Electric Railway Association, the industry's trade body, estimated the rate of return in the industry had been only 1.61 percent in 1902, 1.78 percent in 1907, and 2.64 percent in 1912.[8] By that time, using the measure of additional miles of track built, the industry had virtually ceased to attract new investment. The mileage of single track in the industry had been 8,123 in 1890, 22,597 in 1902, 34,382 in 1907, and 41,065 in 1912. By 1917 the figure had climbed to 44,835, an increase of only 1.8 percent.[9] Other measures indicated that the industry was approaching maturity at the time of the jitney episode. The number of revenue passengers per inhabitant rose from 32 in 1890 to 61 in 1902, to 85 in 1907, and to 100 in 1912. This figure peaked at 109 in 1917. Revenue passengers increased almost monotonically from over 2 billion in 1890 to 11,305,000,000 in 1917.[10]

In 1918 the industry was experiencing serious difficulties. Many of these were war-related, but others could be viewed only as a consequence of secular forces operating against the industry. The war-related problems were to some extent inevitable. The industry had

8. *Proceedings of the Federal Electric Railways Commission* (Washington, D.C.: Government Printing Office, 1920), p. 129.

9. Ibid., p. 73.

10. Ibid., p. 77.

an extremely inflexible pricing structure with a five-cent fare enforced nearly everywhere either by franchise or by municipal regulation. The effects of the draft, expansion of factory employment, and the strength of the union, the Amalgamated Association of Street Railway Employees, caused labor costs to rise by 85 to 90 percent in 1918. Many of the basic materials used by the industry rose in price by about the same amount, and the price of inputs used also for military purposes increased even more (for example, asbestos by 560 percent).[11] The industry's output declined both absolutely and relative to population. The number of revenue passengers fell from 11,305,000,000 to 11,109,000,000; revenue passengers per inhabitant decreased from 109 to 106, about a 3 percent decline. The industry's mileage rose by only 115 miles, a 0.3 percent increase over 1917. The rate of return in the industry dwindled to 0.9 percent.[12]

The industry's problems were severe enough to cause the federal government to enquire into the problem. Secretaries Redfield of Commerce and Wilson of Labor in 1919 proposed establishment of a Federal Electric Railways Commission to report to the U.S. president on the industry's problems. It was stated that fifty or more urban systems were in receivership including those in New York, Providence, Buffalo, New Orleans, Denver, St. Louis, Pittsburgh, and St. Paul. On May 31, 1919, sixty-two companies with a combined mileage of 5,912 were in receivership. Sixty companies had gone out of business and had dismantled or junked 534 miles of railway. Thirty-eight companies (without going out of the industry) had abandoned 257 miles.[13]

By the time the commission published its report in 1920, the industry's situation had ameliorated somewhat. Over 500 cities had allowed fares to rise above 5 cents by July 1, 1920.[14] The wartime inflation of costs had abated. The private automobile was at the time said to be less important as a rival to the industry than walking. Practically all of the witnesses for the commission recognized that the industry was incapable of earning a monopoly gain or even a normal rate of return. Consequently, urban transit was the first of the regulated industries to demonstrate that the presumption of perpetuity

---

11. *Report of the Federal Electric Railways Commission* (Washington, D.C.: Government Printing Office, 1920), p. 12.
12. *Proceedings*, pp. 73, 77; *Report*, p. 129.
13. *Report*, p. 7.
14. Ibid., p. 8.

of the monopoly position of the regulated firm was fallacious. Economist Delos F. Wilcox submitted to the commission a lengthy analysis of electric railway problems which he self-published in 1921.[15] His conclusion was that service-at-cost franchises in which municipalities guaranteed that the street railway would break even were only a stopgap, and he advocated outright municipal operation. Only Boston, San Francisco, and Seattle at the time had some degree of municipal ownership.

THE EMERGENCE OF MOTOR CARRIERS

Contrary to the expectations of the time, the decade of the 1920s produced the conversion away from rail transport of passengers to free-wheel transport in America. The pattern of automobile-dependence that was established in that period, both for intercity transport and for urban transport, has persisted to the present and shows no prospect of remission. The difference between the experience in intercity transportation and urban transportation is mainly a consequence of the difference in policies pursued toward the railroads and the street railways and toward the intercity motor carriers and urban buses. The railroads peaked at about the same time as street railways did; by the usual measures of mileage and employment, this was at about 1916. Again, the experience of World War I concealed the fact that the railroads were already a declining industry.

The federal government in 1920, in the course of returning the railroads to private ownership after the wartime period, endeavored to perfect the cartelization of the railroads that had begun with the establishment of the Interstate Commerce Commission in 1887. The ICC was converted from a body which stabilized private cartels known as rate bureaus to an outright cartelizing body with powers of minimum-rate regulation, control of entry and exit, and various powers (which were ultimately unsuccessful) for endeavoring to equalize rates of return between railroads. The Transportation Act of 1920 regulating interstate commerce provided no regulation of motor carriers, but in the Motor Carrier Act of 1935 Congress established cartelization of truck and bus lines under the ICC. Carriage of agricultural products and trucking with vehicles owned by the ship-

---

15. Delos F. Wilcox, *Analysis of the Electric Railway Problem* (New York: n.p., 1921).

per were exempt from regulation. Thus intercity trucking and also bus operation evolved as a cartelized industry with abundant exempt sectors.

In urban transportation the suppression of the jitneys was so ubiquitous that it amounted to a nationwide prohibition of a competitive market in urban transportation. Society's conversion to free-wheeled vehicles for urban transport was entirely on the level of private carriage. The antijitney regulations in U.S. cities essentially made it illegal to use automobiles as common carriers. This situation had consequences both for utilization of the automobile and for organization of transit systems. As society converted to the automobile, it was forced to do so using the automobile only as a private carrier. Since such transportation appeared to have a strong positive income elasticity, the public tended to use it for trips of all sorts, including trips from home to work, for which public transit is usually argued to have its comparative advantage. The prohibition on using the private automobile as a common carrier resulted in the occupancy of automobiles on the home-to-work trip asymptotically approaching one over time, and continues to the present. (These empty seats in cars during rush hours on crowded streets constitutes a serious waste of resources.)

The situation was compounded by the nature of highway user charges: The driver pays for the use of the road by an excise on gasoline which is not differentiated by hour, place, or direction of travel. Consequently, the roads were and continue to be allocated not by a price but rather by a deterioration in the quality of service as the demand for a road increases. That is, one pays for the use of a road with time wasted in traffic congestion and through risk of death or injury in accidents. These costs cannot be shared with others by filling the empty seats in an automobile as a pecuniary charge could be.

Professor Donald Shoup has recently demonstrated that the provision of free parking to employees by their employers tends to have similar consequences on the decision to use the automobile for the home-to-work trip.[16]

With respect to transit the prohibition on the jitneys meant that the conversion from the streetcar to free-wheel transportation would

16. Donald C. Shoup and Don H. Pickrell, "Free Parking as a Transportation Problem," final report under contract DOT–05–90011 (Washington, D.C.: Department of Transportation, 1980).

be done within the context of area-wide monopolies. Linear bus routes as distinct from the jitney experience had had a very limited history up to the immediate post–World War I era. The longest existing bus line was a special case: Because of the city of New York's unwillingness to allow street railways on Fifth Avenue, the Fifth Avenue Coach Company had converted directly from omnibuses to gasoline buses in 1905. Its cost per passenger was thought to be about double that of a streetcar line, however. In 1912 the Cleveland Railway bought three gasoline buses for operating in lightly populated areas. By 1922, when the American Electric Railway Association began issuing annual figures on ridership in the industry, motorbuses provided only 404,000,000 rides of an industry total of 15,735,000,000; nearly 13.4 billion of the industry's passengers were still carried on streetcars.[17]

The electric streetcar had a notable technological improvement in 1916. Charles O. Birney was the engineer in charge of car design for the Stone & Webster utility group, a holding company that owned a large number of street railways. Instructed to develop a smaller streetcar to rival the jitneys more effectively with rail technology, Birney developed a one-man, lightweight, four-wheel streetcar which he called the Safety Car. It has, however, been universally called the Birney car. The original intention was to use the Birney car for more frequent service on high-density lines. In actuality, it was commonly used either on lightly-traveled lines of major systems or for the entire service of systems in medium-sized cities. Birney developed a double-truck version of the car for more heavily-traveled routes. Several thousand Birney cars, mainly of the single-truck version, were produced from 1916 into the 1920s. The trolley coach, though developed in Los Angeles as early as 1910, still carried a negligible number of passengers in comparison.

The urban transit industry peaked in ridership in 1926 with 17,234,000,000 riders, of which 2,350,000,000 were on subways and elevated lines.[18] Rapid-transit technology, essentially a more capital-intensive version of the electric street railway, was suitable for only a limited number of cities. New York's heavy population density, high degree of concentration of economic activity on lower Manhattan Island, and comprehensive water barriers made it the pre-

17. American Public Transit Association, MS input data for *Transit Fact Book* (1974).
18. Ibid.

eminent rapid transit city. Only Chicago, Philadelphia, and Boston had similar geographical properties and thus developed rapid-transit systems during the relatively short period in which investment in this form of transport was economic. The private sector invested in this technology almost entirely between the late 1890s and the Panic of 1907; except for some extensions of the New York system, there was little investment in rapid transit after 1912. About 80 percent of American rapid-transit passengers were on the New York subway. For this reason, and because additional rapid-transit mileage was not, in general, being built, rapid-transit ridership showed little trend of any sort. Ridership peaked at 2,571,000,000 in 1929 but did not fall below 2 billion until 1954.[19]

In contrast, ridership on streetcar lines was declining rapidly. In 1926, when ridership of all sorts on American transit lines peaked, 12,875,000,000 passengers were still on streetcars. This figure fell slowly until the onslaught of the Great Depression, and then fell rapidly. In 1930 ridership was still over 10 billion, but fell by nearly half, to 5,943,000,000, by 1940.[20] In the years of the deep depression of the early 1930s, the industry made a second effort of technological change, rather the reverse of the Birney car. The new effort was to develop a large streetcar with good acceleration and deceleration properties suitable for use on the lines of heaviest density. This vehicle appeared under the name of "the President's Conference Committee streetcar" (or PCC car) in 1934. It became the virtually universal vehicle for new car orders thereafter, and has been universally and correctly evaluated as a great engineering success. It probably gave the electric streetcar some two decades of rivalry with free-wheeled vehicles which the streetcar could not have had with pre-existing designs.

CHANGES IN URBAN PATTERNS OF TRANSIT

The PCC could not, of course, halt the decline of public transit or the conversion to free-wheeled transit vehicles. The ubiquity of the automobile was producing changes in the urban pattern to which public transit, as it was organized, could not respond effectively. The

19. Ibid.
20. Ibid.

old pattern of strip shopping streets leading into a centralized business district of office employment, an amusement-restaurant complex, and a specialized shopping area was slowly replaced with one of free placing of economic activity, based on expectations that most people would arrive by automobile, and goods would arrive and depart by truck. Most newly established economic activity was either in suburban areas of diffuse geographical character or in light-density cities such as San Jose, San Antonio, and Phoenix, which grew to large size after the automobile and the truck became dominant.

In middle-income brackets, the public showed a tendency to turn away from public transit and toward the automobile with increases in income. Only in income brackets so low that increases in income were mainly a consequence of additional members of the family taking employment did this increased income result in an increased demand for public transit.[21] There was an even more limited exception in the form of high-income families among whom a movement to the suburbs produced a demand for main-line railroad commutation for access to a central business district. For the majority of society, however, the tendency to turn away from public transit with increases in income was dominant. The negative income elasticity of demand for public transit in middle-income brackets was associated with relatively low price elasticies of demand for transit.

Given the various adverse forces operating on transit systems, the alternatives to the electric streetcar were proving more attractive. The trolley coach had become a perceptible carrier in the industry's annual output figures in 1928, mainly as a result of the conversion of much of the Salt Lake City streetcar system to double overhead wires. The trolley coach offered the attraction of continued use of a street railway's electrical distribution facilities with limited lateral freedom from a fixed route. It had excellent acceleration properties and hill-climbing ability. It had the usual attractive feature of electric vehicles: favorable pollution characteristics. By 1940 the trolley coach, however, was carrying only 534 million passengers, compared with 5,943,000,000 on the streetcar and 4,239,000,000 on the motor bus.[22]

21. George W. Hilton, *Federal Transit Subsidies* (Washington, D.C.: American Enterprise Institute, 1974), p. 119 n. 4.

22. American Public Transit Association, MS input data for *Transit Fact Book* (1974).

The motor bus had a continuous history of design improvement from the early models of wooden bodies on truck chassis that emerged during the jitney period. Specialized buses were available during the 1920s from General Motors, Fageol, and other producers. The introduction of rear-engined gasoline and diesel buses in the late 1930s proved the principal technological advance, especially as coupled with the automatic transmission.

World War II was to bring a boom in public-transit ridership parallel to that experienced by railroads in intercity passenger traffic. Transit passengers of all sorts rose from 13,098,000,000 in 1940 to 23,254,000,000 in 1945. Expansion of wartime factory employment, restrictions on production of new automobiles, and rationing of gasoline all tended to inflate transit ridership. The peak was actually immediately after the war—23,372,000,000 passengers in 1946. This was some 6 billion above the historic high of 1926 and a figure that could presumably not have been maintained under any circumstances.

Conventional wisdom in the transit industry at the end of World War II was that streetcar lines operated with the PCC car were the appropriate installations for the most heavily-traveled routes, with trolley coaches for intermediate routes or lines with exceptional gradients or pollution problems, and diesel buses for the remaining routes—which were, of course, the great majority. In 1944 the bus had overtaken the streetcar in number of passengers carried per year. Conversion of streetcar systems in intermediate-sized cities such as Des Moines and Gary had been interrupted by World War II, but most were completed by the end of the 1940s. By 1950 the streetcar was carrying 3.9 billion passengers per year and the motor bus, 9.4 billion. Total transit ridership was 17,246,000,000, approximately what it had been at its peak in 1926. Thereafter the industry's decline was precipitous—far greater than any observer of the time apparently anticipated. Ridership fell below 10 billion passengers in 1958, below 9 billion in 1961, below 8 billion in 1969, and below 7 billion in 1971.[23]

Under such drastically declining demand conditions, the electric streetcar lost any claim to economy; none were delivered after 1952. The streetcar survived mainly on systems where long tunnels presented severe ventilation problems as in Boston, Philadelphia, and

23. Ibid.

San Francisco. Trolley bus orders ceased in 1955.[24] Trolley buses survived mainly in hilly cities such as Seattle and San Francisco. Mainly, however, the industry became a relatively homogenous one of diesel buses. About 80 percent of its vehicles were buses for forty or more passengers by 1965. The Chicago Transit Authority, which converted its last streetcar lines to buses of this type in 1958, estimated the saving at about 48 cents per vehicle mile.[25]

Unfortunately, such motor vehicles are optimal for transit use only within the constraints of the present organization of the industry. Their appeal is in the ability to average out the wage of the unionized driver over a large number of passengers. They are of the approximate size of streetcars and provide similar levels of speed and comfort—levels that were demonstrably unable to retain the majority of transit passengers relative to the automobile. Hayden Boyd and his associates have demonstrated that diesel buses of forty or fifty capacity are actually appropriate for suburban services, such as are typically provided by railroad commutation systems. The transit function is better handled by van-type vehicles with the capacity for about eight passengers. Such vehicles would stop less frequently, provide faster service, and be capable of operating more demand-responsively. If the jitneys had been tolerated, it is thought they would currently operate with such vehicles.[26]

THE DECLINE OF THE TRANSIT INDUSTRY

The industry's financial situation inevitably deteriorated under the circumstances of declining demand conditions. The conversion from public transit to the automobile in general occurred most rapidly in the smaller communities. Between 1954 and 1963, 194 transit companies went out of business. The typical medium-sized community in

24. Ibid.

25. *The Industrial Reorganization Act*, Hearings before the Subcommittee on Antitrust and Monopoly of the Committee on the Judiciary, U.S. Senate, 93rd Cong. 2d sess., 1973, pt. 4; 2230.

26. J. Hayden Boyd, Norman J. Asher, and Elliott S. Wetzler, "Evaluation of Rail Rapid Transit and Express Bus Service in the Urban Commuter Market" (Arlington, Va.: Institute for Defense Analyses, 1973); Edward Smith, "An Economic Comparison of Urban Railways and Express Bus Services," *Journal of Transport Economics and Policy* 7 (1973): 1-12.

the country was simply left without a transit system. Automobiles, walking, and taxicabs provided the service.

The year 1963 is considered crucial in the industry's history, for in that year the industry as a whole went into the red by $880,000. The deficit escalated rapidly, passing $100 million in 1968 and $500 million in 1972.[27] Profitable operation was increasingly limited to relatively small carriers, most of which had extensive charter operations. Operation of a citywide system, especially if it had extensive rail mileage, was increasingly looked upon as inherently unprofitable. As private capital flowed out of the dying industry, the systems in most large cities were converted to public ownership by the mid-1960s. Even such conversion proved to be only a stopgap for the largest systems. Those in the four cities with rail rapid transit networks – New York, Boston, Philadelphia, and Chicago – proved beyond the capacity of the city governments to operate. In each case a regional transportation authority was then established to operate the system, mainly by using tax revenues from suburban counties to subsidize the operation in the central city.

Even such devices were clearly inadequate to support the transit monopolies. By the mid-1960s the industry as it had been traditionally constituted – with linear routes mainly, though not entirely, radial from central business districts, fixed schedules, large vehicles, city-wide fares, and a unionized labor force – was clearly threatened with extinction. Inevitably there arose political pressure for a federal program for subsidy of transit. The Urban Mass Transportation Assistance Program had its origins in a provision of the Housing Act of 1961 which provided $25 million for mass transportation demonstration projects. The program was independently funded beginning with the Urban Mass Transportation Act of 1964.

While it is beyond the scope of this paper to examine the consequences of the program in detail, there are some points that should be noted. The program initially entailed capital grants for the replacement of buses, for the building of rail systems, for conversion of remaining privately-owned transit systems to public ownership, and for demonstration projects. So constituted, the program by 1974 was demonstrably unsuccessful.[28] It had at best simply arrested the

27. Hilton, *Federal Transit Subsidies*, p. 3; American Public Transit Association, MS input data for *Transit Fact Book* (1974).

28. Hilton, *Federal Transit Subsidies*, p. 97.

decline of transit. In 1974 Congress enlarged the program with Section V, initiating federal subsidy of operating expenses. Section V tended to bring about extension of transit systems into more lightly populated areas and resulted in some increased frequencies of service. By 1978 to 1979 the federal subsidy amounted to 15.9 percent of the expenses of American transit systems. Passenger revenue had sunk to only 43.6 percent of such expenses; as recently as 1970, passenger revenues had amounted to 82.1 percent of operating expenses.[29] In addition, the entire framework of the UMTA program has tended to strengthen the unions in the industry. Section 13 (c) of the statutory authority essentially gives the unions a veto power over capital expenditures and demonstration expenditures. This assures that capital will be invested in complementarity with members of the unions rather than as substitutes for their services. The Amalgamated Transit Union has a monopoly gain that has been estimated as high as 18 percent—an exceptionally high figure for laborers of relatively low skill level.[30]

The Reagan Administration has proposed phasing out subsidies to the variable expenses of transit systems by 1985. If this is done, the existing linear area-wide transit monopolies will be hard pressed to survive in many municipal regions. The effort initiated with the suppression of the jitneys in 1915 will have come its full course. The alternative forgone at that time, of a transit industry of competitive owner-operators, may then arise simply because the alternative chosen by public policy in that period has finally demonstrated itself to be workable no longer.

29. Ross D. Eckert, "The Party's Over: An Analysis of Alternative Financial and Regulatory Policies for Public Transportation in an Era Without Federal Operating Subsidies," Order DTUM60-82-P-20023 (Washington, D.C.: Department of Transportation, 1982), p. 9.

30. Melvin Lurie, "The Effect of Unionization on Wages in the Transit Industry," *Journal of Political Economy* 69 (1961): 558-72.

Chapter 3

TOWARD FRAGMENTATION
The Evolution of Public Transportation in Chicago

Christine M. Johnson and Milton Pikarsky

PREFACE

A central issue in the often troubled relationship between the public and private sectors in the transportation industry is "coordination." That word appealingly connotes clockwork efficiency, something everyone is for. So, in the name of coordination, public transportation in urban areas has evolved into a single publicly owned, publicly financed, and publicly operated system. Conversely, it is argued that anything less than the public monopoly would result in financial collapse and chaotic competition.

The Chicago area's transportation system—with its long, colorful history and incredibly rich mix of services—offers an unusual opportunity to explore the myths and realities of the coordination versus fragmentation issue as it relates to the delivery of transportation by the public and private sectors. In the following section, we look at the evolution of the Chicago public transportation system as it moved from a chaotic but highly innovative private system to a consolidated public monolith which, we suggest, may be dying. We also look at some of the new systems springing up in the shadow of the giant.

In doing so, we argue that coordination and consolidation under public ownership have had significant, albeit hidden, costs. History suggests that coordination can be achieved through market forces, purchase of service arrangements with the private sector, and other means not involving puouc ownership and operation. We argue further that the need for coordination in future systems may not exist.

In light of our historical experience, we conclude that future urban mobility would be better served by a highly fragmented system of small, independent, sometimes competing systems. These would be owned and operated by a variety of public and private organizations, and financed by those who specifically benefit from the service. Finally we suggest that the role of a public regional institution, such as a regional transit authority (RTA), should not be to own and operate transit systems. Rather it should assume a role of cultivating and conserving private providers as important regional resources. It should discover new markets and facilitate their development by one or a group of the many possible provider/financiers. And, in the role of *information broker*, it should provide the coordinative link among what could become a pleasantly chaotic mix of services.

INTRODUCTION

Public transportation—buses, commuter trains, rapid transit, and taxis—is a well-established topic of social conversation in Chicago, along with the weather, the Cubs, white wine, and City Hall politics. Everyone has a solution "to make the system better," and the newspapers keep these seven million social commentators well informed. A week seldom goes by without a story on some aspect of mass transportation.

If one were to leaf through a file of these clippings over the last four or five years, it would become evident that the regional transportation delivery system is going through a painfully protracted period of transition, marked by the deaths and contractions of the old, established monoliths and the emergence of small, new services. These new services are so limited they are almost invisible in the traditional system of 8 commuter railroads operating 15 lines over 1,067 route miles, 97 route miles of rapid transit, 3,000 CTA buses, and some 6,000 taxis.

The following sampling of clippings give a flavor of the struggle in process in the region:

- On June 30, 1983, the Illinois state legislature approved the largest tax increase in fourteen years, yet adjourned without passing a desperately needed bill containing a $75-million transit subsidy that had been linked to major public transportation system reform, and that had support from both sides of the aisle. The reason: a major lobbying effort by transit labor, which opposed the labor reforms requiring the use of part-time labor and the elimination of the COLA (Cost of Living Adjustment). The result will be a cash crisis during which the RTA (Regional Transportation Authority) will be paying over half of its monthly sales tax generated revenues for interest on a two-year-old, crisis-induced, bail-out loan from the state. The CTA (Chicago Transit Authority) will launch its third round of service cutbacks, layoffs, and fare increases in less than two years. (Five months later, the legislature passed this measure, and the Governor signed it into law on November 9, 1983. The bill required approval by 60 percent of the state house and senate to have immediate effect. The Illinois senate passed the bill with only one vote to spare.)

- In the wake of the 1981 financial crisis, commuter rail fares on the seven lines serving the central city were drastically increased, nearly doubled in many instances. The result was a consumer rebellion and the birth of a new industry for Chicago: the private, for-profit, commuter bus lines that currently transport some 3,000 commuters daily to and from the Chicago Loop over eighty suburban-based routes.

- When Allstate Insurance, General Finance Corporation, Motorola, and other major firms built new headquarters in the fast-developing North and Northwest suburbs, they also "built" their own transportation systems: employee van and bus pools to bring clerical and lower management employees in a reverse commute from the inner city to the suburbs.

- When the rapidly growing suburb of the Village of Schaumburg faced a crisis of growth—namely, acute peak-hour congestion that would have required doubling the capacity of many arterials—the village board adopted an ordinance requiring new developers to take financial responsibility for mitigating the peak-hour congestion caused by the future employer via transit shuttles, car and van pooling, and implementation of staggered work hours.

- In the wake of "empty" suburban buses and persistent political demand for suburban mass transit service, the Regional Transportation Authority inaugurated a "decentralized paratransit brokerage program" where the RTA provides partial funding for some forty-eight separate community-managed and -operated paratransit services.

- In the meantime, a 1981 study of the taxi industry in the Chicago area reports that one of the last remaining forms of private, for-profit urban mass transportation is dying, having lost 25 percent of its suburban fleet between 1975 and 1980—the same period that saw significant expansion of the RTA suburban public service. Within the last eighteen months, one of the oldest and largest taxi conglomerates in the nation has attempted to put its 3,600 taxi medallions on the auction block.

- Other firms are developing new markets through contracted paratransit services, using a mix of vehicles ranging from buses and vans to traditional taxis and station wagons.

- At the other end of the modal spectrum, two private (though publicly subsidized) commuter rail lines have declared bankruptcy. One, the historic Rock Island, has been purchased by the RTA and the other, the Milwaukee Road, under court receivership, is RTA-managed.

- Two associations of private transportation providers have recently formed and are trying to make their voices heard in the transportation decisionmaking process. One is an association of vanpool operators; the other an association of bus, taxi, and livery operators.

- Finally, in December of 1979 the city of Chicago endured a four-day transit strike, the first of significance in fifty years. The downtown Loop, where 80 percent of the peak-hour commuters arrive by public transit, did not shut down—to the surprise of transit labor, many public officials, and central area businesses. Private buses, vans, and taxis were pressed into service, and many temporary carpools were formed. By the third day, absenteeism in the Loop was only 12 percent above normal. The rest of the region was hardly affected.

Consciously or not, the Chicago metropolitan area is struggling to find a service mix that will genuinely meet the mobility needs of a region where jobs, shopping, and homes are decentralized throughout an enormous 4,653-square-mile, six-county region. Yet it is a region that has at its heart an old city built around, and still dependent upon, a monolithic, traditional transit system. The struggle is fueled by the fact that job opportunities for the poor are no longer "downtown," but spread throughout the outlying suburbs of Lake, DuPage, Will, Kane, and McHenry counties—areas ill-suited to traditional transit. Further pressure for nonautomobile mobility solutions comes from growing numbers of working wives, and increasingly influential elderly and handicapped groups, as well as from congestion-clogged suburban arterials.

Underlying this creative struggle are several issues which are being answered as the emerging delivery system takes shape. Among them are:

- *Who will finance urban mobility?* The user? The taxpayers? Or the beneficiaries of the travel: employers, retailers, and the like?

- *Who will operate the system?* One entity or many? A private, for-profit transportation provider? The public? A private entrepreneur for whom transportation is either part of the production costs or part of the package of goods being marketed?

- *Who will own the means of transportation (the buses, the trains, the maintenance facilities, etc.)?* Can ownership and operation be separated? Is it acceptable to buy a vehicle with public money for a profit-making private company?

- *Fragmentation versus Centralization.* Do the cost-controlling and market-niche-tailoring advantages of competitive, fragmented, and overlapping delivery systems outweigh the consumer convenience of a single, consolidated delivery system? Is regional unification necessary?

The combinations of answers to these questions present possibilities ranging from a totally private, fragmented, free-market system to a single, consolidated, monopolistic, government-owned and -operated system. The questions themselves are not new. Indeed, these issues have been addressed numerous times in the 125-year history of public transportation within the region. And, during that time, we have seen the resolution of these issues result in a steady progression away from the free-market/fragmentation extreme toward a publicly owned and operated monopoly.

FROM FRAGMENTATION TO MONOPOLY:
THE BIRTH OF CTA

During the growth period of the mass transportation industry, the mobility needs of 2 million people were met by a chaotic and severely competitive mix of some thirty private mass transportation companies, ten railroads (using six separate terminals!), as well as an assorted mix of taxi, jitney, and livery companies. That realization makes it difficult to argue for the "inherent public need" for a coordinated, unified (and, ultimately, consolidated) public transportation system. The fragmentation of that era would have given today's planner nightmares!

There are four characteristics of this fragmented delivery system that are worth noting in the context of the transition in transportation service delivery emerging in the 1980s.

Innovation

The period between 1880 and 1930 was characterized by a remarkable number of technical and service innovations. Public transportation evolved from horse-drawn railcars to cable cars, steam-powered rapid transit lines, electric cars, motor buses, trolley buses, and jitneys. Considering the fact that there have been few, if any, comparable innovations in the subsequent fifty years (the period dominated by public-sector control and "coordination"), the tremendous private investment in technologies that had relatively short life-cycles becomes all the more impressive.

The innovation came, we might add, in spite of fierce lobbying from already invested companies who claimed that competition from the new system in question would be ruinous. It came in spite of regulations limiting market entry, largely because of a highly fragmented regulatory system. The state, city, and park district all claimed regulatory control of surface transportation and each granted "exclusive" franchises to a number of otherwise competing systems. For example, the introduction of the motorbus would have been long delayed by city regulations had not the Park District granted the motorcoach companies operating privileges over "boulevards," the streets the park district controlled.

Market-Forced Coordination

In 1898, a city council-commissioned "traction investigation" severely criticized fragmentation of the private transportation delivery system:

> The result is that the downtown district is a network of breaks in transportation. A typical instance of this is Clark Street, where cars from the North side and the South side stop on opposite sides of Washington Street, without transfers, as though no passenger over this line from the north could wish to go farther south, and no passenger from the south could wish to go farther north than Washington Street.

The alderman considered the need to change buses and pay an additional fare "fragmentation." A planner of today might call the same situation a zone service or zone fare system! The fact is that each company recovered the cost of traveling a particular distance. The trip from the North side of Chicago to the South side of Chicago should have cost about the same whether the trip was serviced by one company or two, or via two vehicles or one. "Coordination" of transportation has often been a disguised argument for lowering fares. Unfortunately, coordination seldom reduces costs, since it still costs as much to transport a given number of people along Clark street using one bus company or two. Indeed, coordination may increase costs since the coordinator's salary must be paid.

But market forces were at work to force coordination and, ultimately, consolidation. The market would not support thirty-five companies; and competition was fierce! The company that could offer consumers through-transfer service to other lines had a competitive edge. Thus, as the market began to "shake-out," smaller companies and their franchises were selectively bought out by the survivors. Where buy out was not an option, alliances were formed. Ultimately, in 1913, the five major streetcar companies formed an association which appeared to the passenger to be a unified system: the Chicago Surface Lines. It was, in fact, an operating association of five separate companies. Similar pressures resulted in the transit lines consolidating into a single company, and the bus lines merging into the Chicago Motor Coach Company

Bankruptcy

Public transit companies in the region were failing before the turn of the century. Some because of competition from better services, many because the Chicago City Council maintained fares below the cost of recouping invested capital, and others because the "cost" of court- or competition-induced transfers was too much. (Some, of course, failed simply because of poor management.) By the late 1920s, all local transportation lines incorporated in the Chicago Surface Lines and the Chicago Rapid Transit Company were in receivership. Historians at the time suggested principal causes to be (1) liberal use of transfers, (2) fares which had been held too low for too long by the city council, (3) lack of adequate protection from the motorbus, and (4) competition from the automobile.

Belief that Mass Transportation Should be Publicly Owned and Operated

Fragmented mass transportation service was a popular "ain't-it-awful" political issue as early as 1880. Interestingly, the only proposed solution, from that time forward, was public ownership and delivery of mass transit service. Indeed, the question of municipal ownership and operation of mass transportation companies was put to the voters in public referenda no fewer than seven times between 1902 and 1925. In all but two instances, the issue was passed overwhelmingly in favor of government ownership and operation. Acquisition of sufficient public capital proved a formidable barrier to action, however.

Thus, it cannot be argued that the concept of a unified, publicly owned and operated mass transit service resulted from failure on the part of the private sector. Public transportation has been viewed as a "public utility" to be owned and operated by the government almost from the inception of the industry. And, more often than not, the "public utility" concept has had a constituency of the majority of voters.

The formation of the Chicago Transit Authority in 1945 as a public agency with authority to acquire, consolidate, and operate all surface transportation systems in the city (and parts of Cook County) was the culmination of a "good government," popular issue that had arisen more than fifty years before. Its birth was aided, but not caused by, the financial failure of the regulated private companies in the 1920s.

It is interesting to note that throughout the public debate on municipal ownership there are no references to alternative solutions to coordination (that is, requiring particular routings and intercompany transfers or purchasing the service of private transportation companies). Nor, during a time of national debate on the evils of large private-sector monopolies (the Sherman Anti-Trust Act) and the local outcry over the evils of the local taxi monopoly, was there any commentary on the fact that the "unified system" being proposed by the city leaders had all the potential threats of a private monopoly.

We speculate that the reason for this was a genuine distrust of the private sector, which was echoed by Delegate Snyder at the Illinois Constitutional Convention of 1870.

> I say, if there is anything like unanimity in this State upon any one thing, it is upon restricting these railroads, these immense corporations that are growing day by day, and are already priding themselves on their power to control our legislature and all the other departments of the State. . . . it is better that every railway that has ever been constructed within the State should be sunk to the bottomless pit, than that this free people should lose their liberties, and become the slaves of monopolies.

It was also expressed by Delegate Davis, one hundred years later, at the 1970 Illinois Constitutional Convention:

> And I am very much concerned; very frankly, I am very much concerned with the possibility that some of the villages might see fit to subsidize their taxi companies and their local bus lines, all of which or most of which are private *for-profit* companies [emphasis added].

So strong was this distrust of the private corporations that it took an amendment to the state constitution to permit the transference of public funds to private corporations.

As decisions shaping the evolution of the mobility delivery systems of the 1980s and 1990s are made, we should consider several lessons from this formative period in the history of mass transit:

1. A large metropolitan area *can* be served by a highly fragmented mix of competing private transportation companies.

2. Competition among the companies and/or fragmentation in government control may foster the introduction of innovation.
3. Coordination can be achieved through market forces. But, whether achieved publicly or privately, there are often hidden costs which, if the system is to survive, should be accounted for.
4. Bankruptcy, deferred maintenance, poor management, and unreliable service (due to market entry and exit) are the risks of privately provided transportation service in a largely open-entry and competitive market.
5. Historically, there has been strong public sentiment that mass transportation service—profitable or not—should be (1) unified and (2) owned and operated by the public sector as a utility. These are widely held public beliefs that still persist, and they are a strong factor in shaping our urban mobility delivery systems of today as we see through the evolution of CTA to RTA and beyond.

RTA: A NEW APPROACH IN PUBLIC-PRIVATE PARTNERSHIP

The formation of CTA in 1946 resulted in the consolidation of all the major private surface providers in the city into one public system. The system's capital stock was substantially upgraded, and mass transportation service in the city was stabilized—perhaps to the point of rigidity. (A majority of the routes, for example, have not changed since the 1920s and 1930s, in spite of major population shifts.) The system also, for the first time, gave labor unions the capability to "shut the system down." And, in most instances, the threat was enough. Over the last thirty-five years, the Chicago transit unions have become a potent political force, and they have achieved major wage, benefit, and work rule victories for their members. In spite of the fact that transit system productivity has been constant or declining, CTA wages have gone up 147 percent in the last eleven years. Today the average CTA driver earns $13.04 an hour (excluding a 27 percent benefit package), considerably more than teachers and many similarly skilled manufacturing laborers. Further, many argue that labor work rules have severely limited CTA management's ability to adapt to its changing market.

By the late 1960s, CTA was in serious financial trouble. The riders of the old Chicago Surface Lines, who had provided the tax base for its successor, had moved to the suburbs — beyond the taxing authority of the city. The city was hard pressed to support the aging system, whose deficits were growing at an alarming rate. Coincidentally, the commuter railroads, which had experienced a resurgence of growth with the suburbanization of the 1950s, were in or on the verge of receivership. The concept of a Regional Transportation Authority was born as a means of tapping the lucrative suburban tax base.

The idea for an RTA was first mentioned as early as 1965, in an Association of Suburban Railroads' report, which recommended the establishment of a regional transit system to end "wasteful, uncoordinated planning and operations of separate transportation entities." A leader in the concept's promotion was the Chicago & Northwestern railroad, which had the reputation of being an efficient, self-supporting system. Indeed, it had been periodically upgrading its railroad passenger equipment and applying for and receiving authorization for fare increases from the Illinois Commerce Commission. However, by 1972, the passenger losses due to fare increases, competition from the new CTA rapid transit extension, and from suburbanization of downtown jobs, accentuated the leadership role that the railroad's officers played in developing and supporting RTA legislation.

The RTA referendum ultimately passed, but with a battle that articulated the body politic's dissatisfaction with "regionalism." Despite a 71 percent "yes" vote from within the city of Chicago, an avalanche of "no" votes from the suburbs came within 14,000 votes of defeating the proposal. The margin of suburban opposition was stunning; the McHenry, Kane, and Will County voters opposed the measure by 90 percent. In DuPage and Lake counties, the margin of opposition was 75 percent, and in suburban Cook the margin was 60 percent.

With the inauguration of RTA, answers to the questions Who owns, Who operates, and Who finances were, for the first time since 1925, reformulated. This was largely because a bailout of the commuter railroads (a key to placating the suburbs) presented a significant problem. It would be *very* expensive to buy out the rail lines, and the framers of the RTA legislation conceded that it would be difficult for the public sector to quickly acquire adequate expertise to run a railroad. Further, the railroads would not sell the government their tracks, since the tracks were also being used for freight service, and they wanted to retain control over their freight rights-of-way. In addition, the operating employees for both passenger and freight operations had common seniority rights. (Eventually, however, RTA acquired all the railroads' operating equipment and has since financed all facility improvements.)

The concept of purchasing transportation service from a private company was thus born of necessity. It was conveniently carried over to a number of private and public suburban bus operations to give the initial outward impression of a connected, unified regional system. That perception of a regional system was important, since during the referendum campaign RTA was "sold" as a means of developing a "unified regional system," and as "a means to get from Waukegan to Joliet" (despite the fact that few people want to take the trip) with one fare. Unification, like apple pie and motherhood, is hard to argue against. It is equally difficult to deliver when there is not a substantial need for it. RTA set up a number of "token" bus lines which ran through suburban villages, "connecting" them in a skeletal regional system. But many of these routes did not meet local travel needs (which were not regional in nature) and thus the buses ran empty. Indeed, subsequent RTA studies of trip patterns indicate that the region is not a "region" in terms of travel patterns; rather, it is a series of several small regions (consisting of a few neighboring towns), each with some (diminishing) linkage to downtown Chicago.

Political pressure from suburbanites, dissatisfied with the "useless" transit service for which they were now being taxed, caused yet another evolution in the resolution of the owner/operator/financier questions: the decentralized paratransit brokerage program was initiated. Under this program, RTA executes an agreement with a community wherein RTA provides (standardized) capital equipment which RTA *owns*, as well as some *financial* operating assistance for a paratransit service. It is the community's responsibility to *manage* it, *operate* it, and partially *subsidize* it. Currently forty-eight of these programs are in place.

However, in spite of RTA's noble experiments with public-private and community-managed service delivery, there have been enormous pressures to "centralize," "consolidate," and "go public." Indeed, at this writing, RTA seems to be teetering on the edge of imitating

CTA's example in terms of further public ownership consolidation. We need to understand the lessons from these experiments and the pressures that have moved the body politic to imitate CTA to discern the influences that will shape any future system.

Purchasing Service from a Public or Private Provider Is Feasible for Transportation Delivery

Purchasing service from the commuter railroads and public and private bus operations has proved to be successful, in spite of some initial and continuing problems. Three of these are worth noting: the determination of return on investment; the determination of who bears the risk; and the inappropriateness of applying the same type of contract used with a large operator for a small "mom and pop" operation.

Return on Investment. In the initial purchase of service agreements with the railroads, this issue brought out some of the worst fears of the public and private sides of the negotiating table. The rail lines listed huge amounts of capital invested in equipment and rails for which they wanted a return. The government, on the other hand, noted that the railroads had been required by the Interstate Commerce Commission to provide passenger service as part of their freight operating authority and in effect to subsidize passenger operations from freight revenues. Thus, the government reasoned, eliminating this cross subsidy should be sufficient "profit."

Who Bears the Risk? If ridership goes down (or up) who bears the loss or earns the additional profits? RTA experimented with two solutions. With the rail lines, a level of service was purchased for a flat rate that assumed an estimated revenue, which the railroad would keep. If ridership increased, the railroad kept the additional revenue; if ridership went down, the railroad incurred a loss. Additional incentives were built into the contracts to encourage the railroads to invest earnings into marketing their service and improving on-time performance to gain new riders.

With the bus companies, RTA contracted for a level of service and, on paper, kept the passenger revenue. Thus, if ridership went up, the subsidy was less; if ridership went down, the loss was RTA's.

Inappropriate Red-tape. Many very small private providers (usually taxi owners), who had been the sole source of transportation in some suburban communities until the creation of RTA, wanted to continue to provide service under contract to RTA—until they saw the contract, all fifty pages of it! Many operators did not understand the contract and were afraid of some of the requirements—both with regard to reporting and maintenance. Often RTA's bid specifications did not reflect a knowledge of the local market. Thus, the local providers (who did know the market) frequently didn't know how to properly respond to the inaccurate bid request. This overall inability of the large authority to communicate and deal with the "mom and pop" operator has led to extremely strained relationships between the two and a great deal of mutual mistrust. The result has been that RTA has gone the "public" route for most of its feeder and demand-responsive services, destroying rather than fostering a rich mix of local, privately provided transportation resources.

Standardization of Maintenance as a Major Force for Consolidation and Centralization

Once a contract has been negotiated, many operators (public and private) are aware that the contract can be milked for greater profit by *slightly* deferring maintenance, vehicle cleaning, and the like. The desire to prevent such milking, coupled with the belief that substantial economies of scale could be achieved by standardizing and consolidating maintenance, has driven RTA to set meticulous maintenance standards and practices, and to standardize and consolidate (under RTA control) maintenance operations wherever possible.

The cost of this consolidation, standardization, and monitoring has been great in terms of administrative salaries (needed to coordinate and monitor), in terms of seriously strained relationships with contractors, and in terms of lost flexibility. Part of the "standardization" involved using the same vehicles regionwide, whether or not they were appropriate to local needs or whether other, equally acceptable, vehicles existed locally, in private ownership.

An example of the cost of this push to standardize can be found in the paratransit brokerage program. An evaluation of the program by the Urban Mass Transportation Administration (UMTA) reported:

Early in the deliberations, RTA paratransit staff wanted the flexibility of providing vehicles of a variety of types and sizes to serve specific local needs. This, however, was not acceptable to a number of other RTA departments, most of which were oriented to conventional fixed-route service. These departments preferred to deal with proven vehicles that were standardized and could be obtained in quantity. Because RTA staff did not believe any of the "off-the-shelf" equipment would meet their needs, they developed their own vehicle specifications for a 21-foot, lift-equipped, school bus-type, gasoline-fueled vehicle on a truck chassis. This process of vehicle deliberations started in mid-1976, but vehicles did not arrive for the first of the UMTA funded projects until April, 1980. After the vehicles arrived, a series of malfunctions became evident. . . . a key lesson here is that if the equipment is to be purchased, it should be available immediately and have a good operating history. Once the RTA prescribed a vehicle, it committed itself to a number of time-consuming monitoring and maintenance functions which, in some of the projects, severely strained the relationships between local officials and the RTA. A key RTA staff member recommends that, when initiating a paratransit program, contractors with vehicles should be identified, and/or leased or purchased "off-the-shelf" equipment should be secured immediately.

"Unstable" Local Private Providers Force Public Ownership/Operation

In contracting for local service, RTA at times faced a situation where the existing operator was *highly* marginal and had questionable management ability, rolling stock, and maintenance facilities, or where the local operator couldn't or wouldn't understand RTA contracting policies. To RTA, the only alternative was to establish a government owned and operated traditional, standardized service, and, in almost every case, it has opted for this solution. From the perspective of RTA, this may be appropriate since it perceives its charge to be provision of unified regional service — not strengthening, supporting, or developing a variety of local transportation resources. Had that been a perceived purpose, perhaps RTA would have found it appropriate to train local management and seed new firms with young and more forward thinking management. Such an approach might result in a larger base of local service — portions of which are publicly supported, and portions of which are entirely user supported — and a set of services which adapt more easily to changes in the market and legislative largesse.

As it stands now, there is abundant, albeit anecdotal, evidence that local taxi firms have suffered for those "public-oriented" decisions of RTA. The dilemma was and is an extraordinarily difficult one. It involves balancing the "mission" of providing unified, standardized, and reliable service against the prospect of wiping out unique family enterprises that have been around "for years," but whose founders are too staid in their ways to grow into the possibilities presented by the RTA program.

Other Private Providers Aggressively Sought a Public Buyout

With the formation of RTA, some bus and rail companies wanted to cash out, and they aggressively pursued selling to the public sector. Again the Chicago and Northwestern Transportation Company is an interesting case in point. They were the only railroad at the inception of RTA that still owned its operating equipment; the others used equipment that had been purchased with federal dollars by suburban transit districts and leased to them. Northwestern saw the RTA legislation as a means to cash out, *at replacement value*, capital equipment used in operations that, from their perspective, had no future. Although RTA was conceived as an umbrella financing/planning/coordinating body, legislative authority existed for direct ownership and operation.

The combined private sector pressure and the institutional rewards for buy out have been tempting, inasmuch as the institution is still fighting for its political life. When it issues revenue bonds or notes backed by the "full faith and credit of the RTA and the State of Illinois" for a capital or operations expenditure, it gives the state legislature a great deal of incentive to prolong its life for the term of the bonds. Thus, in spite of its initial conception as a broker/coordinator of regional service, RTA is by choice and circumstance evolving into a traditional public owner/operator. It promulgates policies of centralized, standardized, and consolidated maintenance management and service delivery.

Perhaps it is not surprising that the regional public transportation financial problems that brought RTA into being are far from over. In spite of dramatic fare increases, major service cuts and layoffs, a huge deficit is projected for 1983. Ridership continues to fall, and the state legislature has endured two crises without increasing transit funds to the region. At the same time, maintenance expenses and labor costs have climbed so high on the paratransit program that some communities are rejecting RTA's offer of vehicles and partial support and are opting instead to contract directly with local taxi operators as a cheaper alternative.

TRADITIONAL TAXI FIRMS' FINANCIAL PROBLEMS

The other "traditional" transportation provider in the Chicago region—the taxi industry—is also in serious financial trouble. It is faced with many of the same demographic changes as the bus companies, and most taxi companies are prevented by regulation from diversifying and changing their mix of services, equipment, and rates to keep pace. A recent investigation of the taxi industry in the Chicago Region found that:

- Since 1973, there has been a consistent yearly decline in the absolute number of taxis in nearly every county of the region; the suburban taxi fleet has declined by 26 percent through 1981.
- The ratio of taxis to every thousand people has declined from 0.35 in 1975 to 0.27 in 1980.
- The level of taxi demand has dropped from an estimated 33,000 daily passenger trips in 1975 to 27,155 in 1980.
- The average taxi company covers only 96 percent of its costs.
- The number of trips per taxi-vehicle/day has dropped from a 1975 estimate of twenty-six to twenty-one in 1981.

A year after this study was made, one of the oldest and largest taxi conglomerates in the nation, Checker and Yellow Taxi Companies of Chicago, initiated an attempt to sell its medallions to drivers. This further indicates the weakness of this traditional industry.

SOLUTIONS FOR THE FUTURE

It is true that many traditional systems are in financial trouble. In Chicago, this has happened partly because these systems have been unable or unwilling to adapt to significantly changed mobility needs and patterns. But the picture is not hopelessly bleak. Parts of these systems will survive because there remains a strong, viable market for the type of service provided. And, refreshingly, there are numerous new services emerging, specifically tailored to some of the region's changed and unmet mobility needs.

As we describe some of these new services in the sections that follow, we encourage the reader to note that nearly all have developed totally outside the traditional system, often via a regulatory loophole. Most are small-scale and are tailored to a very specific market, often to a specific set of people taking specific trips. The trips are almost always door-to-door, hence the need for connectivity or "unification" is reduced. There is a varied mix of public and private actors assuming the funding, sponsorship, and operator roles. These new services are not "coordinated" into some grand unified regional system. *Significantly, no one seems to care.*

The Commuter Bus Clubs

In 1981 a financial crisis, coupled with the state legislature's refusal to grant additional transit assistance, forced RTA to drastically increase commuter rail fares; in some cases, fares were nearly doubled. Passengers rebelled and, taking advantage of an old series of court decisions that allowed large companies to bus their employees to and from work without ICC or city regulation, commuters formed "clubs" and chartered daily commuter bus service. This was sometimes done with help from school and charter bus companies. The description that follows is largely excerpted from an investigation of the "new industry" by the Metropolitan Housing and Planning Council of Chicago.

The primary market for these services has been among the low- and moderate-income suburbs to the south and west of the city. The organization of the services is simple. A group of residents charter a bus to take them to their jobs in the Loop for a month. They attempt to fill the bus and then divide the cost of the bus for the month among the riders. In some cases, the charter bus company performs this function, making weekly or monthly charter agreements with individual commuters.

These private and unsubsidized buses have been competing very effectively with the traditional RTA system. In the south suburbs, the area with the greatest concentration of subscription service, the average cost per passenger trip is $1.15 for the primary carriers. This fare covers the entire cost of the service, plus, presumably, a small profit. By contrast, the cost per passenger trip on the commuter rail is $1.80 to $2.80, and these fares only cover 69 percent of the *operating cost.* The average *operating cost* of an RTA suburban bus is $1.44 per passenger trip, and this *excludes* the cost of the vehicle.

Subscription bus service has evolved with a small but highly stable ridership. Approximately 3,000 commuters use it every day to reach their jobs in the Loop. This number appears to have remained relatively constant since the fall of 1981, when most of the routes now in existence had been organized. On most routes every seat is sold, and some have waiting lists.

The MHPC report found several key reasons for the relative success that these services have enjoyed. These same factors may play an important role in many of the emerging services of the future.

The Operations Are Small. The scale of the entire phenomenon is microscopic in relation to its competition, RTA. All subscription services together represent scarcely more than 3,000 riders and eighty buses. Most of the private citizen "community coordinators" have only one to three vehicles to supervise. This small scale allows a great deal of attention to detail and, because of the measurable cost savings for every additional rider, high occupancy is encouraged.

The Routes are Tailored to the User Groups. Unlike public transportation, which must attempt to design routes that will attract maximum ridership, subscription bus service has its ridership as a given. The group determines the pick-up points most convenient to its members. The "bar-bell design" (small collection area to small delivery area) of these long-distance express routes obviates elaborate routing and scheduling.

The Service Does Not Require High Residential Density to be Effective. While it is estimated that fixed route service requires about 4,000 residents and jobs per square mile to be moderately successful, subscription service requires only that from 44 to 48 persons who work in the Loop agree on a few convenient pick-up points.

The Operations Are Highly Flexible. Because subscription service is at present unregulated, community groups and bus companies have almost unlimited flexibility to make service adjustments that are mutually agreeable. The ability to make frequent minor adjustments to pick-up and drop-off locations and times, or to vehicle capacity and the like, allows the route to remain tailored to its user group. This is critical to retaining high occupancy and preserving low costs.

At present most subscription bus ridership consists of former commuter rail passengers. Because RTA could not (or did not choose to) reduce any of its peak-hour capacity in response to new alternative services, the revenue loss to RTA from these riders has been estimated at roughly $253,000 per month. And, the MHPC study concludes, the concept has substantial expansion potential in the low- and middle-income suburbs 20 to 40 miles from the Loop.

Vanpooling

In the Chicago region nearly all traditional transit routes lead to the heart of the city. They are of little use to the large office complexes that have located in the rapidly growing, affluent northern suburbs, but which depend heavily on the labor pools of the city and a few inner ring suburbs. Many companies – Allstate, Zenith, Motorola, G.D. Searle, Montgomery Ward, Baxter Laboratories, and others – have facilitated and in some cases underwritten aggressive vanpool employee transportation programs. Today over 200 employer-sponsored vanpools transport some 2,000 commuters to their largely suburban jobs in the region. There may be as many nonemployer, privately operated vans as well.

An important contribution made by companies that sponsor vanpool programs is the assignment of a full- or part-time coordinator who has become skilled in arranging for employee transportation needs, whether it be parking, matching carpools, leasing vans, or, in some instances, contracting for bus service. The coordinator's salary is paid by the company, not the taxpayers. And, while their mission is coordination, it is limited solely to the needs of their company's employees. This group of coordinators has become sufficiently self-aware to form an association for information exchange and to gain a public voice on regional transportation issues of concern to them.

Interestingly, the pooling concept has, over the past several years, been marketed aggressively in this region by three "competing" publicly funded agencies: the State of Illinois Department of Environmental Resources, RTA, and the regional Metropolitan Planning

Organization (MPO), all under the program name, "Chicago Commuter Computer." Although the fierce interagency turf battles have in some instances reached the press (to the embarrassment of all), the program staff privately agree that the competition has forced far greater performance on their part (to "outdo" the other agency) than might have been achieved had the staffs been combined into a single agency.

The Developer as Transportation Sponsor/Financier

The Village of Schaumburg, located at the intersection of two major regional expressways, has experienced unprecedented economic development, population growth, and traffic congestion. In 1980 a traffic consultant reported that the village would need to at least double the capacity of its current arterial system to accommodate existing and anticipated traffic. When both the Illinois Department of Transportation and RTA indicated that funds would not be available to even marginally meet Schaumburg's projected mobility needs, the village recently adopted an unusual zoning ordinance that will require new developers to take greater financial responsibility for the transportation generated by the development.

Social Service Transportation

One of the rationales for using public funds to operate mass transportation systems is to provide mobility to those who cannot use the mainstream automobile/street system, due either to low income or physical disability. However, until recently the traditional system made little attempt to accommodate the physically disabled, and the diverse locations of social service delivery centers vis-à-vis the initiating locations of low-income clients often made use of the public transportation system by this group impractical at best. Because many federally funded social service programs include provision for client transportation, and because many private social service agencies have found provision of transportation indispensable to service delivery, an extensive network of social service transportation has developed in the region—again entirely outside the traditional system.

A 1979 survey found no fewer than 365 separate alternative transportation programs. Some make as many as 1,000 trips per day. Nearly all are client centered, serving only the homes of the clients and a few destinations: social service centers, medical centers, grocery stores, and the like. Some of the services are provided by private bus and taxi companies; others are provided with vehicles owned and operated by the organization itself.

The Emergence of Paratransit Companies

Though taxi and livery companies as a group are facing rough financial times, a few have found regulatory loopholes through which to grow and expand into new markets. Two examples illustrate this innovative approach.

The Chicago-based Cook-DuPage Transportation Company is neither a taxi, livery, nor bus company. New taxi or livery medallions have not been awarded in this city since the 1950s. In addition, permission to operate buses is always heavily contested at the ICC by the major charter companies. Cook-DuPage vehicles (station wagons and buses) are licensed as "medicars," a mode so ill defined in state statute as to have no effective definition, and a service that is virtually unregulated by the city or county. The company provides high-quality social service transportation to a number of agencies. Since there are no rate or shared-riding restrictions, the rates can be based on multiple occupancy and the actual costs incurred in providing the service. In addition, the company reportedly free-lances by servicing large groups of senior citizens at senior citizen housing complexes on selected shopping days for a flat, per-person rate.

On the other hand, there's the Blue Cab Company in Oak Park. Its owner once got a deal on a van, and quickly discovered that since it wasn't a taxi she could experiment with group riding and group rates to the airport. Opportunities developed to use the "nontaxi" for various types of group-contracted services. Social service agencies and a local college inquired about contracting for demand-responsive and subscription service respectively. In the last two years, this small suburban taxi firm has added two school buses, a lift-equipped van, and a minibus to its fleet. Perhaps more importantly, the owner has added a part-time marketing representative. Today, the owner refers to the company as a "transportation company," not a taxi firm. As such, she recently vigorously contested an RTA paratransit program in her community, claiming that her company will provide more hours of service with less advance notice for 20 to 30 percent less than the projected *operating costs alone* of the RTA service.

Courtesy Cars

In spite of (or perhaps because of) some of the strictest taxi, livery, and transit regulations in the country, "courtesy cars" have proliferated in the Chicago region during the past decade. These cars, vans, and buses collect passengers at airports, train terminals, employee parking lots, hotels, condominium complexes, and other gathering points, to deliver them to shopping centers, ball games, hotels, rental car lots, theaters, restaurants, and other social gathering points where the affluent spend money and appreciate the convenience of hassle-free transportation. It is impossible to get an estimate of the number of these vehicles because they are licensed as private vehicles, and, since they claim to operate no differently than offering a friend a ride, they too are totally outside the realm of regulation. At the airport, however, the number of hotel and rental car courtesy vehicles has increased to the point of controversial traffic congestion and occasional threats of restricting their access to the terminal. Other examples include:

- Apartments and condominiums provide shuttles to shopping and transportation terminals;
- A major Chicago department store, Marshall Field, offers shuttle service to shoppers between its downtown stores and transportation hubs;
- Hospitals and universities run regular shuttles between train stations and their complexes;
- Hotels offer courtesy van service to restaurants, shopping, and other points of interest;
- Restaurants and dinner clubs have begun packaging special dinner tours, with transportation provided to and from the evening's specified event;
- In a similar vein, a major retailer, Polk Brothers, has sponsored programs of offering transit passes to any customer visiting its

stores. Sol Polk, one of the founders of the firm, has been personally committed to the inclusion of public transportation in its special offers for more than ten years.

The interesting element of these services, as with the social service and employer-based transportation programs, is that transportation is not dealt with as an end in itself. It is packaged together with the object for which one needs to travel (that is, hotel, shopping, theater, employment, etc.), and it is sponsored by those who want the passenger to make the trip.

What we have just discussed are a sampling of some of the "births," the innovations, taking place in our regional transportation delivery system. There are striking similarities among the seemingly diverse services.

1. They are all small services;
2. They are carefully tailored to a specific set of people and a specific set of trips. Cost recoupment is based exactly on the service provided—not some systemwide average which has been set by political process;
3. They are not coordinated, nor does there seem to be a need for coordination since service is generally door-to-door and connectivity is not an issue;
4. They are frequently packaged as part of the objectives of the regional transportation delivery system;
5. They are frequently sponsored and sometimes financed by those whose enterprises benefit from the resulting travel.

Finally, we note that these innovations have occurred within the cracks of the system, where regulatory authority was either ambiguous or nonexistent.

LESSONS FROM THE PAST AND SPECULATION FOR THE FUTURE

At the beginning of this chapter, we suggested that the responses to three or four primary questions have determined the public transportation systems of the past. And, we suggested, the reformulation of those answers will shape the way urban mobility is provided in the future. With that in mind, we can review these answers and examine both what we have learned from the past and what the "sunrise" systems emerging today seem to suggest for the future.

Consolidation versus Independent, Decentralized, and Potentially Competitive Enterprises

From the beginning of mass transit we have been responding to this set of choices almost with one voice: consolidation! We have gone from the consolidation of the private companies to the consolidation of a single city system to the centralization and consolidation of a regional system. We have done this with the best of intentions:

- *Unification:* To provide through service in the city and later in the region, or at minimum to provide connecting transfer service so that "anyone" could go "anywhere."

- *Economies of Scale:* Consolidating operations and standardizing practices, it has been argued, will improve service and reduce costs.

- *Avoiding Service Duplication:* This appears to be an efficient use of capital resources whether those resources are public or private.

In spite of these reasonable intentions our experience with the consolidated/centralized answer suggests the following conclusions.

Coordination/Consolidation Has Hidden Costs. It may not provide the promised savings. There are substantial costs associated with the coordination and communication required in consolidation. Indeed, some recent research has found *dis*economies of scale in passenger and freight transportation. These information and communication costs have recently become well established in the management literature, to the point that some advocate the *efficiency* of horizontal management structures where product divisions function as a loose collection of independent, competitive, overlapping minicompanies. At the very least our historical analysis suggests that coordination in the form of through service or nominally priced transfers has the effect of substantially lowering revenue with no associated reduction in operating cost.

Service Duplication May Foster Innovation. The competition implied in service duplication has the very beneficial effect of keeping transportation operators "tuned in" to changing consumer needs. A steady introduction of innovation has been the very healthy reaction. Coordination/consolidation solidifies the status quo, substantially reducing the opportunity for new ideas and, as a result, stunting the system's chance to grow and change with the times. Consolidation has contributed to the reduction of a once vibrant, albeit chaotic, industry to a lumbering, moribund giant which has little relevance to the way we live today.

Consolidation Has Brought With It Some of The Worst Excesses of Monopoly Control. Combining the labor forces of several formerly competing companies into a single city or regional system has given transit workers substantial power to cripple a city, without the countervailing risk of losing their jobs entirely. That power has been used to excess both in wage negotiations and in stifling the introduction of (potentially competitive) innovation.

Finally, it cannot be argued that the region cannot be served by a nonunified system. We have seen that the city and surrounding region has been well served by a competing mix of independent providers. The fact that such a system can work was most recently confirmed during the December 17–20, 1979, CTA strike, when a patchwork collection of taxis, school and charter buses, vanpools, and carpools became the Chicago transportation system for four days, under no one's direction. Given that the system emerged overnight from nothing, it functioned quite well.

A glance at the patterns emerging in the sunrise transportation operations suggests that the "unification" argument may also be on weak ground. It is not at all clear that trip demand is regional. Studies of trip patterns indicate that people shop, play, and, in many cases, work reasonably close to home. We have long known from behavioral research that people hate to transfer. That fact is now being reflected in the subscription concept for work commuting, as well as in the packaging of transportation with the travel objective, which we have seen with social services, shopping centers, and dinner clubs. If the service is door-to-door, there is little need for coordination or connectivity. Indeed, this refocusing of service, from systems to people and the specific trips they make, gives significant advantage to small systems that can afford to deal at the "micro" level.

We as a political body have said "yes, yes, yes" to the consolidation and centralization of transportation. Both history and our emerging systems suggest that we try an approach that allows for more systems that are small, independent, and subregional in scope; systems that are focused on the person and trip rather than on system operations; and systems that have the motivation and the flexibility to adapt to future needs.

Who Will Own? Who Will Operate?

Just as we answered the consolidation question, so have we answered these next questions almost unanimously: the public sector. While there have recently been a few weak voices to the contrary among the small private sector operators, the fact is that, as public transportation became less profitable, some large private companies whose owners stood to profit enormously from a public buy out have been the loudest advocates for public ownership.

Public ownership and operation have tended to result in all the problems of centralization and consolidation. In addition, there is strong evidence that "the public" cannot afford the commitment to unlimited blank checks—at least not for an "old style" unified regional system that serves no one particularly well.

We have had success with alternative answers to these questions, particularly with public-private partnerships in the form of purchase-of-service agreements. We have also had success with a completely private approach, both historically and with today's subscription buses. The not-for-profits also seem to be doing well in their niches. The nontransportation providers—the hotels, developers, and employers, with their shuttles and vans—may be the only growth sector in the region's transportation system! The fact is that there is no one superior provider. Perhaps we should keep it that way, to prevent the stagnation and death that the concept of one owner/operator (whether it be public or private) implies.

We note that there is one answer to the owner/operator question that has been particularly offensive to the public sector. Nevertheless, we believe it is worth considering: private sector ownership and operation, *facilitated* by the public sector. RTA has been able to assist employer vanpools, which are privately owned and operated on a not-for-profit basis. The result has been an addition to our regional transportation system at virtually no cost. Couldn't the concept be extended to provide technical assistance to profitmaking transportation providers to help them identify new markets, to upgrade management skills, to share the risk of a new service? Wouldn't this be more productive than competing with these small firms and eventually running them out of business? This approach seems to expand the system at very little public expense, whereas our current approach seems to contract the system and increase public expense.

Both present and past experience, then, suggest that our answer to the owner/operator question should be: many. We would add a footnote to that answer suggesting that we open up a new public sector role of *facilitating* and *encouraging* profitable private ownership and operation.

Who Will Finance?

Historically we have answered this question two ways: the user, and, most recently, the taxpayers. Even during the heyday of referendums advocating public take-over of the private systems, it was always assumed that the user would pay, just as the user pays for electricity and water. However, when it became evident that the previous users would not pay for a service that had become a lesser good (compared to the automobile) and that was inconvenient to new lifestyles, the body politic was persuaded that "the public" *should* finance mass transit operations. The rationale provided was a combination of: energy conservation; air pollution control; urban renewal; mobility for the mobility disadvantaged; and congestion reduction. As long as "the public" was willing to pay, the rationale didn't particularly matter.

It appears, however, that the body politic is changing its mind—but not a full 180 degrees. There is still political support for *some* taxpayer financing of public transportation, just not as much. At the same time the sunrise transportation operations seem to suggest that there are a number of nonpublic financiers. The vanpool and subscription bus services suggest that user-supported transportation is alive and well. Some employers are willing to subsidize employee transportation systems. Developers, retailers, restaurateurs, and others show evidence of some willingness to finance transportation.

Financial institutions, which can sell the tax benefits of capital equipment, have shown interest. Indeed, the business sector's willingness to pay, rather than complain, was clearly demonstrated during the previously mentioned CTA strike. Public and private social service organizations are also actively financing transportation in the region.

Recognizing that there are a number of beneficiaries of a good urban mobility system (including the public at large), perhaps we should try to answer the question of Who Should Finance? by saying, Those who benefit. Our rather scarce public funds could then be reserved for those urban mobility cases where there is a clear general taxpayer obligation to the mobility disadvantaged, or where there is an achievable general public benefit (congestion reduction). The beneficiaries could pool their resources to continue the system just as it is. It is likely that some pooling of resources will go on simply because there continue to be many beneficiaries of a downtown-oriented system. This is being done now with employer-subsidized passes and retailer-subsidized tokens. But it is also likely that some targeting of resources will prove beneficial and efficient, as in user-side subsidies for the poor and handicapped or for subscription buses and vanpools.

In retrospect we have advocated a future urban mobility system composed of a number of small systems, owned, operated, and financed by a variety of actors. If this is the case, what is the role of a public institution like RTA? We might rashly conclude that none exists. But the fact is that there is still a need for taxes to be collected and disbursed wisely. Apart from this fiduciary role, we believe that an RTA-type institution can play an invaluable *facilitating* role. In this role, RTA would be *accountable* for conserving our mobility resources and developing new ones. It would be charged with striking a Solomon-like balance between the regulation of markets and the introduction of innovation. RTA would also provide information to citizens on what could become a bewildering array of services. It would not, however, own or operate any systems.

In essence, the government role would be to insure that the service that is needed, exists—irrespective of who owns, operates, or finances it—and that those who need the service know where and how to get it.

Chapter 4

USE OF PRIVATE COMPANIES TO PROVIDE PUBLIC TRANSPORTATION SERVICES IN TIDEWATER VIRGINIA

James C. Echols

THE IMPETUS FOR PRIVATE CONTRACTING

It is becoming increasingly clear that fixed-route transit services are not appropriate to the low-volume ridership levels generated by low-density development. The costs of fixed-route bus services are increasing so fast that they are becoming too expensive to be financed by the cities, which are already strapped for funds to continue existing levels of service. Even in old established residential neighborhoods, bus ridership is declining while operating costs are increasing.

The Tidewater Transportation District Commission (TTDC), a regional transit authority organized in the Commonwealth of Virginia to plan, operate, and regulate public transportation services in the five-city area of Chesapeake, Norfolk, Portsmouth, Suffolk, and Virginia Beach, became aware of these facts some seven years ago. Of the 1,092 square miles encompassed by the District, about one-third is urbanized. The central cities of Norfolk and Portsmouth are completely urbanized, as is the northern third of Virginia Beach and small portions of Chesapeake and Suffolk. The remainder of the area is largely rural, with agriculture being a major industry. (Table 4–1 gives population and population density of each city.) The density of much of the area is below the level appropriate for regular fixed-route bus services.

Table 4-1. TTDC Characteristics.

City	1980 Population	Population Density (Persons Per Square Mile)
Chesapeake	114,486	335
Norfolk	266,979	5,037
Portsmouth	104,577	3,606
Suffolk	47,621	116
Virginia Beach	262,199	1,012
District	795,861	729

The metropolitan region has low-density housing and employment areas typical of many mid-sized metropolitan areas throughout the country. Current development continues to be toward low-density, single-family residential growth on the edge of the existing built-up areas. Employment and shopping locations are continuing to disperse from the old downtown areas into low-density industrial parks and regional shopping centers. This trend is continuing even in the face of rising household and commuting costs.

TTDC provides public transportation services to each city under an agreement that permits each city to receive as much service as it is willing to pay for. Costs are allocated according to vehicle hours of service, and revenues are allocated according to passenger fares. State aid, which supplements local operating funds, is provided for maintenance materials, fuel, and supplies. The prevailing local funding constraints of the member cities, along with the high costs of doing business as usual, are the principal reasons TTDC undertook the use of private operators as a way to lower the cost of providing public transportation.

When reviewing its financial outlook and service delivery program during 1976, TTDC management confronted a situation where: (1) the costs of its fixed-route bus services were high and forecast to go higher; (2) fare revenues were low and forecast to go lower; and, (3) subsidy amounts were too high to be financed by the local cities and were forecast to go higher each year. TTDC concluded that it was beyond its power, in the near future, to substantially reduce the costs of fixed-route bus services (due to increasing wage and fuel costs) or to substantially increase ridership (due to continued dispersal of jobs and homes). This situation is presented in Figure 4-2, which plots

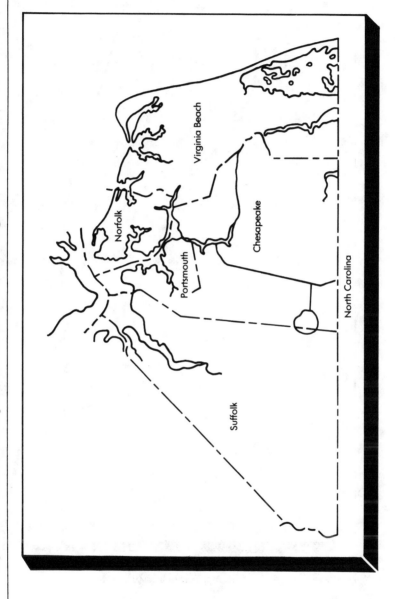

Figure 4-1. Tidewater Transportation District Commission, Virginia.

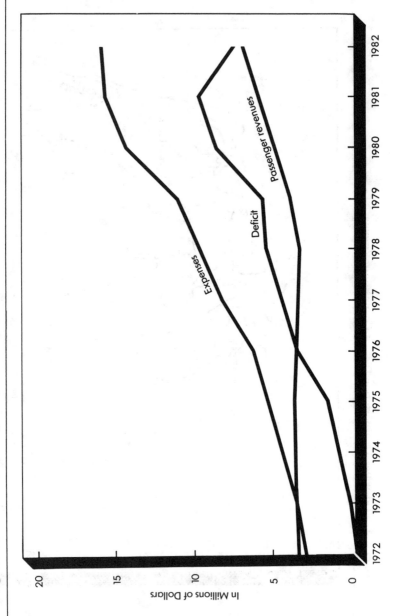

Figure 4-2. TTDC Transit Expenses, Revenues, and Deficit.

costs, revenues, and deficits for the ten-year period following public acquisition of the local transit system.

Thus, TTDC was faced with a subsidy that would continue to increase significantly each year if the existing bus service program were continued. Given the limited amount of subsidy money available from the cities, the options before TTDC were either to reduce its transportation services or to develop a way to provide them at lower cost. TTDC chose to develop lower cost services, and the use of private operators is part of that strategy.

COMMUTER SERVICES

In addition to contracting with private firms to operate regular commuter transit services, the present use of private providers also includes the operation of carpools, and buspools for daily peak-period commuter trips. Since peak-period services are very expensive for transit agencies to provide, substantial cost reductions can result from converting regular scheduled bus routes to private, citizen-operated services such as vanpools. Thus, active marketing of vanpools is an integral part of TTDC's service program. "Peak shedding" from publicly operated buses to privately operated vanpools and buspools is one way the use of private providers has had a significant impact on reducing public transportation costs in Tidewater. TTDC's commuter vanpool program carries approximately 1,000 employees to and from work each weekday in less time and at lower cost than the regular bus service and at no cost to public funds. Indeed, vanpooling saves a substantial amount of public funds. At a bus load factor of forty during the peak period, it would have required approximately twenty-five extra TTDC buses at a capital cost of at least $3,000,000. And allowing for operating expenses of $30 per bus-hour, and four hours per round trip, this service would have cost about $660,000 per year, which is about 4 percent of the total TTDC operating budget.

Buspools, where a private citizen drives a bus to and from work and carries up to forty fellow workers, have application at large employment sites. This type of commuter service also costs less to the rider than the regular bus service, and again at no cost in public subsidy funds. (Information on these types of privately provided commuter transportation services is presented in Chapter 4.)

PURCHASE OF SERVICES

The objective of TTDC's service delivery program is to provide an alternative mode of transportation, at less cost to both the rider (than driving alone) and the transit operator, in low- and medium-density areas. TTDC first proposed to experiment with shared-ride taxi service as a new mode of public transportation. It is less costly than bus service, uses private providers of transportation, and is suitable for public transportation in low-density areas.

Conceptual development of shared-ride taxi service at TTDC started in 1977. Dial-a-ride transportation was then under active development and demonstration in a number of communities throughout the country. TTDC, in cooperation with the City of Virginia Beach, was considering ways to respond to the travel needs of its suburban locations, which were then unserved by public transportation. Some form of demand-responsive transportation seemed appropriate. It was felt that shared-ride taxi services could be designed and operated for the work, shopping, personal business, school, and social-recreation trips between major activity centers and low-density areas.

TTDC's first effort to understand this travel demand was to survey potential users of the new services. Five suburban activity centers were selected, including a shopping mall, hospital, community college, and office park. People arriving at each activity center were asked eleven questions including origin/destination, mode, trip purpose, and demographics. It was concluded from the survey results that there was only a small potential ridership for shared-taxi, even under the best of service conditions.

Although the results were discouraging, conceptual development was pursued. In early 1978, a Request for Proposal (RFP) was drafted to solicit the interest of taxi companies in providing shared-ride taxi service at a regional shopping center. The objectives included meeting the transportation needs of those people not served by other forms of public transportation and strengthening the taxi market. The RFP requested information on fare structure, service area, requests for service, level of service, and coordination among taxi operators. The RFP proposed that the fare be set so that the service was self-supporting and profitable for the taxi company.

TTDC received expressions of interest from two taxi companies in the city of Norfolk. Initially they thought the RFP was for elderly and handicapped services, in which they were keenly interested at the time. Still, they appeared interested in the shared-ride taxi concept; but they, as Norfolk companies, would have difficulty operating exclusively in the separate jurisdiction of Virginia Beach. No Virginia Beach company had expressed interest. In reviewing their proposals with the private firms, both companies declined to continue in the development of shared-ride services.

Although no service was ever implemented at the shopping center, these early efforts did lay the groundwork for several arrangements with taxi companies in 1979. One was contracting with three companies to provide elderly and handicapped services.

ELDERLY AND HANDICAPPED SERVICES

TTDC was operating two kinds of van service for the elderly and handicapped: (1) a dial-a-ride service for the clients of social service agencies—operated under contract to the agencies, and financed by them; (2) a dial-a-ride service for other kinds of transportation needs of the elderly or handicapped—financed by TTDC, with a nominal fee to users. The local cab companies asked to take over the second service, under contract to TTDC, arguing that they could provide it at a lower unit cost per ride. They were already obtaining significant revenue from the transportation of patients under the Medicaid program and viewed the proposed service as a logical extension of that market.

Based on the desire of the elderly and handicapped community to expand transportation services and with the urging and endorsement of the Elderly and Handicapped Advisory Committee, TTDC contracted with three independent cab companies to provide door-to-door services for elderly and handicapped citizens not affiliated with a social service organization. Each person wishing to use the service had to be registered with TTDC after being certified as elderly or handicapped by a social service organization. TTDC then issued an identification card, which permitted the person to call one of the cab companies under contract and receive a trip for a fare of $1.00. The cab company transported the person at the regular meter rate, ob-

Table 4-2. Provision of Door-to-Door Elderly and Handicapped Services by Private Taxi Companies.

Month	Number of Trips Provided	Cost of Service	Cost Per Trip
May 1979	123	$ 756	$ 6.15
June	109	451	4.14
July	59	355	6.02
August	264	623	2.36
September	146	388	2.66
(Begin Contract Taxi Service)			
October	1,146	6,933	6.05
November	2,205	9,713	4.40
December	1,464	26,346	18.00
January 1980	1,641	23,963	14.60
February	1,410	14,321	10.16
March	2,660	46,616	17.52
April	2,797	43,616	15.59
May	2,618	29,257	11.18
June	3,518	20,531	5.84
July	2,839	34,546	12.17
August	5,029	61,055	12.14
September	3,211	38,971	12.14
(Contract taxi service terminated)			
October	881	9,507	10.79
November	880	9,034	10.26
December	1,121	11,467	10.23

tained a receipt for the trip, and billed TTDC for the difference between the meter fare and the $1.00 passenger fare.

Since the unit cost of the taxis was lower, if the total number of trips had remained constant, the total TTDC subsidy for elderly and handicapped services would have declined. We actually anticipated some increase in trip taking, but the size of the increase proved surprising: demand expanded by factor of ten. This was further enlarged by the cab companies, who wanted to expand their total revenue, and hence encouraged users to make more, longer, and lower priority trips. The cabs even agreed to wait while the rider participated in shopping or recreational events, hence raising the unit cost of service provision. The combination of the unexpectedly high latent demand for transportation, and the operational problems of rationing the total amount of service, eventually led to severe financial problems.

The taxi program lasted for one year before the cost became prohibitive, and TTDC terminated the program altogether and returned to its own limited service. The rapid expansion of riders carried, and the cost of the program while using private taxi companies, is presented in Table 4–2.

TTDC now operates the service with its own personnel and limits service provided to stay within its budget. This is a very substantial reduction from the unrestrained taxi level that was being provided, and it resulted in a strong, but short, reaction by handicapped citizens. Trips currently being provided to unaffiliated handicapped citizens are primarily for work and medical purposes. Trips must be requested a day in advance, and most of the available supply is consumed each day as soon as reservations are permitted. The Advisory Committee continues to monitor these services and meets monthly to review and advise on ways to improve and expand the service.

SHARED-RIDE TAXI SERVICES

Adjacent to the city of Portsmouth is a low-density, rural area of Chesapeake called Deep Creek, which had several established and rapidly developing subdivisions in 1975 when the private bus system serving it was acquired by TTDC. It had two bus routes which extended from Portsmouth, serving it on approximately sixty-minute headways. One route was immediately terminated upon public acquisition because of high deficits. Service on the other route was later reduced to two-hour and longer headways, as declining ridership and increasing costs produced a steadily worsening deficit per passenger—TTDC's principal performance indicator. After much public comment, a third route was extended to the area to improve service in the fall of 1978. However, deficit per passenger continued to increase, and Chesapeake city officials asked TTDC either to provide service alternatives to the existing bus service or to terminate the service altogether.

TTDC and Chesapeake city officials had several discussions in early 1979 concerning ways to provide a basic level of public transportation in the areas where fixed-route bus service was not appropriate. TTDC suggested a shared-ride taxi service to replace the poorly performing bus route. TTDC's presentation to the city council indicated that such service would be better, since it could pick up people at their homes; and since subsidy costs would be lower, as a result of both a lower operating cost and a higher fare for the user. The city council did not agree that such a travel arrangement should be supported by city funds, as they believed that cab service was a high-quality service mainly used by upper-income people, and it decided to terminate the bus service and not replace it with an alternative.

After an interval of six months, public requests to reinstitute the bus service built to a point where the city council agreed to restore fixed-route bus service over the old route. This bus route performed more poorly than the previous one, since costs were now higher and riders were fewer, and thus the deficit per passenger increased over the previously unacceptable high level. Faced with the dilemma of citizen demands for service, including a standing-room-only crowd in the city council chambers during a public hearing on restoring service, and the unacceptable cost of continuing the current bus service, the city council agreed to try a new way of providing a basic public transportation service in the area.

The major change was to terminate the fixed-route bus service and operate a flexible service tailored to carry residents of the area to either a regular bus route in Portsmouth or to an activity center such as Tower Mall. The flexible service would use a taxi- or van-type vehicle, would be available on an on-call basis, would pick up at the home, and would cost the rider $1 per trip (twice the regular bus fare).

An analysis of the alternative services—fixed-route bus and shared-ride taxi—showed that the taxi service would be cheaper. This is illustrated in Table 4-3. Based on the above analysis, shared-ride taxi services to be provided by a private provider were selected for imple-

Table 4-3.   Alternatives Analysis for Deep Creek, Month of July 1979.

	Vehicle Hours	Cost	Passengers	Revenues	Deficits	Deficit/ Passenger
Current TTDC Bus Service	239	$4,660.00	1,170	$526.00	$4,134.00	$3.53
Estimated Shared-Ride Taxi Service (Private Operator)	338	2,704.00	650	650.00	2,054.00	3.16

mentation in September 1979. This service change resulted in a sub-stantial cost savings to Chesapeake.

Based on the city council's acceptance of the concept and on favorable experience with the service, TTDC proceeded in its devel-opmental efforts. An opportunity arose as a result of complaints about congestion at Tidewater's largest shopping mall, Military Circle Mall. Both the mall's owners and city officials were concerned with improving traffic access. TTDC suggested that a shared-ride taxi ser-vice might help.

With the cooperation of the mall's management and merchant's association, an operational plan for service was developed and imple-mented. The final plan provided for services from the mall to an adjacent subdivision, Kempsville, located in Virginia Beach. This provided benefits to two cities and allowed a Norfolk taxi company to operate the service on a fully paid cost per hour basis. The service was to be an experiment during the 1979 Christmas season. It began on November 15, 1979 with taxis dedicated to the service Monday through Saturday, 9:30 a.m. to 10:30 p.m. The fare was a dollar each way. Because of poor ridership, one taxi was eliminated on Decem-ber 4. Ridership never exceeded about fifteen in a day and service was terminated on January 1, 1980. The taxi company charged $8 per vehicle hour, which was less than a third of the cost of bus service.

While this particular experiment failed, TTDC continued to con-centrate on the initiation of shared-ride services in low-density neigh-borhoods that were unserved by public transportation and on the substitution of shared-ride or small bus services for lightly patronized bus routes. In addition to variably routed shared-ride van services, TTDC proposed substituting fixed-route service to be operated by private operators for selected evening and weekend TTDC bus ser-vices, particularly since ridership on some TTDC bus services operat-ing after 7:00 p.m. dropped significantly. TTDC analyzed evening and weekend ridership statistics to select several routes which war-ranted lower capacity and lower cost service. Also, since evening bus service had been terminated in Portsmouth several years before, TTDC proposed reinstituting public transportation service in one or two corridors.

All known private operators of transit services in the area were contacted, apprised of TTDC's interest in contracting for the opera-tion of selected low volume routes, and requested to express any interest in contracting for the services. TTDC also offered to help them obtain the proper equipment for the services.

TTDC's program was to: determine potential markets; remove institutional and legal barriers; market the service; develop the appropriate service arrangement including coordinated dispatching; underwrite the start-up and developmental cost of the service during the trial period; and monitor the services.

It was anticipated that TTDC would contract for substitute services to be provided by local taxicab and other private transit operators. TTDC would plan the service, develop specifications, and solicit bids from qualified service providers. TTDC would then monitor the service contract and conduct appropriate data collection to evaluate the effectiveness of the service.

Promotion of these services was considered essential. Since they would serve primarily specific neighborhoods, localized advertising would be used, particularly direct mail, door-to-door, and newspaper. Also, personal selling by TTDC's Transportation Service Representatives would be employed to inform neighborhood groups, businesses, and other local associations. Brochures, posters, and other materials would be produced to support promotion activities.

CONTRACTING FOR SERVICES

Taxicab companies were solicited to bid on the provision of the various shared-ride and van-type services. There are two major cab companies in the area and six smaller firms. The two dominant firms were approached by TTDC for comments and expressions of interest in shared-ride services. As noted, the two firms were doing a substantial Medicaid business and continued to suggest that they could do more business for the elderly and handicapped, including contracting with TTDC to do all its special services for the handicapped at standard meter rates and using their standard taxi vehicles. However, both firms perceived general shared-ride services provided on a contractual rate basis as a threat to their market and declined to bid.

In response to statements by the large taxicab company owners that they were being bypassed, and by the desire of TTDC to foster general ride-sharing by taxis, particularly to and from the airport, TTDC formed a Taxi Study Committee. All taxi companies were invited to become members, as well as the various departments of each of the five cities that are part of TTDC. Initial committee meetings covered the general subject of group riding and coordination of public transportation services. In later meetings the two major taxi firms were represented by an attorney, who repeatedly expressed concern over issues such as unnecessary regional control, interference in fare levels, and increased competition. The two firms also retained a consultant to develop their position and present a report to the Committee. The two companies subsequently withdrew from participation on the Taxi Committee and ended all discussion of participation in shared-ride services.

The Request for Proposals for operation of the shared-ride services was kept simple. The services were described and a minimum of specifications were developed, as shown in the Appendix. The proposals were solicited on the basis of low bid per vehicle hour. The contract contained provisions for insurance, facilities and equipment, supervision, fare collection, and so forth.

Two smaller companies responded, and both were engaged to provide service. Yellow Cab of Chesapeake was contracted to provide several shared-ride services at $14 per vehicle hour, which was less than half the cost of providing conventional bus service. Airport Limousine Company was contracted to provide one service-area (the only one it bid on) service at $14 per vehicle hour. TTDC leased, at its standard van rental rates, to Yellow Cab Company several 12 passenger vans from its inventory of vehicles used for vanpooling and other uses.

Contracting for the operation of fixed-route small bus services on a low-volume route to Portsmouth and on weekends on several routes in Norfolk followed a similar pattern. No large private operators expressed interest in the service. One small operator submitted a bid for the Portsmouth route and several pieces of the Sunday substitute service in Norfolk. He requested TTDC assistance in acquiring small buses and vans to use on the services, and TTDC leased him the vehicles. The contract for the operation of those services was $14 per vehicle hour; again less than half the cost of the bus service formerly operated. The operating costs of large bus, fixed-route services by TTDC, which is typical of many transit authorities, are compared with small vehicle services operated by private operators in Table 4–4.

After the companies that would provide the service were solicited, operating procedures for each service were finalized and incorporated

Table 4-4. Comparison of Average Cost Per Vehicle Mile.

	TTDC Transit Bus	Commuter Vanpool	Private Operator Shared-ride and Small Bus	TTDC Operated E&H Vans
Depreciation	$0.17	$0.15	$0.15	$0.15
Maintenance	0.37	0.07	0.07	0.07
Fuel	0.32	0.14	0.175	0.175
Insurance	0.09	0.05	0.025	0.09
Administration	0.15	0.01	0.265	0.068
Operator	0.64	0.00	0.24	0.33
Total Cost Per Mile	$1.74	$0.42	$0.925	$0.883

into brochures. These brochures describe the service area, fares, and pick-up procedures. They contain a map of the service area and were widely distributed door-to-door in the service areas and by local merchants.

MONITORING CONTRACTED SERVICES

Services that were contracted for operation by the private companies are monitored extensively in several ways. The principal monitoring device is the monthly evaluation report.

Each month operational information including in-service hours, cost, ridership, revenue, cost per hour, and average fare are obtained and reported for each contracted service area. The operating deficit and the deficit per passenger, the principal measure of effectiveness used by TTDC, are derived and reported. This information is used to make decisions to add, delete, or modify services. A sample monthly evaluation report for Deep Creek, the service area previously discussed, is given in Table 4-5. An evaluation report for the service area in the Ocean View section of Norfolk, which is the highest density area where shared-ride van services were substituted for a fixed-route bus service, is presented in Table 4-6.

TTDC Service Representatives conduct activities to monitor the operation of contracted services. Service Representatives ride each vehicle and interview both operators and passengers. The Service Representatives also compile information gained from complaints which they receive on the services. This information is used to help

Table 4-5. Monthly Evaluation of Deep Creek Service Change to Private Operator.

	Number of Passengers	Cost	Revenue	Deficit	Deficit Per Passenger
TTDC Bus, August 1979 Average Monthly for Bus Routes #41 and #43 (Chesapeake Only)	1,134	$5,786.00	$ 396.00	$5,390.00	$4.75
September Contract Service	277	2,093.00	277.00	1,186.00	6.55
October	523	2,457.00	523.00	1,934.00	3.70
November	659	2,704.00	659.00	2,056.00	3.10
December	786	2,600.00	786.00	1,814.00	2.30
January 1980	864	3,150.00	864.00	2,286.00	2.65
February	858	3,150.00	858.00	2,292.00	2.67
March	915	2,898.00	915.00	1,983.00	2.16
April	1,150	3,276.00	1,150.00	2,126.00	1.85
May	1,125	3,528.00	1,125.00	2,403.00	2.13
June	1,053	3,024.00	1,053.00	1,971.00	1.83
July	1,256	3,276.00	1,256.00	2,020.00	1.63

plan service changes and improve marketing efforts. Based on their analysis, these representatives continue extensive marketing efforts with local merchants, civic groups, and within major activity centers in the contracted service areas.

Ridership is extensively analyzed in several ways. Trip manifests are analyzed to determine origin-destination information, average trip length, and passengers per vehicle hour. This analysis continues to provide useful insight concerning travel patterns, major activity centers, travel time, vehicle productivity, and vehicle scheduling.

Riders are also surveyed by TTDC staff, who ride the vehicles and administer questionnaires. Past surveys obtained information on trip purpose, origin-destination, rider demographics, rider satisfaction with the service, and how the rider found out about the service. This analysis is valuable in planning marketing strategies and in obtaining the rider's perspective on service operations. Also, ridership can be analyzed in other ways to find out specific information, such as transferring between this contracted service and bus service, and fare collection.

Table 4-6. Monthly Evaluation of Ocean View Service After Change to Private Operator.

	In-Service Hours	Cost	Passengers	Revenue	Deficit	Deficit/ Passenger
Fixed-Route Bus (Route 14) Before Change	300	$8,940.00	1,680	$ 570.00	$8,370.00	$4.98
Contract Service (1980) Nov. 23–Dec. 31	370	5,698.00	1,556	653.00	5,045.00	3.24
January 1981	300	4,200.00	1,242	522.00	3,678.00	2.96
February	280	4,312.00	1,085	434.00	3,878.00	3.57
March	310	4,991.00	1,223	428.00	4,563.00	3.73
April	300	4,830.00	1,461	511.00	4,319.00	2.96
May	310	4,991.00	1,460	511.00	4,480.00	3.07
June	300	4,830.00	1,617	566.00	4,264.00	2.64
			(Fare increased from $0.50 to $1.00 July 5, 1981)			
July	310	4,991.00	1,323	1,323.00	3,668.00	2.77
August	310	4,991.00	1,361	1,361.00	3,630.00	2.67

Another type of monitoring is an operations analysis. TTDC has conducted a covert check of the contract service operations, using staff or a private security firm who pose as riders. The information gleaned from such activities is invaluable in spotting operational problems such as theft of fares, driver discourtesy, poor dispatcher/ driver coordination, inefficient routing and scheduling, improper vehicle speeds and layovers, and physical problems with vehicles while moving and at stops.

As it turned out, many operational problems indeed are spotted and reported. Drivers took fares from passengers and did not deposit them in the farebox. Fareboxes were broken and pilfered. Drivers carried friends and their family members free. Riders had difficulty identifying the van, especially at night. Dispatcher/driver coordination was often lax, and riders sometimes waited hours for a pick-up. Vehicles were not always clean. Drivers traveled out of the service area or took unexcused breaks.

A number of actions were taken to remedy those problems. TTDC has increased its supervision and assigned an individual to manage paratransit and other contract and special services. Closer monitoring of the contract services has been implemented. Drivers have been dismissed. Specifications for more appropriate vehicles have been developed. Other private operators than those currently under contract have been solicited to provide additional services.

In addition to the TTDC staff, the riders themselves are acutely aware of the cleanliness of the vehicles, the skill and attitude of the drivers, and the drivers' general knowledge of public transportation service. The nonriding public also observes and comments on aspects of this service. Furthermore, the union representing TTDC bus drivers and mechanics notes and makes frequent observations about how poorly or how well the contracted services are being operated.

ISSUES CONCERNING THE USE
OF PRIVATE OPERATORS

The initiation of new paratransit services generated concern and reaction among a variety of groups that provide transportation services. This was not surprising, as any action taken to change the status quo and implement a new service area generally meet with at least an equal reaction by those who will be affected by the service change.

This reaction process finally results in a service that has been tempered by competing or opposing interests. After the resistance process had run its course, paratransit services provided under contract by private operators were accepted into TTDC's regular service delivery program for public transportation.

One implementation issue was the impact on bus operator jobs. TTDC's regular transit bus operators and mechanics are represented by a collective bargaining agent, Local Division 1177 of the Amalgamated Transit Union, AFL–CIO. During the public hearing that was held to receive comments on the proposed paratransit services, an attorney for the union presented a prepared statement in opposition to the new services and in favor of continuing regular bus services. The union also wrote to the state funding agency to protest funding of the new services and initiated a suit in the federal district court alleging violation of Section 13(c) of job projection provisions. The state funding was made available, and the court suit was later dropped as part of a collective bargaining agreement.

During the term of the project, the union officers observed the new operations very closely and reported by word-of-mouth on any difficulties, from appearance of drivers to off-route trips to cleanliness of vehicles to possible mishandling of fares. Additionally, the Union officers talked steadily about widespread concern among the employees regarding possible loss of jobs if the new services were successful. Although no employees were furloughed for any reason as a result of the contracted services, the union presented job security as a major fear of the employees. The federal court suit claiming Section 13(c) rights against service changes, as well as two suits in state court on part-time drivers and contracting-out claims, were all settled out of court, partly in exchange for adding to the collective bargaining agreement a new job classification that permitted the contracted-out TTDC van and small bus services to be operated at a cost competitive with the private operators.

Another implementation issue was the impact of the new services on existing providers of similar services, the private taxicab companies. During the early project planning stages, the TTDC staff assumed that the taxicab companies would welcome the type of services to be provided by the project, as they would represent a new market and the possible expansion of their business. During the public hearing prior to implementing the services, a cab company representative spoke against the new services on the grounds that they would result in a loss of jobs for cab drivers, since the project services would attract riders who were currently using cabs (or would if no alternative were available) and thus result in less cab business. This concern was presented even though it was widely advertised that the new services would be provided through contracts with private taxi-cab companies. Further, the owner of a large taxi company wrote the state to protest funding of the project as a subsidized intrusion against private enterprise.

As we have seen, the major taxicab companies in the area declined to bid for the services to be provided. During the course of the operation of the contract services, these taxicab companies sought and obtained through the Virginia General Assembly approval of a bill that "clarifies" the enabling legislation for transportation district commissions to ensure that taxicab companies shall not be regulated by the district commissions. In response to this concern, TTDC changed the name of project services from "Maxi-Taxi" to "Maxi-Ride" as a way of distinguishing the group of shared-ride services from the regular, exclusive-ride services provided by private taxicab companies.

It is a curious note that both the bus operators and the cab operators perceived the new services to be a threat to job security, even though one group would clearly get more jobs.

OBSERVATIONS

The *continuation* of current transit services and patterns is easily carried on by transit authorities without generating new concerns by users or providers of the services. Everyone can relate to and understand how a regular bus route works. However, developing new services and new operating arrangements tends to generate many impediments that must be overcome before implementation can be accomplished.

An initial obstacle to be overcome is the reluctance of the governmental and the private sides to work together. Both seem afraid of losing ground to the other. Rather than attempting to expand the market for transit services, most of their energy is directed toward preventing the loss of current riders on each existing service.

Providing new services and using private operators represent a change in the status quo and therefore generate reaction from existing providers of transportation services. Several large taxi companies, as a specific example, have viewed our neighborhood bus substitution services as an infringement on their market and have resisted expansion of these services. They have declined to bid on operating the services under contract, and they have sought changes in TTDC's enabling legislation to restrict the scope of its services.

New services are outside the experience of the transit unions and are resisted because the results are unknown and they are perceived to threaten job security. For example, substituting low-capacity neighborhood services for regular bus services means that the transit system needs fewer bus drivers, and, in this case, the union reacted strongly (including initiating law suits) to a decrease in the size of the bargaining unit, even if no employees were laid off as a result of the service changes. Individual driver employees see new services as an eventual threat, even though they may not be furloughed, because they may affect wage and benefit levels in the long run, by permitting the operation of services at lower wage costs.

Based on TTDC's satisfactory experience with using private operators in several areas, and in recognition of the proposed expansion of this part of the service program, the union sought to add a new job description to the bargaining unit at a contract renewal. A new position, called "mini-bus" operator, was created at $4.00 per hour (compared to $9.68 per hour for a regular operator), with no work rules and reduced benefits. This new position permits TTDC to operate shared-ride and small vehicle services at a cost no higher, or even less, than that of a private operator. As a result of this change in its cost structure, TTDC has begun to use its own mini-bus operators in some services that were contracted to private firms.

Developing new services requires a large amount of policy board and management insight and initiative since there is not much precedent. New services will need substantial revision between the time of proposal and implementation. Designing a dependable, useful, and timely monitoring system for contract services has been a significant and difficult task of this project. The purchase of public transportation services, as well as the shared-ride and small vehicle concept, is new to TTDC, and this has presented organizational problems. These problems include: control of fare revenues; supervision of services operated by other organizations; coordination of rider complaints; acceptance by Union officials and TTDC planning and operating staffs; and developing working relationships with service providers.

One can understand that change comes hard. Altering the traditional fixed-route public transit system into a variety of services tailored to people's travel needs is definitely a difficult process. However, with the prospect of restricted and even reduced public funding, transit operators must change their ways of doing business if they are to continue to provide services at all.

TTDC's service delivery program incorporates the belief that there is a high potential for payoff in developing less costly and more demand-responsive services, through a wide range of public transportation services. The tremendous effort required to effect change will be repaid many times over if we can continue to provide services that would otherwise be dropped because they are too expensive to subsidize. In our example of substituting neighborhood van-type services for bus routes, both taxi company and transit system employees resisted the change. And yet, if transit is to continue in many neighborhoods and thus sustain those employees' jobs, we must find new ways to provide at least basic public transportation services. As the agency responsible for the public transportation in Tidewater, TTDC must balance the people's need for transportation with the difficulties involved in providing the appropriate service.

APPENDIX
MAXI-RIDE SERVICES' REQUEST FOR BIDS

The Tidewater Transportation District Commission (TTDC) is responsible for the development and provision of public transportation services in the Tidewater area. One element of the transportation program is shared-ride or "Maxi-Ride" services.

Maxi-Ride is a family of services using small vehicles, such as taxi cabs and vans, to provide both demand-responsive and fixed-route service. It may be door-to-door within a fixed area or may operate along a specified corridor.

TTDC purchases some of these shared-ride services from local transportation providers such as taxi-cab companies. This request solicits bids to operate vehicles in Maxi-Ride services as described in the attachment. As a minimum, each proposal must give the following information:

1. Name, business address, telephone and principal contact of the firm;
2. Experience of the firm in providing similar flexible services;
3. Capability of the firm to provide the necessary dispatching, drivers and vehicles;

4. Familiarity with the service area;
5. The bid cost per vehicle per hour of operation. This cost must be firm for six months.
6. The vehicle hours and miles of operation per day;
7. Number of vans, 12 or 15 passenger, to be leased from TTDC to provide the service.

All fare revenues charged to riders will belong to TTDC. It is the responsibility of the service provider to insure that the appropriate fares are collected, secured and given to TTDC. TTDC will provide tickets, transfers and fareboxes as may be necessary for fare collection.

The service provider will invoice TTDC monthly for services provided. Ridership statistics, similar to a taxicab manifest, must be supplied with the invoice. The provider will be responsible for the accuracy and security of fare collection and statistical reporting. As this is an experimental program, supplemental, periodic reports may be required. TTDC will be responsible for the planning, marketing and coordination of Maxi-Ride services in cooperation with the service providers. TTDC will provide all promotional materials; however, the provider is expected to promote Maxi-Ride to help assume its success. All other services, facilities and equipment necessary to provide Maxi-Ride, including radio and telephone communication, are the responsibility of the provider.

Chapter 5

PRIVATE COMMUTER VANS IN NEW YORK

Jay H. Walder

INTRODUCTION

Throughout New York City, privately operated, profitable commuter vans are playing an increasingly important role in the provision of transportation services. The proliferation of these operators has been most evident on Staten Island, where newspaper reports and television news shows have highlighted the growing confrontation between van operations and established mass transit services.

New York City officials have become concerned about these vans for a number of reasons. They believe that the vans are stealing passengers from the city's own express bus system, hence decreasing profits; they believe the vans are operating illegally and are not giving sufficient regard to safety and insurance considerations; and they believe the vans are increasing traffic congestion.

In this chapter, I make a detailed cost analysis of the city's express bus service and find that, contrary to the city's belief, the express buses are losing money—about 85 cents lost per passenger, or $4.7 million per year. I find that the express buses are not only losing money as a whole, but also on a route-by-route basis. Hence rather than harming the express bus service, or "skimming the cream" off its routes, the private vans are actually helping to reduce the city's transit deficit. I also examine the safety implications and find that these can easily be handled within the existing regulatory framework, and that the traffic congestion effects will be slight.

MASS TRANSIT AND COMMUTER VANS

Staten Island is the only New York City borough not connected to Manhattan by means of fixed-rail rapid transit. Thousands of Staten Island residents commute to work each day by means of express bus service or the Staten Island ferry. This section describes the current mass transit services and the competing private commuter van services that have recently developed.

Express Bus Service

The New York City Transit Authority (NYCTA) operates twelve weekday express bus routes between the two boroughs. Most routes operate only during the rush hours, with headways ranging from five to twenty minutes, and a fare of $2.50 each way. Both lower and midtown Manhattan are served, with the bulk of service concentrated in lower Manhattan. The current NYCTA policy is to attempt to provide each passenger with a seat on this premium-fare, long-distance service. In total, approximately 21,400 passengers are carried to and from Manhattan each weekday morning.

Private franchised express bus service is also provided on Staten Island. Figure 5-1 compares NYCTA-operated and private franchised express bus routes. Domenico Bus Company service is provided through New Jersey to points to midtown Manhattan; the ability to travel interstate allows the private operator to reduce travel time to midtown by approximately fifteen minutes. Routes and fares are regulated by the Bureau of Franchises of the NYC Board of Estimate. The same $2.50 fare is charged. While many of the private bus lines in NYC receive operating subsidies, government subsidies to Domenico have historically been of only a nominal sum.[1]

---

1. Geoffrey Clarke, Gary Grobman, and Douglas Jacobs, "Provision of Express Bus Service in New York City" (Cambridge, Mass.: JFK School of Government, Harvard University, May 1982), table 4-7. (Unpublished.)

Figure 5–1. Map of Staten Island, New York, and New Jersey.

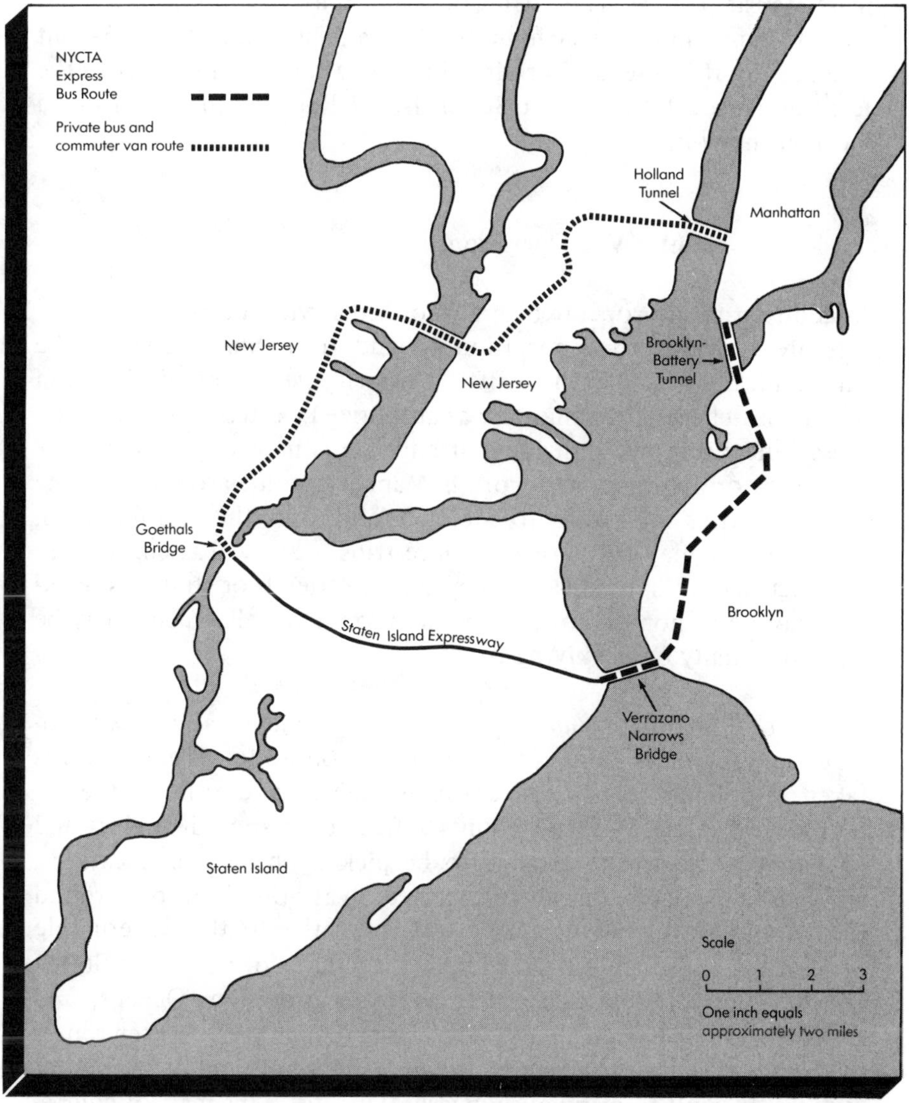

Staten Island Ferry

The traditional Staten Island Ferry also remains a major part of the mass transit picture. The ferries operate on a 24-hours-a-day basis, with fifteen minute rush hour headways. The round-trip, 25-cent fare is paid at Whitehall Terminal in Manhattan. Connections to the ferry are made by means of Staten Island Rapid Transit trains or a local bus network.

Commuter Van Operations

In addition to city operated or authorized service, private van operators are providing transportation to and from Staten Island. The vans typically seat eleven to fifteen passengers, operate during rush hours, and charge the same fare as authorized express buses. Beyond these generalizations, individual arrangements may vary widely. The van operator may park and work in Manhattan, ride around until the afternoon trips, or return to Staten Island after the morning runs. The operator may make one or more trips per day. Passengers may ride regularly or sporadically; they may be friends or strangers. Pickups may be at homes, street corners, or bus stops. Payments may be made on a daily or weekly basis.

Extent of Commuter Van Service. It is difficult to accurately estimate the extent of commuter van service on Staten Island. Counts taken at popular boarding locations probably underestimate the extent of van service. These counts reflect only sporadic riders and regular passengers who arrange to be picked up at these locations, and ignore regular riders who are picked up at other locations around the island. Surveys along major traffic arteries to the eastern side of Manhattan probably overestimate the volume of vans from Staten Island, since they also count vans from Brooklyn, Queens, and Long Island. Moreover, many Staten Island vans take shorter routes through New Jersey to reach midtown Manhattan. Finally, commuter vans are difficult to distinguish in visual surveys. Vans may, of course, serve other purposes than commuter transport.

Despite these shortcomings, surveys have provided a rough measure of the extent of commuter van services. Approximately 150 to

200 van trips are made between Staten Island and Manhattan each weekday morning.[2] Assuming an average of twelve passengers per van, between 1,800 and 2,250 residents utilize these services on a daily basis.

Van Impact on Other Transit Modes. What is the former mode of transit for van passengers? Are vans competitors to express buses, the ferry, or personal cars and carpools? To answer this question, graduate students at the New School for Social Research polled van passengers during the afternoon rush hour.[3] Surveys were distributed over a three day period at a van loading point in lower Manhattan. The results of this poll are presented in Table 5–1. It should be noted that the small sample size and nonrandomness of the population make it impossible to draw strong conclusions. Nevertheless, it is interesting to note that 74 percent of the van passengers who completed the survey formerly rode NYCTA express buses.

Regulatory Jurisdiction. Regulatory authority for van operations falls in a gray area of state and local control. Controversy exists as to what types of transportation services must be franchised by NYC as "bus lines" and what types must be licensed under state law as "contract carriers" of passengers.[4] State Transportation Law defines a bus line as a motor vehicle

> operated for the use and convenience of the public, usually along the same route or between stated termini, or on a fixed or stated schedule, carrying passengers for hire. . . .[5]

If vans are operating as bus lines, regulatory authority rests with the Bureau of Franchises of the NYC Board of Estimate.[6] Applica-

2. Barbara Belovin, Emily Griske, Tom Hauser, and Kurt Richwerger, "Commuter Vans and Surface Transportation in Manhattan" (New York: New School for Social Research, December 1982), p. 4. (Unpublished.)

3. Ibid., p. 7.

4. Normally, for-hire, nonmedallion vehicles are under the jurisdiction of the NYC Taxi and Limousine Commission (TLC). However, the TLC's authority extends only to vehicles carrying eight or few passengers. Regulatory uncertainty regarding private paratransit operations is not uncommon. See Chapter 3 of this volume for a similar example in the Chicago Rapid Transit District.

5. New York Transportation Law, sec. 2(12).

6. New York City Charter, chap. 14, sec. 362. New York Transportation Law, sec. 80 (6) (McKinney 1982) exempts privately owned bus lines operating within the city from New York State Department of Transportation control.

Table 5-1. Former Mode of Transit for Current Van Passengers.

Mode	Number of Passengers	Percent of Total Passengers
NYCTA Express Bus	28	73.7
Private Express Bus	7	18.4
Local Bus to Subway or Ferry	2	5.3
Car	1	2.6
	38	100.0

Source: "Commuter Vans and Surface Transportation in Manhattan."

tions to operate local or express bus routes within the city must be approved by this office.

Alternatively, the vans may be operating as contract carriers of passengers. A contract carrier is defined as a person or corporation who engages in the transportation of passengers other than the operation of a bus line.[7] Contract carrier permits are issued by the New York State Department of Transportation (NYSDOT) and are outside the authority of the city.

In the past, contract carrier permits included all passenger operations that were *not conducted along a defined route or fixed schedule.* Moreover, NYC permits were specifically issued for service "provided on a regular daily basis for a defined group *between a residential neighborhood and a work-related central location in the metropolitan area*" (classified as "Commuter Club Service").[8]

Recently, the State has restricted the issuance of contract carrier permits to applicants operating entirely within the boundaries of NYC. All applicants providing commuter club service,

> must present *substantial evidence that existing mass transportation facilities are inadequate* by virtue of their lack of proximity to the neighborhood origin points of the users, or that users cannot reasonably avail themselves of existing facilities.[9]

In addition, permits for commuter club service have the following relevant restrictions: (1) maximum seating capacity of twenty pas-

7. New York State Department of Transportation, Case 29812; The Establishment of Regulatory Policy Regarding the Grant of Permits to Contract Carriers or Passengers Within the City of New York (7 July 1982), p. 2. (Unpublished opinion.)

8. Ibid., p. 3.

9. Ibid., p. 10.

10. Ibid., p. 10.

sengers; and (2) operators may not solicit passengers along the routes and at the stops of existing bus line and subway operations.[10]

Under these guidelines, the burden is on the applicant to present evidence that the existing mass transit facilities are inadequate. Many of the commuter vans that received permits under the old policy will not qualify under the current policy. Thus, while there is ample power to regulate vans, the current inclination is to be restrictive.

While the city has committed both transit police and Staten Island highway police to stopping and ticketing vans, the effort has been ineffective. An estimated 95 percent of the first 400 tickets issued were dismissed in city traffic court. This result is attributable, in part, to the legal ambiguity surrounding van operations. One judge noted that he must frequently dismiss charges against van operators because no penalties have been specified by law.[11] Moreover, police officers are unclear as to what laws are being violated. Charges filed in criminal court have ranged from running unfranchised bus lines to accepting hails without a taxi medallion to operating without a limousine license.[12]

Summary

Commuter vans have become an important part of the transportation service on Staten Island. Approximately 150 to 200 vans carry residents to and from Manhattan each weekday, often for the same fare as public and private express buses. Many former express bus riders have expressed a preference for this unconventional service. In total, the vans may be diverting as many as 17 percent of NYCTA express bus riders.

The body of law under which the vans operate is in need of clarification at both the state and local levels. The current restrictive policies lead to a confused environment.

COSTS AND REVENUES OF THE EXISTING NYCTA EXPRESS SERVICE

There are three major objections to the commuter vans: they may be causing financial harm to the NYCTA by "skimming the cream" off

11. "City Franchise Seems to Have Lock on Bus Transport, *Staten Island Advance*, 11 May 1982.
12. "Fans of Vans Say Bans Violate Rights," *Staten Island Advance*, 10 May 1982.

its express bus runs; they may not be as safe as the NYCTA express buses; and they may add to traffic congestion. All of these issues are examined below. I begin by looking at the costs and revenues of the existing express bus system and find that it is operating at a deficit. Since the commuter vans do not require a public subsidy they are not harming the NYCTA, but rather are helping to improve its financial state.

Profitability of the Express Buses as a Whole

Suppose the existing Staten Island express service did not exist. What would happen to the costs and revenue of the NYCTA? I calculate the cost savings first (from eliminating the service), then the resultant revenue loss.[13]

Marginal Savings. Since the relevant unit for analysis is the entire express service, it is important to note that a change of this magnitude will affect the necessary fixed overhead on Staten Island. There are currently two depots, Yukon and Castleton, operating on Staten Island. Because of capacity constraints, the NYCTA plans to retrofit a third depot (Edgewater) on the island. The capacity and number of express buses at each depot are listed in Table 5-2.

If the express service were closed, 145 buses would be shifted and the immediate need to reopen Edgewater depot would be alleviated. The NYCTA would save the one-time cost of retrofitting the depot, plus the annual overhead and operating costs associated with the express service.

Table 5-3 contains estimates for the marginal savings from closing the express service. No savings are attributed to the one-time expense

Table 5-2. Express Buses at Staten Island Depots.

Depot	Capacity	Express Buses
Castleton	125	30
Yukon	242	115
Edgewater	125	NA

13. Jay H. Walder, "Commuter Van Service on Staten Island," M.P.P. Policy Analysis Exercise (Cambridge, Mass.: JFK School of Government, Harvard University, April 1983), p. 31.

Table 5–3.   Effect of Closing All Staten Island Express Service.

	Marginal Savings (Annual $)	
	Lower Bound	*Best Estimate*
Total Express Service	14,590,819	18,711,458

of opening the Edgewater depot. Therefore, the figures in the table actually underestimate the true marginal savings. As calculated here, the best estimate of the marginal savings is approximately $18.7 million per year.

Marginal Revenue Loss. It is assumed that all revenue collected from current express riders would be lost to the NYCTA system. The simplest and most accurate method for estimating this revenue loss is to count the actual fare box intake. Unfortunately, the NYCTA does not separate fares collected on express and local service. In the absence of this information, I have used ridership estimates to indicate revenue received. This is possible since there are no discounts for express service; all passengers pay the $2.50 fare.

Surveys conducted by the NYCTA provide recent ridership data. Visual surveys were conducted of express buses entering Manhattan during the morning peak. Since the majority of express service is a peak-only service, it is possible to extrapolate from this survey. If NYCTA-operated Staten Island express service were eliminated, the annual revenue loss would be approximately $13.9 million (from the loss of 5,574,284 passengers).

Total Net Revenue. As Table 5–4 indicates, express service is currently operating at a loss. Even the lower bound savings outweigh the estimated loss in revenue. NYCTA-operated express Staten Island bus service is clearly unprofitable, with an average loss of 85 cents per passenger, or $4.7 million annually.

Profitability of Individual Routes

Even though the express bus system loses money as a whole, it is possible that individual routes on it might be operating at a profit. So I next take up a route-by-route financial analysis of the system. Al-

Table 5-4. NYCTA Staten Island Express Service Net Revenue.

Route	Marginal Savings (Annual $)		Marginal Revenue Loss	Deficit (Annual $)		
	Low Estimate	Best Estimate		Low Estimate	Best Estimate	Per Passenger ($)
Total Express Service	14,590,819	18,711,458	13,935,710	−655,109	−4,775,748	−0.85

though the analysis shows that some routes do better than others, none of them earns enough to cover its costs.

Marginal Savings. Table 5–5 contains estimates for the marginal savings from eliminating individual routes. The best estimates for the annual savings range from $327,000 for the smallest route to $7.6 million for the largest. Similarly, lower bound annual savings range from $251,000 to $5.8 million per route.

It must be stressed that these estimates do not include any change in fixed overhead. If a number of routes were jointly eliminated, the service change may be large enough to affect fixed overhead. If so, these figures underestimate the marginal savings.

Marginal Revenue Loss. For each route that is closed, it is assumed that no passengers would continue to ride NYCTA-operated service. That is, all revenue currently collected on the route would be lost to the system. As I indicated above, the NYCTA does not separate fares by route. Table 5–6 uses survey data to approximate the revenue loss.

Table 5–5. Savings Estimates from Eliminating Staten Island Express Routes.

	Operating Characteristics (Annual)			Marginal Savings (Annual $)	
Route	Hours	Miles	AM Peak Buses	Lower Bound	Best Estimate
Yukon Depot					
X9/11/13	121,666	2,361,522	68	5,829,018	7,556,478
X12	18,309	351,536	11	895,616	1,166,281
X15	13,564	275,590	8	664,676	867,003
X17/19	37,431	758,698	21	1,805,977	2,347,340
X18	5,173	102,362	3	251,277	326,919
X20	7,510	138,176	4	352,229	453,786
Castleton Depot					
X10	34,684	648,932	16	1,544,110	2,244,643
X14	14,304	266,446	10	723,766	1,085,487
X16	4,775	97,282	4	261,440	400,812

Table 5-6. NYCTA Staten Island Express Service Marginal Revenue Loss.

Route	Passengers (Annual)	Marginal Revenue Loss (Annual $)
Yukon Depot		
X9/11/13	2,547,112	6,367,780
X12	356,616	891,540
X15	327,152	817,880
X17/19	752,094	1,880,235
X18	115,824	289,560
X20	150,876	377,190
Castleton Depot		
X10	877,824	2,194,560
X14	323,850	809,625
X16	122,936	307,340

Net Revenue. Table 5-7 indicates the annual net revenue for each of the current routes. The results of this analysis are sensitive to the estimation of marginal savings. Closing individual routes will save the NYCTA up to $1.2 million per route.

Profitability of Individual Runs or Service Expansions

In a manner similar to the above analyses, I examined the consequence of decreasing the service on individual routes (increasing the time intervals between buses), and found that such service cuts would have a net positive effect on the financial condition of the NYCTA.[14] And finally, I analyzed the financial consequence of expanding the express bus service so as to "compete more effectively" against the commuter vans, and found that this would only increase the NYCTA operating deficit.[15]

14. Ibid., p. 43.
15. Ibid., p. 38.

Table 5-7. NYCTA Annual Net Revenue by Route.

Route	Marginal Savings (Annual $)		Marginal Revenue Loss (Annual $)		Net Revenue (Annual $)	
	Lower Bound	Best Estimate	1981 Count	TA Survey	Low Estimate	Best Estimate
Yukon Depot						
X9/11/13	5,829,018	7,556,478	5,012,870	6,367,780	538,762	-1,188,698
X12	895,616	1,166,281	886,233	891,540	-4,076	-280,048
X15	664,676	867,003	851,438	817,880	153,204	-15,565
X17/19	1,805,977	2,347,340	1,979,298	1,880,235	74,258	-368,042
X18	251,277	326,919	310,368	289,560	38,283	-16,551
X20	352,229	453,786	428,250	377,190	24,961	-25,536
Castleton Depot						
X10	1,544,110	2,244,643	1,830,973	2,194,560	650,450	-413,670
X14	723,766	1,085,487	788,823	809,625	85,859	-296,665
X16	261,440	400,812	327,940	307,340	459,000	-72,872

Summary

Commuter vans are offering a reasonable service, without subsidization by the city. Moreover, they are increasing the profitability of NYCTA express bus service: If NYCTA bus service replaced the vans, an already existing operating deficit would likely increase.

Likewise, since closing the existing express service, either in part or as whole, would decrease the operating deficit of the NYCTA, it ought to consider such options. This might involve contracting out existing service to the private bus operators who already operate in the area, or else simply permitting the private bus and van operators to expand as they wish.

Finally, if the NYCTA wishes to continue operating all of the current routes, it should cut back service in areas best served by commuter vans. The vans can supplement NYCTA-operated service to improve the system's financial position without detracting from service.

PASSENGER SAFETY AND TRAFFIC CONGESTION

The previous discussion has focused exclusively on the cost and revenue implications of alternative responses to the commuter van situation. From a fiscal perspective, either of the recommended options involve continued use of commuter vans to connect Staten Island and Manhattan. This section takes a broader perspective and considers social costs that may be imposed by the commuter vans. In addition to revenue considerations, the City has expressed concern that the vans: (1) may be operating without adequate safety standards or insurance coverage; and (2) may be adding to rush hour traffic congestion problems.

Safety and Insurance Coverage

While the city's concerns for safety and insurance are legitimate, they are nonetheless indicative of the current regulatory confusion surrounding commuter van service. Restrictive regulatory initiatives have fostered an atmosphere in which public safety concerns have not been attended to.

A regulatory structure to ensure adequate safety standards and insurance coverage already exists. In part, the issuance of a New York State Department of Transportation Contract Carrier Permit requires a test of the fitness, willingness, and ability of the applicant to perform. The criteria normally considered to make this determination include:

- the *transportation experience* and background of the applicant;
- the ability to obtain *insurance coverage* to satisfy DOT requirements; and
- the ability to obtain a *DOT safety certificate of inspection* prior to placing vehicles in service.[16]

In short, commuter vans licensed by the state conform to reasonable safety and insurance standards.

The city has sought, however, to limit the number of state permits for use exclusively within the city's boundaries. This restrictive policy has led to a proliferation of unregulated vans, with minimal safety or insurance oversight. A more cooperative atmosphere would ensure reasonable safety and insurance standards.

In addition, visible permiture (e.g., a special license plate or marking) would aid passenger awareness and enforcement efforts. Enforcement could appropriately be focused on vans operating without a proper permit. Passengers would notice if the van was properly marked and could make appropriate decisions whether to ride. Moreover, passengers could aid the enforcement effort by notifying the proper authorities of unlicensed vans.

It is important to point out that price regulation is not necessary. The vans operate in an open competitive market that more than adequately ensures against price gouging. If an individual operator tries to raise his price above the competitive level, passengers have an opportunity to make other arrangements.

The point to be stressed here is that an integrated transit system with commuter vans does not have to cause the city to sacrifice its concern for public safety. At the state level, an adequate regulatory structure already exists to satisfy these concerns. Alternatively, the

16. New York State Department of Transportation, Case 29812, p. 6.

city government could handle this function. What is required in either case is a cooperative, rather than combative, regulatory atmosphere.

Traffic Patterns

Concern has also been expressed about the impact of commuter vans on rush hour traffic patterns. Vans may add to congestion problems on the crowded roads connecting Manhattan to the outer boroughs. Moreover, in the downtown area, vans have been reported to stop in designated bus lanes and no-standing zones, obstruct moving traffic, and park illegally.

The important measure here is the marginal increase that vans may add to already serious traffic problems. Given this, three questions must be answered:

1. Do the vans represent a large proportion of the vehicle traffic entering Manhattan?
2. Are the vans diverting passengers from automobiles or mass transit?
3. If the vans are obstructing Manhattan traffic patterns, can the problem be alleviated?

Proportion of Vehicle Traffic. Table 5–8 compares van trips to vehicle trips across the East River in the morning peak. The most complete data are for the Brooklyn-Battery Tunnel, where the highest percentage of van crossings are thought to occur. The data on total vehicle trips are from 1980, when gasoline prices were signifi-

Table 5-8. Van Versus Vehicle Trips.

Artery	Number of Van Trips	Number of Vehicle Trips[c]	Van Trips as a Percentage of Vehicle Trips
Brooklyn-Battery Tunnel[a]	190	10,150	1.9%
Brooklyn-Battery Tunnel[b]	172	10,150	1.7%
Manhattan Bridge[b]	31	9,460	0.3%
Williamsburg Bridge[b]	14	9,790	0.1%

a. NYCTA Van Count.
b. "Commuter Vans and Surface Transportation in Manhattan," New School for Social Research, December 1982. (Unpublished.)
c. Tri-State Regional Planning, Hub-Bound Travel: 1980.

cantly higher than they are now. This collection of data probably underestimates the current number of daily vehicle trips. At the Brooklyn-Battery Tunnel, vans represent only 1.7 percent to 1.9 percent of the total daily vehicle trips to Manhattan during the morning peak. For the other bridges, the percentages are much lower.

To judge the effect of this increased traffic, it is necessary to know how current traffic volume relates to the maximum capacity of the roadways. Average traffic speed falls slowly as traffic volume increases until the volume approaches maximum capacity, after which average speeds drop rapidly.[17] If, as I expect, the roadways are already at maximum capacity, the marginal increase in traffic congestion may be relatively large.

One way to reduce traffic congestion problems is through the increased use of contra-flow lanes for commuter vans. Contra-flow express bus lanes are currently provided on certain expressways leading to Manhattan. Until recently, the Traffic Bureau of the N.Y.C. Department of Transportation also issued permits to van operators for use of the contra-flow lanes. As part of the City enforcement campaign, all commuter van permits were revoked in June 1980.[18] If the vans were permitted to use these lanes, much of the congestion problem would be alleviated.

Diversion from Mass Transit.   In themselves, vans are not necessarily adding to congestion problems. To the extent that passengers are diverted from automobiles, the vans may actually be helping to alleviate the problem. As reported in the first section of this chapter, a New School survey found that most van riders were former express bus riders. Assuming fifteen passenger vans, it takes approximately three fully loaded vans to replace one fully loaded (all seats full, no standees) express bus. Since most of the road capacity used by a van or bus is for spacing between vehicles, the road space occupied per passenger will undoubtedly be higher with a van than a bus. The van may have an advantage, however, in that its smaller size relative to buses allows for greater maneuverability on crowded roadways. Thus, while vans are diverting passengers from larger buses, their marginal increase to traffic congestion may be relatively small.

17. John R. Meyer and Jose A. Gomez-Ibanez, *Autos, Transit and Cities* (Cambridge, Mass.: Harvard University Press, 1981), p. 186.

18. *Staten Island Advance*, 11 May 1982.

Obstruction of Traffic Patterns. Vans have been reported to obstruct the flow of traffic in lower and midtown Manhattan. Operators who choose to remain in Manhattan rather than deadhead back to Staten Island may park illegally or stop in no-standing zones. In the evening rush, vans may obstruct cars and buses while waiting to load up.

While concern about these problems is legitimate, steps can be taken to minimize their adverse effects. The City could designate a number of "van stops," where van operators could pick up and discharge passengers. Informal stops of this type have already been established in parts of lower Manhattan. While the stops could be relatively small, it is important that they be scattered throughout the City. This type of action would help to alleviate problems at designated bus stops. An enforcement program could also be added, whereby frequent offenders would have their permits revoked or suspended.

While a program of this type would not eliminate traffic problems, it would help to alleviate some of the city's concerns. In addition, the reduction in buses on the city streets should also help traffic to move more freely.

CONCLUSION

I have analyzed the role of commuter van operations in the provision of transportation services on Staten Island, where approximately 150 to 200 vans carry commuters to and from Manhattan each weekday. The city has expressed concern that: vans are siphoning off revenue that would otherwise accrue to the mass transit system; the vans are operating in an unregulated environment without adequate safety standards or insurance coverage; and the vans may be adding to rush hour traffic problems.

My primary conclusion is that the vans are not siphoning off revenue from the NYCTA express bus system. Contrary to general perception, NYCTA express buses are operating at a loss, with a deficit estimated at $4.7 million per year, or 85 cents per passenger. Moreover, if express buses were to replace the vans, the system's financial position could only be expected to get worse.

Second, I conclude that commuter vans do not have to sacrifice public safety. At the state level, an adequate regulatory structure already exists to satisfy safety and insurance concerns. However, the current inclination is to severely restrict the issuance of state permits. A more cooperative atmosphere would ensure reasonable safety and insurance standards. In addition, visible permiture would aid passenger awareness and enforcement of regulatory provisions.

Third, the vans were found to have a negative impact on traffic patterns. Although the vans do not represent a large percentage of vehicle trips to Manhattan, the marginal increase to already congested arteries is probably great. This problem may be alleviated to some extent by increased use of contra-flow express lanes on connecting highways.

Fourth, the city could best respond to the commuter vans in a cooperative atmosphere. An integrated transit system could provide reasonable services at modest cost, and the vans can supplement city services to improve the profitability of the express system.

Finally, the city should reexamine its role in providing express bus service. A traditional justification is that this service cross-subsidizes other less profitable transportation services. This study has shown the opposite. Express bus services are not profitable at the current fare and service structure. Private bus lines have shown an interest in providing the service. Wherever possible, the City should contract out service to these companies. An integrated system of private bus lines and commuter vans could provide reasonable service to the residents of Staten Island at reduced cost to New York City and the public.

Chapter 6

RECENT EXPERIENCE WITH SUCCESSFUL PRIVATE TRANSIT IN LARGE U.S. CITIES

Edward K. Morlok and Philip A. Viton

INTRODUCTION

The most widely used form of public transit in the United States is service operating on fixed routes with fixed schedules, usually provided either by buses on public roads or by rail vehicles operating on a separate right-of-way. Virtually all major bus and rail systems of this type are owned and operated by local government authorities, which have the exclusive right to provide the services as monopolists in their respective service areas. This is in marked contrast with almost all other goods and services in our society (including transport), where there is substantial reliance on competitive private providers, increasingly with little or no regulation as to entry or price. Motivated largely by the rapid escalation of deficits of these public providers, and by what some observers believe to be a lack of adaptation by them to changing travel demands, many now question the wisdom of excluding the private sector from urban transit. This paper summarizes the results of some of our research into the feasibility and desirability of having transit service provided by the private sector. We shall focus on five critical questions around which much of the controversy centers, and briefly indicate their significance.

First: is it true that line-haul scheduled transit service cannot be provided at a profit? For decades, this has been the conventional wisdom — at least in the western world. It follows that if transit service is to be provided at all, it must be subsidized from the public purse. Furthermore, the allegation of inherent unprofitability is used as a reason for government ownership, the rationale being that it is easier and perhaps more appropriate for the government to subsidize a government agency rather than a for-profit firm.

Second: if service is to be operated profitably, what type or types of service should be offered? In order to be profitable, the "product" offered potential travelers by a transit system might have to be different from that currently provided by a typical public transit authority. By "product" we mean the transit service as it would be viewed by a potential user: the prices charged and the qualities of the service, such as route structure, how frequently vehicles operate, the comfort level both on and off the vehicle, and so forth. Unlike almost any other supplier of consumer goods, transit authorities have generally chosen to offer the same product throughout their regions, ignoring differences in the preferences for various combinations of service qualities and prices which lead (in virtually all other markets) to a wide variety of types of goods being offered. This is true whether one talks of durable goods, services, or even other forms of transport; for example, both Amtrak and the airlines offer many classes of service with different prices.

Third: is the service offered by private carriers in general inferior to that offered by public carriers, whose facilities may be undermaintained and excessively crowded? The third question is motivated by the allegation among the public ownership proponents that any possible service offered by a for-profit firm would be inferior to that offered by a public authority. This is presented as another reason why public ownership is desirable.

Fourth: is it true that private carriers generally operate more efficiently and hence have lower costs than publicly owned carriers? In the context of this question, we examine the degree to which private sector operators might be more efficient and therefore able to offer service at lower cost than public carriers in the same situation. This aspect of the research is not completed, but sufficiently so for the answer to be clear.

Fifth: if private firms were allowed to enter the transit market, would they selectively pick services to provide, skimming only the "cream" and leaving the most difficult service to be provided by the public sector or not at all?

In keeping with the orientation of this book, we focus on two of the case studies that we performed in the course of our early research into these questions (in 1978–79), namely the privately operated express bus service in New York City and one profitable privately owned commuter rail service. However, it is important to point out that the conclusions that we present here are based on an analysis of other examples of private sector transit operation and on extensive simulation analyses of the feasibility and desirability of private provision of transit.

DESCRIPTION OF THE CASE STUDY SERVICES

It is useful to begin with brief descriptions of the two systems surveyed. This serves the purpose of providing a basis for future discussion of costs, service quality, and pricing. But it also conveys an appreciation and understanding of the rather unusual institutional setting that permitted these private firms to emerge as profitable providers of public transit, in an industry in which a single public provider has been given the exclusive right to provide transit service in almost all cities.

The bus system we will discuss is one of the many express bus services operating wholly within the city of New York. These systems provide radial central business district-oriented transit service primarily between the city's residential boroughs and Manhattan. They operate in direct competition with the city-owned transit authority's subways and buses. The first service began in February 1968, when a private operator was given a franchise to operate express buses between Queens and Manhattan. Since the initial routes operated by private firms were very successful, both in terms of rider satisfaction as well as profitability, the city transit authority reversed an earlier stance against the provision of express bus service in the city (especially in direct competition with its own subways) and elected to offer this type of service as well. Since then, express service has greatly expanded in scope and now covers all five boroughs of the city with some sixty routes, some operated by private firms and some by the transit authority. This episode alone suggests the value of competition and open entry into transit.

Most express bus services use conventional suburban- and intercity-type transit buses (with features providing greater passenger comfort than conventional transit buses, such as high-backed cushioned seats, parcel racks, reading lights, and ample air-conditioning and heating) and operate primarily in mixed traffic on public streets, although the transit authority and some private operators use conventional transit buses on their express routes. Recently, the city has attempted to improve service by providing exclusive bus lanes, and considerable extension of such lanes is being contemplated. All of the routes are designed to connect residential areas with the Manhattan CBD. Route lengths vary in length from 8 miles (13 kilometers) for a route connecting Park Avenue to Wall Street to 27 miles (43 kilometers) from Staten Island to midtown Manhattan via New Jersey. However, most routes are from 12 to 18 miles (19 to 29 kilometers) long.[1]

Most of the express bus routes are operated by private carriers. A franchise to operate a bus and pick up passengers on public streets in regular service must be granted by the New York City Board of Estimate's Bureau of Franchises before service can be initiated. Similarly, requests to modify the terms of service must also be processed through the bureau. The ultimate decision rests with the Board of Estimate, and the process can take up to thirteen months—actually a relatively short time in comparison to time required for any major construction of new transit routes.

The Board of Estimate is also responsible for approving fare structures and changes. Unlike most regulators, the board has readily granted fare increases to cover cost increases. In 1968 the basic fare on those routes operated by the Transit Authority was $1.00, while the private operators charged $1.15. In 1973 the private carriers charged $1.25, and in 1975 all carriers increased the basic fare to $1.50 (compared to 50¢ on the subway or local buses). Recently additional fare increases have been granted, up to $2.50 for express bus rides (compared to 75¢ on the local buses and subway). The

1. In Chapter 7 Giuliano and Teal suggest that the market for commuter bus service is rather small; but the evidence adduced is for trips at least twenty-five miles long. This is of course considerably longer than the distances observed for profitable service in the New York area.

Table 6-1. Financial Picture.

Selected NYC Express Bus Routes, 1972				
Number of Routes	*Operator*	*Total Cost[a]*	*Total Revenue[b]*	*Profit (Loss)*
7	Transit Authority[c]	$2.02m	$2.34m	$0.32m
6	Queens/ Steinway	2.44	3.07	0.63
5	Riverdale	2.47	3.11	0.64
1	Pelham	0.52	0.60	0.08

C&NW Commuter Rail			
Year	*Total Cost[a]*	*Total Revenue*	*Profit (Loss)*
1965	$14.3m	$15.7m	$1.4m
1970	19.2	21.0	1.8
1973	23.7	24.2	0.5
1974	26.4	27.7	1.3
1975	28.6	28.5	(0.1)

a. Cost includes all expenses of operation, maintenance, administration, and depreciation of capital stock (buses, facilities, etc.).

b. Revenue is that from the relevant passenger operation—fares plus incidentals such as advertising.

c. Includes Manhattan and Bronx Surface Transit Operating Authority. Total revenue was adjusted upward to reflect a uniform $1.15 fare, assuming that passenger traffic remained the same as with the actual $1.00 fare for the routes of these two operators. All other operators had the $1.15 fare for the entire year.

Source: Morlok, Viton et al. (1979), pp. 2-23, 2-34.

board's willingness to grant fare increases is undoubtedly one of the reasons that private carriers are willing to enter the market.

Since carriers are not required to report revenues and costs for their express bus operations separately from other operations, we have no complete financial accounting. However, Table 6-1 shows the relevant data for a selection of operators. The ratios of total income to total cost (including depreciation) ranged from 1.15 to 1.26; these are levels of profit comparable to many other business activities and indicate a financially healthy enterprise.[2]

2. In Chapter 5 Walder concludes that NYCTA's express bus service is unprofitable (contrary to the Authority's belief). It is important to bear in mind that we are concerned here primarily with privately operated express services, which must of course be profitable,

For purposes of this research, we focused our attention on one express bus operator, New York Bus Service (NYBS). NYBS was chosen because it is the only system that operates express buses almost exclusively, having little other income. All other express bus operators, including of course the city-owned Transit Authority, operate a combination of express buses and local buses, extensive charter service, or both, and the only data on service and expenses for bus systems are systemwide.

NYBS services have characteristics typical of most other express bus routes in the city. Its four routes connect four residential areas in the Bronx with the Manhattan central business district. Stops are frequent in the residential areas, followed by an express portion where stops are made only on call at distances of between 1 and 4 miles, and then frequent stops in the CBD. NYBS has had a profit similar to the other self-sustaining carriers shown in Table 6-1.

The second operation to be examined was the self-sustaining commuter or regional rail service provided by the Chicago and North Western Railway Company (C&NW) in the Chicago metropolitan area.[3] This railroad had three suburban routes radiating from the Chicago CBD. When in the late 1950s a new management took over the C&NW, it undertook the radical step of attempting to make the suburban services profitable by modernizing the equipment and tailoring the service to the postwar market. It continued to operate profitably until 1975. In 1974 a regional transit authority was created in Chicago, and it intervened in a fare-increase proceeding by the railroad, offering to give the railroad a lump-sum subsidy in lieu of the fare increase. The RTA's policy was to hold fares constant, with the RTA making up the operating deficit. In 1977 the rolling stock was purchased by the RTA, and the C&NW operated RTA trains under contract to the RTA. Although the C&NW presumably could have continued under private for-profit operation, especially if its publicly owned competitor, the Chicago Transit Authority, were to charge

---

as they continue to operate (in the case of some carriers) refusing subsidy. Also, the deficits of those private express bus operators who do accept subsidies are quite small, all deficits in 1980 being less than 10 percent of total operating revenues (from passengers, advertising, etc.) (New York State Department of Transportation, 1982, pp. 69–70).

3. We use the term "commuter rail" in this paper, although "regional rail" is increasingly used to describe the services we analyze. The word "commuter" is now widely used to denote service for work trips only, whereas all the (bus and rail) services we considered operated in nonpeak periods and in both directions, and served points all along their lines.

fares close to costs; however, it was only reasonable to include the rail system in the RTA, for otherwise the RTA would not be truly regional, and its regional tax support would be in jeopardy.[4]

All three C&NW commuter routes radiated from a single terminal located in the northwest corner of the CBD. Line lengths were 52, 36, and 63 miles (83, 57, and 101 kilometers) for the North Line, West Line, and Northwest Line, respectively; the latter had a spur to Lake Geneva, Wisconsin, for a maximum length of 71 miles (114 kilometers). The change of management in the 1950s led to three important sets of operating changes in the service.

The first was that the old equipment was replaced by air-conditioned, double-deck commuter cars ("gallery cars"), and the steam locomotives were replaced by modern diesel-electrics. Many of the cars were equipped with cabs from which the locomotive could be controlled: this allowed a "push-pull" operation, with the engine remaining at one end of the train, and it substantially reduced costs by eliminating yard switching. The second change was the introduction of flash-type commuter tickets, which were merely shown ("flashed") to the conductor instead of being collected. This enabled train crews to be reduced and resulted in further cost savings. Finally, the management focused on suburb-to-CBD markets and withdrew from very short-haul, intra-Chicago markets that were better served by local transit. Some city stations were eliminated, especially those adjacent to rapid transit stops. At the same time, parking facilities were considerably expanded, making the system in effect a rail-auto service rather than a traditional walking-access service.

These changes took place under the scope of regulation by the Illinois Commerce Commission. Like most regulatory bodies, the Commission was reluctant to grant fare increases: the C&NW overcame the reluctance by linking the fare increases to proposed equipment purchases or service improvements. Commuters favored high-quality service, even at increased fares; thus there was virtually no opposition to fare-increase proposals during the period of modernization.

Table 6–1 shows the costs and revenue through 1975. The commuter rail service operated at a profit from 1965 to 1974, the period

---

4. An interesting aside is the support of C&NW for public take-over, mentioned by Johnson and Pikarsky in Chapter 3. As they point out, the C&NW anticipated a "buyout" at replacement rather than current value of depreciated stock – such a windfall no doubt being preferable even to continued long-term profitally.

of private management and before the Regional Transportation Authority began its subsidy and take-over program.

These, then, are two major private transit systems that have managed to be self-sufficient during a period of generally increasing transit deficits. How have they managed this feat? Two explanations suggest themselves. First, the systems may be more efficient than others, and hence have lower expenses. Second, they may be offering a different (and more attractive) type of service than more conventional transit systems, increasing their passenger traffic and revenue.

Two different approaches to these questions may be distinguished. The first, which we take up in detail in the following sections, is to analyze them through case studies of the operations. The second is to attempt to formulate a model of decision-making by providers and users of transit service and, within the context of such a model, analyze "scenarios" of privately produced service. Our research encompassed both approaches. Since the second approach is unavoidably more complicated than is appropriate to discuss in detail here, we provide next a brief overview of the models and their principal results.

In very general terms, the modeling analyses took the following form. They focused on a radial urban corridor, in which express bus service is to be provided connecting the central business district with a suburban residential area. The transit operator is presumed to be a profit maximizer, meaning that he or she selects the fare, schedules (or frequency) of buses to operate on each route, and the number of routes (and hence coverage of the residential area), all in order to maximize profit. For a given distribution of income and other characteristics of the travelers, the percentage using transit is estimated using a standard urban travel modal-split model by comparing the costs and quality of transit to the cost and quality of the alternatives, in this case assumed to be riding in an owner-driven automobile. Characteristics of the consumers and of the transportation corridor can be varied over any range desired in order to ascertain the sensitivity of the results and feasibility of private for-profit operation under these conditions.

The analyses performed encompass a very wide range of these characteristics, including variations in total travel in the corridor (including both auto and bus users) from 500 passengers per peak hour (and correspondingly lower volumes in other periods) to 5,000 persons per hour. Bus and automobile speeds were also varied, including auto line-haul speeds between 25 and 50 miles per hour, and bus speeds over a similar range for the express portion and down to 8 miles per hour for the local portion. Income and other features of the population were also varied over a range encompassing typical population characteristics in residential districts.

The basic result of these analyses[5] (Viton 1980; Viton, Morlok et al. 1982) was that operators of conventional large buses, with the same costs as existing publicly owned operators (this feature has a significance that will become apparent later in the paper), could operate a service profitably at corridor passenger volumes down to 2,000 passengers per hour during peak periods under typical conditions, and down to about 800 passengers per hour with conditions favorable toward transit. Considering that a passenger volume of 2,500 persons per hour (in about 1,700 automobiles per hour) is a typical volume on a single lane of an urban expressway during the peak period, the minimum volumes required for profitable private operation of transit are low indeed. Furthermore, in all cases the transit operator had a substantial range of fares and services for which profitable operation was possible. This suggests that service could be provided with far from perfect information, and that a private operator could enter the market profitably with almost any reasonably well-conceived service, and then experiment with variations in fares and service quality in order to find the most profitable point if he or she so chooses. Profitability is emphatically not a knife-edge problem.

As examples of the sort of analyses and results that these models can generate, consider the following situation.[6] A private entrant serves a transit market, consisting of a circular residential area of radius 4 miles, connected to a CBD by a limited-access highway 8 miles long. Within this market, the private carrier faces competition only from the private car. The private carrier is assumed to be free to set its fare and to provide service by designing a route structure (routes are laid out on the radii of the residential area) and running buses on those routes. Consumers choose between this service and

---

5. P. A. Viton, "On Competition and Redundancy in Urban Transportation" (Berkeley: University of California, Institute of Urban and Regional Development, 1980); and P. A. Viton, E. K. Morlok, et al., "The Feasibility and Desirability of Privately Provided Transit Services," final report to UMTA, project no. PA–11–0027 (Philadelphia, Penn.: University of Pennsylvania, Civil Engineering Department and Regional Science Department, 1982).

6. Taken from Viton, Morlok, et al., "Privately Provided Transit Services," ch. 3.

Table 6-2.   Example of Profitability Analysis.[a]

Commuters/ Peak Hour	System Profit Per Day, $	Fare, $	Routes	Buses Per Hour	Overall Bus Share
5000	11041	1.60	9.0	38.7	0.387
4000	7998	1.53	8.0	30.2	0.378
2000	2437	1.25	5.3	13.5	0.338
1000	309	1.05	3.7	6.7	0.254
800	22	0.97	3.2	5.0	0.213
600	—b	—	—	—	—

a. See text for explanation of market structure and other conditions.
b. Positive profit not possible.
Source: Viton, Morlok et al. (1982), p. 3-13.

the private car by utility maximization: essentially, they compare costs and service on the two modes. The demand function is known to the private carrier.

Using costs and demand data from the San Francisco Bay Area, the following questions may be addressed. First, when is profitable operation possible, and what sort of service will be offered by a profit-maximizing carrier? Table 6-2 shows, for various corridor travel volumes, the answers to these questions. Profitable operation is possible when travel volumes exceed 800 per peak hour; fares, as one might expect—and consistently with the case study of actual bus operations presently to be described—are considerably higher than normal transit fares.

Next, what combinations of fare levels and bus frequency will yield positive profits? Here we are interested in the range of such combinations: if it is narrow, then profitable entry may be difficult, due to information or search costs. By contrast, a wide range of profitable combinations suggests that profitable entry is a comparatively simple matter. Figure 6-1 shows the range of profitable combinations (the numbers shown are profit per day) for the case just described: clearly it is a very wide range indeed.

Further analyses were done to determine the effect of having a private carrier enter a market in which there was also a publicly operated transit system.[7] The public system would presumably be subsidized and could offer a lower fare. This is precisely the situation that exists in New York City, where subway and bus lines parallel some of

7. Viton, Morlok, et al., "Privately Provided Transit Services."

Figure 6-1. Range of Profitability.[a]

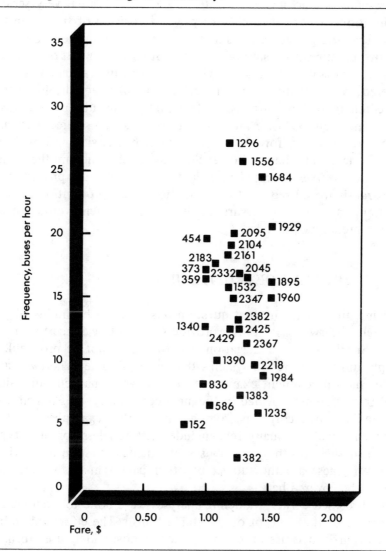

a. Same structure as Table 6-2, but 2,000 commuters/peak hour assumed throughout.
Source: Viton, Morlok et al. (1982), p. 3-21.

the express routes. As would be expected, under this condition it is quite possible and indeed relatively easy for the public carrier to reduce fares or improve service quality to the point where the private operator could no longer operate at a profit. This has very serious implications for the feasibility of private provision of transit, in the sense that the public carrier must be restrained from predatory competitive practices that simply drive the other carrier out of business. This is probably one reason why more private carriers have not entered transit at the present time.[8] But another equally important impediment to their entry is the fact that public authorities are usually granted an exclusive monopoly to operate the service, with any competition simply forbidden. The express bus services in New York are among a small handful of exceptions to this rule, another being the jitney service operated in Atlantic City. Entry of private firms into transit would require the elimination of the prohibition of competition, as well as the assurance that public carriers would not engage in predatory practices.

THE ISSUE OF PROFITABILITY

Turning directly to the first question posed at the beginning of this chapter, the two case studies provide sufficient evidence for an answer. Specifically, the allegation that transit cannot be profitable is simply untrue—there are systems that are profitable! The two cases are perhaps preeminent examples of the conventional scheduled linehaul transit being provided in the most common type of transit market, radial urban corridors. A number of other examples could be included, including many that include currently less common types of transit such as jitneys, minibuses, and demand-responsive services. However, these are the subject of other papers in this volume and will not be covered here.

As discussed earlier, modeling analyses were done to examine the generality of the concept of profitable transit. These focused on bus transit, partly because buses are by far the most widely used form of public transit in the United States, and also because such systems can

---

8. For example, in Chapter 7 Giuliano and Teal point out that private commuter operators in Boston, Hartford, and Houston have cited the introduction of competing services by subsidized transit authorities as the reason for their abandoning service.

be implemented more quickly than rail. In addition, there is considerable evidence that properly designed bus systems, operating on public streets in some cases and operating on their own exclusive rights-of-way in others, can provide the same or higher quality service at lower capital and operating costs than rail systems. The issue of the conditions under which capital-intensive systems can achieve similar results is far from settled. Nevertheless, the C&NW experience, as well as the earlier experience of other rail operators such as the Red Arrow Lines in Philadelphia, suggests that rail systems can be profitable, too.

SERVICE CHARACTERISTICS

The question of the level-of-service and pricing of the two self-supporting transit services (relevant to our second and third initial questions) is addressed here, in two parts. We first compare the service levels of these systems to those of other U.S. systems in order to ascertain whether the self-sustainability could be attributed to an unusual price-service package. That is, we compare service quality in the self-sustaining services to service quality in other U.S. transit systems. Second, it is important to be market-specific in order to assess the potential viability of the services. If, even with levels of service different from an industry norm, the self-sustaining systems cannot compete with alternatives already present in the transit market, one would not expect them to attract the necessary patronage for long-term survival. Thus, we shall also compare the service levels of the self-sustaining systems to the service levels of alternative means of travel in the same markets.

For purposes of comparison, we shall discuss the concept of service quality, structured into four primary categories of urban transport service characteristics. These categories, together with their operational meanings, are shown in Table 6-3. The characteristics revealed as important by previous literature are included.

The service quality on NYBS express routes is far higher in most respects than typical city transit bus routes. First, as may be seen from Table 6-4, the average speed is faster due to the limited-stop operations. In addition, there is an explicit general policy of providing a seat for all patrons. Data limitations prevent a direct comparison of this feature with other systems, but data on average system

Table 6-3. Primary Service Characteristics of Public Transport Systems.

Category	Characteristics
Service availability	Origin-destination areas Time period of service Traveler and trip types served
Information	Maps and timetables Real-time information sources
Price	Fare
Level of Service	Travel time (access, wait, on-vehicle, transfers, etc.) Predictability of arriving as planned Schedule delay Comfort Personal security Activity options while traveling Interruptions of journey (transfers)

load factors are indicative of the differences between NYBS and typical transit services. Because these express buses usually pick up and discharge passengers only near the ends of the routes, the load on express buses is essentially constant. Thus, one would expect such express buses to have a much higher load factor than the normal transit buses. But the load factor on the NYBS operations is about the same as other bus systems, as revealed in Table 6-4. This suggests that other bus systems have a higher ratio of passengers to seats past the peak-load point, and hence that they are more likely to have standees than NYBS. This is consistent with the common observation of many standees, and in some cases extreme crowding, on large city transit buses during peak periods.

By contrast, NYBS has a policy of trying to give a seat to all passengers. This is accomplished primarily by operating more buses for a given passenger volume, but some real-time dispatching during periods of very short-headway operation is also used by express operators. This avoids the unused seats that otherwise would result from variations in passenger demand. Comfort aboard these express buses is also better than normal: all are air-conditioned; seats are fully cushioned, with high backs; and overhead luggage racks are provided for baggage and packages. Among all these aspects of service, only with respect to headway is the NYBS about on a par with other systems.

Table 6-4. Selected Level of Service Characterization of U.S. Bus Systems.

System	Average Headway (min.)		Average Weekday Operating Speed (mi/hr)	Average Load Factor (pssgr-mi/seat-mi)		Estimated Average Fare ¢/mi
	Weekday	*Peak*		*Weekday*	*Peak-hour*	
Boston	11.3	7.1	15	0.37	0.37	5.4
Chicago	22.0	16.0	12	0.35	0.51	10.1
Cleveland	32.4	16.2	11	0.29	0.79	11.7
New York[a]	13.0	8.7	18	0.25	0.27	11.0
NYBS (express)	25.9	15.0	18	0.36	0.46	8.8
Philadelphia	26.0	13.0	15	0.36	0.45	5.7

a. Average for New York includes NYBS.
Source: Morlok, Viton et al. (1979), pp. 4-22 – 4-24 (1972 data).

Travel information is available by telephone, by mail, and from drivers while on board the buses. The four NYBS routes differ in the times during which service is provided. Two (Co-op City and Parkchester) operate every day, while the Pelham Bay and Throgs Neck services do not run on Sundays. The former two routes operate on weekdays from early morning (5:00 to 6:30 A.M.) to late evening (11:00 to 12:00 P.M.), with additional departures provided for late night theater-goers. Both operate from 10:00 A.M. to 8:00 P.M. on Sundays. The Pelham Bay and Throgs Neck services run on weekdays from early morning (6:00 to 6:30 A.M.) mid-evening (9:00 to 9:30 P.M.) and on Saturdays from 9:00 A.M. to 8:00 P.M.

As would be expected for routes serving long trip lengths, NYBS fares are much higher than those of other bus systems: more than three times that on the next most expensive system. Average revenue and average trip lengths are plotted in Figure 6-2. Here it can be seen, however, that the fare per mile is in the same vicinity as that of other systems. Thus the key difference between the private and public bus systems is that the former base fares on distance traveled in contrast to the flat fare of most public systems.

The C&NW commuter rail service, like the other self-sustaining transit operations, has information readily available. Telephone and mail information service is provided; timetables may be picked up at stations. Once on board, information is readily available from conductors or trainmen. Service is provided from approximately 6:00 A.M. to 1:00 A.M. Parking facilities are readily available: the average number of spaces per station is 292. By contrast, for other Chicago-area rail services, the Burlington Northern provides 229, the Milwaukee Road 100, Illinois Central Gulf 128, and the Rock Island 188. In Philadelphia, the former Penn Central commuter lines provided 74 spaces per station, and the former Reading Company lines 50.

Table 6-5 provides quantitative level-of-service data on major U.S. commuter rail lines. The C&NW does not run at headways significantly shorter than other commuter rail services, nor is its average speed higher. Like most commuter railroads, it has a policy of attempting to provide a seat for all passengers during the peak. And, in contrast to the other self-supporting services studied, the average fare per mile on the C&NW is about the same or a little lower than on other systems studied (Figure 6-3).

Figure 6-2. Average Fare Versus Average Trip Length for Various U.S. Bus Transit Systems.

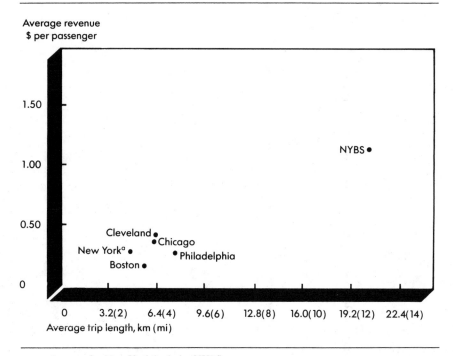

Average revenue
$ per passenger

a. Average for New York includes NYBS.
Source: Morlok, Viton et al. (1979), pp. 4-22-4-24 (1972 data).

To conclude this section, it appears that, compared to other U.S. transit systems, the self-sustaining services go to special lengths to ensure that system information is readily available, and to provide a seat for (virtually all) patrons even during the weekday peak. Their average vehicle speeds are somewhat higher than average; and (not mentioned above), the vehicles of both systems are free of graffiti and dirt. Shelters or more elaborate waiting facilities are provided. Fares charged per mile are about the same as on other systems, but absolute levels are higher, due to longer average trip lengths.

The other aspect of service quality that must be discussed is the within-market comparison. How does the service offered compare, not to average U.S. transit service, but rather to the alternatives facing travelers in their own markets? We compare the money and

Table 6-5. Selected Level of Service Characteristics of U.S. Commuter Rail Systems in 1972.

System [b]	Average Headway (min.)		Average Weekday Operating Speed (mi/hr)	Average Load Factor (pssgr-mi/seat-mi)		Estimated Average Fare ¢/mi
	Weekday	Peak		Weekday	Peak-hour	
Boston	42.0	15.0	31	0.51	0.64	5.91
Chicago [a]	43.0	26.0	31	0.35	0.57	4.55
C&NW	59.1	18.2	32	n.a.	n.a.	4.47
New York	33.4	14.1	33	0.44	0.57	4.55
Philadelphia	48.0	22.0	33	0.41	0.64	4.97
San Francisco	48.7	7.1	34	n.a.	n.a.	2.91

a. Average for Chicago includes C&NW.
b. Commuter rail only, not including rail rapid and light rail.

Source: Morlok, Viton et al. (1979), pp. 4–20 – 4–34 (1972 data).

Figure 6-3. Average Fare Versus Average Trip Length for Various U.S. Commuter Rail Systems.

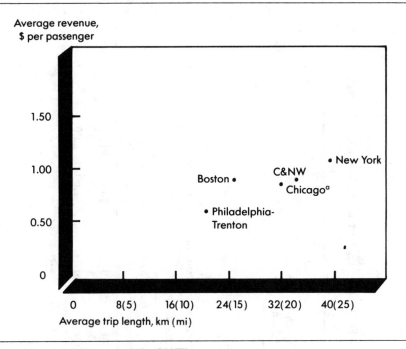

a. Average for Chicago includes C&NW.

Source: Morlok, Viton et al. (1979), pp. 4-20 – 4-34 (1972 data).

time costs for representative trip distances for the two systems in question.

For New York City trips, we compare in Table 6-6 the service of the express buses with that provided by the subway, the most widely used alternative mode from the Bronx to the Manhattan CBD. As has been pointed out, the express bus fare is considerably above that for the subway – $1.50 versus $0.50. However, the level of service on NYBS bus routes is generally better than that on subway or bus alternatives. Using NYBS's Co-op City route as an example, a 1976 rider survey found that passengers on the express buses experienced very slight increases in travel time (door-to-door) as a result of switching from NYBS buses, average travel time being 64.4 minutes via NYBS and 66.2 minutes via the express bus. Subway train headways are about the same as those of the bus during peak periods, but during the other periods the subway headways are typically 20 minutes or

Table 6-6. Comparison of Time and Cost of Self-Supporting System and Alternative Travel Paths for Selected CBD-Oriented Trips.

Express Bus versus Subway (1978)

Origin Point	Fare	Expected Travel Time
Bronx (Co-op City)		
NYBS	$1.50	64.2 min.
Subway	0.50	64.1

C&NW Commuter Service versus Auto (1975)

Origin Point	Approximate Trip Distance	C&NW Fare		Auto Cost[a]		Expected Travel Time	
		10-ride	Unlimited Monthly	Scpt.	Std.	C&NW	Auto
Oak Park	20 km.	$0.90	$0.60	$0.90	$1.00	37 min.	27 min.
Des Plains	30	1.25	0.75	1.25	1.50	56	44
Warrenville	50	1.60	1.10	1.60	2.00	83	63

a. "Scpt." is subcompact; "Std." is standard-sized automobile. Costs are average operating cost, plus cost of parking.

Source: Morlok, Viton et al. (1979), p. 5–23.

more, and the bus headways are typically one hour during weekdays. But the bus service provides timetables and adheres to them closely (as inferred from passenger responses on actual service reliability), and thus waiting time for the bus in nonpeak periods is likely to be less than for the subway. Added to this is the fact that many passengers on express buses had to transfer between transit routes at least once on their prior mode, exacerbating the waiting time difference between the express bus and conventional transit.

The travel environment of the express bus is usually superior to that of other forms of city transit, especially subways. For example, in a typical weekday peak, at the maximum load point entering the Manhattan CBD, the average express bus held 47 riders and provided between forty-five and fifty-two seats; while a subway car carried 138 passengers but provided only forty-nine seats.[9] Shelters are provided at most express bus stops. Personal safety is also considered to be far greater on the buses than on the subway.[10]

For Chicago-area trips, we compare trips by the C&NW and trips made by car, assuming 2 persons per car. Typical results are given in Table 6–6. The fares on the C&NW travel are shown under two alternatives: tickets are bought under either a 10- or 25-ride plan, or an unlimited monthly ride plan. As shown in the table, the lowest C&NW fares are consistently less than even subcompact auto costs. (Of course, more extensive carpooling would alter this conclusion.) On the other hand, the average travel times by train are generally higher than the corresponding auto travel times.

What one finds in the C&NW service is a combination of service quality and price that makes a very attractive transport package from the viewpoint of travelers in the region. That this is the case is borne out by a survey conducted in the area served by the Chicago and North Western Railway's northwest line in 1973. This survey was of approximately 1,000 households selected at random. It was undertaken by a conference of mayors of suburban communities, in order to assess the adequacy of transportation and other services in the area. In this survey, 76.7 percent of the respondents indicated that

9. Tri-State Regional Planning Commission, "Interim Technical Reports" (New York: Tri-State Regional Planning Commission, 1976), pp. 6, 16; (1977), pp. 12, 16.

10. New York City Department of Transportation, "Better Integration of Transportation Modes Project," final report (New York: NYCDT, 1977), p. 268.

Table 6-7. Chicago and North Western Fare Increases, Traffic, and the Consumer Price Index, 1969-1974.

Year	Fare Increase, %	CPI Increase, %	Passengers		Passenger-miles	
			Millions	% Change	Millions	% Change
1969			25.729		528.6	
	5	5.9		-2.7		-2.2
1970			25.046		517.9	
	6	4.3		-1.1		+0.6
1971			24.763		521.1	
	7	3.3		-0.6		-0.5
1972			24.606		518.3	
	5.25	6.2		+0.8		+0.6
1973			24.812		521.4	
	7	11.0		+2.6		+2.5
1974			25.452		534.4	

Source: Morlok, Viton et al. (1979), p. 2-33.

they felt the C&NW commuter service was very good or excellent, and 93.6 percent rated it average or better.[11]

There is a final feature of these services that bears emphasis. In a period of inflation of all costs, the prices of these services must necessarily increase to keep pace with cost, if self-sufficiency is to be maintained. One might think that such fare increases would diminish ridership. This is not necessarily true, as the C&NW experience indicates. Table 6-7 presents the fare increases initiated by C&NW in the period just before it was taken over by a public authority and no longer operated for profit. As can be seen, these fare increases were generally equal to or slightly greater than the increase in the Consumer Price Index. Nevertheless, traffic continued to grow over this period.

What does all this mean in terms of the questions posed at the outset of the chapter? These findings on product offerings—service quality and fares—are directly relevant to the second and third questions. Turning first to Question 3, it is clear that these private carriers offer a service that is generally superior in service quality than that offered by public authorities. And the results of the simulation analysis (of how an operator attempting to maximize profit would behave) also

11. O. A. Morlok, "Attitudes and Mode Choice Behavior," (M. S. thesis, Loyola University, 1974), p. 45.

suggest that, in general, such an operator would provide higher quality service. There is no indication that costs would be reduced by such tactics as undermaintenance; in fact a detailed comparison of the C&NW and other commuter lines operated by public authorities revealed that the C&NW performance was far better in features that are strongly influenced by maintenance, such as on-time performance and overall rider satisfaction with the service.[12] While any organization, public or private, could skimp on maintenance in order to make short-run gains at the expense of the long run, there is no evidence in these studies to suggest that this is a significant problem in private sector operation.

Turning to Question 2, part of the answer as to how a profit can be made is that high service quality produces high passenger demand. Also, fares are graduated by distance, in both the case-study systems and in the results of simulation analyses. (In the case of the regional bus services, which by regulation have a flat fare, the distance-relatedness results from the fact that these passengers have a longer average trip length than passengers on the city transit systems, as revealed in Figure 6-3. This is a very crude form of distance relatedness, but nevertheless it does exhibit this property.) Other aspects of the answer to Question 2 will be covered in the next section.

COSTS

In this section, we ask whether or not the costs of private transit systems are lower than those of comparable (mainly public) systems (Question 4). However, before proceeding to the discussion, an important conceptual question must be resolved. When we speak of one transit operation as being less costly than another, we generally mean that its *average cost* (total cost per unit of output) is less than that of the other. But in this case it would be inappropriate merely to compare average costs. For as we have seen, the self-sustaining services provide a level of service higher in some important respects than that usually provided. Also, passenger traffic and capacity can differ significantly between any two systems. Thus what is required is a

---

12. E. K. Morlok, "Innovation in Urban Transportation," final report to UMTA, project no. PA-11-0022-3 (Philadelphia, Penn.: University of Pennsylvania, Civil Engineering Department, 1980).

way of incorporating the level of service, capacity, and traffic into the description of the transit system.

Our standardization is in two steps. First we compute the physical resources that a comparison (public) system would need to produce an equivalent service level as a base (private for-profit) system. Having done this, we then calibrate cost models and use them to calculate the costs that a comparison system would experience in providing the capacity and service level of the base system. The cost model used here for the bus comparison is a unit-cost model: the principal cost accounts are assigned to various units of resources and outputs; and these computed unit costs are assumed to be constant over the entire range of system outputs.[13]

The comparison is particularly simple in the case of the express buses. The buses operated by the various systems are identical in size. Hence to provide the same capacity and headway as the express service of New York Bus Service, it is only necessary to operate the same number of bus-miles and bus-hours and to employ the same fleet size as that system. Unfortunately no consideration of features other than capacity and service frequency could be incorporated into the analysis, as there are no comprehensive data on vehicle condition, on-time performance, and so forth.

The results of the cost comparison, using 1975 cost data, are shown in Table 6-8. The table gives the estimated total operating cost of producing the service level of NYBS at the unit costs of various comparison systems. As can be seen from the table, NYBS is far from being a low-cost system. For the other carriers in New York City, NYBS is a less costly system, but the differences are slight—6 percent at most. Indeed, it is significantly more costly than all the carriers located outside the New York metropolitan area. This is undoubtedly due to higher wage rates in New York City, a subject to which we shall return. Thus we may conclude that it is not primarily due to a cost advantage that New York Bus Service is able to be profitable.

No satisfactory cost model was available with which the costs of commuter rail operations could be analyzed, so one was developed for this research similar in spirit to the bus cost model used for the

---

13. Details are given in E. K. Morlok, P. A. Viton, et al., "Self-Sustaining Public Transportation Services," final report to UMTA (Philadelphia, Penn.: University of Pennsylvania, Civil and Urban Engineering Department, 1979).

Table 6-8. Bus Cost Comparison.

System (Location)	Cost	Index of Cost[a]
New York Bus Service	$4.012m	1.00
Liberty Lines (New York)	4.094	1.02
New York City Transit Authority	4.145	1.03
MBSTOA[b] (New York)	4.080	1.02
MSBA[c] (New York)	3.181	0.79
Jamaica Bus Lines (New York)	4.265	1.06
Chicago Transit Authority	3.186	0.79
SEPTA[d] (Philadelphia)	3.065	0.76
Transport of New Jersey	3.154	0.79
CDTA[e] (Albany)	1.995	0.50
Binghampton County Transit	1.891	0.47

a. Estimated total operating cost of providing NYBS 1975 capacity and level-of-service in dollars/year.

b. Manhattan and Bronx Surface Transit Operating Authority.

c. Metropolitan Suburban Bus Authority.

d. City Transit Division, Southeastern Pennsylvania Transportation Authority.

e. Capitol District Transportation Authority.

Source: Morlok, Viton et al. (1979), p. 3-17.

last comparison.[14] We estimated the costs in 1975 of providing the C&NW's capacity and service level on four other commuter rail operations. Two—Penn Central and Reading—were rail services operated under contract to the regional transit authority by the railroads, wherein the authority specified fares and service to be offered, and, along with local governments, purchased the cars and other new capital stock to provide the service on the railroad's tracks. The other two were private railroads providing service on their own, presumably for profit, although, in contrast to the C&NW, neither railroad seemed to pay much attention to its commuter service.

Table 6-9 presents the results of the analysis. It is evident that all of the other carriers are higher cost carriers (in the sense used here) than the C&NW. The variation is from 22 percent higher cost in the case of the Milwaukee Road to 83 percent higher in the case of the Penn Central—a very substantial difference. Thus in the sense used here the C&NW is certainly an extremely efficient railroad. Low costs clearly are one reason why the C&NW has been profitable in providing its commuter service. A separate study, which compared the C&NW's costs to those of the Long Island, the only entirely pub-

14. Ibid.

Table 6-9. Commuter Rail Cost Comparison.

System	Cost^a	Index
C&NW	$26.356m	1.00
Burlington Northern	39.134	1.46
Milwaukee Road	32.825	1.22
Penn Central	49.209	1.83
Reading Company	34.764	1.29

a. Estimated total operating cost of providing C&NW 1975 capacity and level-of-service in dollars/year.
Source: Morlok, Viton et al. (1979), p. 3-26.

licly owned commuter railroad, at that time, 1980, resulted in the same conclusions regarding the lower cost of the C&NW. (These results are not in comparable form and hence cannot be presented in Table 6-9.)

These results led to an intensive study of the C&NW's costs and its choice of technology, or means of providing rail passenger service, in order to discover why it was so much cheaper and whether or not the same techniques could be used on other railroads. The conclusions of that study[15] were that in modernizing its service in the late fifties and early sixties the C&NW developed—partly in conjunction with a car-builder, a diesel locomotive manufacturer, and with the cooperation of its employees union—a technology that was both cheaper in first (capital) cost and in operating cost than other rail passenger technologies. While no one innovation was startlingly new and major, the overall result was substantial. Furthermore, the technology was reflective of the mainstream of North American *freight* railroad development—diesel powered locomotives, low capital cost facilities, easy to maintain but functionally attractive equipment. This was and is in marked contrast to the conventional wisdom and technological epitome of rail transit, which tends toward very high capital costs for facilities and equipment, numerous advanced components that are difficult (and expensive) to maintain, and often rather spartan accommodations for passengers (for example, the three to two seating on New York, Connecticut, and Pennsylvania regional rail coaches). The comparison is consistent with the hypothesis that a for-profit firm is likely to be more attentive to costs and to innovate in cost-effective ways.

15. Morlok, "Innovation in Urban Transportation."

Are there similar opportunities for efficiencies in bus systems? Hardware options are not so apparent there as in rail systems, so our initial focus has been on labor costs, which typically account for 70 to 80 percent of operating costs. This research is continuing, but one very significant early finding is that firm size can have a tremendous impact on wage rates. Variations in wage rates for drivers on the order of two to one are found in the same labor market. The higher wages are associated with firms that are large in size, tend to have a monopoly position, and are subsidized (Morlok and Krouk 1983). Again, this suggests that small private firms, operating competitively, would have much lower costs than the large monopolistic firms that have characterized transit in most of this century.[16]

THE CREAM-SKIMMING ISSUE

Discussing this issue (the fifth of our questions) is difficult because it is not at all clear what the "cream" of transit is. In fact, there appears to be no cream; past studies suggest that virtually all service provided by public authorities loses money, especially based on fully allocated costs.[17] However, the relative contributions to system deficits undoubtedly vary considerably, estimates being are dependent upon the choice of output measure (for example, loss per passenger or per passenger mile).

Nevertheless the issue can be dealt with—at least in part—by examining the types of service that private firms do, or could, operate at a profit given available evidence. One service that may be considered a major source of deficits is long routes with highly peaked traffic.[18] But this is precisely the type of service that has been operated profitably by both New York private bus lines and the C&NW Railway! There is no evidence of cream-skimming in these instances— quite the contrary.

Another type of service operated by private carriers is on low-volume routes, where an innovative service delivery system, such as taxicabs, may be used in lieu of conventional buses. (This type of

---

16. The relative costs of private and public providers of transit are discussed by us in Chapter 10.

17. R. L. Oram, "Peak-Period Supplements," *Progress in Planning* 12 (1979): 81–154.

18. R. Cervero, "Transit Cross-Subsidies," *Transportation Quarterly* 36 (1982): 377–89; Oram, "Peak-Period Supplements."

service is covered in other papers in this volume.) Often the provider is a private firm operating under contract to the regional transit authority. The authority involves the private firm because the arrangement reduces costs and hence the authority's deficit. Again this could hardly be called cream-skimming.

Another—less common—type of service is typified by the Atlantic City jitney, which provides short-haul service at a much lower fare than the minimum or base fare of most transit systems, but at a profit. Again it is hard to conceive of how this could be considered "cream" traffic.

If fares must be kept below costs for social reasons—for example, to assist low-income users—the obvious mechanism of direct user subsidy could solve the problem. The subsidy would be targeted to the needy groups, eliminating the waste of subsidizing all passengers regardless of need, and the carrier could charge an appropriate (market) fare.[19]

The available evidence simply does not support the allegation that certain types of service could not be provided by private for-profit firms. There may be definitions of "cream" transit traffic not covered by this discussion, and these would have to be addressed when presented. But considering the notions of cream traffic known to us, the evidence suggests, if anything, that private operators are oriented more toward noncream traffic than cream traffic.

CONCLUSIONS

In this chapter we have examined five questions that are central to the feasibility and desirability of using the private sector to provide conventional fixed route, scheduled transit service. These five questions do not exhaust the issues, but space limitations prevent more extensive treatment, as is covered in the Morlok, Viton, and coauthors references, and on which this chapter is based.

The general conclusion that emerges is that provision of fixed route transit by private firms appears both feasible and desirable. What is not known is how to accomplish this—how to get there from here.

---

19. P. A. Viton presents some preliminary results on various forms of subsidy in "Eliciting Transit Services," *Journal of Regional Science* 22 (1982): 57–71.

There are two aspects to the problem. One is the question of how to organize the provision of service. At one extreme we could have essentially free entry and direct competition, as in most other industries, including much of the transportation sector. Another model would be to have private firms contracting with a regional authority that would decide what service each firm would provide, and so forth. And there are all sorts of combinations in between. We do not know at this time which would be most appropriate.

The second problem arises once the best arrangement is identified (for any particular area or market): how is the transformation to be accomplished? Resistance to any such change is to be expected. It might come from the transit authority management, whose role is drastically changed at best and eliminated at worst.[20] It could also come from transit labor unions that will no longer be bargaining with a publicly subsidized monopolist. Indeed, it may not be possible to unionize a reorganized transit industry with many small, and probably very diverse, firms. Creative genius will be required to develop the right mix of incentives and compensation in order to cause the system to move, while treating those displaced fairly and humanely.

20. We do not wish to imply that all transit management would oppose such change. Many surely would embrace change that would improve transit; other chapters of this volume, especially, 3, 4, 11, and 13, provide a few examples.

Chapter 7

PRIVATELY PROVIDED COMMUTER BUS SERVICES
Experiences, Problems, and Prospects

Genevieve Giuliano and Roger F. Teal

INTRODUCTION

In response to the growing fiscal problems facing the U.S. public transportation industry, attention has increasingly turned to the possibility of expanding the role of privately provided bus services in the urban commuter transportation market.[1] Compared to public transit agencies, private providers have relatively lower labor costs and more scheduling flexibility.[2] Since labor costs make up the largest proportion of transit operating costs, private providers have a distinct advantage in supplying such services. The critical issue, however, is not whether private providers can provide commuter transit services at lower cost. Rather, it is whether these services are economically viable without subsidies, and whether, if subsidies are necessary, public agencies and private providers are able and willing to jointly provide these services.

---

1. Portions of this chapter appeared in our article "Increasing the Role of the Private Sector in Commuter Bus Service Provision," *Built Environment* 8 (1983). Reprinted with permission of the publisher, Alexandrine Press, Oxford, England.

2. Anne Y. Herzenberg, "Who Should Run Boston's Buses?" (M.S. thesis, MIT University Press, 1982); Southern California Association of Governments (SCAG), *Commuter and Express Bus Service in the SCAG Region* (Los Angeles: SCAG, Transit Section, February 1982).

If private providers are capable of supplying commuter bus services without subsidies, public transit agencies could turn over existing services to them, and regulatory constraints could be relaxed in order to promote freer entry into the commuter bus service market. On the other hand, if subsidies are required, private bus service expansion involves significant institutional problems: labor constraints, subsidy issues, and transit agency control over service provision.

Based on our recent study of privately provided commuter bus services in seven metropolitan areas in the United States, we conclude that some significant problems stand in the way of a major increase in such services, whether they are unsubsidized or subsidized. Our research examined different types of privately provided commuter bus services in urban areas, having a variety of transportation situations and institutional arrangements. We found that a similar set of economic and institutional factors affected the potential for successful private bus operations across these diverse settings, and, given the present configuration of these factors, we are not optimistic about the prognosis for significantly increasing the role of private bus operators in commuter transportation.

TYPES OF PRIVATELY PROVIDED COMMUTER BUS SERVICES

Unsubsidized Commuter Bus Services

Commuter bus services can be classified as regular route, subscription, or buspool. The primary distinguishing factors are the employment status of the driver and the extent to which demand is preorganized.

Regular Route Service. This is the traditional form of commuter bus service and closely resembles public transit commuter express services. It operates on a fixed schedule and usually involves several bus runs daily. Demand is not preorganized; trips can be purchased either singly or through weekly or monthly passes. Drivers are usually full-time bus company employees with guaranteed minimum pay for each morning or afternoon piece of work. Routes, fares, and schedules are typically regulated by the state regulatory authority. Over the past several years, unsubsidized services of this type have declined in most areas. Table 7–1 indicates that, of the seven areas included in the study, only the Boston area has a significant amount of privately provided regular-route service.[3]

Subscription Bus Services.   These are targeted at a specific employment location and group of passengers. Fares are paid in advance on a weekly or monthly basis, and the passenger receives a reserved seat. Subscription service is usually contingent upon a minimum revenue: Operation begins only when a sufficient number of passengers have been obtained, and service is suspended if ridership falls below the required minimum. Subscription services may be organized by employers, employees, or by the bus company itself. The bus company provides both vehicle and driver, and drivers are paid on an hourly or shift basis. Since most subscription services consist of only one round trip per day per bus, the trip is usually provided as an adjunct to other services, for example, charter or school bus operations. Subscription service may or may not be regulated, depending on the nature of state regulatory laws. Among the case study areas, unsubsidized subscription services were found only in the Los Angeles area.[4]

Buspools.   These have many variants: carpool-type operations where the owner-driver sets rules, collects fares, and is employed at the destination site; employer-sponsored services that utilize worker-drivers and employer-owned equipment; and bus company-organized services which also utilize worker-drivers. The key feature of buspools is that the driver's major source of income is full-time employment at the job (destination) site. Worker-drivers are consequently paid relatively little: a free commute plus a small wage or a percentage of revenues. Buspools are frequently a "no frills" service which utilize older vehicles with few amenities. These low labor and equipment costs make it possible to break even with relatively low fares. Although buspools are not necessarily operated on a formal reservation

3. The New Jersey-New York City commute corridor is the other area in the United States that has a significant amount of private, unsubsidized regular-route service. See Edward K. Morlok and Philip A. Viton, "Self-Sustaining Public Transportation Services," vols. 1 and 2, final report #UMTA–PA–0017–80–2 (Philadelphia: University of Pennsylvania, November 1979).

4. Unsubsidized subscription services exist in a few other areas in the United States, notably Chicago.

Table 7-1. Survey of Private Commuter Bus Service in Seven U.S. Metropolitan Areas.

	Unsubsidized			Subsidized (by Public Funds)	
	Regular Route	Subscription	Pool[a]	Regular Route	Subscription
Hartford, Conn.	1 route	0	25 buses[b]	6 routes	0
Newport News, Va.	0	0	54 buses	0	0
Norfolk, Va.	0	0	90–100 buses	0	0
North San Francisco Bay Area, Calif.	0	0	0	0	27 buses
Boston, Mass.	200 buses	0	25 buses[b]	0	0
Houston, Texas	0	0	0	13 routes (112+ buses)	0
Los Angeles region, Calif.	0	24 buses[c]	84 buses[d]	6 routes (11 buses)	0

a. Owner-operator buspools not included.
b. Some of these are apparently subscription services sponsored by employers.
c. At least six are partially financed by user-side subsidies.
d. At least five are partially financed by user-side subsidies.

basis, tickets are usually purchased weekly or monthly. The regulatory status of buspools depends upon the particular form of organization, and it varies from state to state. In terms of both the number of areas and the number of buses, buspools are the most prevalent form of private, unsubsidized commuter bus services found in the seven areas studied.

SOURCES OF SUBSIDIES FOR PRIVATE BUS SERVICES

The sources of subsidies for private bus services are public transit agencies, transportation funding agencies, and private employers.

Transit agencies are the most likely candidates to subsidize commuter bus services because they either have jurisdictional rights over service provision and/or they are the primary recipient of all transit subsidies within their service area. This combination of service monopoly and fiscal control typically means that the transit agency is the only public agency able to contract for commuter service. There are a few instances of other funding agencies subsidizing commuter bus services. In California, for example, Yolo, Ventura, Riverside, and Los Angeles counties subsidize private express bus services with discretionary state transportation subsidies. However, in the seven areas studied, the bulk of subsidized service is provided under contract to transit agencies.

Currently, private employers play a minor role in subsidizing commuter bus services in urban areas. Some employers in the Boston and Hartford areas have organized subsidized subscription bus service for their workers, and Hughes Aircraft in Los Angeles organized and subsidizes a regular route operation to its El Segundo work site. More commonly, employers subsidize employee commute trips through transit pass programs or vanpool and carpool programs. In both Houston and Los Angeles, many major employers have large vanpool programs, and most employers in Houston offer transit fare subsidies as well. In the Los Angeles area, a few employers provide subsidies to employees which can be applied to any bus service (public or private) that serves the job site. Direct contracting by the employer is unusual (SCAG 1982).

EXPERIENCES WITH PRIVATELY PROVIDED COMMUTER BUS SERVICES

Unsubsidized Regular-Route Service

Of the seven areas studied, only Boston had a significant amount of regular-route commuter bus service. Approximately fifteen bus companies, which collectively own a fleet of over 300 intercity buses, provide scheduled commuter service into the Boston core. The commuter bus industry in the Boston region is predominantly composed of small operators; only four of the fifteen companies own more than 20 intercity buses.[5]

Interstate bus service in Massachusetts is tightly regulated by the state's Department of Public Utilities (DPU) which awards routes, approves schedules, and determines the fares which may be charged. In general, DPU pursues a policy of granting route authority to a single carrier. In exchange for these monopoly service rights, however, DPU seeks to keep bus fares low. The low fares have made it difficult for all but the largest companies to generate sufficient profits to buy new buses, and many carriers now own fleets which are considered excessively old by bus industry standards.

Private regular-route service is heavily commuter oriented. While some carriers operate all-day schedules, the bulk of the service is provided during the peak commuting hours. Private commuter buses serve most of the major radial corridors into downtown Boston, although they are particularly concentrated in areas which do not have commuter rail service. Patronage is comparable to the region's commuter rail system; it is estimated that approximately 12,000 to 15,000 commuters in the region (about 1 percent) use the private buses. The private commuter buses have a much larger modal share than commuter rail in some corridors. In the region's most heavily congested corridor, the private buses carry nearly 5 percent of all commuters, or almost twice as many as the commuter rail service. The private regular-route industry thus remains a significant factor in the Boston commuter transportation system.

The commuter bus operators service a predominantly long-haul clientele, with most routes being 25 miles or more in length. With

---

5. Tramco, Inc., *A Study to Develop Recommendations Designed to Upgrade Intercity Bus Service in Massachusetts* (Cambridge, Mass.: Tramco Inc., April 1980).

few exceptions, the routes originate outside the service district of the Metropolitan Boston Transit Authority (MBTA), the region's transit agency. There is a simple reason for this. MBTA has exclusive service rights (except for a few grandfathered private operators) within its district, and, consequently, many of the best commuter express bus routes are preempted by the transit agency. The good routes which remain tend to be too lengthy to be served by MBTA buses, but are often paralleled by commuter rail lines. The private commuter bus option in Boston remains viable in spite of these regulatory and competitive obstacles because 20 percent of the region's employment is concentrated in downtown Boston, where parking is very expensive and highway access is severely congested.

The restriction to long-haul service has significant economic implications, for it sharply limits the ability of the companies to use their labor and equipment productively. Most buses are unable to make more than a single round trip during the peak period because of the long routes (a round trip can require 1½ to 2 hours on many of the routes), and virtually all demand is in the peak direction. While every company strives to efficiently utilize its labor and vehicles, opportunities to do so in the off-peak period are limited. Charter work is concentrated on weekends or does not easily fit into the time between peak periods, and other scheduled service, such as school transportation, utilizes different equipment and often different drivers.

The experiences of the largest commuter bus company in the Boston region illustrates the economic situation for regular-route operations. This company has provided bus service for fifty years, and currently owns seventy buses for its regular-route operations. It operates in the most heavily traveled corridor in the region, the transports about 7,000 passengers (not all in commuter service) on an average weekday. During 1980 and 1981, it grossed approximately $5 million per year from regular-route services. In 1981 it lost money, due in part to a strike, while in 1980 it made a profit of approximately 6 percent of total revenues. The company's routes vary in length from 28 to 72 miles, with the average passenger trip length on these routes ranging from 25 to 60 miles. Given these long trip lengths and the heavily one-way demand, it is difficult to generate adequate fare revenue. The company shows a profit only because it is able to generate approximately $2.80 per passenger in fare revenue. However, recent fare increases have resulted in ridership losses. In 1982 an increase of approximately 8 percent resulted in a 9.5 percent loss of riders. At these fares the bus service is more expensive than vanpooling, and the number of vanpools in the company's service area have been increasing.

It bears noting that this company appears to be quite efficient and well-managed by commuter bus industry standards. Its 1981 operating costs (including depreciation) were approximately $1.65 per revenue mile, well below the contract costs to public agencies of privately provided commuter bus service elsewhere in the United States. Moreover, the company's labor costs represent less than 55 percent of its total operating costs, much lower than the comparable figure for most public transit agencies. Nonetheless, the company has had difficulty making a profit in recent years.

Despite these problems, the financial strength of the company and the strong commuter market it serves probably guarantee its continued viability. Many smaller bus companies in the Boston region dependent on only one or two routes, however, are not so fortunate. A few have gone bankrupt during the last several years, and many are apparently losing money on their commuter operations.[6] Unenlightened regulation, basic problems with industry economics, and competition from other modes are threatening the well-being of the commuter bus industry in Boston.

Buspool Services

A significant amount of buspool service exists in both the Norfolk and Newport News areas in Virginia, and in the Los Angeles region. The services and the operators themselves are quite different in the two regions. Buspools in Los Angeles have been primarily organized by two large companies and appeal to a service-conscious commuter, whereas buspools in Norfolk and Newport News have been initiated by many individual entrepreneurs as well as several companies, and appeal to a price-conscious commuter.

There are two large buspool providers in the Los Angeles area, each with thirty to thirty-five buspools currently in operation. Commuter Bus Lines, Inc., (CBL) derives about 75 percent of its revenues from its commuter buspool services, whereas Antelope Valley

6. Ibid.

Bus, Inc., is more heavily dependent upon charter and contract operations, and obtains about one-third of its revenues from buspools.
Both companies use essentially the same method to initiate and operate buspools. They market their services at large employment sites,
typically containing several thousand workers. CBL and Antelope
Valley are interested only in long-haul service, with routes at least
25 miles in length from first pick-up point to the work site. Most
routes are 30 to 50 miles in length. They will start up a new bus only
when a sufficient number of workers (usually twenty) have agreed to
use the service and one member of the group has agreed to become
the driver. Once the service has started, the driver and the passengers
are encouraged to recruit other riders, as they are informed that a
certain load factor must be maintained to continue the service. If
ridership stabilizes at twenty-five to thirty daily users, the buspool is
typically viable.

Although the commuter services provided by CBL and Antelope
Valley properly fall into the category of buspools, they are treated as
regular-route operations by the California Public Utility Commission
(PUC), which regulates intercity bus service. According to California law, all carrier services available to the public on an individual-
fare payment, non-subscription basis are subject to regulation. Consequently, these buspool services must obtain route authority and
must have their fare schedules approved by PUC. Where potential
competition exists with other private carriers or with public transit
agencies, applications are usually protested.

As in most regulatory situations, PUC's regulatory system is designed to protect companies with existing service rights, rather than
to facilitate service development. Duplicate route authority is usually
not granted, and PUC is even reluctant to authorize a new service
when dormant route authority exists. COMBUS, a subscription bus
operator in Los Angeles, has route authority for many services it no
longer operates or never did, but it strenuously resists efforts of
other providers to initiate services that would infringe on these markets. To prevent protests by public transit agencies, private buspool
operators must sign agreements stipulating that the transit agency has
the right to start competing services at some future time.

Even when there is absolutely no problem with an application for
new route authority, it still requires thirty to ninety days to be approved. but once a group of sufficient size has been assembled to
start a buspool, there is the danger that it will disintegrate if the ser-

vice cannot begin for several weeks. Thus it is not uncommon for operators to begin the service simultaneously with filing an application that they are confident will be uncontested.

Both CBL and Antelope Valley utilize used intercity coaches to provide service. CBL's operation is representative and will be described here. CBL uses forty-five buses for its buspool operations. All are at least nineteen years old, and the oldest is a 1953 model. The company purchased these vehicles for a mere $400,000, although it has spent large sums on repairs and upgrading. A stringent preventive maintenance program keeps the vehicles in top condition. CBL has traded off depreciation against maintenance: due to the low purchase price, CBL's depreciation on the vehicles is minimal (less than 5 percent of total costs), while maintenance expenses represent nearly 30 percent of total costs.

CBL's operating cost is quite low, averaging about $1.25 per vehicle mile in 1981. The efficient use of driver labor is one important reason for the low costs. With no deadheading, drivers are paid only for productive time. Consequently, payments to buspool drivers represent only 11 percent of the total cost of CBL's buspool service, as compared to over 25 percent for privately provided regular-route operations. In addition, both CBL and Antelope Valley pay their buspool drivers a percentage of the buspool fare revenues, thereby tying their income directly to the productivity of their buses.

In 1982–83, CBL grossed approximately $1.1 million from its buspool services, yet made only a small profit. It was able to make the profit, moreover, only because it raised fares approximately 12 percent during 1982. The fares remain quite modest, ranging from $16 per week for a 25-mile trip to $24 per week for a 50-mile trip, or approximately 5 to 6 cents per mile. CBL can apparently make a profit at load factors of 60 to 70 percent, which it is managing to maintain so far.

Both CBL and Antelope Valley have been plagued by competition from vanpools, some of which have been created directly from buspools. The vanpools are very strong competitors in the long-haul market, as they can offer fares which are comparable or slightly lower than CBL and can also provide a more personalized service. Since current buspool load factors are only slightly above the break-even point, a loss of even a few riders can lead to a buspool's demise. Rather than merely complain about vanpool competition, however,

CBL has chosen to use the regional ridesharing agency's data base to identify potential new markets for buspools and has persuaded the ridesharing agency to market buspool services along with vanpooling and carpooling. CBL believes that bus service has more amenities than vanpools—more legroom, a less crowded vehicle, less social pressure to interact—and attempts to capitalize on this in its own marketing activities.

Buspools in Norfolk and Newport News are much different than those in Los Angeles. Some buspools are provided by bus companies that are predominantly charter carriers, but the majority are organized by individual entrepreneurs. The number of buspools operated by these individuals range from two to thirty-two. Commuter buspools are not regulated in Virginia, and therefore there are no legal restrictions on entry, routes operated, or fares.

Whereas the buspools in Los Angeles attract a primarily white-collar ridership, the buspools in Norfolk and Newport News are low-cost services aimed explicitly at blue-collar workers. Virtually all buspools serve three huge naval bases and shipbuilding facilities, which employ thousands of workers. Most buspool vehicles are used school buses, and no amenities are offered in terms of seating quality or leg space. Fares are quite low, ranging from $6 to $12 per week, or approximately half the Los Angeles level. Riders are obviously attracted by the low fares and the attempt to provide pick-ups as near their residence as possible. Travel times are longer than by automobile because of the numerous pick-up points and because there is little peak-period congestion on the highway system. In Los Angeles, in contrast, buses make only two or three pick-ups at central locations and then travel in express mode to the work site, making the travel time reasonably competitive with the auto.

Because they are operating a no-frills, low-cost service, the Norfolk-Newport News buspool operators have found that viable routes can be as short as 10 miles in length, although most routes range between 15 and 30 miles. Breakeven load factors are reported to be as low as 50 percent. Precise operating costs of the buspools are difficult to obtain, but a reasonable lower level estimate is 60 to 70 cents per mile, exclusive of operator profit. These exceptionally low costs have two sources: the minimal acquisition costs of the vehicles ($2,000 is a representative price for a used school bus), and the labor contribution of individual owners who maintain the vehicles and keep financial records but are compensated only out of profits. Including profit, the operating cost is approximately $0.90 to $1.00 per mile.

Vanpools are also becoming a problem for buspools in Virginia. Several buspool operators assert that vanpools have been formed directly off of their buses, and all are concerned about the future profitability of buspool services. Although the vanpools are more expensive, they offer a considerably higher quality of service that appeals to many workers. Moreover, vanpools are easiest to form at the same employment locations as buspools, and this is where ridesharing agencies have concentrated their efforts.

Subsidized Regular-Route Service
For a Transit Agency

The Metropolitan Transit Authority of Harris County, Texas, (Houston MTA) has utilized local private bus operators to provide express bus service since its inception in late 1978. As of 1982, five different private operators were under contract to provide service on thirteen express routes utilizing a total of 112 buses. These private contractors provide approximately 23 percent of MTA's total service.

While the motivation for utilizing contract service is usually financial, this was not the case in Houston. Rather, MTA was committed to a program of rapid service expansion which could not be accomplished with MTA resources alone. This service commitment was the result of enabling legislation which formed the Transit Authority and authorized a 1 percent local sales tax to finance it. Political support for the legislation was obtained by proposing a vastly expanded express bus system for area commuters.

MTA inherited an aging and badly maintained fleet, inadequate maintenance facilities, and an outmoded route system from the previous city-owned transit system. At the same time, MTA had to find some way to satisfy commuters in a service area of some thirteen hundred square miles, and the agency turned to the private sector for assistance.

Private bus operators were readily available, as three of the current contractors had been operating routes in the I-45 corridor as intercity carriers. Since the enabling legislation also granted MTA regulatory authority within its service area, the local portions of these routes were absorbed by MTA and then contracted out to the same carriers to continue their operation.

Three factors make the contracting situation in Houston unique. First, the Houston MTA enjoys a favorable financial position due to the local sales tax revenue. In the 1982 fiscal year, for example, the sales tax generated $162 million, or 76 percent of MTA's total revenue. The operating deficit is easily covered, and a sizeable capital fund has accumulated as well. Understandably, MTA has so far had no need to consider cost effectiveness in service decisions.

Second, MTA has a political commitment to service expansion, and given the availability of funds, its first priority was to provide a high quality, reliable service. This priority translated into stringent vehicle requirements and performance standards for the private operators, and in effect made it possible only for relatively large bus operators to successfully provide the service.

Finally, MTA turned to the private sector during a time of need, but perceives contract service as a stopgap measure that will eventually be eliminated as MTA operational problems are overcome. Thus the amount of contract service has remained stable; new services are initiated by the MTA as vehicles become available. The transit union initially accepted contracting because of MTA's assurance that it is an interim strategy. The union contract limits contract service to 15 percent of total service; an emergency limitation of 25 percent is currently in effect. It bears noting, however, that since MTA (and its predecessor) had never operated these express services, Section 13(c) of the Urban Mass Transportation Act of 1964 is not an issue in MTA contracting.

Financial Aspects of MTA Contracting. MTA's concern for service rather than costs is clearly demonstrated in the contract costs and provisions. The private providers are paid the going charter rates, ranging from $375 to $475 per day per bus, depending on route mileage. On a per revenue-vehicle hour basis, contract service costs range from $69 to $94 (see Table 7–2).

Contracts have a duration of three years plus two yearly renewal options. The service price is fixed for the first two years and is negotiable thereafter. The contractor supplies both vehicle and driver and is responsible for all aspects of the service except the route schedule, which is set by MTA. Contract provisions also include vehicle specifications, performance standards and penalties, and back-up

Table 7-2. MTA Private Operator Contract Revenue.

Operator	Contract Revenue Vehicle Hours/ Month[a]	Contract Revenue/ Month[a]	Estimated Annual Revenue[b]	Average Revenue/ Revenue Vehicle Hour
A	4,384	$317,943	$3,684,855	$72.53
B	2,596	242,876	2,814,933	93.56
C	2,365	162,318	1,881,266	68.63
D	1,575	123,750	1,434,263	78.58
E	383	27,570	319,536	72.02
Total	11,303		$6,449,998	

a. These are totals for all routes operated by each company.
b. Based on one month actual data.

vehicle requirements. Contracts are written for a minimum quantity of service, and MTA has the option of requiring additional service up to a prespecified maximum on three days notice. The volume of MTA business available has been such that there is little competition; all of the local private operators capable of contracting are involved.

Several aspects of MTA service contribute to its high cost. First, vehicle requirements call for luxury coach-type vehicles (preferably new), which cost upwards of $100,000. Back-up vehicles are also required to assure service reliability. These vehicles must remain available during weekdays; that is, they cannot be used for charter service. Because of the relatively short duration of the contract, these vehicle costs must be depreciated rapidly.

MTA's option to adjust the level of service to be provided with only three days notice also adds to costs. In practice, this means that contractors must be prepared to provide the maximum level, even though they may never be asked to do so. This provision also makes it very difficult for small operators to bid on the service, as they usually cannot obtain vehicles on short notice, nor can they afford to purchase vehicles which might never be adequately utilized.

In an effort to control contract service costs, MTA has negotiated recent contracts on the basis of revenue-vehicle hours (RVH) rather than a daily rate per bus. MTA's position is that the private operators should be paid only for the service provided. Private operators disagree, pointing out that there is little chance of utilizing the vehicle during the midday, and that the driver must be paid a minimum guarantee no matter how many hours the service requires. Although private drivers are not unionized in Houston, driver wages range from $75 to $100 per day including fringes, and there is usually a half-day guarantee for each morning or afternoon piece of work. One operator pays part-time drivers $25 for single trips. Private bus operators claim that they must be competitive with MTA in order to keep their drivers, and point out that the express runs are more difficult to service than charters and should be paid accordingly.

Impacts on Private Operators.   It is clear that MTA contract service has been profitable for the private operators. Contract service is a guaranteed revenue source (at least for the duration of the contract), and the rate of pay is generous. Indeed, two of the Houston providers stated that their contract bids included a 15 percent profit. It would appear, however, that the greatest benefits have accrued to the largest bus operators, and that the contract service requirements discussed above have effectively eliminated small operators from participating. This in turn has reduced the competition for the contracts. At least two small operators (who performed as subcontractors) had to give up contract service and subsequently went out of business. In both cases, vehicle reliability was the problem. MTA charges $100 plus the cost per hour for late runs (more than fifteen minutes late), and $250 plus the cost per trip for missed runs. In spite of the compensation rate, a small operator cannot afford to incur very many of these penalties.

A second barrier for small operators is the short start-up time allowed in the contract. Service begins one week after the contract is signed, which means that vehicles must be acquired *before* the operator has been awarded the contract. The effect of this provision has been to restrict the small operators to a subcontractor role, as only a large operator can afford to take the risk involved in bidding for the contract.

Yet contract service has become a major source of revenue for participating operators. Although precise figures were not available, the contract service provided at least 50 percent of each operator's total revenue. Private operators are not concerned about their dependence on MTA, because they are convinced that contract service is here to stay. They cite MTA's long history of operating problems, the poor morale and training of MTA employees, and the great demand for commuter services in the Houston area as reasons why contract services will continue. They also maintain that private operators are more efficient, and that comparable MTA service would be much more costly.

Subscription Service For a Transit Agency

The Golden Gate Bridge, Highway, and Transportation District (GGBHTD) in the San Francisco Bay Area has, since 1971, sponsored a privately provided subsidized subscription bus service into San Francisco. The subscription bus services, which are called "club buses," were initiated in the 1960s by commuter groups in Marin, Sonoma, and Napa Counties, which contracted with private bus companies to operate the service. The club buses served areas north of the Golden Gate Bridge that were not served by the private commuter services of Greyhound, then the only public transportation in this area.

Initially, GGBHTD's subscription bus program involved six clubs running fifteen buses. The original cost of subsidizing the program was quite modest, and the commuter clubs essentially ran the program themselves. The carriers were responsible for providing the vehicles and drivers, and were selected by each club on the basis of competitive bids. GGBHTD paid 50 percent of the cost of the contracts, with fares covering the other 50 percent. The District had minimal administrative responsibilities beyond paying the bills and stayed entirely out of operational matters. In 1972, GGBHTD took over the commuter bus services of Greyhound and established its own transit operation. Golden Gate Transit substantially expanded both service and patronage during the mid-1970s, and it instituted a number of new commuter express routes. Even so, the club bus program continued to grow, utilizing twenty-one buses by 1977, because Golden Gate Transit could not offer convenient express service from all areas north of the Golden Gate and could serve only a limited number of destinations in San Francisco.

During the latter part of the 1970s, fiscal limitations ended Golden Gate's service expansion. The peak-to-base ratio was nearly five to one, and the deficits associated with peak service had become substantial. Nonetheless, GGBHTD had established a policy goal of preventing an increase in peak-period vehicle use of the Bridge. In order to accommodate the steadily increasing commuter demand and yet avoid providing more transit, GGBHTD developed a vanpooling program. The vanpool program, a carpool program, and the club bus services were all incorporated into the newly created Ridesharing Division in 1980.

Placing the subscription bus program in the Ridesharing Division raised the issue of the appropriate level of subsidy support for the club buses, as the only subsidies involved in vanpooling and carpooling were for the District's administrative costs. Management wanted to eliminate operating subsidies from club buses as well, on the theory that this was a ridesharing mode and ridesharing should not be subsidized. As an initial move in this direction, club bus fares were raised to 55 percent of costs in 1981–82 and to 60 percent of costs in 1982–83.

Although operating subsidies are a source of contention, the District is aware that the subscription service is more cost-effective than regular transit service. Regular transit cost per trip ranges from $1.38

to $2.30, while club bus cost per trip ranges from $1.24 to $1.74, depending on trip length. Moreover, the subscription service generates less deficit per passenger.

In addition to changing fare policy, placing the program in the Ridesharing Division had the effect of formalizing relationships between GGBHTD, the clubs, and bus contractors. Contractors were required to meet more stringent performance guidelines and were penalized financially if they missed runs, were overly late, or substituted substandard equipment. After years of dealing informally with club leaders, these new policies caused considerable resentment on the part of some operators. The Ridesharing Division also took over the competitive bidding process, changed the procedure by which routes were bid, and stimulated more competition. Because all of the contractors are small companies, the Golden Gate Transit contracts represent a substantial portion of their business, ranging from 30 to 80 percent. The net result was that some existing contractors lost business and one contractor went out of business as new competitors bid lower prices.

In spite of these organizational problems and the recent fare increases, the subscription bus program continues to flourish. The program now totals twenty-seven buses, and commuters continue to pressure the District for more service. These additional runs are priced to cover a greater proportion of costs; the most recent route covers 65 percent of operating costs. Given the lower subsidies of the subscription service compared to regular transit, it is possible that GGBHTD will continue to financially support the program, especially given the strong constituency which has developed.

Other Contract Services

Three other contracted commuter bus services, all in the greater Los Angeles area, also bear mentioning. Two of these are regular-route operations and the third is a subscription service. The County of Los Angeles has been contracting for express bus service from the Santa Clarita Valley to downtown Los Angeles since 1980, and it has used both Commuter Bus Lines and Antelope Valley Bus as the providers. Because more than 50 percent of the miles are deadhead miles, the service is about twice as expensive as these companies' buspool services and is comparable in cost to the contracted Houston express bus operation. Nonetheless, the cost per revenue-vehicle mile (including vehicle costs) is only 42 percent of the cost of the regional transit agency's park-and-ride services.

In Ventura County, an organization of private employers is providing subsidized subscription bus service to employees at several major industrial parks in an effort to expand their labor market. Both state transit subsidies and CETA funds have been used to subsidize the operation which, although targeted at low-income workers, is open to anyone. Riders must subscribe for one week at a cost of $8, and currently the service is carrying nearly 300 passengers per day in eight buses. The provider uses school buses. Vehicle and driver utilization during the off-peak hours is a problem, and both are often left idle at the destination end of the trip. Despite this problem, the cost is only about $50 per revenue-vehicle hour. Lower driver wages, the use of inexpensive equipment, and the decision not to deadhead the vehicles unless they have other productive work account for the low costs.

Hughes Aircraft, a major aerospace company located in El Segundo, California, began operating its own employee commuter bus service in late 1982. Hughes has a contract with a private bus company to operate buses on ten routes, each about 12 to 15 miles in length, which serve residential areas with relatively high concentrations of Hughes employees. The employees pay 75 cents a ride, and Hughes subsidizes the remainder of the cost. Whether the service will attract sufficient riders to prove economically viable remains to be seen. Current ridership of approximately 525 one-way trips per day is about half of what is necessary to achieve Hughes's original financial goal for the service. At the present level of ridership and service, an annual subsidy of about $250,000 would be required. The subsidies are an essential element of the bus service, for otherwise fares would be too great to attract passengers out of their cars. The bus service is an extension of Hughes's employee ridesharing program which includes contract (subsidized) park-and-ride service and privately provided (unsubsidized) buspools and vanpools serving commuters traveling longer distances. The initiators of the bus service view it as a way to compete with the automobile for trips too short to be economically served by these other ridesharing modes.

ECONOMIC ISSUES IN THE PROVISION
OF PRIVATE COMMUTER BUS SERVICES

Financial Status of the Private Bus Industry

If commuter bus services are to be provided by the private sector, a private bus industry must exist to operate such services. This needed industry infrastructure, however, is currently not well positioned to assume a larger role in commuter transportation. As is well known, regular-route operations within the intercity bus industry in the United States have been in decline for the past three decades. Since 1950 the only growth in the bus industry has occurred in charter and tour operations, which now are estimated to generate 50 percent of the industry's revenues. In contrast to regular-route service, charter services operate with a revenue guarantee, which means that a company can make money on these operations as long as its buses are kept busy. It is not surprising that regular-route commuter operations have all but disappeared in view of the decline in transit ridership and the advent of low-fare subsidized commuter transit services. Only in Boston and the New York/New Jersey region does there apparently still exist a significant amount of unsubsidized regular-route bus service into the regional core.

Labor and Vehicle Productivity Problems
for Commuter Bus Services

Private operators, like their public transit counterparts, have difficulties in providing peak-period commuter services in a cost-efficient manner. Commuter service requires the use of vehicles and drivers for only a few hours a day, and demand is often in only one direction of haul. The key to efficient operation, however, is full utilization of labor and equipment.

In order to achieve better utilization of resources, private operators usually attempt to integrate commuter service with charter or other contract services. Subscription service and contract regular-route operation face particularly difficult problems in service integration, as many such services consist of a single round trip per day. In Houston and San Francisco these services are provided by charter bus companies with regular charter drivers and equipment. Some charter work is available for the drivers and buses during off-peak periods, but most work is on weekends or at night. Thus drivers are often idle between morning and afternoon runs.

Despite these difficulties, private operators are able to operate less costly services than public transit because of compensation and work rule conventions which are less favorable to labor. Regular-route and subscription drivers are paid a fixed rate per day or half-day, and all drivers are guaranteed a half-day minimum, but there are no split-time or spread premiums, and overtime is usually paid only after twelve hours. Wage rates are lower and employer-paid benefits are substantially less for private drivers than for transit agency drivers. Also, private drivers can be utilized for maintenance and other work during off-peak hours. As a result, direct operation costs for privately provided regular-route service can be as much as 50 percent less than transit agency costs for similar services.[7] However, as Table 7–3 indicates, actual service cost differences observed in our research were much smaller.

Privately provided subscription and regular-route services are still relatively expensive. Suburb to central business district (CBD) express service costs $50 to $80 per vehicle service hour in large urban areas – considerably more costly than typical urban transit, but less expensive than comparable transit agency peak-period express service. This high cost reflects capital charges as well as labor expense. With new intercity coaches costing from $100,000 to $150,000, any service which makes only limited utilization of vehicles will result in high hourly charges for capital recovery. As much as 20 percent of the cost per hour can be attributed to capital recovery when no regular alternative weekday uses are available for the vehicle, particularly if it is new or of recent vintage. While used buses have lower depreciation charges, the difference may be offset by higher maintenance costs. Depreciation is thus one facet of bus economics where the private sector is at a significant disadvantage compared to public transit.

As Table 7–4 indicates, the only truly cost-efficient form of privately provided commuter bus service is the buspool. In addition to the driver compensation arrangements described earlier, costs are further reduced by utilizing old and spartan used vehicles and making

---

7. Herzenberg, "Who Should Run Boston's Buses?"; SCAG, *Commuter and Express Bus Service in the SCAG Region.*

Table 7-3. Unit Costs of Regular-Route Express Service.

	$/RVH	$/RVM
Public Transit[a]		
SCRTD Park-n-Ride (Calif.)	$84.91[c]	$5.82
GGBHTD Express (Calif.)	73.07	3.12
OCTD Park-n-Ride (Calif.)	70.33	4.22
Subsidized Private[b]		
Los Angeles County (Calif.)	$78.91	$2.43
Houston MTA (Texas)	78.89	2.74
Conn-DOT (Conn.)	60.01	2.15
Unsubsidized Private		
Boston	N/A	1.69

a. Public transit operating costs exclude depreciation.
b. Private total costs, including depreciation.
c. All costs are in 1981 dollars except SCRTD and OCTD costs, which are 1982 estimates.

Table 7-4. Unit Cost of Subscription, Buspool, and Vanpool Service.

	$/RVM	$/PASS-MI
Subscription Service		
Public Transit (Calif.)	$6.01[a]	N/A
Subsidized Private (Calif.)	2.67	$0.066
Unsubsidized Private[b]	2.00	0.060
Buspool		
Unsubsidized Private[c] (Calif.)	$1.25	$0.042
Unsubsidized Private (Va.)	$0.80–1.00	$0.03–0.05
Vanpool[d]		
Unsubsidized Public (Conn.)	$0.53	$0.044
Unsubsidized Private (Calif.)	0.49	0.041
Unsubsidized Public (Va.)	0.47	0.039

a. Estimate for FY 1982; all other costs are actual 1981 dollars.
b. Average round trip = 70 miles.
c. Average round trip = 80 miles.
d. Assume 70-mile round trip; twelve passengers in fifteen passenger van.

minimal use of garage facilities. Vehicles are usually parked at or near the driver's home, and the vehicle is brought into the garage only for scheduled maintenance and repairs. In this way, overall service costs are kept to an absolute minimum. It is important to note, however, that most contract services are for regular-route or subscription type operations, not buspools.

How Large a Market for Unsubsidized Commuter Bus Services?

The economic success of unsubsidized private commuter bus operations in the New York City, Los Angeles, and Boston regions, and the recent establishment of private bus services in Chicago, has suggested to some transportation analysts that a significant market for unsubsidized commuter bus services may exist in a number of urban areas around the United States.

Two of the most striking characteristics of existing private commuter bus services are that most have been in operation for many years and that they predominantly serve specialized markets: strong CBDs with heavily congested highway access and very high parking costs, workers commuting long distances to large employment sites, price-conscious workers willing to accept equipment with fewer amenities in return for cost savings, or some combination of these markets. While these markets are not insignificant, neither are they widespread. For example, even in the largest metropolitan areas, only 8 to 10 percent of all workers live twenty-five or more miles from their place of employment.[8]

The market for profitable unsubsidized commuter bus services is further limited by competition from two sources: public transit services and vanpools. Competition from heavily subsidized public transit agencies is a two-fold problem for private providers. First, transit agency services may preempt the best markets. In many of the largest metropolitan areas, commuter rail serves the long-haul trips into the CBD. In addition, when the only available long-haul transit is bus service, the transit agency or a state regulatory body may prohibit other providers from operating in the transit agency's markets.

---

8. Arthur B. Sosslau, *Home to Work Trips and Travel* (Washington, D.C.: Federal Highway Administration, Highway Statistics Division, December 1980).

Second, in spite of their substantially lower costs, private providers cannot compete with transit agency fares that routinely reflect subsidies of 50 percent or more. Implementation of express commuter service by the local transit agency was cited as the reason for abandoning commuter routes by private companies in Hartford, Houston, and Boston.

Some observers have argued that private bus services could attract commuters that public transit cannot by offering a higher level of service at a premium fare. The willingness of commuters in Boston and from New York to New Jersey to pay relatively high fares (by transit standards) for commuter bus service would appear to support these claims. But these commuters are the very ones who, by virtue of their trip lengths and work destination, would be attracted to collective transportation in any case. Golden Gate Transit has demonstrated that it is possible for a public transit agency to offer high quality *subsidized* commuter bus service at high fares and attract large volumes of users. Private providers cannot successfully compete against a public transit agency providing regular-route or subscription service at subsidized fares.

On the other hand, only private providers are capable of providing truly low cost commuter bus service, as exemplified by the buspool operations in Los Angeles and Norfolk-Newport News. But vanpooling is another low cost alternative. Vanpool services have become the most effective competitors for commuter bus services. They are really a smaller version of buspools or subscription services and as such have the same flexibility. In addition, as Table 7-4 indicates, vanpool and buspool costs per passenger mile are quite similar.

Vanpools also have other advantages. In some areas vanpools enjoy tax advantages which are not available to private carriers. For example, vanpools in Connecticut are exempt from the state gasoline tax. Vanpooling has also had the benefit of aggressive marketing and support by public agencies. Finally, private employers have been willing to sponsor vanpool programs and absorb some (or all) of the administrative expense. As a result, vanpool programs have become the predominant form of private (unsubsidized) commuter services in six of the seven case study areas.

Contracting for Commuter Bus Service

Costs of subsidized contract services are quite sensitive to contract provisions and service arrangements. The most obvious source of service cost differences are vehicle requirements. Unlike public transit operators, private operators must cover vehicle depreciation costs in order to stay in business, and these are true costs, in that private operators must either purchase the vehicles outright or lease them at the market rate. Thus vehicle specifications can make the difference between a high or moderate cost contract, as is illustrated by the cost of the Ventura County subscription service ($50 per RVH) which uses school buses and the Golden Gate club bus service (nearly $80 per RVH), which uses over-the-road coaches. Vehicle costs are also related to the expected duration of the contract. If the service is viewed as very short term, the contractor's incentive is understandably to depreciate the vehicles as quickly as possible. Finally, back-up vehicle requirements, as in the Houston case, add a further cost dimension as, again, the contractor must be compensated for maintaining an idle vehicle for possible breakdowns.

A second major source of contract costs are performance standards and penalties. When breakdowns or missed runs carry large financial penalties, the contractor must be especially attentive to fleet maintenance and driver reliability. Again, building in the flexibility necessary to avoid these penalties requires more investment in maintenance as well as higher pay rates and guarantees for drivers.

Closely related to performance standards is the transit agency's administration costs of the contract service. The transit agency may or may not allocate administrative costs to the service, but the more rules and regulations are imposed, the more agency employees become involved in the service. The Houston MTA, for example, has several employees involved in contract negotiations, schedule development, and on-site monitoring of the contract service. Frequent monitoring also adds to the private operator's costs, as employees must be made available to deal with the MTA and generate the required service statistics. If the full potential of cost savings associated with contracting are to be realized, it is essential that contract provisions which add to service costs be kept at a minimum.

INSTITUTIONAL ISSUES AFFECTING
PRIVATELY PROVIDED COMMUTER
BUS SERVICES

Regulation

Unsubsidized commuter bus services in most U.S. metropolitan areas are subject to economic regulation. Most commonly, a state regulatory commission has jurisdiction over common-carrier private bus operations, and a bus company must obtain a certificate in order to initiate a new service. When competing services exist, or another operator alleges competition, the new entrant must demonstrate that existing services are inadequate to serve the market, or that a new service will in some way improve the overall quality of service in the market. Transit agencies are sometimes particularly zealous in protecting their service rights, even when new services do not constitute direct competition. In addition, other private carriers with dormant route authority may oppose new entry into a market in order to protect future interests. Most state regulatory commissions tend to favor the status quo, and opposition to new entry may be successful even when the actual competitive impacts are minor.

An even greater obstacle to private commuter bus operators exists when the transit agency itself is the regulatory body within its service district. Under these circumstances, private bus companies have little chance to develop new markets if the transit agency views their services as threatening rather than complementary. In Boston, private carriers must apply to the regional transit authority to operate routes within its service district, and basically are not allowed to directly compete with transit services. In contrast, transit agencies in Norfolk and Newport News have no desire to exercise their regulatory powers. In their view, private commuter bus service provides a substitute for more peak-period transit. But such attitudes are quite enlightened by transit industry standards; many agencies still believe that their peak-period services are the most profitable, despite ample evidence to the contrary (Oram, 1979).

Another serious problem is that of regulatory lag. A commuter bus operator will usually file an application for a new route only when enough ridership for profitability has been secured. However, if the operator must wait several months from the time of filing to the time of receiving a permit, the prospective ridership may evaporate. Even expedited regulatory procedures, instituted in response to complaints of slow decision, require at least thirty to sixty days from filing to permit issuance. As discussed earlier, Southern California bus operators sometimes initiate service without permits because of this problem.

Regulatory lag can pose an equally serious problem with respect to fare changes. Boston area bus operators complain that the state regulators are extremely tardy in granting fare increases, and that their profitability is being jeopardized by this practice. A recent state DOT study largely confirmed these claims. Given the relatively low profit margins of most unsubsidized bus services, timely fare adjustments are a necessity if the services are to remain economically viable.

Monopoly Organization of Public Transportation

One of the most vexing issues confronting the potential expansion of privately provided commuter bus service is the monopoly organization of public transportation which prevails in almost all U.S. urban areas. The transit monopoly creates four major obstacles to privately provided bus service. The first, as discussed earlier, is market preemption, either in the form of the transit agency using regulatory power to prevent private operators from providing service, or in the form of providing highly subsidized services against which private operators cannot compete.

The second major obstacle which the transit monopoly creates for private providers is the monopolization of subsidies. With few exceptions, all transit capital and operating subsidies are allocated to public agencies, and usually pass directly to the transit agency. Private transportation providers can obtain subsidies only through these public agencies. Some transit agencies do contract for various types of services, including commuter bus service in a handful of cases, but this is uncommon. Lacking access to these subsidies except on a contract basis, private bus operators are at a substantial disadvantage in developing new services.

The third obstacle is the mindset of transit management. Even when transit was privately owned and operated, the industry was composed primarily of local monopolies. The traditional attitude of transit management has been that a single organization should control all aspects of service provision. Most transit managers see no reason to give up control over service by engaging in contracting, not understanding the high costs of their own peak-period services. In addition, they are quite reluctant to weaken their political position by relinquishing their status as the sole provider of public transit services.

Finally, the monopoly organization of transit has also allowed the establishment of a quasi-monopolistic labor supply with institutionalized rights and privileges. Both Section 13(c) of the Urban Mass Transportation Act of 1964 and provisions in local labor contracts can represent formidable barriers to service contracting. Section 13(c), which applies to all transit agencies which receive federal transit subsidies, in effect prohibits management from using these subsidies in such a way that unrecognized transit workers are adversely affected. For example, a transit agency which accepts federal subsidies could not contract for part of its peak-period bus services and then lay off agency drivers who were no longer needed, unless it was willing to pay compensation to the affected employees. Lacking the incentive to control labor costs because of the availability of subsidies, management has agreed to contracts which provide additional obstacles to private contracting. In Los Angeles, for example, the transit agency is flatly prohibited from contracting for any regular bus service. As discussed earlier, the Houston MTA contract operation is limited to a percent of total service. These various manifestations of the monopoly organization of transit pose serious constraints to any significant expansion of either subsidized or unsubsidized privately provided commuter bus service.

CONCLUSIONS

The evidence presented by our case study research clearly suggests that under the present circumstances opportunities for greater participation of private bus operators in commuter transportation service provision are quite limited. Privately provided unsubsidized public transit services must compete with the low fares of subsidized public transit services on the one hand and the high quality of service provided by vanpools on the other. Consequently, private unsubsidized regular-route and subscription services are no longer economically viable in most urban areas. Without exception, bus companies in the case study areas had no plans to initiate new unsubsidized services, and in most cases were eliminating existing services. Only bus-pools have managed to grow in recent years.

While economic viability is the major obstacle for unsubsidized services, institutional problems stand in the way of expanding subsidized services. Private bus operators are usually quite enthusiastic about subsidized service because it provides them a guaranteed source of revenue. At the same time, the cost to the sponsoring agency is usually lower than transit agency-provided service. Existing institutional arrangements, however, are what prevent these potential cost savings from being realized. Transit agencies in most urban areas have direct access to subsidies, and consequently they control the structure of service provisions within their service area. With very few exceptions, transit agencies are unwilling to share service provision with private providers, even when the incentive of fiscal problems exist. If an increased role for private providers is to be achieved, then, institutional change must take place. Allocation methods for subsidies must be more flexible, and sponsors must become more willing to decentralize the supply of commuter transportation.

Chapter 8

THE TAXI IN THE URBAN TRANSPORT SYSTEM

Sandra Rosenbloom

INTRODUCTION

Taxis carry more passengers than all U.S. mass transportation systems put together.[1] Moreover, these taxi services carry a larger share of those considered transit-dependent than do public transit systems: In 1969 over 70 percent of all taxi passengers came from households with incomes under $10,000 per year. In that same year, that group accounted for only 64 percent of the passengers on all mass transit modes.[2]

The role of the taxi in the urban transport system has been highlighted by both the recent interest in deregulation of transportation industries and the recent emphasis on the private delivery of public services. While the urban taxi is heavily regulated in most U.S. cities,

The author would like to thank C. Kenneth Orski, Gorman Gilbert, and Roger Teal for information on interesting taxi public-private partnerships and Karen Martin for research assistance. The author would also like to thank Charlie Lave for his constructive comments. Special thanks to the students in CRP 680A who cheerfully—and with uncontained enthusiasm—critiqued and criticized an early draft, adding immeasurably to the organizational structure.

1. Sandra Rosenbloom, "Urban Taxi Policies," *Journal of Contemporary Studies* 4 (Spring 1981).

2. John Meyer and Jose A. Gomez-Ibanez, *Autos, Transit, and Cities* (Cambridge, Mass.: Harvard University Press, 1981), p. 76.

there is evidence that, if deregulated, private taxi services could possibly provide or replace many public transport services.

This chapter examines two potential roles for the taxi. The first role is as a free-enterprise, deregulated operator. The second is as a contractor to government enterprises in the private delivery of public services. Both roles have aroused substantial interest because taxis are likely to have cost advantages over direct public operations in the delivery of a range of transportation services.

Of the two potential roles described here, the taxi as a free-enterprise, deregulated operator has been the most discussed. There is a large body of compelling literature that argues that the deregulated taxi could meet a substantial number of urban transport needs—now badly or expensively met by public authorities—and could do so at a profit. In fact, the argument is often made solely on ideological grounds: The competitive free market in search of profit will always provide better and more efficient services.

Unfortunately, an examination of empirical data on regulatory reform of the taxi industry to date shows few of the benefits claimed by proponents. This chapter reviews the actual experiences of those communities where taxis have been permitted some measure of economic freedom, considers why the expected benefits of taxi deregulation did not occur, and focuses on the transferable lessons of these experiences.

A later section examines the experiences of the taxi in its second potential role: as a contractor to public enterprises, generally for services that cannot be financially viable without public subsidy, no matter how delivered. It is ironic that most of the really interesting taxi "success" stories fall into this second category, yet it is the least discussed in the literature. There are a growing number of cities where taxi operators, acting as partners with public enterprises, are efficiently and effectively providing a range of transport services. This chapter describes some of these experiences and focuses on their transferable lessons.

Perhaps the most important conclusion to be drawn from the analyses presented here is that "success" has both an operational and an institutional dimension. Proponents of regulatory reform have long held that the taxi would be an operational success if indefensible institutional barriers were dropped. Yet evidence indicates that, firstly, the taxi is not necessarily a "success" when deregulated, and secondly, that overcoming institutional barriers is a formidable task.

Quite often "indefensible barriers" can indeed be defended on sound policy grounds. Even if our experience with the deregulated taxi were better, it is still useful to question whether the benefits out-weigh the political, administrative, and economic costs of achieving such institutional changes.

On the other hand, taxis as contractors to public enterprises have a far better track record when measured against both operational and institutional criteria of success. It seems wise, then, to focus greater attention on achieving more taxi involvement in public-private partnerships.

REGULATORY REFORM OF THE TAXI INDUSTRY

The Economic Case for the Private Taxi

Taxicabs are strictly regulated in most American cities today. Laws restrict the number of taxis in service, the kind of transportation and nontransportation services that may be provided, the fares that may be charged, the number and kind of passengers that may be served, and even the color and logo of individual cabs. In the few U.S. cities where taxis have traditionally been less regulated, for example, Washington, D.C., and Atlanta, there are many more cabs per capita.

Local and, occasionally, state restrictions on taxis have existed for many years. These restrictions grew out of a number of events and as a response to several specific local concerns. Early on, threatened transit operators sought restrictions against taxis, which had developed the habit of racing along fixed trolley lines and picking up trolley passengers waiting at stops. Some economists argued that taxis were a declining-cost industry so that competition between numerous small operators decreased efficiency and increased costs to riders. Localities were uneasy about public safety; they were concerned with the sometimes violent forms of competition between taxis, as well as criminal behavior on the part of some individual drivers. Moreover, local city councils were concerned with ensuring service continuity and area coverage.

The answer to these problems seemed to be a permanent relationship between a selected few operators and the local legislative body. By and large, local regulatory bodies saw exclusive franchises, with significant restrictions on fares and permissible services, as the way to deal with all these situations and concerns.

In the last decade, arguments against such exclusive franchises, and the controls on fares and services that accompany them, have been strongly advanced. First, there has been a significant intellectual attack against regulation in general; second, public concern over rising transit deficits and declining service has made the economic-efficiency claims of the deregulation advocates look especially interesting.

The major proponents of taxi regulatory reform have argued persuasively that deregulation would bring a number of significant benefits: freedom of entry would cause an expansion of taxi service, hence serving more people; competition resulting from removal of fare regulations would cause decreased fares; the search for profitable market niches would lead to innovations in the kinds of taxi service available and to expansion of various demand-responsive modes of public transportation; ridership on conventional bus and rail transit would actually increase because of better taxi feeder service to these line-haul modes; transit deficits would fall as taxis took over those services where public transit is inherently inefficient—low-density suburban service and peak-hour service; and finally, removal of shared-ride restrictions would allow the kind of low-fare, high-service jitney operation that works so well in the rest of the world.

The benefits of deregulation are based on the positive features of small-scale and competitive operations. Proponents assume that competitive markets are inherently more efficient than public ones and that small private providers will avoid the diseconomies of scale associated with large public operations. Taxis as private, small-scale entrepreneurs with the flexibility to pool resources may offer higher labor and equipment productivity even when wage rates are not appreciably lower.

The major deregulatory advocates have been economists, and, until recently, they had to use gross comparisons between heavily regulated and lightly regulated U.S. cities to "prove" the superiority of the competitive market and the inevitable benefits of deregulation. My own early work appeared to support the theoretical arguments. Table 8-1 shows the kind of numbers common to this discussion since the late 1960s: Cities with no or minor regulations have far more taxis than the restricted cities. I used a number of economic indicators to determine what was the most important determinant of

Table 8-1. Taxis Per Capita, Selected American Cities.

	1960		1970		1976	
	Number of Taxis	*Taxis per Thousand Population*	*Number of Taxis*	*Taxis per Thousand Population*	*Number of Taxis*	*Taxis per Thousand Population*[a]
Not Restricted						
Atlanta	1,300	2.7	1,900	3.9	1,900[b]	3.8
Washington	10,180	13.3	9,144	10.2	8,079	10.7
Honolulu	947	3.2	1,400	4.3	1,600	4.6
Company Franchise or Public Convenience Restriction						
Los Angeles	885	0.4	855	0.3	696	0.2
Kansas City, Missouri	542	1.1	542	1.1	542	1.0
Dallas	n.a.	n.a.	435	0.5	439	0.5
Fort Worth	n.a.	n.a.	197	0.5	197	0.5
Numerical Restriction						
Miami	431	1.5	431	1.0	431	1.2
Boston	1,525	2.0	1,525	2.3	1,525	2.5
Chicago	4,600	1.3	4,600	1.3	4,600	1.4
New York	11,722	1.5	11,722	1.5	11,722	1.5

a. 1976 estimated population.

b. Estimate provided by the Atlanta Police Department, 1976.

Source: Sandra Rosenbloom, "Case Studies of United States Taxicab Regulation," in *Economic Regulation of Urban Public Transportation* (Washington, D.C.: National Academy of Sciences, Transportation Research Board, September 19–22, 1977).

the variation among the cities.[3] As Table 8-2 makes clear, no economic variable comes close to explaining the differences in the numbers of taxis. Washington, D.C., for example, a somewhat deregulated city, had hotel and convention business relatively similar to that of other regulated cities on a unit-taxi basis.

Unfortunately, the problems with this kind of analysis are many. First, the number of cabs licensed is not equivalent to the number of cabs being operated. Many District of Columbia and Atlanta drivers work part-time, driving only when they feel like it. Moreover, data on the numbers of cabs are usually available only for the largest municipality in the area; nearby suburban cities license taxis that may provide some service to the larger city. Whether a cab is used by one, two, or three drivers and the number of service hours per day are not shown in these figures. Lastly, none of the deregulated cities in the early analyses had tried to deregulate fares or even permissible services. In short, these tables, and the assertions based on them, said little about the impact of regulatory reform on the taxi industry.

Proponents often augmented their arguments with the experiences of Third World countries with private, unregulated transport services. This reasoning is enjoying a new vogue. Columnist Neal Pierce of the *Washington Post* summarizes the argument well:

> In Africa, in Asia, in parts of Latin America, one finds flourishing, privately owned profitable modes of public transportation that are able to provide city residents with relatively fast, frequent and convenient service—and all at affordable prices. Private public transportation takes many names, shapes, and organizational forms from Argentina to Zaire. It is characterized in many cases by fleets of collective taxis, jitneys, and microbuses that cruise the streets and provide door-to-door or mainline service.
>
> The alternative systems are a success story by all service criteria.[4]

If deregulation seems such an obvious answer to many urban transport problems, why has it been tried so rarely in this country? Proponents answer that effective political opposition has been created by: (1) drivers, franchised taxi companies, and transit operators; and (2) seemingly irrational responses by public authorities. In short it

---

3. Sandra Rosenbloom, "Case Studies of Domestic Taxicab Regulation," in *Economic Regulation of Urban Transportation* (Washington, D.C.: Transportation Research Board, National Academy of Sciences, 1977).

4. As quoted in Gabriel Roth and George Wynne, *Free Enterprise Urban Transportation* (New Brunswick, N.J.: Transaction Books, 1982), p. v.

Table 8-2. Taxis per Selected Indices of Economic and Tourist Activity.

	City Retail Sales (1000)			CBD Retail Sales (1000)			Hotel, Motel Receipts (1000)			Service Industry Receipts (1000)		
	1963	1968	1972	1963	1968	1972	1963	1968	1972	1963	1968	1972
Not Restricted												
Atlanta	1.3	1.3	1.0	4.3	n.a.	5.9	6.2	3.8	2.0	4.7	4.1	2.2
Washington	7.4	5.8	5.1	25.0	n.a.	19.4	11.8	8.7	7.4	23.5	16.4	7.5
Honolulu	1.9	1.8	1.2	17.1	n.a.	21.4	2.8	1.8	1.0	7.4	5.6	2.9
Company Franchise or Public Convenience Restriction												
Los Angeles	0.2	0.2	0.1	2.8	n.a.	2.3	0.7	0.5	0.6	0.6	0.4	0.2
Kansas City, Missouri	0.7	0.5	0.4	3.9	n.a.	4.6	2.3	1.9	1.3	2.5	1.8	0.9
Numerical Restriction												
Miami	0.7	0.5	0.4	4.0	n.a.	3.1	2.5	1.7	1.2	2.1	1.7	0.8
Boston	1.3	1.0	0.9	3.8	n.a.	3.5	3.5	2.7	n.a.	3.6	2.7	1.4
Chicago	1.0	0.7	0.6	6.8	n.a.	5.4	2.7	2.2	2.2	2.1	1.7	1.1
New York	1.2	1.0	0.8	5.0	n.a.	3.8	2.7	2.5	2.5	1.7	1.3	0.9

Source: Sandra Rosenbloom, "Case Studies of United States Taxicab Regulation," on *Economic Regulation of Urban Public Transportation* (Washington, D.C.: National Academy of Sciences, Transportation Research Board, September 19–22, 1977).

is common to blame most resistance to the private taxi on short-sighted self-interest and institutional barriers.

An Empirical Assessment of the Free-Market Taxi

Recent empirical developments in the United States promise to illuminate both the role that less restricted taxis can play in the urban transportation network and the problems involved in removing those restrictions. Several U.S. cities have attempted regulatory reform. Four of these cities have been extensively studied by UMTA: San Diego, Portland, Seattle, and Indianapolis. I conducted research in San Diego, as well as Seattle.[5]

Indianapolis. In Indianapolis, additional entry was accomplished beginning in 1972 by reissuing out-of-service licenses and not by regulatory change. But the relative relaxation of control on entry was accompanied by a net *decrease* in the number of licensed taxis in service. Moreover, the city experienced several problems: The quality of vehicle maintenance declined significantly, and complaints about taxi service were reported to have tripled between 1973 and 1976. The police were particularly opposed to the relaxed entry controls; they reported difficulty in enforcing insurance and safety requirements. In 1977, police found one firm of 18 taxis operating the largest drug ring ever uncovered in the city.[6]

Portland. In 1979, Portland's regulatory reform allowed companies to set their own rates (up to a maximum) using either a flat rate or the meter for different types of services. The local reforms also allowed existing companies to deploy additional taxis, but there were serious efforts on the part of local officials to discourage independent operators. While the number of licensed taxis increased slightly after the reform, the numbers were small and UMTA analysts found little change in the traditional operating practices of the industry.

5. For analyses of Portland, Seattle, and San Diego, see Rosenbloom, "Urban Taxi Policies."

6. Gorman Gilbert and Pat Gelb, "Indianapolis Experience with Open Entry in the Taxi Industry," for the Mass Transportation Service and Methods Demonstration Program, UMTA Report MA–06–0049–80–15 (Cambridge, Mass.: Transportation Systems Center, 1980).

Although there were initial fare differences among the companies, within six months of the reform all companies were charging the same fare.

Seattle.   Seattle enacted comprehensive regulatory revision in May of 1979, after six years of debate. Controls on taxi entry were significantly relaxed, and operators were allowed to set their own fares. Over the last three years the number of cabs has increased 25 percent, and the number of independents has more than doubled. But demand for taxi service has apparently been dropping at an equal rate (25 percent), due in part to service refusal rates on the part of operators and an aging vehicle fleet (the average age of Seattle's taxis increased 50 percent between 1979 and 1981). Most of all, the 25 percent increase in the number of cabs did not represent increased citywide service because most of the cabs were congregating at the airport.[7] There were no reported service innovations in Seattle, and although individual rate setting was permissible, all operators were charging the same fare within six months of entry, clearly engaging in informal price fixing.

Taxis were more competitive at the Sea-Tac airport; in 1981 the airport authority felt compelled to impose a ceiling on fares at the airport, in the face of increasing complaints about exorbitant fares. There is currently some sentiment for stronger licensing at the airport and even for a reenactment of citywide entry controls. The city estimates that it is spending more money to enforce the remaining vehicle restrictions than it ever did before; this is ironic since local officials supported open entry partly to reduce the administrative costs of holding frequent rate hearings and of issuing licenses.

Atlanta.   Atlanta has frequently been used as an example of a city with historical open entry. This is because the city had a large number of illegal "cars for hire," generally operated in minority neighborhoods by black drivers. In 1965 Atlanta officially opened entry, in effect legalizing the undocumented operators. Both old and new operators then moved to the airport and major hotels, effectively decreasing taxi service in other parts of the city and in minority

---

7. Paratransit Services, *The Experiences of U.S. Cities with Taxicab Open Entry* (Chapel Hill, N.C.: October 1983). (Processed.) See also for references to Atlanta and San Diego.

neighborhoods. Complaints about problems at the airport became severe, and a study undertaken for the International Taxicab Association reported that the Atlanta Chamber of Commerce was so concerned about the airport problem that it donated staff resources to draft a new ordinance controlling taxi service. In 1981 entry controls were reestablished. There appears to be no impact on the total number of cabs in service.

San Diego. San Diego is the only city that can be described as initially successful at taxi reform. In 1978 the city council removed a per-capita ceiling on licenses, and in January of 1979 began issuing a number of new permits each month. Today San Diego has about a hundred new taxis, or a 25 percent increase in the number of cabs since reform. However, while the regulatory changes encouraged non-traditional services (such as jitney-type competition to the transit system) and rate-setting by operators to be geared to such special services, most taxi operators currently provide traditional services at the *same* rate. The largest number of new entrants were airport-based, increasing taxi supply for tourists but not fulfilling any urban transport functions.

As in Seattle, demand apparently dropped slightly as supply was expanding. This made the airport situation even more chaotic. Drivers' waiting time at the airport increased significantly. There were more numerous incidents of drivers refusing short trips and of drivers refusing to wait in line to try and serve passengers. Price gouging was rampant through 1981. The airport authority attempted to deal with the problem by issuing limited permits for service at the airport, but this was not successful. In August 1983 the city placed a moratorium on entry permits, and there is some local sentiment for re-regulation of the industry.

Transferable Lessons

The International Taxicab Association study, cited earlier, examined nine cases of entry relaxation, including the ones described here. The study reported that most, although not all, of the cities studied experienced some increase in the actual number of taxicabs in service: Spokane and Fresno were two cities that experienced significant decreases in the number of taxis after open entry. But the ITA-sponsored survey concluded that it was not possible to predict the impact of open entry on industry size, because so many other variables were involved.[8]

Another common theme in the cities studied by ITA was a problem at the airport, with problems being most severe for cities with the most sizeable increase in taxis in service. The ITA-sponsored study found no evidence of service or fare innovations. At the same time most of the cities involved reported significantly higher costs in enforcing remaining vehicle and driver restrictions.[9]

These experiences reveal that taxis were not particularly successful in an operational sense when deregulated. More importantly, they created enough problems to make them very unsuccessful institutionally. Deregulated taxis behaved in ways that concerned business people and citizens, and ultimately came to concern policymakers.

When comparing these experiences to an operational criterion of success, it becomes clear that most anticipated economic outcomes did not materialize. The irony is that free-market private taxis simply don't act like entrepreneurs in a free market. In spite of a small number of energetic competitors creating problems for tourists and at airports, taxi operators in most "reformed" cities were not very enterprising, energetic, or competitive. In spite of some fairly substantial official latitude, both the companies and individual drivers failed to act with much initiative.

Second, putting these experiences to an institutional test raises severe questions of cost effectiveness. Most of the reforms took significant administrative staff time and political resources to implement. Regulatory revisions, although often marginal, faced tremendous opposition, which in turn created serious political and administrative costs for advocates. Regulatory reform in Seattle was debated for over six years; in Atlanta, for four years. In all of the cities described above, administrative staff spent months preparing for hearings and meetings. Seattle and San Diego have incurred significant expenses in advertising to the public new taxi services and rates. Now many of the cities are expending considerable resources on maintaining taxi-related safety and other standards in deregulated markets.[10]

Not surprisingly, then, there is increasing evidence that resistance to regulatory reform comes not only from entrenched interests but from some critical analysts. Proponents have been too quick to over-

8. Paratransit Services, *Experiences of U.S. Cities.*
9. Rosenbloom, "Urban Taxi Policies."
10. Paratransit Services, *Experiences of U.S. Cities.*

look the problems associated with deregulation, or to accept them as a necessary price for a free, working taxi market. They argue that because deregulation was relatively limited, these cities did not serve as tests of the basic market concept and that, over time, taxi operators may become more assertive, inventive, and innovative enough to use their new powers to provide better or cheaper service. But state and local policymakers who have expended considerable resources to achieve even these limited reforms are probably not very satisfied with these comments. Many decide that the costs, both financial and political, are not worth the gains. Often they evaluate the gains much less enthusiastically than long-time proponents have.

Furthermore, with taxi deregulation local elected officials lose control not only over aspects of the industry where the legitimacy of their control is questionable, but also over aspects that do require their attention: insurance, vehicle safety standards, and public and passenger safety. Local officials have legitimate concerns about service continuity, area coverage, and how the city looks to tourists; their constituents charge them with tasks that proponents do not.

The positive analogy to underdeveloped Third World countries also seems strained. In examining public reaction to these cities' relaxed controls, it is not at all clear that Americans would like the bazaar-like atmosphere of the truly free-market industries in Kuala Lumpur, Singapore, or Cairo. Although none of the "reformed" cities have come close to these models, aspects of free-market competition have already proven distasteful and problematic: Tourists and locals alike are unable to deal with differential fares, service refusals, and the legal and illegal activities of enthusiastic drivers at the airport.

Some proponents have argued that it is not citizens who are unhappy with a competitive market, but officials and regulators. Analysts long ago noted that regulatory agencies prefer to control a few large enterprises rather than large numbers of small entrepreneurs. In this volume, Johnson and Pikarsky (Chapter 3) argue that officials have a need to organize, centralize, and control public services. But the question is still worth considering: Do the relatively high-income citizens of the United States desire the kind of free-for-all transport markets that work so well for the very low-income citizens of some Third World countries?

Deregulated Taxis; A Summary

Very few of the expected benefits of deregulation have occurred, although our limited U.S. experience with regulatory revision has gone nowhere as close to free-market situations as strong advocates would like. But the institutional reality is that local regulatory reform usually occurs in the United States as an incremental change to existing regulations. Rarely are existing regulatory systems entirely abandoned, nor is that goal espoused. It seems clear that this is the political and administrative climate in which any future U.S. reforms will be made.

If nothing else, these experiences suggest that whether or not "real" deregulation or privatization of the taxi could have substantial benefits, it is unlikely that such real deregulation will occur. We would do better to assess new roles for the taxi within existing regulatory structures.

THE TAXI-TRANSIT PARTNERSHIP: CONTRACTING FOR PUBLIC SERVICE

Some quite extraordinary changes in the nature of the taxi industry are taking place across the United States, often unheralded and unnoticed. U.S. cities are increasingly contracting with taxis to provide a range of services, generally as *partners* with the local transit authority or city government. Rarely are these changes accompanied by ideological rhetoric.

In fact, the most interesting feature of the wide range of "new" services being provided by taxi operators is that they generally evolved as a response to community needs and not because policymakers thought private service to be inherently "right." They were all specific responses to definite problems. As one analyst commented,

> The intense pressure currently being placed on government budgets by transit deficits calls for a closer look at the opportunities for substituting taxicabs for large buses on light routes, and for the redeployment of high capacity buses to routes where they will be more productive.[11]

11. Ronald F. Kirby, "Innovations in the Regulation and Operation of Taxicabs," in *Taxicab Innovations: Services and Regulations*, Proceedings of the National Conference on Taxicab Innovations, Kansas City, May 5-6, 1980 (Washington, D.C.: Government Printing Office, 1981), p. 13.

Almost all of the newer services call for the taxi to operate in non-traditional ways. The traditional taxi has long provided an *exclusive ride* service. People who knew each other could form prearranged groups for travel from one single destination to another, but drivers were generally forbidden from grouping strangers or serving multiple destinations. Most of the newer services are based on some form of *shared ride*, often operating in a many-to-many mode. Because of such differences, these newer services may require at least some regulatory change.

The formal arrangements between private providers and local communities can take a number of forms. Most commonly the public agency contracts with a private provider for one or more specific services, including:

(A) Traditional fixed-route transit or demand-responsive services in low-density areas or late at night, often in lieu of existing fixed-route services;
(B) Feeder services to fixed routes;
(C) Paratransit services for special target groups such as the poor, the elderly, and the handicapped;
(D) Involvement in a user-side subsidy program; and
(E) Brokerage services matching travelers to the most cost-effective provider for each service.

Each of these services will be discussed below. This section will conclude with an analysis of the conditions that accompanied or facilitated the implementation of such partnerships.

(A) Low-Density or Late-Night Service

Phoenix.[12] The city of Phoenix contracts with a local taxi operator, Arnett Cab, to provide several types of public transit service to supplement or replace services provided by the Phoenix Transit System. The Sunday Dial-A-Ride, begun in 1981, is a demand-responsive service operated with both conventional taxis and lift-equipped vans throughout the entire city. The service is operated between 8:00 A.M.

---

12. Personal conversation with Ed Colby, city of Phoenix, October 14, 1983; Maricopa Association of Governments, *1981 Ridership Survey of General Purpose Dial-A-Ride Systems in Maricopa County* (Phoenix, Ariz.: December 1981).

and 5:00 P.M., door-to-door, and it generally requires only 30 to 40 minutes advance notice. Although the service is designated for the general public, over 60 percent of the ridership is elderly travelers paying even lower fares. Average ridership in mid-1983 was 295 riders each Sunday.

The same taxi operator contracts with the city for full-time, demand-responsive service trips within the 16-square-mile Paradise Valley service area with dedicated vehicles. About 190 people per day use the service, and 35 percent of these transfer to the Phoenix Transit System. Roughly 35 percent of the ridership is elderly or handicapped. The city also contracts for a limited service in the Moon Valley area of Phoenix. Ridership has been low; the service was initially discontinued and then reinstated.

The city of Phoenix negotiates contract charges with Arnett Cab each year; the 1983 charge was $16.69 per vehicle hour for Checker cabs and $17.69 per vehicle hour for wheelchair vans. Farebox revenues for the Sunday Dial-A-Ride covered 12 percent of the cost in 1981; the service currently operates at an annual subsidy of $104,425—considerably less than the $600,000 that would have been necessary to operate Sunday scheduled service in the city. Revenues on the Paradise Valley service covered about 12 percent of operating costs in fiscal year 1980–81; currently the annual subsidy is $145,500. The Moon Valley Dial-A-Ride, which was originally discontinued in 1981 when revenue equalled 3 percent of total operating costs, now carries 34 riders a day at an annual subsidy of $45,655.

It is also important to note that city staff members feel it necessary—for good service delivery—to develop an ongoing relationship with one operator rather than seeking competitive bids.

Ann Arbor.[13] In March 1982 the Ann Arbor Transportation Authority (AATA) began contracting with a local taxi operator to provide late night shared-ride taxi service in this community of 208,000 people. The Transit Authority considered its own dial-a-ride service costs to be too high for night service, and a grant from UMTA Services and Demonstration made it possible to explore a role for the

13. Personal conversation with Christopher White, Planning Coordinator, Ann Arbor Transit Authority, October 1983; G. Christopher White, "Late Night, Shared-Ride Taxi Service in Ann Arbor, Michigan" (Paper prepared for the Policy and Planning Committee, American Public Transit Association, October 1983).

taxi. The service, Night Ride, operates from 11:00 P.M. to 6:00 A.M., seven days per week, with an average wait time of fifteen to twenty minutes. No one has been refused service, but there have been waits of forty minutes and more during heavy demand periods.

The taxi operator was chosen through competitive bidding, although there are only two operators in the community. The transit authority thought that the service might lead to loss of regular exclusive riders, so it made an effort to get the two companies to develop a joint proposal for the required service. (Both companies were required by their franchise to operate all night and were known to have excess capacity available during night hours.) However, the companies were unable to agree to cooperate. Veterans Cab won a two-year contract by bidding a lower subsidy per vehicle hour. In September 1983, Veterans was again the successful bidder for FY 1984.

The firm operates three dedicated taxis each night, although only one taxi is usually in service between 2:00 A.M. and 6:00 A.M. The taxi operator keeps all fares and, in addition, receives a subsidy per vehicle hour. Veterans is responsible for all drivers' wages, fuel and maintenance costs, and dispatch service. AATA pays for the special phone line and all marketing.

For the first year of operation, Veterans bid a $6.00 subsidy per vehicle hour. However, it had erroneously predicted higher ridership and thus greater revenue from fares than actually transpired. In March 1983, the subsidy per hour was raised by AATA to $7.50 per hour. Because average ridership is roughly 3.3 passengers per vehicle hour, the taxi operator is now making approximately $10.95 per vehicle hour rather than the $12.75 it originally expected.

Ridership has been increasing slowly but steadily; currently, during most of the year average monthly ridership is between 1,200 and 1,300 people; the figure drops to 1,100 during summer months. During the first year of operation, the average Night Ride subsidy per passenger was $1.80. The second year average subsidy per passenger is $2.30. Both figures include only direct costs and not overhead, administration, or evaluation costs.

Night Ride was originally funded for eighteen months by the UMTA Demonstration Program, but the AATA Board of Directors recently voted to continue the service with local funds after the end of the demonstration period.

Tidewater Transportation District Commission. [14] The Tidewater Transportation District Commission (TTDC), centered in Norfolk, Virginia, has tried a number of contract services with taxi operators. Although many of the services were not successful, and the remaining services are relatively limited in comparison to the previous examples, the district's experiences may give some transferable insights about private contracting. The operational details of the TTDC taxi services are described by James Echols in Chapter 4. I will concentrate on the institutional issues that provide lessons for other areas.

There were some institutional problems in implementing taxi contracts; several taxi operators needed permission to operate in cities in the district where they were not licensed. Transit district union members were also very concerned about the possible loss of jobs and monitored service closely. Several taxi companies already providing contract services for the elderly and handicapped were disturbed about the loss of exclusive-ride passengers and refused to participate. The original name of all nine services was "Maxi-Taxi," but protesting taxi operators forced a name change to Maxi-Ride.

In analyzing why some services were successful and others were not, the TTDC staff concluded that shared-ride services replacing existing transit services and serving one major activity center were the most likely to succeed. Subsequent ridership studies showed no relationship between ridership and the ability to use the service to transfer to another bus line or the service area population, size, or density. Ridership was, however, slightly related to lower average family incomes.

Although the district did put original services up for competitive bid, the staff made every effort to circumvent this by getting all local taxi operators involved and assisting them in formulating bids. It appears that the staff would have been more willing to fashion a solution allowing all operators to become involved in a cooperative rather than competitive system.

14. Personal conversation with A. Jeff Becker, Service Development Manager, Tidewater Regional Transit, September 30, 1983; Tidewater Transportation District Commission, *Unified Work Program, Paratransit Service Development* (Norfolk, Va.: June 1983).

(B) Taxis as Feeder Services to Line-Haul Transit

San Diego Transit.[15]   The San Diego Transit System (SDTS) began DART, a transit feeder service in the 6-square-mile Paradise Hills area of San Diego, in 1982. Paradise Hills had been served by a direct SDTS line until 1978, when route changes in other parts of the system forced the rerouting of this line. The remaining services suffered drastic patronage losses, and the average per-passenger subsidy was $3.80 when DART was begun in 1982.

The DART system is operated under contract by the San Diego Cab Owners' Cooperative Association, a group of major independent owner/operators. This association was the first formed after the 1977 deregulation of the San Diego taxi industry. SDTS had originally hoped to reduce costs by allowing drivers to provide regular exclusive-ride taxi services along with DART services. However, due to conflicts in peak periods such arrangements were not actually possible, and it became necessary to dedicate drivers to all DART services to guarantee reliability. Because the transit system was worried about the problems of enforcing performance standards on lease drivers, the association agreed to pay regularly assigned lease drivers an hourly wage comparable to what they could average operating an exclusive-ride service.

DART was originally envisioned as providing two types of services: The first was a peak-period, fixed-route feeder service to the regular municipal carriers in the area; the second service was to be demand-responsive and off-peak, requiring only an hour's advance notice. Three months after DART was implemented, the peak-period service was modified, and the less productive of the original two fixed routes was changed to demand-responsive service. The remaining fixed route is on a 30-minute headway and serves one SDTS transfer location. The demand-responsive service provides transportation not only to two other transit transfer points, but to all locations within Paradise Hills. Most nontransfer service serves riders traveling to shopping malls.

15. Personal conversation with Sandra Showalter, Paratransit Coordinator, San Diego Transit System, September 30, 1983; Sandra Showalter, "The DART System: San Diego Transit's Taxi Feeder Project" (Paper prepared for the Policy and Planning Committee, American Public Transit Association, October 1983).

The cost of current services averages $10.00 per vehicle hour. While the original subsidy per passenger was $4.33, decreasing costs and increasing ridership lowered the average subsidy to $2.18 by October 1983. If a percentage of the fares paid on other lines by riders transferring *to* DART were attributed to DART's revenues, SDTS staff members estimate that actual per passenger subsidies would be between $1.69 and $1.75. It is a telling point that DART was begun with an eighteen-month UMTA Demonstration Grant, but it has been continued by San Diego Transit because the service operates within system productivity standards.

Memphis.[16]   In January 1983, the Memphis Area Transit Authority (MATA) requested bids from seven qualified local operators (five of whom were taxi companies) for the provision of a fixed-route taxi feeder service in two areas of Memphis. Both areas had been served by line-haul transit until late 1982. The contract was awarded to Memphis Transportation Company (Veterans Cab). Service began in May 1983 and operates in the morning and afternoon peaks only, between 6:00 A.M. and 9:00 A.M., and again between 3:00 P.M. and 6:00 P.M. Adults pay 85 cents per one-way trip and 10 cents for each transfer; senior citizens and the handicapped pay 50 cents, while students pay 60 cents.

By August 1983, average ridership had grown to twenty-one passengers per day on one route and seven per day on the other. Approximately 10 percent of the ridership is elderly or handicapped. There has been a significant increase in riders transferring to or from other MATA transit services—about half of the August 1983 ridership comprised transfers.

The operating expenses of the project are being covered by the transit authority. All planning, marketing, and data collection costs are being financed through an UMTA Demonstration grant (UMTA is also analyzing other MATA non-paratransit services). Cost data are not yet available; it is too early to evaluate this project.

16. Personal conversation with Kerry D. Roby, Director of Service Development, Memphis Area Transit Authority, September 29 and October 28, 1983.

(C) Taxi Services for the Elderly and Handicapped

In April 1976, DOT issued regulations defining the responsibilities of federally aided transit systems for the elderly and handicapped. Specifically, aided systems were ordered to provide "special services" targeted to these disadvantaged citizens. While local authorities chose a number of service delivery mechanisms to meet these regulations, a common option was to contract with a local taxi operator. Sometimes the taxi operator provided all required services using its own lift-equipped vehicles as well as conventional taxis. In other cities, the taxi operator leased special vehicles — bought with UMTA funds — from the transit authority. In some communities, as described in the following section, taxi operators provided service in conventional taxis only to those people who could ride in them.

In many instances, these public-private partnerships have not changed the ways taxi operators have traditionally operated.[17] The poor, including the elderly and handicapped, have always made up a substantial percentage of the ridership of most taxi operators — contrary to the conventional wisdom, which sees the taxi as a luxury mode of travel. In fact, a number of Texas cities initially sought taxi contracts for such special services in order not to negatively affect the traditional business of local taxi operators. Now many contract taxi operators find themselves providing similar services to their traditional customers and simply being reimbursed differently.

There is a substantial case study literature on these types of services which is beyond the scope of this paper.[18] Conclusions from this literature are summarized at the end of this section of the paper. But two lessons seem to stand out and will be discussed here.

17. Roger Teal et al., "Shared Ride Taxi Service as Community Public Transit," Institute of Transportation Studies for the Urban Mass Transportation Administration, Report DOT-1-8-14 (Washington, D.C.: U.S. Department of Transportation, Office of Technology Sharing, 1980).

18. The interested reader is advised to look up the following references for case studies: "Cost-Effectiveness of Transportation for Handicapped Persons," prepared for the National Cooperative Highway Research Program, Project 8-27, draft final (Knoxville, Tenn.: Transportation Center, 1980); "Market Opportunity Analysis for Short-Range Transportation Planning," NCHRP Report No. 209 (Washington, D.C.: National Research Council, National Cooperative Highway Research Program, 1979); *Paratransit: State of the Art Overview* (Cambridge, Mass.: U.S. Department of Transportation, Technology Sharing Program and the Transportation Systems Center, 1981); Sandra Rosenbloom, John Hickman, and Alessandro Pio, "Cost-Effectiveness Measures for Transportation for the Elderly and Handicapped," Research Report DOT-TX-11-0009 (Austin, Tex.: The University of Texas at

(1) *Segmenting Markets Creates Cost Savings.* First, using taxi contractors to serve specific market segments within the elderly and handicapped population generally creates real economies. In 1979, I chronicled the experiences of the six largest cities in Texas, all of which had been using taxis in innovative ways since the mid-1970s.[19] Austin and San Antonio are particularly interesting because each transit operator is using contract taxi services for a segmented market – the ambulatory elderly and the handicapped. Non-ambulatory passengers are served directly by the transit systems' own wheelchair lift-equipped vans. The Minneapolis-St. Paul Metro Mobility System also provides an example of the cost savings that result from separating ambulatory from non-ambulatory riders.

San Antonio.[20] In San Antonio, VIA, the transit district, has a verbal agreement with one local taxi operator, Yellow Cab, to provide all needed service for the ambulatory; dispatching is done by VIATRANS, the special service arm of VIA. Eligible users, who are certified by VIATRANS, pay the driver 50 cents each; the authority pays the taxi operator the difference between the meter fare and that amount. The average taxi fare is $6.00 (1984 dollars), while VIATRANS directly provides transportation services for the non-ambulatory at an average cost of $11.00 per trip.

VIATRANS also contracts with a regional office of the Texas Department of Health and Mental Retardation (MHMR) to carry its clients. Monthly usage varies between 1,500 and 2,000 one-way passenger trips, including the MHMR contract passengers.

Austin.[21] In Austin, the municipal transit system contracts with one of three local taxi operators to provide special transit service

Austin, Council for Advanced Transportation Studies, 1979); Systan, Inc., *Paratransit Handbook: A Guide to Paratransit System Implementation*, vol. 1, for the Urban Mass Transportation Administration (Palo Alto, Calif.: 1978); and *Transportation and the Elderly and Handicapped: A Literature Capsule* (Cambridge, Mass.: U.S. Department of Transportation, Technology Sharing Program, Office of the Secretary and the Transportation Systems Center, 1977).

19. Sandra Rosenbloom, "Local Responses to Meeting the Transportation Needs of the Handicapped: The Experience of Six Texas Cities," *Transportation Research Record* 784 (1980): 39.

20. Rosenbloom, "Six Cities"; personal conversation with Richard Guerra, Assistant Manager, VIATRANS, San Antonio, Texas, September 30, 1983.

21. Rosenbloom, "Six Cities"; personal conversation with O. J. Grahm, Coordinator, Austin Transit System STS, October 17, 1983.

(STS) to the ambulatory elderly and the handicapped. All eligible riders pay 60 cents per person. STS service is available from 6:00 A.M. to 10:00 P.M., Monday through Friday; more limited service is available on the weekend.

There is no ridership guarantee to the taxi operator who provides service in regular, nondedicated vehicles. The operator is *limited*, however, to 130 trips per day. The total STS system operates approximately 450 one-way passenger trips per day. The average cost for the 320 non-ambulatory trips carried by the transit system in its own vehicles is over $13.00 per passenger; the transit system pays the taxi operator a flat rate of $6.65 per person regardless of trip length or time of day.

Minneapolis-St. Paul. [22]   Service is provided to the elderly and handicapped citizens of Minneapolis and St. Paul by Metro Mobility, a broker that contracts with six taxi operators, one chaircar company, and one nonprofit transportation. Funding is by the state of Minnesota. (The project is discussed here rather than later in the brokerage section because of the great cost differences in serving different market segments.)

Three taxi operators provide service in regular nondedicated taxis in each of the two cities; the six companies are paid on a grid-zone base designed to be comparable to meter fares. The initial charge ("the drop") is 85 cents, each stop is 35 cents, and the charge per zone is 60 cents. Eligible riders pay 60 cents during the off-peak hours and 75 cents during the peak. The operators collect the fares, calculate their daily trips at the rates described above, and bill Metro Mobility for the difference between fares and allowable charges.

In September 1983, the entire system carried 11,000 one-way passenger trips in Minneapolis and 3,600 in St. Paul. The overwhelming number of trips in both communities were provided by taxi operators. The average subsidy per passenger trip for *all* passengers was $10.00 in September, including dispatch, administrative, and eligibility screening costs. But the average subsidy for the ambulatory

22. Sandra Rosenbloom, Carole Schlessinger, and Henry Dittman, "Ridership Patterns in Transportation Services for the Elderly and Handicapped," Research Report DOT-TX-11-0011 (Austin, Tex.: The University of Texas at Austin, Center for Transportation Research, 1980); and personal conversation with David Naibitch, Metro Mobility, Minneapolis-St. Paul, October 29, 1983.

passengers carried in standard taxis was only $3.62 in direct costs and $1.92 in administrative and other costs. One of the reasons that ambulatory passengers have been cheaper to serve is that their average trip length is roughly one-half that of wheelchair users (who are carried only by the private chaircar and the nonprofit system).

It is interesting to note that Metro Mobility did not engage in competitive contracting. Funds were simply divided among the existing taxi companies in proportion to the number of total operating permits they owned.

(2) *The Increased Costs of Nondifferentiated Service.* When examining the cost patterns for specialized services by taxi operators, the second complementary lesson is a logical outcome of the first: Such partnerships do not necessarily lead to lower costs when the taxi operator is required to provide the full range of service for *all* handicapped riders. The leading cause for observed cost differences is the great reduction in vehicle productivity that occurs when passengers who require substantial driver assistance and lengthy boarding and deboarding time are served. This loss in performance affects the entire system, often because the sporadic nature of the ridership of the severely handicapped makes it difficult to adequately plan for such time delays.

In 1978 my associates and I examined the cost patterns of sixty-seven systems for the elderly and handicapped, for which at least partially reliable cost data were available.[23] Generally, private taxi costs were not lower than comparable public agency costs when the operator was required to provide equivalent levels of service for both ambulatory and non-ambulatory elderly and handicapped people. Analyses of subsequent reports show similar patterns.[24] The effective loss of vehicle productivity is so high when transporting severely handicapped people in a large service area that any labor or other savings are often lost. The longer average trip lengths only exacerbate the problem. Most of the productivity advantages of shared riding turn into a disadvantage for these riders.

23. *Cost-Effectiveness of Transportation for Handicapped Persons.*
24. Rosenbloom, *Ridership Patterns.*

(D) Taxis and User-Side Subsidies

Traditionally the *provider* of transportation services has been subsidized when subsidy is required. But analysts have argued that in those cases where subsidies are justified, the *user* should be given the amounts required.[25] Many areas have experimented with user-side subsidies, and the UMTA Demonstration program has funded and monitored several applications. Most of the existing programs directly involve taxi operators.

In 1979 the Transportation Systems Center (TSC) did a preliminary assessment of thirteen user-side subsidy applications, including five UMTA-funded projects. All five of the UMTA Demonstration projects used taxis; three used both taxis and buses.

The TSC report concluded that a user-side subsidy was an effective mechanism for selected target groups such as the elderly and the handicapped. Costs were reasonable, and administrative expenses were not generally high; in small communities the average total cost per trip (including administration) was between $1.80 and $2.00 (1978 dollars). Since most projects paid one-half of direct trip costs, the average subsidy per passenger was between $1.00 and $1.30. In medium-sized cities or service areas under 50 square miles, the subsidy was between $1.50 and $2.25 per trip (1978 dollars).[26]

Although adequate taxi service was required to ensure that users were able to take the trips they needed, TSC found no evidence that competition among providers increased quality as well as quantity of service. Many taxi operators were hesitant about participation because of their fear that reimbursement waits would be sizeable. Some smaller companies were extremely unwilling to participate because of the increased paperwork.

A user-side subsidy program for the elderly and the handicapped in Milwaukee had a different impact on private providers in the area. Milwaukee County, with a 1980 population of almost one million, began a user-side subsidy program in June 1978, which now allows

25. Ronald F. Kirby and Gerald K. Miller, "Short-Range Public Transportation Improvements," Report 3072–01 (Washington, D.C.: The Urban Institute, 1983); Donald F. Kendall, "A Comparison of Findings from Projects Employing User-Side Subsidies for Taxi and Bus Travel" (Paper delivered at the UMTA Regional Seminars on Interim and Specialized Transportation for Handicapped and Elderly Persons, August 1979).

26. Kendall, "A Comparison of Findings."

people in wheelchairs or with aides and the blind to use any participating taxi or chaircar company in the 237-square-mile service area.
The program requires the users to pay the first $1.50, and the pro-
gram then pays the remaining cost, up to a maximum of $9.50 for
wheelchair users and $6.50 for other eligible users. In an attempt to
consider the application of the Milwaukee concept elsewhere, the
Urban Institute calculated average trip costs for the system at $8.91
(1980 dollars); deducting the user's $1.50 leaves a subsidy per pas-
senger trip of $7.41.[27]

Taxi operators in Milwaukee integrate riders into their regular
operations, although there is no shared riding. Overall the taxi operators have seen increased business, and the chaircar industry has expanded from one to three providers. All providers have apparently
increased service quality to attract new riders and keep old ones;
they offer longer service hours and greater flexibility.[28]

Two programs offering slightly modified user-side subsidies to the
general population are of interest. Hopkins, a suburb of Minneapolis
with three or four taxi companies, began a shared-ride service using
contract taxi service in September 1978. The service became a user-
side subsidy in June 1980.[29] Ten-ride ticket books now cost $8.00,
with a half-price discount for certain low-income people. The user
simply gives a coupon to the driver, who redeems it with the city for
a specified amount; the average payment to operators was $2.10 in
January 1981. Because the operator is paid per passenger, shared riding is encouraged. Original program cost when the service was operated under contract was $2.20 (1980 dollars).

The city of Santa Fe, New Mexico, has been using local taxi companies to provide services in lieu of public transit since April 1982,
employing a modified user-side subsidy.[30] The city directly funds
the service, mobilizing UMTA Section 5 operating assistance to cover
half the deficits. The city simply pays any eligible taxi operator one-
half the full meter fare for any citizen.

Riders must use coupons that are distributed free, in books of ten,
at four locations in Santa Fe. The coupons have space for both the
driver and the passenger to record and agree on trip details. At the

27. Ibid.
28. Ibid.
29. Ibid.
30. Personal conversation with Richard Montoya, city of Santa Fe, New Mexico, September 30, 1983.

end of the trip, the rider pays half the meter fare and surrenders one coupon. Cab drivers then turn in both their driver logs and the filled-in coupons to the city for reimbursement of the remaining half of the fare. The taxi operators provide all dispatch services and use their existing vehicle fleet. The average taxi fare is reported to be $4.00, although the total annual passenger subsidy (derived by dividing total annual expenditures by total number of passengers) is $2.28. The total annual subsidy is $228,000 for an average daily ridership of 274 passengers.

(E) Brokerages and Taxi Services

Transportation brokerages are an organizational strategy designed to more effectively deliver a variety of transportation services. The brokerage itself is not a transportation service different from those discussed above; it is simply a way of organizing the delivery of those types of services. In such an arrangement, one central administrative organization, which may or may not be a direct service provider, coordinates the existing transportation resources of the community with the transportation needs of individual citizens and of the agencies serving them.

Taxi operators have been involved in all of the well-known brokerages. In some examples, taxis are only a minor part of the whole brokerage operation. In others the involvement of the taxi operator is essential to the operation of the system. The brokerages with the most taxi involvement generally provide elderly and handicapped services.

Houston.[31]   Houston, Texas, has a very large brokerage operated through the Metropolitan Transit Authority (MTA); all costs are covered by local funds. MTA itself provides no special transit services; it currently contracts with one social service agency transportation system, the largest cab company in the area and one private bus operator to provide transportation services to elderly and handi-

---

31. Sandra Rosenbloom and David Warren, "A Comparison of Two Brokerages: The Lessons to be Learned from Houston and Philadelphia," *Transportation Research Record* 830 (1982); personal conversation with Jim Laughlin, Coordinator, Metrolift, Houston Metropolitan Transit Authority, October 14, 1983.

capped citizens and to any agencies that contract with MTA for service. The involvement of Yellow Cab is central to the system. The taxi company receives all calls for service and provides dispatching for all contract providers.

The Houston Metrolift service operates with a 24-hour advance notice, using dedicated vehicles, most of which are radio and lift-equipped. Eligible residents of the 1,700-square-mile area served by the transit authority pay 50 cents for trips under 4 miles and $1.00 for longer trips. Agencies purchasing Metrolift service pay varying amounts from $0.85 to $3.10 per trip.

MTA pays Yellow Cab and the bus company for all vehicle hours provided, with no maximum. In 1983 the charge was $15.50 per vehicle hour for taxis. Yellow Cab is paid under a separate contract for dispatching services. MTA provided approximately 6,000 trips per month in 1983; most were agency-purchased trips. The average subsidy per passenger, not including administrative costs, was $7.34.

MTA obtains its contract providers through a "competitive" bid process, but in fact the process is far more collaborative than competitive. From its inception, MTA had to have the support of the social service network; one way to achieve this cooperation was to contract with some of the small social service transportation systems, even though their costs were higher than were those of the taxi operator. However, all but one of the social service providers have ceased to provide service.

Pittsburgh.[32]   The brokerage in Pittsburgh, ACCESS, was forced to develop a similar mechanism to accommodate the social service network and to gain its trust. The ACCESS program was begun in 1979 through a UMTA Demonstration grant and continued through state and local funds.

ACCESS contracts with five taxi operators and four local social service systems to provide service in dedicated lift-equipped vans and some standard taxicabs. Although ACCESS has a very formal bid process, the service area was divided into a large number of zones, and bids were requested by zone. This was designed to ensure that the existing social service providers could become involved. In the

---

32. *The Port Authority of Allegheny County's ACCESS Program: A Demonstration Retrospective* (Cambridge, Mass.: Multisystems, Inc., 1982); Sandra Rosenbloom and David Warren.

first quarter of 1982, the average cost per vehicle hour for dedicated equipment was $15.93.

ACCESS also provides contract service to agency clients. By 1981 agency-contracted trips accounted for half of all trips, substantially increasing productivity because most agency trips are regularly scheduled. ACCESS averaged 16,200 one-way passenger trips per month in mid-1982. At that time the average subsidy per passenger trip was $11.69; $1.45 of that amount was for administrative costs alone (and did not include liability insurance or demonstration monitoring and evaluation costs).

(F) Transferable Lessons

It is interesting to note how little of the success of shared-ride taxi projects can be ascribed to the traditional economic variables discussed at the outset of this paper. While taxi services generally have been cheaper than comparable public transit costs, this has been due mostly to lower labor costs, not to competitive forces, private operator expertise, higher vehicle utilization, or public diseconomies of scale. In fact one is struck by the limited impact of competitive forces, the absence of limited-scale economies, and a general inability to achieve high vehicle productivity.

Successful taxi public-private partnerships have in fact been achieved more through collaborative effort than through competition; more because of the availability of UMTA (and occasionally state capital) than through private entrepreneurship; and more through the application of a delimitated concept to a well-defined community problem than through general interest in the inherent superiority of private operators. These observations have important implications for other communities interested in utilizing the potential of the taxi.

Economies of Scale and Productivity: Inconclusive Evidence. Taxis are thought to be more cost-effective than public operations because transportation services can be characterized by significant diseconomies of scale: Smaller private operators may operate more cheaply than larger enterprises. In addition, smaller operators have the flexibility to offer existing underutilized capacity at relatively low marginal costs; in fact the provision of new service may be possible at lower marginal costs given the existing infrastructure.

However, an examination of the systems described in this paper suggest that the data do not support these assumptions. In several cities, including Phoenix, Pittsburgh, Houston, and Philadelphia, it was only the more established and larger taxi or other systems that were able to provide the range of needed services at an acceptable cost. In Philadelphia a major nonprofit provider was able to show lower cost patterns than were competing private firms, even when the impacts of subsidies were discounted. Smaller firms in several cities, such as Houston and Dallas, were not willing to bid on proposed services because they were not large enough to deal with the cash-flow problems created by contract options, and they had insufficient staff to handle necessary paperwork. In other cities like Chicago, Pittsburgh, and Phoenix, small operators had higher costs, sometimes significantly higher, than larger taxi operators. Private taxi and other operators were not at all competitive with public operations in several services for the non-ambulatory handicapped, because the large public systems were able to provide services at lower marginal cost.

The evidence on productivity is inconclusive as well. The officials of almost every system described in this paper, and some reviewed in the literature, tried to get contract operators to mix subsidized riders or trips with their regular exclusive-ride service. This has been possible in a few communities, like Minneapolis, Austin, and San Antonio, and with the use of user-side subsidies. But in many cases the dispatch capability to do such integration of service was missing; in other cases, lease drivers refused contract riders in favor of more lucrative trips. In many cases, services begun as integrated operations displayed such dismal performance that the only solution was to assign dedicated drivers/employees to dedicated vehicles, at some loss of productivity.

Competition and Cooperation. The competitive spirit in search of profit, which seeks to lower the cost and increase the diversity of available service, has often been absent in these examples. Roger Teal concludes in his intensive study of the taxi-transit partnership in California, a state with many such examples, that

> Given the resistance to major change which we have observed among many taxi operators, . . . it seems likely that the taxi market will seek out new markets and offer new services primarily to the extent that these strategies represent the *only* path for profit *maintenance* . . . the taxi industry in large cities

is less likely to pursue paratransit options, since its natural inclination to avoid change can more easily be accommodated by virtue of the nature of its market. . . . While central city operators can be expected to seek out social service contracts for subsidized [traditional taxi] service they may well resist any move into shared ride. [Emphasis added.] [33]

The environment itself, particularly in many smaller communities, is hardly competitive. Kirby notes,

[G]enuinely competitive procurement approaches tend to be the exception rather than the rule. In many instances there is only one local operator with the managerial and financial capabilities to compete for any contracts. Moreover many local funding programs are quite small in scale, and the costs of a formal competitive procurement process would be burdensome. [34]

Of course, the reverse side of this situation is the lack of creativity on the part of many local officials. Many localities respond only to crisis situations; officials do not actively seek ways in which the use of taxis would improve community service. [35]

Federal policy has had an impact on the response of local officials. Until recently, as Kirby and Kemp note in Chapter 12 of this volume, UMTA policy was less than clear on the use of federal assistance funds for private service provision. Although UMTA funds have been used successfully for such provision, many commentators have noted the "chilling effect" of previously unresolved UMTA policy. (Recent policy positions from UMTA strengthen the ability of transit authorities to contract with private providers. The recently issued UMTA Paratransit Policy encourages public agencies to use private providers when they can provide, without subsidy and at a profit, currently subsidized transit services. But the policy also acknowledges that even when subsidies are required, private operators may still be the more cost-effective provider.)

Many local policymakers tried to generate ways to reduce competitive elements because they saw problems in genuine competition. In

33. G. J. Fielding and Roger Teal, eds., *Proceedings of the Conference on Taxis as Public Transit*, Conference co-sponsored by the Institute of Transportation Studies, University of California (Irvine, Calif.: Institute of Transportation Studies, 1978), p. 15.

34. Kirby, "Innovations," p. 87.

35. Eugene R. Leyval, "Regulatory Reform at the Municipal Level: Toward Increasing Taxi Productivity and Affordable Paratransit," in G. J. Fielding and Roger Teal, eds., *Proceedings of the Conference on Taxis as Public Transit*, Conference co-sponsored by the Institute of Transportation Studies, University of California (Irvine, Calif.: Institute of Transportation Studies, 1978), p. 127; Kirby, "Innovations," p. 13.

both the Houston and Pittsburgh brokerages, officials felt it was necessary for the long-term stability of the project to involve a wide variety of operators, whether they were cost-competitive or not. Officials in other cities were extremely worried about the advantage that the first bid winner would achieve if truly competitive bidding were held; these officials felt that allowing one provider to operate for one or two years would effectively reduce the ability of all other providers to compete with that operator in the future. Many officials informally reported being afraid of lawsuits or general political controversy if all operators were not involved. Thus, while many areas had a formal competitive bid, city staffs worked with all affected operators to achieve acceptable bids and to devise ways to award either multiple or collaborative contracts.

Some areas simply did not see competition to be a positive factor and actively avoided it; Project Mobility in Minneapolis-St. Paul is one example. Phoenix, San Diego, and a number of California systems sought a long-term relationship with one taxi operator.[36] In most cases, the public staffs felt that competition would be destructive or that they could better assure service quality in a long-term relationship. Even when the first bid was awarded competitively, as in Austin, San Antonio, and in a number of California cities, continuation contracts were not awarded competitively.

(G) Public-Private Partnerships: A Summary

Overall, taxi operations have been cheaper than the public services that they replaced or than those public services that could be implemented in their stead. The extent to which these cost patterns represent differences in the level of service provided, differences in service productivity, and differences in labor costs is not very clear.

The most successful partnerships have involved the bigger and more sophisticated operators, who had often already ventured into public-private partnerships with human service agencies. These larger taxi operators were able to deal with some payment delays, they had the staff to meet paperwork requirements, and they had the experience or sophistication to negotiate satisfactory arrangements with public operators.

---

36. Teal et al., "Shared Ride Taxi Service."

Officials interested in fashioning public-private partnerships with local taxi operators could not depend on competition to motivate taxis operators to come forward with innovative suggestions. Officials often had to reach out to these private operators with specific service proposals. And officials could not count on the profit motive to interest operators in participating; they often had to be prepared to cover the financial and even administrative risks that those operators perceived would result from their involvement.

Overall, nonlocal risk capital was a key ingredient in the successful implementation of most public-private taxi partnerships. Most of the successful projects described here and in the literature were funded by UMTA (or with state funds) as demonstration projects.

At the same time, it should also be noted that cost factors were not the only issue that motivated local decisionmakers. Just as often it was a reluctance to hire permanent union or civil-service drivers for new services whose subsidies seemed insecure. Sometimes the transit authority did not want to get into the "paratransit" business.

Public officials sought or accepted some reduction in competitive forces and involved a variety of community providers in order to achieve politically acceptable solutions. They often were willing to forego competitive contracting, at least in subsequent years of service, in order to achieve continuity of service and accountability.

CONCLUSIONS

Specific conclusions have already been presented in the two summary sections above. Here we address a more general point about the successful implementation of transportation strategies. The success of the taxi depends on two separate but related factors: First, whether private taxis can deliver needed transportation services and do so better or cheaper than the public sector; and second, whether taxis can do so, given the institutional constraints imposed by the American political, social, and economic structure.

Taxi deregulation has not addressed either factor and has been relatively unsuccessful, no matter how success is measured. Most regulatory reforms did not bring large increases in the quality or quantity of taxi services, at least throughout the city, and fare or service innovations were almost non-existent. Just as significantly, such regulatory reforms were quite difficult to achieve in the American local political structure (and one might argue, from the evidence here, for good reason). So even in those cities where deregulation or relaxed entry might arguably bring more or better transportation services, it would be difficult to achieve.

Taxi public-private partnerships have addressed both factors. First, they have delivered the services needed by the public sector and have generally done so at a lower cost. And they have done so even when services were not competitively offered or delivered. Second, the flexibility of these partnerships fits well into the existing institutional infrastructure: Contracts can be successfully fashioned in a number of ways—competitively or not, small- or large-scale—and still be effective and responsive to community needs.

The private taxi operator has tremendous potential to increase the quality and quantity of transport service in a community. Innovative taxi services hold great promise for a number of U.S. cities, if these cities develop services and strategies in response to their own specific needs and operating environments. In order to fashion effective taxi public-private partnerships, cities must develop practical implementation strategies that match their requirements and resources to the resources and expertise of local taxi operators.

Chapter 9

THE OVERSEAS EXPERIENCE

Gabriel Roth

INTRODUCTION

While public transport in the United States – and in most of Western Europe – seems to be inextricably entangled in a vicious circle of rising costs and declining ridership, other countries provide many examples of urban public transport that combine financial viability with high service quality.

- In Manila, the owners of 28,000 fourteen-seat licensed jeepneys, and the reputed owners of a similar number of unlicensed ones, compete fiercely for the right to provide unsubsidized public transport.

- In Singapore, operators of school buses are permitted to provide high-quality daily transport for business people, as business hours do not clash with school hours.

- In Hong Kong and Kuala Lumpur, minibus owners fortunate enough to have licenses are reported to recover their investments in two years, despite competition from one another and from franchised conventional services.

- In Calcutta, full-sized private buses make profits, while similar buses operated by a state-owned company suffer substantial losses, even on better routes.

- In Nairobi, drivers of private minibuses often earn enough to buy their own vehicles, and some even diversify by buying farms.

- In Mexico City and Caracas, shared taxis provide fast, low-cost service to all urban areas, including many unserved by the regular bus services.

- In Northern Ireland, a major portion of public transportation is provided by shared-ride taxi services run by owner-operators. Fares are generally lower than those operated by the regular city bus service, and it is estimated that these shared-ride services account for about half the daily trips in their traffic corridors.

- In Buenos Aires, private microbuses account for 75 percent of all transit trips and 54 percent of total trips. These buses thrive because they offer more flexibility, higher speeds, and greater frequencies than the publicly operated system. Their labor productivity is very high, and they operate at a profit.

All the systems mentioned above differ from the conventional services found in the United States in that they are not operated as monopoly franchises for or by government authorities. These systems, which have been designated as informal or intermediate public transport, have been described by Sigurd Grava, a professor of economics at Columbia University and former U.N. Transportation Adviser based in Manila, as follows:

> At first glance they all appear to be different, but this is primarily because of variations in hardware—from bicycle rickshaws to sleek European minibuses. The institutional structure and basic operations are quite similar: Private individuals acquire the highest technology vehicle that they can afford, and respond to the mobility demands of their neighbors at a tariff that most of them can pay.[1]

The systems can be described as "successful" in that they provide services that are frequent, affordable, and unsubsidized. Comfort standards and speeds are generally superior to those provided by the conventional services.

Before examining the factors associated with the success of these systems—and of numerous others—it might be helpful to look at two

---

1. Sigurd Grava, "Locally Generated Transportation Modes of the Developing World," *Urban Transportation Economics*, Special Report 181 (Washington, D.C.: National Academy of Sciences, Transportation Research Board, 1978), pp. 84–95.

in detail: The private bus associations in Buenos Aires and the "Black Taxis" of Belfast.

EXAMPLES

The Buses of Buenos Aires

Buenos Aires, the capital of Argentina, has a population of nine million living in an area exceeding 1,500 square miles. It has a variety of transport modes, the most important being the microbus or "colectivo," in the local jargon, which accounts for 54 percent of all trips and 75 percent of public transport trips.[2] The buses seat twenty-three, with room for at least thirty more. Most are built locally by Mercedes-Benz and are painted in bright colors. Route numbers and destinations are painted on.

The *colectivos* were developed in the 1920s when, as a result of a general economic crisis, many people could not afford to take single-ride taxis. Groups of passengers therefore used the vehicles, with fares being paid by each passenger individually. The taxis ran on fixed routes chosen by the taxi drivers themselves. The shared-ride taxi quickly showed certain virtues of its own and was favorably received by the general public: It offered more flexibility, higher speeds, and greater frequencies than the underground and electric tramways. The colectivo vehicle developed from a seven-seater to an eleven-seater; subsequently it grew to fourteen and seventeen seats, finally reaching the twenty-three seat which is the typical unit of today.

Because the microbuses offered stiff competition to the public tramways and underground system, the government established in 1936 a public agency called the "Corporate Enterprise." It was supposed to have had a total citywide monopoly in the provision of mass transport services. Acquisition by the government began in 1938, not without resistance, but in 1942 the government stopped the process, leaving a good many of the original firms still operating. By 1951 the Corporate Enterprise was in financial difficulties, and the government took over the function of control. Urban public transport thus came to be split between the remaining private firms

2. Ezequiel Ogueta, "Bus Transportation in the Buenos Aires Metropolitan Area" (Paper presented at Eighth International Road Federation World Meeting in Japan, 1977).

which ran the *colectivos*, and the state-owned *Transportes de Buenos Aires*, which ran buses, trams, trolleybuses, and the metro. After this, says the official history, "the public transport system, in the hands of the state, continued to deteriorate." By 1959 its deficit amounted to US$120,000 per day—over US$40 million a year. In 1962 *Transportes de Buenos Aires* was itself wound up, and the buses and all transport services except the underground were "handed over to private enterprise."[3] The tramways were abandoned in the same year, except in the neighboring city of La Plata, where they lingered on until 1965; the trolleybuses ceased in 1966. The *colectivo* operators thus returned to the center of the stage.[4]

The microbuses still operate profitably and provide a level of service that is praised by all visitors to Buenos Aires. The organizational unit of the service is the route association (*empresa*), which is an association of owner-drivers empowered to serve just one route; it is described in more detail in the section on route associations. The services are regulated by the Ministry of Public Works and Services, which fixes fares and minimum frequencies for individual routes and governs the formation of new *empresas*.

The public benefits from the competition that occurs between different *empresas*. As routes overlap for long distances, competition is keen. New *empresas* can be formed with the permission of the authorities, and routes readily changed. Labor productivity is high: Each vehicle produces 1.3 to 1.6 million passenger-miles per year, so average labor productivity is around 480,000 passenger-miles per year per person employed. The total fleet is composed of 13,000 microbuses; on average, 60 microbuses are used on each route, about 4 per route-mile.

The Black Taxis of Belfast[5]

To counter the argument that profit-making urban transport works only in developing countries, mention should be made of the "black

3. Ministerio de Obras y Servicios Publicos, "Estudio Preliminar del Transporte de la Region Metropolitana" (Buenos Aires, 1972).

4. John Hibbs, "Urban Bus Transport in Buenos Aires—The Colectivos" (Paper presented to the 53rd Annual Meeting of the Transportation Research Board, Washington, D.C., January 1983).

5. R. F. Amos, "Shared Taxis in Belfast" (Paper presented at the PTRC Summer Annual Meeting, University of Warwick, July 1978).

taxis" of Belfast, Northern Ireland, which emerged in the early 1970s following disruption of conventional bus service by civil disturbances. These vehicles — called "black taxis" because they are actually ex-London taxis, most of which are black — appeared first in Catholic working-class areas of Belfast and later also in Protestant areas. Although the taxis are normally operated by owner-drivers, they are regulated by local taxi-owner associations that limit the number of taxis operating in their areas of influence and decide who operates them and under what conditions. By 1977, the total number of taxis operating was estimated to range between 500 and 600.

The black taxis operate a high-frequency shared-taxi service at relatively high speeds. Passengers are picked up or set down along fixed routes between the city center and the particular areas served. To speed up the system, dispatchers are employed to organize passengers into taxi loads for different destinations. Fares are fixed and, most surprising to transport experts, are generally lower than those offered by the regular city bus service. On the other hand, comfort standards are low, with as many as eight adults in each vehicle at peak periods. But, in general, the consensus in Belfast is that the service provided by the black taxis represents an efficient and economical form of public transport. This is reflected in their patronage which, on weekdays, is estimated to cover about 50 percent of all public transport trips on the main routes they serve. The key to the financial success of the black taxis seems to be their relatively high load factors, which range from 43 to 82 percent, compared to bus load factors which range from 15 to 46 percent.

Four main criticisms are leveled at the black taxi operators. First, the full costs of insurance are not paid. Safety standards are enforced by the taxi associations themselves, but there have been problems with insurance, stemming from the fact that the insurance companies are generally unwilling to insure the black taxis other than as private cars.

Second, the drivers have been accused of competing aggressively for passengers, of overloading, and of inconsiderate driving behavior (parking in restricted zones to pick up or drop off passengers, making U-turns, and so forth). Such complaints against taxi drivers are not uncommon in other cities, in Ireland and in the United States.

Third, the services have been criticized on the grounds that the conventional bus services are faced with unfair competition; unfair because the publicly owned bus company has to meet uneconomic social obligations, such as providing services at peak periods and late at night, when costs cannot be covered by revenues. This point is related to the economics of cross subsidies, which are discussed elsewhere.

And finally, the black taxis are accused of "raising money for terrorism." This kind of criticism is irrelevant to a book that is concerned only with transport characteristics. It might be noted, however, that no one nowadays accuses franchised government transport companies of raising money for terrorism, or for any other purpose. Given the alleged interest of groups in Belfast to *raise* money for sectarian causes, it is significant that they chose to do so by providing shared-taxi services, rather than conventional bus services.

FACTORS ASSOCIATED WITH SUCCESSFUL PUBLIC TRANSPORT SYSTEMS

The success of these alternative, informal services has been known for many years, but the reasons for it were not clear. Recent work by Sigurd Grava and by A. A. Walters has identified four key factors associated with these forms of mass transport: (1) ownership is private; (2) operating units are small; (3) vehicles are small; and, (4) route associations provide effective organizational frameworks.[6]

Ownership

That publicly owned bus companies sustain losses is not entirely surprising, as many of the systems taken over by government authorities tend to be the ones that cannot be run at a profit by private operators. However, the large losses under public ownership seem to have little relationship to increases in service levels. The losses appear to be due to: (1) the higher cost levels (especially wages) that can be "afforded" by subsidized systems, and (2) the inability of publicly owned operators to resist pressures from politicians to hold down fares and expand underutilized services. For example, evidence from

6. Grava, "Locally Generated Transportation Modes"; A. A. Walters, "Costs and Scale of Bus Services," World Bank Staff Working Paper No. 325 (Washington, D.C.: World Bank, 1979).

Great Britain, Australia, and India shows that, where public and private bus companies operate in similar conditions, the costs of the former substantially exceed those of the latter.

Great Britain. In 1980, the U.K. Transport and Road Research Laboratory published a report on the economics of publicly and privately owned bus companies.[7] A comparison of fares in two areas showed that, for a wide range of journey lengths, the mean fare charged on rural and interurban runs by private operators was 25 percent lower than that charged on similar services provided by publicly owned operators. Further economic analyses by the laboratory indicated that the private operators' lower fares stemmed largely from lower unit costs, rather than from higher loads or other possible causes. The report concluded that at least some of these lower unit costs were due to the following factors:

1. Lower garage costs resulting from the use of low-cost premises;
2. Less expenditure on items associated specifically with large networks, for example, on bus stations, information offices, bus shelters, and stop signs;
3. Lower staff costs resulting from greater flexibility. Part-time drivers were used, and many full-time employees combined driving with administration or vehicle maintenance;
4. Lower staff costs resulting from lower wage rates and less advantageous working conditions. A 1978 survey indicated that the earnings of drivers in the private sector, although similar to the average for manual workers in all industries and services, were 10 to 15 percent lower than in the public sector;
5. A greater proportion of one-person operations;
6. Lower loan repayments. Public sector companies tended to borrow more than those in the private sector, and debt-service costs were correspondingly higher;
7. Use of a greater proportion of smaller vehicles.

Australia. The Australian private bus industry plays a major transport role in that continent, carrying (in 1981) 29 percent of all public transport trips, compared to the 35 percent carried by govern-

7. R. J. Tunbridge and R. L. Jackson, "The Economics of Stage Carriage Operation by Private Bus and Coach Companies," Transport and Road Research Laboratory Report 952 (Crowthorne, England: Transport and Road Research Laboratory, 1980).

ment buses and trams and 24 percent by railway. The industry consists of over 3,000 private bus and coach operators owning nearly 14,000 buses and employing about 20,000 people. The firms tend to be small, with 90 percent of the firms owning ten or fewer buses. About half of the distance traveled by the buses is on fixed-route public transport service; about a third on school services; and about a fifth on charter work. In many remote areas, private operators provide the only available public transport services.

In 1975 (the latest year for which data are available), fifty-five of Australia's sixty-eight centers were dependent for public transport services on the private sector. In the remaining thirteen urban centers, public transport is provided by both private and government bus services, the private share being 52 percent in New South Wales, 46 percent in Queensland, and 83 percent in Victoria. The government services in all three states operate at a loss. In Queensland and Victoria, the private operators receive subsidies to enable them to provide service at fares designated by the authorities. In New South Wales (for example, in Sydney and Newcastle), the private operators receive no subsidies, which leads to the paradoxical situation that the western suburbs of Sydney receive sparse, self-financing bus services, while the center and eastern suburbs enjoy government-subsidized services of higher quality. The authorities are considering the introduction of government services to the western suburbs, but are reluctant to do so because of the high costs that would be involved.

Studies carried out by the consultants R. Travers Morgan Pty. Ltd., and reported in 1979 and 1983[8], have shown that the unit costs of urban bus operators in Australia are only between one-half and two-thirds of those of the publicly owned operators providing similar services. Thus, in each city in which a comparison could be made, and in each year compared, the costs of the private operators were substantially lower than those of the public ones (see Figure 9-1).

The reasons for the differences in costs were reported to have been due to the following differences.

8. Ian P. Wallis, "Private Bus Operation in Urban Areas—Their Economics and Role," *Traffic Engineering and Control* (December 1980); Wallis, "Private Bus Route Services—Problems and Prospects" (Paper presented to the Australian Transport Research Forum, Canberra, May 1983).

Figure 9-1.   Australia: Average Operating Costs per Kilometer for Public and Private Bus Operators.

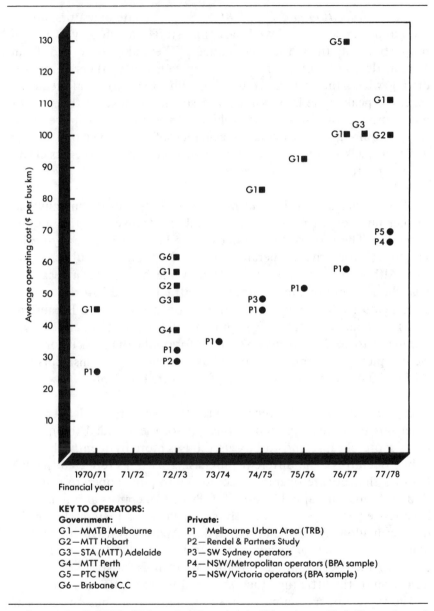

KEY TO OPERATORS:
Government:
G1 — MMTB Melbourne
G2 — MTT Hobart
G3 — STA (MTT) Adelaide
G4 — MTT Perth
G5 — PTC NSW
G6 — Brisbane C.C

Private:
P1   Melbourne Urban Area (TRB)
P2 — Rendel & Partners Study
P3 — SW Sydney operators
P4 — NSW/Metropolitan operators (BPA sample)
P5 — NSW/Victoria operators (BPA sample)

Source: Ian P. Wallis, "Private Bus Operation in Urban Areas — Their Economics and Role," *Traffic Engineering and Control* (December 1980).

Crew Wage Rates. Basic wage rates for public operators' crews were about 11 percent higher than those for the private operators.

Labor Utilization and Flexibility. Some private operators, unlike the public services, employed part-time staff, though only as a small proportion of their total employees. They also benefited from greater flexibility of staff. For example, many workers combined driving with other duties, thus minimizing the extra staff required to cover peak periods, sickness, and so on. Almost all the staff of many private operators were able to drive buses and drove them when required. In particular, mechanics often carried out driving duties in peak periods, and drivers carried out much of the bus cleaning and routine maintenance work.

Maintenance and Administration. Private operators generally had smaller numbers of maintenance and administrative staff than public operators. The ratio of total employees to buses owned was typically 1:0 to 1:5 for private operators, but 2:0 to 2:5 for public operators. Although public operators often averaged a greater mileage per bus, the low proportion of nondriver staff employed by private operators made a substantial contribution to their lower costs. Because of this factor alone, total staff requirements for private operators was estimated to be 25 percent lower than for public ones. As labor costs were typically 70 percent of total bus company costs, this explained a 15 to 20 percent total cost saving for private operators.

Capital Facilities. In general, private operators tended to have older bus fleets than the public ones. Also, they tended to buy new buses more cheaply and to buy used buses more frequently than the public operators. The different purchasing patterns reflected the difficulties that private operators, compared to public operators, had in finding funds for capital investment. Private operators also tended to have less elaborate and less costly depot facilities than public operators, even allowing for their relative sizes. Many private operators had open-air maintenance facilities rather than under-cover ones, and they provided very limited recreational facilities for staff—possibly a reflection of the little time their staff had for recreational activities.

The typical operating costs of public and private bus operators in Australia are summarized in Table 9-1.

Table 9-1. Australia: Typical Public and Private Operating Costs.

Cost Item	Public Operator (% of operating costs)		Private Operator (% of public operator costs)	
Wage/Salary and Related Costs:				
1. Driver wages	43.1[b]		30.2[b,c]	
2. Traffic staff salaries	3.8		1.9[d]	
3. Vehicle repairs/maintenance wages/salaries[a]	11.7		4.0[e]	
4. Administration and general salaries	3.9		2.5[f]	
		62.5		38.6
5. Driver on-costs[g]	9.3		2.1[h]	
6. Other staff on-costs[g]	3.7		1.0[i]	
		13.0		3.1
Non-wage/Salary Costs:				
7. Direct operating costs—fuel, tires, etc.	6.4		6.4[f]	
8. Vehicle repairs/maintenance, materials, etc.[a]	3.7		2.7[f]	
9. Depreciation	6.0		5.0[j]	
10. Interest	3.2		3.5[k]	
11. Insurances, licenses, and registration	3.5		4.5[j]	
12. Miscellaneous general	1.7		1.0[l]	
		24.5		23.1
Totals	100.0		64.8	

a. Includes workshop and stores costs.
b. Includes leave provisions.
c. Assumed 70 percent of public operator.
d. Assumed 50 percent of public operator—in practice traffic staff also probably carry out other functions.
e. Assumed—from analysis of various private operators by comparison with public operators; in practice much of the maintenance carried out by drivers.
f. Assumed—based on inspection of various operators' accounts.
g. Includes payroll tax, superannuation, and pension payments.
h. Assumed at 7 percent of private driver wages.
i. Assumed—represents 12 percent of private nondriver wages/salaries.
j. Assumed.
k. Assumed—grants for new buses not generally available to private operators.
l. Assumed—allows for higher registration and license fees for private operators.
Source: Ian P. Wallis, "Private Bus Operation in Urban Areas—Their Economics and Role," *Traffic Engineering and Control* (December 1980).

Calcutta. One of the largest, most densely populated, and poorest cities in the world, Calcutta, supports a population of some 10 million in an area of fewer than 600 square miles. Private buses first appeared in the city toward the end of the nineteenth century, but were banned in 1960 when all bus services were vested in the Calcutta State Transport Corporation (CSTC). From the start, CSTC suffered from managerial and financial problems and, in 1966, was paralyzed by strikes. In response to public demand before the 1966 elections and to its need for ready cash, the government of West Bengal sold permits that enabled 300 private buses to operate. These operated at a profit, although they charged the same fare (equivalent to about US1/2¢ per mile) as the money-losing CSTC, and although they had inferior routes. By the late 1970s, some 1,500 full-sized private buses were operating in Calcutta, in addition to about 500 private minibuses. Today, the private buses account for about two-thirds of all bus trips in Calcutta, and do so *without subsidy*. Meanwhile, the CSTC, which operates the best routes at the same fares, has to be subsidized to the equivalent of US$1 million a month by a government that is desperately short of funds for other purposes.

The success of the private bus operators in Calcutta has been attributed to three factors.

Keeping Vehicles on the Road. As soon as a private bus breaks down it is repaired, often on the road, with needed parts, if necessary, being bought on the "black market." The CSTC, in contrast, has to go through "channels" to obtain spare parts and only half of its buses are generally on the road.

Fare Collection. The private bus crews (who are paid a percentage of the revenues) make greater efforts to collect the fares than CSTC employees. "Fare evasion" is estimated to be 25 percent on CSTC buses and negligible on private buses.

Higher Labor Productivity. The state corporation's staffing levels, at 50 employees per bus (1980), is one of the highest in the world.

Size of Operating Unit

The organizational unit supplying public transport ranges from the one-person bicycle rickshaw in east Asia to fleets containing thousands of buses in cities such as New York, Chicago, London, Bombay, and Bangkok. Numbers of employees per bus also vary widely, from under two in Australia to fifty-eight in the *Office des Trans-*

ports en Commun du Zaire (OTCZ) of Kinshasa.[9] (As only about 50 percent of OTCZ buses are on the road at any time, the staffing works out at 116 people per working bus.) Attempts have been made to assess the effect of fleet size on the efficiency of public transport systems, but the results are not conclusive. A study comparing firms of different sizes in Britain reported that unit costs increase with fleet size, while the opposite effect was found in India. For the purpose of this book, it will be sufficient to note that there is no clear evidence that increases in the size of bus fleets result in lower costs or higher profitability.

On the other hand, there is clear evidence — from Manila and elsewhere — that large bus fleets incur financial losses under the same conditions that small operators (owner-drivers) make profits. Although operators the world over are reluctant to admit to making profits, the pressure to obtain permits to provide service and the prices at which permits in some cities change hands, or are hired out, are sure indications of profitability.

In the early 1970s, Bangkok had twenty-four franchised bus companies, all of which provided service for a basic fare of about US 4¢. In 1976, following recommendations by European consultants, the government decided to amalgamate the twenty-four companies and to create the Bangkok Mass Transit Authority. The plan was carried through despite the protests of many of the operators. Shortly after the buses were taken over by the city, the fares were raised by 20 percent, yet the system started to operate at a deficit. By 1979, BMTA was losing the equivalent of over US$25 million a year, while an estimated 7,000 privately owned minibuses were running at a profit. The main reasons for the switch from profit to loss seem to have been improved wages to bus crews and reduced utilization of vehicles.

The reasons for the financial viability of the small transport firm, be it a mover, a taxi driver, or a bus operator, are well known and typical of other types of small business in the service sector. The owner is willing to work longer and less regular hours than is a paid bus driver in a large fleet. He will clean his own vehicle (or enlist the help of family members) and is likely to do the routine servicing and maintenance himself. He will not have his own depot but will service his vehicle on the street or at a local garage. His recordkeeping will

---

9. Jan Podoski, "Public Transport in Developing Countries," *UITP Revue* 4 (1977).

be minimal; just sufficient to keep the tax inspector at bay. He will make a greater effort than a paid driver to collect fares from passengers and to ensure that the amounts collected do not get lost on the way. An extra driver can be employed if two shifts a day have to be run.[10] Some facilities, such as a two-way radio service, can add to earnings without the owner relinquishing control of his vehicle.

There is also evidence that a high level of service over a wide area can be provided by small firms, as long as the organizational structure of the industry is appropriate. Taxis are a case in point. While some may be operated as one-person firms, and some in large fleets, there is no need for any formal coordination to achieve an acceptable level of service. Taxis find their way to where the business is most profitable and provide an example of *coordination through competition*. Obviously, a single operator cannot cover a whole route, but a route can be covered by a large number of individual operators organized, if necessary, as a route association.

Size of Vehicle

One of the established (but questionable) principles of public transport operation is that large vehicles are more economical to operate than small ones. The reason given is that, with over two-thirds of bus operating costs being labor costs, it pays a bus company to have large vehicles—even if they are full for only a fraction of their working lives—so as to avoid the additional labor costs that would be required to meet peak demand with small vehicles. This reasoning, though perfectly logical, may be questioned on two grounds.

The first is that the capital cost *per seat* seems to increase with the size of the vehicle. For example, operators in San Juan, Puerto Rico, can expect to pay $17,000 for a minibus seating seventeen ($1,000 per seat), but $140,000 ($2,800 per seat) for a full-sized bus seating fifty. Thus a full-sized bus can cost almost three times as much per unit of passenger capacity than a minibus. One reason for this may be that small vehicles can be mass-produced and bought "off the shelf," while large ones tend to be specially made-to-order and assembled as separate units. In 1981, for example, Washington, D.C., not to be outclassed, ordered thirty-three M.A.N. (a German

---

10. Amos, "Shared Taxis in Belfast."

bus manufacturer) seventy-two-seat articulated ("bending") buses at $271,877 each—over $3,750 per seat!

But there is a second reason favoring the small bus which, while subtler, may be more important. For a given route capacity, small buses provide more frequent service than large ones and, therefore, result in less waiting time per passenger. This factor might not matter to a franchised operator who has to bear the costs of his crew but not the waiting-time costs of his customers; hence the preference of monopoly operators for big vehicles. However, where competition is allowed, those who provide public transport have to respond to the needs of the passengers, most of whom dislike waiting for buses. To reduce waiting, it is necessary to use small vehicles providing frequent service. It is significant that when, as we saw earlier, the private bus operators took over the municipal service in Buenos Aires in 1962, one of their first actions was to replace the large municipal buses with smaller ones. More generally, whenever a private operator has the freedom to choose the size of his vehicle, he generally chooses something less than a full-sized bus. The small bus has other advantages: as it holds fewer passengers, it is easier to fill with people starting at one point and wishing to travel to another, so it tends to stop less frequently than large buses; and, being more maneuverable, it can often make its way more quickly along congested streets.

The Route Association

In order to make the maximum contribution in the provision of transport, however, the individual unit does have to work within an appropriate organizational framework. For example, a taxi looking for business has to be recognized by the public as being available for hire. If it is a vehicle intended to carry more than one person, its destination has to be clearly indicated. It is also important for the intending passenger to know the fare that is being charged, and the places at which vehicles for hire can be readily found. Some of these features are provided by route associations, which are to be found in many cities in Latin America, Africa, and Asia.

The essence of the route association is that each vehicle remains under the control of its owner or owners, both as regard driving and maintenance. What is shared is the route, that is, the members of the association ply a specified route in conjunction with others, thus offering travelers frequent service. Fares are generally fixed by the association, but not invariably: In Hong Kong and Istanbul, for example, higher fares may, at the discretion of the operator, be charged in peak periods when demand is higher and traffic congestion more acute. (Peak period charges are the norm for Washington, D.C., taxis, which are allowed to charge higher fares in peak periods than in off-peak ones.) The revenues in some associations are retained by the individual members; in others, they are pooled among the members.

The precise organization of a route association varies from city to city. Any group operating a route has an interest in limiting its numbers and also in ensuring that its members work harmoniously with one another. This means that conditions must be imposed on entry (possibly an entrance fee) and that rules are laid down to prevent members from "stealing" traffic from others in the association. In many cities (Buenos Aires, Manila, Calcutta, Hong Kong), route associations compete with one another so that no group has a monopoly over an entire route.

In Buenos Aires, the route association is known as an *empresa.* The owners joining an *empresa* have to abide by its rules, which govern such matters as schedules and fares. The empresa is the formal employer of the drivers and assumes all the responsibilities arising from the labor laws. The vehicle owners choose and replace the drivers, and they pay the operating expenditures of the vehicle. The income goes to the vehicle owners, who either turn it over to a common fund for distribution among members of the empresa, or pro-rate it according to the mileage run by each vehicle, or divide it through any other method that the empresa may choose. Each month the empresa charges each of its members for a share of the administrative expenditures corresponding to each vehicle, the salaries paid, goods and services supplied for maintenance, and, in the event that the company is financing the purchase of a vehicle, an installment payment.

The investments in vehicles and in repair facilities are part of the company's capital. A successful operation results in an increase in the value of its shares, which cannot, however, be sold in the free market. Any disputes within an empresa are settled at a members' meeting. Each vehicle is generally entitled to one vote. One of the typical characteristics of the empresas is the large number of members: although a member can own several vehicles or several members can

t service at less cost than public
ten, but not always, less costly
ter sections of this chapter to a
which private-sector operations
ly. We conclude by considering
such circumstances.

osts of public and private provid-
is discussion into perspective by
ver the past three decades. Most
operated at the beginning of
had been taken over by public

osts per vehicle-mile of operating
950 to 1980. (All of these costs
sing the Consumer Price Index,
nstant dollars.) The most impor-
, which show the average costs of
es—buses, streetcars (or light rail
the period 1950 to 1980. Even
1980 average-cost level is over

osts, 1950–1980 (in dollars per
n).ª

d	(C) Both (A) and (B)	(D) Commuter Rail
	1.38	n.a.
	1.56	n.a.
	1.65	n.a.
	1.71	n.a.
	2.07	3.56[c]
	2.63	n.a.
	3.11	5.93[b]

sumer Price Index.
n, "Impacts of Subsidies on the Costs of
ransportation."

own one vehicle, on average there is one partner per vehicle. About one-third of the members work as drivers of their own vehicles.

A key factor in the success of the private buses in Calcutta is the route association. These associations—generally one for each route—were formed voluntarily and spontaneously by the private owners. Each owner retains control over the operation and maintenance of the vehicle and receives the fares collected on it. The associations have rules to govern relationships between the members; for example, vehicles have to run on time. This is important because a bus running late tends to pick up more than its fair share of passengers, at the expense of the next bus. Owners of buses that do not keep to time are fined, the fines being distributed among the other members. In some instances, the fines are reported to be proportional to the delay, at a specified rate per minute, and paid directly to the owner of the following bus.

CONCLUSION

The private bus operations described in this chapter vividly illustrate the proposition that, given a suitable organizational framework, privately operated buses can provide and expand transport services without subsidy while a municipal enterprise is unable to do so. The key advantage of the private operations is that, in order to survive, the operator has to seek out and efficiently provide services that the public wants to use and is prepared to pay for. The municipal operator is under no such constraints and is unable to resist political pressures to raise costs and serve underutilized routes. The objective of the public operator is often the provision of services deemed desirable by politicians and administrators, rather than meeting the needs of travelers.

In the first quarter of the century, the jitney demonstrated the viability of informal public transport in the United States. Even after U.S. jitney services were regulated out of existence, the superiority of this mode continued to be confirmed in many countries overseas. Perhaps the time has come once again for the public to decide whether Americans should be allowed to use such services again.

vate firms do in fact produce tra
firms. Because private firms are
than public operators, we turn i
discussion of the circumstances
would be expected to be less c
briefly the question of how to cre

BACKGROUND

Before turning to the comparativ
ers of transit, it is useful to put
considering trends in transit costs
U.S. transit systems were priva
this period; by its end, almost
authorities.

Table 10-1 presents the average
transit in the United States from
have been adjusted for inflation,
with the costs presented in 1980
tant figures are those in column (
operating conventional transit veh
vehicles), and rapid transit cars—f
after adjustment for inflation, tł

**Table 10-1. Trends in Transi
vehicle-mile, adjusted for infla**

Year	(A) Bus and Streetcar[b]	(B) Rail Ra Transi
1950	n.a.[d]	n.a.
1955	n.a.	n.a.
1960	n.a.	n.a.
1965	n.a.	n.a.
1970	1.87	3.20
1975	2.45	3.93
1980	2.95	3.79

a. 1980 constant dollars, adjusted using Co
b. Source: Pucher, Markstedt, and Hirshr
Urban Public Transport," p. 158.
c. Source: Morlok, "Innovation in Urban
d. n.a. indicates not available.

own one vehicle, on average there is one partner per vehicle. About one-third of the members work as drivers of their own vehicles.

A key factor in the success of the private buses in Calcutta is the route association. These associations — generally one for each route — were formed voluntarily and spontaneously by the private owners. Each owner retains control over the operation and maintenance of the vehicle and receives the fares collected on it. The associations have rules to govern relationships between the members; for example, vehicles have to run on time. This is important because a bus running late tends to pick up more than its fair share of passengers, at the expense of the next bus. Owners of buses that do not keep to time are fined, the fines being distributed among the other members. In some instances, the fines are reported to be proportional to the delay, at a specified rate per minute, and paid directly to the owner of the following bus.

CONCLUSION

The private bus operations described in this chapter vividly illustrate the proposition that, given a suitable organizational framework, privately operated buses can provide and expand transport services without subsidy while a municipal enterprise is unable to do so. The key advantage of the private operations is that, in order to survive, the operator has to seek out and efficiently provide services that the public wants to use and is prepared to pay for. The municipal operator is under no such constraints and is unable to resist political pressures to raise costs and serve underutilized routes. The objective of the public operator is often the provision of services deemed desirable by politicians and administrators, rather than meeting the needs of travelers.

In the first quarter of the century, the jitney demonstrated the viability of informal public transport in the United States. Even after U.S. jitney services were regulated out of existence, the superiority of this mode continued to be confirmed in many countries overseas. Perhaps the time has come once again for the public to decide whether Americans should be allowed to use such services again.

Chapter 10

THE COMPARATIVE COSTS
OF PUBLIC AND PRIVATE
PROVIDERS OF MASS TRANSIT

Edward K. Morlok and Philip A. Viton

INTRODUCTION

If there is a primary driving force behind attempts to substitute private urban transportation for publicly provided forms, it is surely the belief that substantial cost savings would thereby result. As other chapters in this book document, the deficits of public systems show little sign of abating. With the public purse under severe pressure at all levels of government, the hope of realizing economies by shifting to private-sector operations is a natural one. One may distinguish at least two ways in which this could be done: first, by having a private carrier provide just what had previously been provided by the public system. This approach, often involving some form of contractual relationship, is probably the simplest method of realizing cost savings. At the other extreme, a private carrier could be left free to decide on the service to be produced: here cost savings as well as a more demand-responsive quality of service are the hoped-for results. Is the possibility that such a carrier will act as a monopolist, to the detriment of the public, real enough to cause concern? This question too resolves into a cost question, as we show below. Thus, for a number of reasons, it is important to analyze the costs of providing transit under various organizational forms.

In this chapter we address the cost issue, in two related aspects. After a brief review of cost trends, we survey the evidence that private firms do in fact produce transit service at less cost than public firms. Because private firms are often, but not always, less costly than public operators, we turn in later sections of this chapter to a discussion of the circumstances in which private-sector operations would be expected to be less costly. We conclude by considering briefly the question of how to create such circumstances.

BACKGROUND

Before turning to the comparative costs of public and private providers of transit, it is useful to put this discussion into perspective by considering trends in transit costs over the past three decades. Most U.S. transit systems were privately operated at the beginning of this period; by its end, almost all had been taken over by public authorities.

Table 10-1 presents the average costs per vehicle-mile of operating transit in the United States from 1950 to 1980. (All of these costs have been adjusted for inflation, using the Consumer Price Index, with the costs presented in 1980 constant dollars.) The most important figures are those in column (C), which show the average costs of operating conventional transit vehicles – buses, streetcars (or light rail vehicles), and rapid transit cars – for the period 1950 to 1980. Even after adjustment for inflation, the 1980 average-cost level is over

Table 10-1.   Trends in Transit Costs, 1950-1980 (in dollars per vehicle-mile, adjusted for inflation).[a]

Year	(A) Bus and Streetcar[b]	(B) Rail Rapid Transit[b]	(C) Both (A) and (B)	(D) Commuter Rail
1950	n.a.[d]	n.a.	1.38	n.a.
1955	n.a.	n.a.	1.56	n.a.
1960	n.a.	n.a.	1.65	n.a.
1965	n.a.	n.a.	1.71	n.a.
1970	1.87	3.20	2.07	3.56[c]
1975	2.45	3.93	2.63	n.a.
1980	2.95	3.79	3.11	5.93[b]

a. 1980 constant dollars, adjusted using Consumer Price Index.
b. Source: Pucher, Markstedt, and Hirshman, "Impacts of Subsidies on the Costs of Urban Public Transport," p. 158.
c. Source: Morlok, "Innovation in Urban Transportation."
d. n.a. indicates not available.

two-and-one-quarter times that of 1950. Underscoring this increase is separate data for the individual modes, but these are available only beginning in 1970. Even in this ten-year period, both bus costs and rail rapid transit costs increased, although in the rail case a slight reduction in average cost has been observed recently—undoubtedly due to the opening of some new, highly automated lines. Commuter rail costs are also available only for a limited portion of this period, but again the data reveal a very substantial increase in cost, during a period when service continued to evolve from private ownership and operation to operation either for or by public authorities.

As Charles Lave details in Chapter 1, U.S. transit in the same period went from a situation in which revenues exceeded costs to one where revenues covered less than 40 percent of operating expenses and virtually none of the capital expenditures necessary to build new lines, rebuild old ones, or purchase vehicles. Yet, at the same time, a few transit services remained profitable, mainly ones in private hands. Some of these had passenger fares that were no higher than those of public authorities, suggesting that their profitability may have been due to lower costs. This suggests that it is important to examine the relative costs of private and public operators of transit.

PRIVATE VERSUS PUBLIC COSTS: THE EVIDENCE

In order to amass any significant amount of data regarding the relative costs of private and public organizations providing transit service, it is necessary to use data from a wide variety of sources, because there are relatively few instances of private-sector participation. In some cases, private firms provide transit service in the same metropolitan area as public ones; in others, there has been a transition from public to private provision—in a few cases, the transition has been in the opposite direction—such that costs can be compared directly.

The first type of comparison to which we turn is of the cost of providing service for entire systems operated by public organizations or by private firms. To be useful, the data must be for comparable service by the private firms and public authorities. Also, it is important that the comparisons be made between organizations in the

Table 10-2.   Comparison of Average Costs per Vehicle-Mile on
Private and Publicly Owned Transit Services in Various Nations.

Location	Service Type	Year(s)	Ratio of Private to Public Costs
Australia[a]			
Melbourne	Urban Bus	1970–77	0.55–0.58
Other areas	Urban Bus	1972–73	0.50–0.65
United Kingdom[b]	Local Rural and Inter-urban Bus	1977	0.58
United States			
Cleveland[c]	Urban Bus	1982	0.60
Los Angeles[d]	Peak Period-Only Express Bus	1982	approx. 0.50
New York City (N.Y.) Suburbs[e]	Urban Bus	1980	0.53

a. Wallis, "Private Bus Operations in Urban Areas," p. 606.

b. Tunbridge and Jackson, "The Economics of Stage Carriage Operation," p. 6.

c. Cox, "Deficit Control Through Service Contracting," p. 25.

d. Southern California Association of Governments, *Commuter and Express Bus Service in the SCAG Region.*

e. Calculated from data in U.S. Department of Transportation, Urban Mass Transportation Administration, *Second Section-15 Annual Report*; see also Cox, "Contracting for Public Transportation Services," p. 3.

same region, for one would expect regional differences in some costs, especially wage rates.

Table 10-2 presents data from previous studies on the ratio of costs per vehicle-mile of providing bus service by private firm and public authority. In each of these instances, the buses are essentially of the same size, and other features, such as the quality of seating and the extent of such amenities as air conditioning, are essentially identical. The results are striking. For U.S. cities, private carrier costs are about half of public costs, with the mean values being 50 percent to 60 percent. Studies have also been carried out in Australia and in England, and the data there reveal a similar pattern. Private costs are typically in the range of 50 percent to 65 percent of public costs. While these data necessarily involve comparisons between different routes (operated by different companies), and there may be some cost differences due to inherent features of those routes, the reduction in cost for the private operator is so large that it is unlikely that cost reduction could be due solely or even primarily to any such features. It must surely be due in large measure to differences in the cost structures faced by private firms and public authorities.

Table 10-3. Examples of Cost or Deficit Reduction from Contracting.

Location and Service	Savings
Hammond, Indiana All local bus service[a]	Reduced cost by approx. 50%
Yolo County, California Local and commuter bus service[b]	Reduced cost by approx. 50%
Norfolk, Virginia Local bus service[c]	Reduced cost by more than 60%

a. Private Communication with P. T. Coulis, Yellow and Checker Cab Co.
b. Private Communication with W. Bourne, Commuter Bus Co., Sacramento.
c. Private Communication with A. J. Becker, Tidewater Transportation District.

We turn next to instances where private firms have actually taken over the provision of public transit service, providing essentially the same service to the public. Examples of this are, naturally, very few in number, for the trend has been largely in the opposite direction. However, the rapid increase in costs and deficits of public authorities in recent years has caused some local governments to attempt to find less expensive ways of providing public transit service; in a few instances, they have decided to have transit service provided under contract by private firms rather than by a government-owned transit authority.

Table 10-3 presents the cost savings, as reported by these organizations, resulting from the switch to private provision of transit service. In all cases, there was competitive bidding. The general pattern is clearly one of substantial savings, on the order of 50 percent. Furthermore, by the very nature of the contracting process, these are situations where the costs of both private and public providers are reportedly for the same service, so no other factors (such as differences in service quality) should influence costs. It is also important to note that these savings have been realized both in large metropolitan regions as well as smaller areas. However, as the number of instances of this type of contracting is very small, it is important to examine other evidence as well.

Additional information on comparative costs comes from two studies on the impact of public takeover of private transit systems in the United States in the post–World War II period. Both studies involved mathematical models of the effect of public takeover and of subsidies. While the models are complex and their presentation would be far beyond the scope of this chapter, it is useful to review their conclusions because they bear directly on the issue of private versus public costs. One of these studies, by Anderson (1983), examined the impact of takeover and subsidies on costs; she concluded that, for the United States as a whole, the average operating cost per bus-hour increased 28 percent as a result of public takeovers and subsidy programs. The implication is that public agencies have simply been unable to provide transit service as cheaply as private firms.

The second study, by Pucher, Markstedt, and Hirshman (1983), attempted to examine the effect of subsidies on the costs of government-owned systems; the authors concluded that the availability of federal—as well as state and local—subsidies increased costs substantially. They also concluded that a major impact of subsidies was to permit wage increases, a topic which we will examine later. Furthermore, the use of dedicated taxation to provide funds for the transit authority led to greater increases in costs than would have been the case with nonearmarked levies. The conclusions of both studies are thus entirely consistent with the data presented earlier, that private companies may be able to provide transit service at less cost than their public counterparts.[1]

---

1. A 1983 study by I. Philips and J. W. Rat, "The Effectiveness and Benefits of Financial Support for Public Transport," has been referred to as refuting this evidence of the cost escalation due to public ownership and subsidization. (See, for example, P. J. Goldsack, "Transit Subsidies," *Mass Transit* 10 (November 1983), p. 12.) Their study actually does not compare public versus private ownership and the costs that would prevail under each. Rather it examines trends in various characteristics of transit services over time, with all of the data for western nations being from publicly owned or subsidized carriers. Furthermore, the analysis allegedly demonstrates that public transit has become more efficient as a result of subsidization; in fact, the only data or statistics used to support this are measures of output per employee, such as passenger-miles or vehicle-miles per employee, which could increase if the carrier became less efficient in an economic sense (due to factor substitution). So one cannot really accept the conclusion that these carriers have become more efficient; the data do not indicate that they have become less efficient either. The wage rate increases experienced by the carriers surveyed were allegedly necessitated by general increases in wage rates and transit's undesirable working conditions (such as long hours). That wage rates in general are increasing in an economy does not mean that wage rates for transit must go up by the same amount. It may be that carriers at the beginning of any analysis period were paying more than was really necessary in order to attract workers of the desired skill level, and that this difference has simply continued. The discussion in the section on competition in this chapter indicates that transit authorities in the United States are paying more than is necessary to bus drivers. The recently negotiated "community wage rate" of San Diego Transit illustrates this perfectly: Drivers on new services outside the city are paid at a rate one-half that of the standard wage rate for the system.

Third, in addition to these direct comparisons of private and public costs, there have been a number of studies of the degree to which public carriers are inefficient, particularly in comparison to private firms. While most of these rely on indirect evidence that is not as compelling as that presented above and on comparisons between systems that may be in different localities or have other dissimilar features which make for complexities in the analysis, the conclusions of these studies generally support the hypothesis that private carriers are cheaper than public ones. Many of these studies have been undertaken by knowledgeable persons working in the transit field who have no particular bias towards public or private ownership. As one example, we quote from the report by Richards (1983, Para. 15) on a study of the problems and future of public transport in Southeast Asia, written for Martin and Voorhees Associates of London and Hong Kong:

> We have also sought to establish that such evidence as is available suggests that operators are not always as efficient as is possible, and those in public ownership tend to be less efficient than in private ownership. Furthermore, a significant proportion of the funds provided to subsidise operating costs leaks away into decreased productivity and higher operating costs.

While it is clear that private firms can provide transit service at substantially lower costs, they may not necessarily do so. For example, the five private firms that still operate local bus service in New York City have costs per vehicle-mile that are only slightly lower than those of the Transit Authority. The critical factor appears to be the nature of the arrangements for service. In this case, the private operators have traditional monopolistic operations and a guaranteed city subsidy to cover their deficits. Under these conditions, the end result may be little incentive toward low-cost, efficient operation.

Further supporting this idea are the results of a recent study of noncompetitive service contracting by regional public authorities (Ho, 1981). In some of the cases (Worcester, Massachusetts, and a number of towns in Connecticut), it appears that service contracting was slightly more expensive than public provision of the service by public authority. In addition, other disadvantages of noncompetitive contracting were cited, such as lack of incentives for efficiency and cost-cutting by firms in ways that could lead to service degradation with fixed-cost contracts. All things considered, noncompetitive contracts with private firms appear generally unattractive.

It remains clear that, in a significant number of instances, the observed costs of private carriers are substantially lower than the costs of public providers. But private firms are not always cheaper. If we wish to discover why this should be so, we will have to delve deeper into the economic characteristics and operating possibilities for carriers. The examples presented here point us toward four factors: competition may lead to lower costs; there may be systematic differences in labor costs; there may be alternative and less costly ways to produce a given quantity and quality of service; and there may be economies or diseconomies associated broadly with firm size. The next sections discuss these possibilities in detail.

COMPETITION

The idea that competition would work to keep costs down hardly needs support. While market imperfections can thwart it in some cases, the effect of competition on costs and prices is so widely seen that few would question its validity or importance. The previous section's examples illustrate the power of competition to keep transit costs low. The best and clearest examples are in service contracting: Noncompetitive service contracts in Worcester, Massachusetts, and various Connecticut cities resulted in costs somewhat higher than those of the public authorities that replaced them, with other service disadvantages; in contrast, competitive bidding resulted in private firms being able to provide the transit service at far less cost — typically 50 percent less — than the public authority could.

But there need not be overt competition among prospective service providers to provide enough pressure to keep costs low. All that is necessary is the possibility that another, more efficient firm could enter the market if the present provider becomes too costly. This helps explain why some private firms, operating under contract, provide efficient service even though they do not face overt competition. The threat of a potential competitor provides the incentive to keep costs below those of the potential alternative operator.

Of course, if there is only one alternative operator and it has high costs, then this source of pressure on costs is weakened. This appears to be the case with New York City's private local bus operators; the city's transit authority is probably the only operator that would be willing to take over any significant number of additional routes.

Local-service bus operation, under the traditional franchise and regulatory arrangement, simply does not promise sufficient profit to induce new firms to be ready to enter the business, even with subsidies.

In the rare instance when transit firms try to make a profit without government subsidy, competition with alternative means of transport would work to contain costs and assure service quality. The express bus services in New York City and a commuter rail service in the Chicago area demonstrate this. In both cases, rider satisfaction is very high, and fares are no higher than those for comparable service on publicly owned or subsidized systems.[2] One would expect firms to eschew subsidies only if they had complete control over fares and service, for otherwise it would be possible for regulatory restrictions on these to lead to deficits and ultimately bankruptcy. However, in the two examples cited, regulation was present, but the regulatory bodies recognized the need for profit and permitted fare and service changes so that profits were obtained.

LABOR COST DIFFERENCES

The second explanation of private firms' lower costs is that they may pay less for their inputs. With vehicles purchased in national markets and fuel in regional markets, it is apparent that the most likely source of price variation lies in the price of labor, or wages and benefits. Since operating labor costs account for typically 30 percent to 50 percent of the total cost of operations, wage rates and work rules have received particular attention. Most research on labor costs has focused on drivers' pay, partly because data on drivers is more readily available than that for other workers. However, we cannot rule out the possibility of substantial cost savings at the management level; this question remains to be studied.

The most comprehensive study of these issues was done in the Philadelphia metropolitan area, chosen for the wide variety of organizations providing passenger transportation service, the variety in those services, and the fact that it is a single labor market. Consistent with other studies of labor costs, it was found that driver pay per unit of work performed (vehicle-mile driven) increased substantially with increases in the organization's size, the effective wage rate in the

2. These are reviewed in detail in Chapter 6.

Table 10-4. Driver Costs as a Function of Firm Size and Vehicle Size (in dollars per vehicle-mile).

	Firm Size: Total Operating Revenue, $1,000/yr.		
Vehicle Size	$400	$100,000	$275,000
5 passengers (taxi)	0.22	0.33	0.52
11 passengers (van)	0.24	0.35	0.54
25 passengers (minibus)	0.28	0.39	0.59
45 passengers (charter bus)	0.35	0.46	0.66
66 passengers (transit bus)	0.43	0.54	0.73

Source: Calculated from equation (3.2) in Morlok and Krouk, "Variations in Driver Wage Rates and Opportunities," p. 111.

larger organizations being twice that found in the smallest. Furthermore, this holds even with a wage adjustment for the difficulty of the job, as reflected in the size of the vehicle operated (measured by its capacity).

Table 10-4 reveals this pattern, which shows driver costs (in dollars per vehicle-mile) as a function of firm size and vehicle size. For example, reading across the bottom row, we see that driver costs increase from 43 cents per vehicle-mile to 73 cents per vehicle-mile as the firm size as measured by revenue grows from $400,000 per year to $275,000,000 per year.[3] This result is for sixty-six-passenger transit buses, and the change is even greater for the other kinds of vehicles shown. That is, costs in the largest firms are about double that of the smallest ones. Looking down the columns, we see that driver costs increase as the size of vehicle increases. This clearly suggests that if a single regional monopoly transit organization were to be replaced with a number of smaller organizations, the wage bill would be expected to diminish substantially. The halving of total

3. All but one of the different types of passenger carriers included in the data had average speeds of about 18 to 22 mph, so rates per hour would be approximately proportional to the mileage rate. The pay rate for that one carrier was adjusted to the standard of 20 mph for the analysis.

operating costs found in aggregate comparisons of the sort presented in Tables 10-2 and 10-3 is entirely consistent with this finding for wage rates.

There are actual examples of this pattern of lower wage rates prevailing in small transit firms. The large Alameda-Contra Costa (AC) Transit System (840 buses) in the San Francisco area pays its drivers $12.21 per hour. But two small transit operators in the same area— County Connection Transit and Community Transit—pay only $8.48 and $5.25 per hour. In the Philadelphia area, the small, private Schuylkill Valley Lines had paid its drivers about 70 percent of the wage rate of the regional transit authority before the authority took over the service. Since then, the drivers' union has successfully negotiated with the authority to reduce the pay difference (Cook and Lounsberry 1982). In the Boston area, a recent study found that the transit authority's labor costs are up to three times those of private, nonsubsidized operators (Herzenberg 1982). And an evaluation of the Rochester, New York, paratransit service for the Urban Mass Transportation Administration concluded that driver wage rates in a private firm were probably less than half the rates paid by a public operator to unionized drivers (Newman et al. 1980).

Thus, there is considerable evidence that private firms can hire people to drive transit vehicles at wage rates far below those prevailing in the transit industry. These private firms are generally much smaller than the publicly owned regional transit authorities, and their small size appears to be a crucial feature leading to lower wage rates. This size-related explanation, rather than private ownership, is also consistent with the preceding examples of lower wage rates for both private transit operators and small, publicly owned transit agencies.

Further emphasizing the importance of organizational size to wage rates is that the same pattern has been observed in all types of industries (Masters 1969) and is not limited to transportation or even transit. Economists and persons concerned with labor-management relations have attempted to explain this pattern (see, for example, Levinson 1967) and the following seem to be the most important reasons. First, workers seem willing to trade off high wages for the increased recognition of their work and increased importance of their position in a smaller firm. Second, differences in wage bills per unit of output may be due to more efficient labor utilization in small firms, which have fewer work rules that lead to some workers being paid while no work is being performed. In a small firm, there tends to be a lack of anonymity among workers, and workers in jobs that require a full effort would be aware and resentful of other workers having a soft job or nothing to do. Third, firms with smaller market shares may face more intense competition than larger ones, and hence would have little opportunity to provide workers with higher wages. Finally, it has been observed that smaller firms are less likely to be unionized than larger ones, in part because unions target their organizing efforts on firms where the increase in membership is likely to be greatest.[4] In addition, in the case of transit, firms that are successful in keeping wages low seem to choose their workers carefully. Often they try to hire persons who want part-time work only and who are not the main breadwinners for their families.

FACTOR SUBSTITUTION AND EFFICIENCY

In this section we examine another possible reason for cost savings in small private firms. It arises directly from the observation that a given service may be produced using different combinations of inputs (termed factor substitution), some of which will be cheaper than others. In this section, we briefly list some alternative production processes and discuss their potential for cost savings.

In order to make these possibilities more concrete, it is useful to consider them in the context of a specific example. Consider a route that is operated in both the peak and other periods throughout weekdays. As is typical in transit, many additional bus runs are required during peak periods to serve passengers flowing into or out of the central business district. In contrast, there are few passengers traveling in the reverse peak direction.

Some of the possible options for producing bus transit service using different combinations of inputs, that are likely to influence costs significantly are the following (Morlok and Viton 1983):

- Provide bus storage spaces near the CBD for morning peak-period runs that can be terminated downtown, rather than returning empty to a suburban garage. This would reduce the bus-miles and driver-hours required to provide the service. (The reverse pro-

---

4. We would not wish to be misunderstood on this point. This is an explanation, not a prescription. Union power provides, and historically has provided, a vitally necessary counterbalance to the power of management, especially when the firm is an oligopsonist.

cess could occur in the evening.) Given the cost savings suggested in the previous section, the benefits of such a policy could be considerable.

- Operate the additional peak-period runs with either part-time labor or with so-called worker-drivers, who work at another job at the work-site end of the morning run. Such a driver need be paid only for the time actually worked as a driver and, unlike a full-time driver, not for a full day regardless of the time spent actually driving a bus.

- On a long route connecting the CBD and outlying residential areas, where passenger traffic declines with distance from the CBD, terminate some runs part-way along the route. This adjusts the capacity provided to passenger traffic and has the effect of reducing bus-miles, drivers required, and buses required. Often this is done with buses that continue to serve the outlying areas by running express service to the CBD. This reduces travel time and fleet and driver requirements even further.

- Substitute small buses for large ones. This would enable more frequent service to be offered while providing the same capacity. While it might be thought that such a change would always increase costs, this is not true. The reduced running time (due to fewer passengers boarding and alighting each vehicle, and greater maneuverability in traffic), reduced wage rates associated with the smaller vehicle, and possible wage reductions resulting from provision of service by a small firm rather than a large regional public authority (see the prior section), among other factors, can easily result in substantial cost reductions.

While these options do not exhaust the range of possibilities, they do illustrate the variety of technological or production-process options available to bus transit management. In addition, they show the interrelationships between organizational options (for example, small firms) and technological options in the structure of transit provision.

SCALE ECONOMIES

An important reason often adduced for having transit services provided by a single regulated entity is that it is less costly for all service to be provided by one firm than by many. In this section we suggest, first, that for bus transit the claim does not appear well founded; and second, that it has important implications for the feasibility of decentralization of this mode.

The evidence on this question has been studied by Viton (1981), using a data set covering almost all public firms in the United States in 1975; it is not likely that developments since then would substantially alter the conclusions. The results of the statistical study may be summarized as follows: Taking as the single measure of output the number of vehicle-miles provided, it emerges that up to the output of a moderate-sized system (about 5.5 million vehicle-miles annually, the size of the public system in Albany, N.Y.) essentially constant costs prevail, with possibly slight decreasing costs for systems providing relatively little output (less than 1 million bus miles annually). Moreover, at the level of the largest urban systems, quite large diseconomies prevail. That is to say, for very small systems, increases in output result in cost per unit of output declining; for firms producing between 1.0 and 5.5 million vehicle-miles per year (the latter being the size of the Albany, N.Y. system), average costs do not vary with output; and for the largest systems, increases in output increase average costs. These results imply that small-scale entrants would not experience higher costs than large-scale providers, if their scale of operation did not exceed about 5.5 million miles annually. Moreover, it is possible that they would experience lower costs than the largest firms.

The implications of this for the question of small-scale cost-effective entry are immediate. Entry is almost always feasible in medium-sized or larger cities; moreover, there may be a considerable cost advantage in decentralizing the largest firms, which operate in a region of increasing (long-run) average cost. In all but the largest markets, one would not expect to observe more than six to ten minimally sized firms; but on cost grounds alone there can be no objection to fewer firms each providing about six million annual miles, which would have medium-sized urban areas served by one or two firms.

One or two firms is a decidedly small number; and the question is immediately raised of the potential exercise of monopoly power in that situation. The answer is reassuring. Absent legal restrictions on entry (through exclusive route franchises), monopoly power will not persist. This is because nonlegal barriers to entry (start-up costs) appear to be slight, and the minimum optimal scale is small. Were a carrier to charge high fares and earn large profits, the opportunity would exist for another firm to enter, undercut the fare of the existing competitor, and still earn a profit. With no legal or administrative barriers to entry, this would surely occur. In the language of Baumol, Panzar, and Willig (1982), urban bus transit markets are "contestable."

To summarize the results of this section: Available evidence from public-sector firms suggests that provision of service by small-scale transit agencies is possible and may result in cost savings over the largest agencies. In fact, obtaining such cost savings is one of the primary reasons for the appearance of county-level (or other small area) transit authorities in regions already served by large regional authorities. Nevertheless, the evidence of lower costs for smaller public-sector providers is limited and must be treated cautiously.

PEAK-PERIOD COSTS

In discussing the cost of public transportation services, one important feature is the variation in the cost of providing service by time of day, particularly during weekdays. The reason for this cost variation is the extreme peaking of transit travel, both temporally, with the vast majority of trips concentrated during periods of travel to and from work, and by direction, most trips being made to work places such as the central business district in the morning and away from it in the evening.

The typical pattern of this peaking is shown in Figure 10-1. As it indicates, it is not uncommon for peak-period transit travel to be two to five times the average for nonpeak periods. One useful measure of the temporal peaking of travel is the percentage of all daily trips that occur in the hour of maximum travel. If travel were uniformly spread over the twenty-four hours in a day, then this percentage would be 4.2 percent; more reasonably, if it were spread over sixteen hours (allowing eight hours for rest), then it would be 6.3 percent. Actual data on transit systems reveals the following percentages (Levinson 1982: 285):

Rail rapid transit:	14–17 percent
Bus:	
large cities:	10–12 percent
medium-sized cities:	12–16 percent
small cities:	12–20 percent

Figure 10-1. Typical Patterns of Peaking.

Passengers per unit time

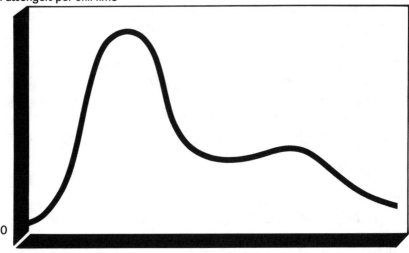

0

Time of day

a. Inbound (toward the central business district).

Passengers per unit time

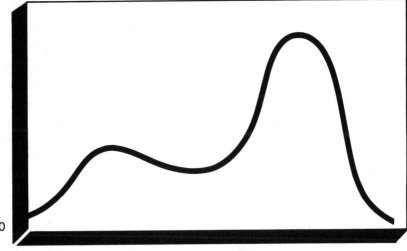

0

Time of day

b. Outbound.

Two aspects bear discussion. First, the peaking of transit is more pronounced than that of travel in general. This peaking reflects the somewhat specialized nature of transit service, which is not equally well-suited to all types of trips. Transit usually serves only some locations in an urban area and is not designed to accommodate such trip types as food shopping or transporting infants with stroller. (Of course, the service might be redesigned to better accommodate such trips.) Secondly, systems designed to serve some types of trips well, may discourage other types. The higher peakedness of rail rapid transit illustrates this. Such systems achieve high average speeds through infrequent stops, making them less suitable for nonpeak travel, which is typically shorter in distance and not as CBD-oriented as peak trips. In addition, the auto is generally preferred to the bus as a feeder to such systems, meaning that non-CBD stations are often surrounded by parking lots, and not final trip destinations. This specialization has a price in terms of practical usefulness for other trip types. All this is not to argue against attempting to match the specific needs of particular trip types, but rather simply to point out that much of transit matches only limited trip types. A more creative approach would be to try to make transit service, or at least the expensive fixed facilities, suitable for a variety of trip purposes more reflective of the full spectrum of trips made in an area.

The impact of this peaking on the cost of providing transit is substantial. First, to accommodate such large peak-period loads, additional vehicles that will only be utilized during those peak periods are required. This means that the additional expense incurred to accommodate peak-period passengers in the peak direction of travel will include the full cost associated with purchasing additional vehicles. Drivers must also be hired to operate these vehicles. Typically they must be paid for a full day's work, even when there are insufficient bus runs in the middle of the day to utilize their time fully. (A detailed discussion of work rules and pay arrangements for transit drivers appears in Lave (1983).) Thus, the full cost of these additional drivers also results from the peak-period demand. All of this leads to an extremely high (incremental) cost associated with additional peak-period services compared to that part of the service that operates throughout the day.

A number of studies have attempted to ascertain the relative cost of peak and off-peak services. Specifically, these studies attempt to determine the marginal or incremental cost of peak services, as compared to the additional costs of services that would operate only during periods such as midday or early evening. We draw upon two that were selected because, in a recent study of bus route-crossing procedures for UMTA, they were identified as the most appropriate for accurately estimating the costs of such services (Cherwony et al. 1981: 92). One study of the Chicago system, using the Northwestern model, estimated the peak-period incremental costs of adding or subtracting a bus run from a route as 3.6 times the cost of doing so in the base period (Morlok et al. 1971). Another study, employing data for Bradford, England, using the second (Traverse Morgan) model, concluded that peak costs are 2.4 times those of the midday period (Cherwony et al. 1981: 69). Since the technologies, labor management agreements, and relative costs of different resources used are roughly the same in these two nations, these results are probably indicative of typical values for western nations in general.

CONCLUDING REMARKS: FORMS OF PRIVATE-SECTOR INVOLVEMENT

Although the primary focus of this chapter is on the relative costs of private- and public-sector provision of public transportation, it is appropriate—given particularly our tentatively optimistic conclusions regarding the cost-saving possibilities inherent here—to address briefly the ways in which the private sector can be involved in providing urban public transportation. There are basically two ways: have the private sector provide transit as a contractor to existing public transportation authorities, or have private firms engage directly in the provision of transit service as independent providers, with no involvement by any transit authority.

The general form of contracting would be for the transit authority to contract with private firms for the delivery of specific public transportation services. The contract would specify the route or routes on which the private firm would operate, the schedules of runs to be made, the type of vehicles to be operated, and so forth. This service would be provided for a fixed amount of money, to be paid by the authority to the firm. All revenue from passengers, collected on board the vehicles, would then be turned over to the authority, and this could be used to help offset the cost of the service. This type of arrangement has actually been undertaken in a few cases. Most typically it is carried out as if the transit authority were actually providing the service directly, with the buses identified with the transit authority, and the public often being completely unaware that the service is being provided through contract. In a few cities, all service is contracted with private firms, while in others only especially expensive services have been contracted out, such as additional peak-period runs. From the standpoint of economic efficiency, the contractor has every incentive to provide the service at least cost, thereby maximizing profits, given the fixed gross revenue payments from the public authority.

There are, however, a number of potential problems with contracting. First, since the aim of the exercise is to capture cost savings associated with private sector involvement, it is important to design a mechanism which reveals when the contract terms are too generous or too restrictive. A particularly simple way to do this is through competitive bidding. This in turn requires careful consideration of the contract packages, to ensure that as many firms as possible can bid. Second, as discussed by Simpson in Chapter 13, contracts must be designed to provide the contractor with the incentive to perform correctly; such an incentive will generally be a net-revenue incentive. Third, if the contract specifies the service levels to be offered, thought must be given to cost-effective ways of monitoring the service. This is so because, with fixed-price contracts, an easy way to reduce costs and increase profits is to skimp on service. Thus, it is essential to have provisions in the contract that reward firms that perform well and that punish those that perform badly. In the extreme, provisions must exist for canceling a contract quickly if service is unsatisfactory. The problem of getting rid of contractors that perform poorly is also reduced by having contracts with many different firms simultaneously thus ensuring that there are others who could fill voids quickly.

The question of "service" may be approached in two ways. The first, and the one most often observed in contractual arrangements (for example, the contract between the Chicago RTA and the C&NW railroad), is to specify detailed characteristics and require the contractor to provide those levels. The principal difficulty with this is that there is no assurance that such service levels correspond to what people actually want. There is, however, a simple way of guaranteeing this. The market, as has often been observed, provides a direct way of revealing a failure to meet consumer desires. This fact suggests that an appropriate way to monitor service is not via arbitrary standards of vehicle cleanliness and so forth, but rather by rewarding those carriers who tailor their service to consumer needs, as revealed by the number of passengers actually served. This has the added advantage of being administratively simpler than monitoring service quality and efficiency of production directly (usually done by arbitrary standards such as bus-miles operated per driver per day). Indeed, except possibly for some minimal level-of-service provisions, there appears to be little reason for a contracting agency to get involved in detailed service considerations at all. (See Viton (1982) for a discussion of service provision along these lines.)

Contracting under these circumstances approaches the other general arrangement: simply to have private firms provide transit service, just as private firms provide other types of goods and services offered to the public. These firms would have a great deal of managerial discretion over the routes to be operated, fares to be charged, and service features such as frequency and capacity. There seems to be an almost infinite variety of ways in which such service could be arranged. At one extreme, transit could be provided by whatever firms wished to enter the business, with each firm having complete discretion over its service and fares. At the other extreme is the old model of having monopolies by area, or at least by route, with a public regulatory body setting the fares and other service features.

This was the arrangement for most U.S. transit during the period before public takeover. It had a number of unattractive features. For one, any sort of monopoly power increases the possibility of "excessively" high costs and diminishes the incentives on management to be efficient. Secondly, such complete regulatory control means that public bodies can force firms out of business by virtue of their decisions. Third, a regulator may end up prescribing the wrong service-quality/price mix.

On the other hand, total deregulation may be far from optimal. In particular, it might mean that low-income areas or low-demand regions would receive no service at all (cf. the modelling evidence on private entry discussed in Chapter 6; but note that cost savings on the scale suggested here as feasible would reduce significantly the range of unprofitable service). Elimination of service to transit-dependent people would certainly be wholly undesirable as a matter of social policy. A more attractive alternative would be somewhere between the two, with some public control, but no firm given a regional or even large-area monopoly. Firms would have considerable freedom to decide on the fares to be charged and the quality and capacity of services.

The questions raised here, and elsewhere in this volume, seem to us to be the vital ones for the formation of a better public policy toward urban transportation. They have as yet received scant attention. We believe that policy research might profitably be focused, first, on adducing additional evidence on the public versus private questions that have been the principal focus of this chapter; and second, by turning more directly to issues of organizational form and incentives. If unacceptable levels of transit deficits are to be reduced, these are the questions that must be addressed.

Chapter 11

REDESIGNING LOCAL TRANSPORTATION SERVICE

C. Kenneth Orski

INTRODUCTION

Small communities across America are faced with a fundamental choice regarding their local transportation service. On the one hand, they can accept falling ridership and increasing operating costs as the price of maintaining conventional fixed-route transit systems. This option offers them the prospect of continued deficits and a steady decline in ridership, as the systems struggle to remain solvent by periodically cutting service and raising fares.

The alternative is to concede that the traditional approaches to providing transit service are no longer effective in spread out, auto-mobile-oriented cities, and to begin gradually to restructure transit service to better reflect today's realities. A community transit system of the future might retain a core network of traditional bus services along routes with high ridership, but elsewhere it would offer users more flexible transportation options, tailored to meet different needs. The restructured system would encourage competition among service providers, lift restrictions and eliminate barriers to free entry of alternative providers, and establish incentives for them to be efficient and responsive to community needs.

There is a growing realization that the market for traditional transit service is progressively diminishing. Buses operating on fixed routes and set schedules worked well in the days when most homes and jobs were located in cities, when a large proportion of the urban population lived within walking distance of bus routes, and when travel destinations were sharply focused on the central business district. Today, we are confronted with a vastly different set of circumstances. Trip origins and destinations are widely dispersed; the largest residential, shopping and employment centers are often found in the suburbs; and travel patterns resemble Brownian motion—they appear random in nature and are taking place in every direction all at once.

SOURCES OF CURRENT PROBLEMS

Changing Demographic Patterns

Within metropolitan areas, suburban population growth has been far outstripping that of central cities in every region of the country. From 1950 to 1980, the population in the ten largest urban areas decreased by over 35 percent, while population outside the central cities rose by more than 60 percent. This trend appears to continue during the decade of the eighties. The residential migration, coupled with massive shifts of employment to suburban locations, has fundamentally modified the nature of metropolitan travel. The majority of workers today are "lateral" commuters, that is, they both live and work in the suburbs. The Census Bureau's last national study of commuting, *The Journey to Work in the United States: 1975*, showed that about eighteen million workers lived and worked in the suburbs, about sixteen million lived and worked within central cities, and about nine million workers lived in the suburbs and commuted into the city to work. Another four million workers were "reverse" commuters, living in the central city and commuting out to jobs in the suburbs. Recent census data show that the proportion of commuters who live and work in the suburbs has increased in virtually every metropolitan area during the 1970s.

Regular transit was never designed to cope with the dispersed living and travel patterns that have developed since World War II. Public transit was predicated on the existence of concentrated flows of people along predictable routes—a market that could be satisfied with a single type of service provided throughout the day in defined travel corridors. What has emerged instead is an increasingly fragmented market. Contemporary travel demand varies not only by trip destination, but by time of day, by age group, by price elasticity of demand, even by level of comfort desired. There is no longer a homogeneous traveling public; instead there are many different traveling publics, each with its own set of needs and preferences.

Despite these changes, most cities have made little attempt to adapt transit systems to the new markets. By and large, public transit systems continued to function in the same way as before the suburban migration. Cities went on operating large buses on radially oriented fixed routes and providing a single type of service throughout the day, seemingly oblivious to the fact that demand for such service was dwindling, as more and more commuting, shopping, and recreational trips began and ended in the suburbs, and travel origins and destinations became ever more dispersed.

In sum, transit ridership has been eroding because cities have failed to respond creatively to the changing conditions of the marketplace. Far from learning from the mistakes of the private transit industry and fashioning services to respond to the more diverse and scattered travel patterns in contemporary communities, the public agencies that took over the operation of the former private transit systems, perpetuated the practices of their predecessors, and condemned transit to a continued slide into insolvency.

Just how serious the decline in transit usage has been can be seen from the 1980 census data. Between 1970 and 1980 the number of people commuting to work on public transportation fell by close to half a million, a decline of 7 percent, despite a significant increase in the workforce. In terms of modal choice the shift has been even more dramatic. Only 6.4 percent of all workers rode public transit in 1980, down from 8.9 percent in 1970. A significant decline in the proportion of people using transit occurred in virtually every region except the West, as can be seen in the Table 11-1.

It is tempting to blame this erosion in transit ridership on the Americans' love affair with the automobile. But recent census data belie this theory. Almost half of the respondents in the Census Bureau's 1980 Annual Housing Survey said they did not use public transit because it was not available, and another 25 percent cited difficulties with using transit. Only 13 percent of the respondents said that they simply preferred to use their own private cars, and less than 1 percent said that they did not use public transportation because it

Table 11-1. Workers Using Public Transportation, 1970 and 1980.

	Rate of Transit Use		Change, 1970–1980	
	1970 (%)	1980 (%)	Number (000s)	Percent
U.S. Total	9.0	6.4	−487	−7.3
Northeast	19.1	14.2	−596	−16.7
North Central	6.7	4.9	−187	−13.3
South	5.0	3.3	−82	−7.3
West	4.6	5.0	378	66.6

Source: Philip N. Fulton, U.S. Bureau of the Census, Population Division, Journey-to-Work and Migration Statistics Branch, Washington, D.C. (1983).

was too expensive. Thus, about 75 percent of all the interviewed workers who commute by car did not use public transit not because they preferred the automobile, but because transit could not conveniently serve their needs.

During the 1970s the impact of eroding ridership went almost unnoticed because of a rapid growth in federal operating subsidies. Between 1972 and 1980 federal operating assistance to mass transit grew fivefold, from $200 million to over a billion dollars a year, and helped to cover the widening gap between fare revenues and operating expenses. In a larger sense, however, these subsidies have done the cities a disservice, for they masked transit's underlying structural weaknesses and encouraged city officials to expand services into low-density areas without regard to economic soundness. The result was to compound the already precarious state of transit finances. However, the threat of shrinking federal subsidies and the reality of state and local budget restraints are forcing cities to confront the balance sheet. Local officials evidence a new, more questioning attitude, greater willingness to challenge the conventional planning wisdom, and greater receptivity to innovative solutions. Increasing numbers of transit agencies and local governments are reassessing the logic of traditional approaches and exploring new ideas about how transit should be organized, provided, and paid for.

A recent Census Bureau report, commenting on the continued decline of transit ridership during the decade of the 1970s, put it this way:

It has long been a fundamental assumption of planners that mass transit would provide the ultimate remedy for the urban transportation problem by reshaping urban form and modifying consumer behavior. On the contrary, the principal lesson to be learned from the 1980 census is that for transit to retain its public, it must better adapt itself to the changes in urban form and consumer preferences that are taking place around it.

Declining Transit Productivity

The growing mismatch between where transit goes and where people want to go has been a source of transit's mounting costs and declining productivity. Transit operating costs have grown significantly in recent years, increasing nationwide 160 percent between 1967 and 1980 alone. Cost per revenue hour of operation, a key indicator of transit efficiency, rose from $29.00 in 1979 to $38.00 in 1982 – a 31 percent increase in just three years. Operating expense per vehicle mile increased from an average of $1.02 in 1970 to $3.11 in 1980. These cost increases substantially exceeded the general rate of inflation in the economy. In inflation-adjusted constant dollars, the unit operating costs grew by 62 percent.

With increased suburbanization and near-universal automobile availability, the demand for transit service is concentrated into a few morning and afternoon hours. It is not unusual for transit systems to run two or three times as many buses during rush hours as during midday hours. Consequently, a large proportion of transit resources, including drivers and vehicles, remains idle most of the day. Adding to the problem are union-imposed work rules that restrict the use of part-time drivers and the proportion of "split shifts" that drivers can work. Under typical work rules, transit systems often find themselves paying their drivers nine hours pay for five hours of driving, the extra pay being compensation for having to work split shifts. As a result, peak-hour transit service has become very costly to run.

Also contributing to the declining productivity and cost escalation has been service expansion into low-density suburbs, which has been made possible by rapidly increasing federal operating subsidies. Suburban services generate less ridership (and, therefore less revenue) than central city services because of lower population densities; they are also more expensive to operate because of the long deadhead distances that empty buses have to travel between garages and endpoints of suburban routes. Yet is is precisely in the suburbs that the greatest expansion of service has occurred, as transit authorities push bus routes further and further out in the hopes of gaining a wider political constituency. While the intent behind these efforts may be commendable, the cost of extending bus service out into low-density suburbs, far beyond transit's traditional territory, is prohibitive. According to a recent General Accounting Office study of transit productivity, peak-period commuter runs into the suburbs require four times as much public subsidy per passenger as local central city services.

Toward a Service Redesign

If public transit is to play a constructive role in American communities once again, it must be reexamined and restructured to provide services that are appropriate to today's markets. The International City Management Association, in its report, *Public Transit in Small Cities and Counties*, offers these thoughts to communities in search of transit solutions:

> The resurgence of public bus systems in small urban areas over the last decade probably will come to an end. Data from the survey indicate that, although traditional fixed-route, fixed-schedule transit service has been maintained or reintroduced in many communities, a significant portion of the operating and capital costs of this service is financed with federal and state dollars. Without a much greater investment of local funds, many of these systems will not survive the elimination of federal transit aid. Although current budgets for small-city transportation systems are modest in comparison with larger urban systems, the expenditures on a per rider basis are not. Thus, from both an economic and utilization standpoint, these smaller fixedroute systems will be harder to sustain, and a valid question can be raised as to whether they should be.
>
> A major challenge facing small city administrators and local elected officials will be managing the transition from federally funded operations to locally affordable, flexible transportation systems that include a range of services. Fiscal realities will require diversifying service options and increasing the role of the private sector in providing public transportation.
>
> The federal phase-out of transit assistance clearly presents an immediate threat to small transportation systems, but it also presents an opportunity. The new financing reality will force a long-overdue reassessment of current services and delivery mechanisms, and can be a catalyst for innovative, flexible approaches that communities can afford.

In the sections that follow, we examine some of these innovative approaches and assess their promise for improving mobility and helping American communities achieve greater transportation self-sufficiency.

OPTIONS FOR THE FUTURE

In considering how to respond to the changing times, American communities are faced with several alternatives. On the one hand, they can maintain their present transit systems and try to enhance performance, productivity, and cost-effectiveness through internal management improvements. Reappraisals of this type have become quite common recently, as transit authorities strive to cut costs and trim fat in response to tighter local budgets. The utility of such analyses has been demonstrated. The city of Cincinnati, for example, reportedly saved $900,000 a year by reducing late evening and weekend service, yet the move affected only a hundred regular transit riders.

Another option is to make the transit system fiscally more self-supporting by increasing fares to a level that better approximates the true cost of providing service. In the past, local officials have deliberately maintained low fares in pursuit of two objectives: First, low fares were felt to be necessary because those who most need public transit service are least able to afford it; second, low fares would attract riders who would otherwise commute by car. Upon closer analysis, however, neither argument is compelling. There are more efficient ways of accomplishing the equity objective, such as by subsidizing needy individuals rather than the entire system. The mechanism is the so-called user side subsidies, which are employed in over one hundred communities to provide low-cost public transportation and other social services (food stamps, housing vouchers, and so on) to needy persons. With regard to the use of low fares to entice automobile commuters, all available evidence suggests that low fares have little influence on the white-collar commuter's choice of mode. Suburban commuters are much more sensitive to service quality—on-time performance, guaranteed seating, riding comfort, and convenience—than they are to cheap fares. Thus, there is no reason to keep fares low in the hope of luring auto drivers to transit. On the contrary, there are good reasons to raise fares for peak-period commute trips, which typically cost one-third more to operate than off-peak or base-period trips.

Management can also improve system efficiency through more efficient use of labor by negotiating part-time labor and work rule changes (for example, increasing the proportion of split shifts that drivers can work).

Marketing may also play a limited role in revitalizing transit, although the utility of spending large sums on advertising and other promotional activities seems questionable. The power of advertising, effective as it may be in persuading people on how to spend their discretionary income on consumer products, is not likely to have great influence on their travel behavior. As we have seen, most people ignore transit not because they have a negative attitude toward it or possess insufficient information about it, but because they cannot conveniently use it. No amount of advertising and promotion will persuade the public to use transit if the buses do not go where people want to go.

SERVICE REDESIGN

In sum, conventional strategies—labor productivity improvements, service cutbacks, fare increases, and advertising—afford a certain measure of relief, but do not offer a lasting solution to the problem of eroding ridership and escalating deficits. If cities are to place their transit systems on a truly sound footing, they must consider more fundamental changes in the way transit is organized, provided, and paid for. We call such changes "service redesign."

Much of the public debate about transit still reflects the old assumption that the only choice is between raising revenue or cutting service. Money and service are seen as the only variables: More money produces more or better service; less money results in less or poorer service. Inherent in the concept of service redesign is a third alternative: more efficient and less costly delivery of services. Service redesign directs attention to the way services are organized, managed, and delivered: the factors that determine how much revenue the present level of service requires and how much service the present level of revenue produces. From the standpoint of service redesign, cost reduction is not tantamount to less or poorer quality service; it may mean more or better service, delivered with the help of more efficient and less costly providers.

A starting point for redesigning transit systems along more effective lines is to adopt a market-oriented, user-sensitive approach to service delivery. The demand for urban transportation has long ceased to be (if it ever was) a monolithic market that could be satisfied with a single type of service provided throughout the day and throughout the entire metropolitan area in a uniform manner. Today the market is highly segmented, demanding a spectrum of diversified services that cater specifically to the transportation needs of different groups of users and adapt to the changing demands throughout the day.

Service redesign involves the consideration of a full spectrum of transportation techniques and practices. They include:

- Encouraging commuters to form vanpools and carpools instead of simply adding more peak-hour buses.

- Substituting flexible forms of transportation (such as shared taxis) for regular transit in low-density areas, where transportation demand is too low to justify fixed-route, fixed-schedule service.

- Contracting for service with private operators when such operators can provide an equal level of service at a lower cost.

- Encouraging private carriers to provide unsubsidized services, and facilitating their entry into the commuter transportation market.

- Enlisting business sponsorship of selected transportation services, for example, employee ridesharing programs and downtown shopper shuttles.

- Encouraging community-based and social service organizations to operate volunteer transportation programs.

- Promoting commuter "bus clubs" and other cooperative transportation arrangements in suburban communities and housing developments where provision of regular transit service would be very expensive.

- Decentralizing transit service and contracting the size of service districts in order to achieve greater efficiency and responsiveness in the provision of service.

- Providing land use and development incentives (for example, reduced parking requirements or density bonuses) to encourage developer-sponsored transportation management programs, such as carpool and vanpool programs.

- Providing user-side subsidies, that is, free or discount transit passes to needy individuals, and charging others the full cost of transit service.

The desire to offer more diversified services that are closely tailored to various needs leads in turn to a greater variety of service providers and greater competition in service provision. The traditional assumption that the public interest requires a single public agency to be the sole supplier of transit service within a region is no longer accepted as dogma. Increasingly, local officials view transit agencies as "full service providers"—brokers and coordinators who identify the region's transportation needs and ensure that those needs are satisfied in the most cost-effective manner through a variety of operators, both public and private.

Applying the Concept of Service Redesign

One example of an imaginative approach to service redesign is the programs of the Tidewater Transit District Commission and the Peninsula Transportation District Commission in southeastern Virginia. There is a substantial demand for peak-hour service in both service areas. The addition of buses to accommodate this demand was considered; however, because fixed-route service in the area only returns 45 percent of its cost from the farebox, the decision was made to seek other alternatives, such as van-, car-, and buspools, where users not only pay full operating costs but also the local share of capital (vehicle) costs. The strategy of both commissions has been not to expand fixed-route bus services but to do everything possible to substitute flexible services. Both transit districts provide ridesharing services, including a fleet of over a hundred vans for vanpooling and fifty vans (under contract to social service organizations) for special services for the handicapped. They also acquire buses and lease them to individuals who commute in buspools. For local service where performance analysis has shown fixed-route service to be cost-ineffective, the Tidewater Transit District contracts for shared-ride taxi service. This strategy has been tested in the city of Chesapeake, where two lightly used bus routes have been replaced with on-call taxi service. Ridership has increased, while cost has decreased by 43 percent. Deficit per passenger fell from $4.75 in August 1979 to $1.85 in April 1980.

Fare policies also help the two transit districts to manage peak demand. A zone system, together with peak-period surcharges for express service, makes long-distance commuting pay more of its own way. Bus routes are constantly reviewed for performance. Each year resources are shifted from the lowest performing routes and added to those with the highest performance. Paratransit is promoted as a substitute for those areas from which regular bus service is removed.

MAKING BETTER USE OF
PRIVATE PROVIDERS

An essential strategy of service redesign is to involve a more diverse group of providers, to open up the system to private operators, and to stimulate greater competition in service provision. Privately contracted services can often be purchased for less than it costs the public transportation agency to provide the service itself. Savings of 50 percent or more are not unusual, and these savings can be returned to the public via higher service levels, lower subsidy levels, or a combination thereof. One example is Tidewater District's contract with a local taxi company for on-call service in low-density residential neighborhoods. The service costs the transit authority $16.00 per hour, as compared to $33.00 per hour to operate its own buses.

The city of Phoenix contracts with a private taxi company to provide service in low-density areas and on Sundays. Approximately 240 riders use the service each Sunday. The city pays the taxi company a unit price of $16.25 per vehicle hour in use, plus all fares collected. The city estimates that it is saving $600,000 a year in net operating costs by contracting with the taxi company instead of providing fixed-route service with its own buses. (Contract services cost the city of Phoenix $1.22 per mile, compared to Phoenix Transit's cost of $2.86 per mile).

A score of communities in California have entered into purchase-of-service contracts with private operators to provide fixed-route and flexible services using sedans, mini- and maxi-vans, and small buses. In San Diego private contracting caused the cost per vehicle mile to drop from $3.65 to $2.39—a cost reduction of 35 percent for essentially the same level of service.

By far the most extensive application of contracting will be in Dallas, where the new Dallas Area Rapid Transit Authority (DART) will contract with private firms or public agencies to perform virtually every aspect of its operation, from preparing blueprints for the new rail system to operating bus and rail systems. By shifting operation and maintenance to the private sector, DART will be able to concentrate on longer range issues: setting general policy, determining annual budgets, monitoring tax and fare revenue, marketing the system to the public, and responding to the public's needs. Through built-in bonus incentives, fines, and 24-hour cancellation provisions, the authority hopes to be able to tailor transit service to its exact specifications.

Beyond the savings in operating costs, recent evidence indicates that the competitive process itself works as an incentive to limit operating cost increases. In Los Angeles, for example, the cost of the privately operated Santa Clarita Valley commuter service has consistently increased by less than the inflation rate. No comparable incentive to control costs exists for public transit agencies, as the rapid rise in transit operating expenses testifies. Finally, the private operator's interest in retaining the contract and obtaining future contracts creates a powerful incentive to assure quality service. A public agency that holds an exclusive monopoly on providing service and is protected from competition lacks that strong motivation. Incentive contracting, whereby a portion of the private contractor's compensation is contingent upon real and measurable performance, can be used as an added stimulus. Such contracts not only encourage the private operator to be efficient, they also protect the contracting agency from an operator who performs poorly. Incentive contracts, properly conceived, can be an important management tool for achieving maximum efficiency.

Finally, a major advantage of contracting with private providers is the flexibility and reduced risk it affords the contracting public agency. Changes in service levels can be implemented quickly. Contractors who perform poorly can be removed, and organizational changes that require reductions in personnel levels can be implemented more easily. There is more freedom to experiment or adjust service levels to meet new circumstances. In sum, private contracting works well because the desire for growth and profits cause the contractor to remain flexible, competitive, and receptive to service modifications that contribute to efficiency. By capitalizing on the profit motive of the private contractors and challenging them through incentive contracts, the transit agency can gain a valuable instrument in carrying out its mission.

Barriers to Contracting

An issue that is often raised in discussions about contracting is its impact on labor and the obstacles placed by existing collective bargaining agreements. While the consequence of contracting—indeed its very purpose—is an eventual contraction in the size of the *publicly* employed workforce, the change can be managed with sensitivity to the rights of employees, and in ways that shield individual workers from layoffs or reductions in compensation. Public transit agencies generally have high enough attrition rates to allow a gradual shift to contracting, without worsening the position of any employee. Furthermore, a growth in the private provision of transit services will necessitate increased staffs on the part of the private firms, so that a bus driver formerly employed by the public agency could possibly find employment with the substituting private firm.

EXPANDED USE OF UNSUBSIDIZED
PRIVATE CARRIERS

Most communities have local taxicab companies which provide door-to-door, personalized transportation service. There are, however, ways to enhance the role of taxicabs in a community and make them a more versatile and attractive mode of transportation.

1. *Shared-ride taxis.* This policy would allow taxis to pick up additional passengers enroute and carry them to different destinations, provided they were all going in the same general direction. In order to make shared-ride taxis more attractive to potential riders, a shared-fare policy could also be adopted, wherein the cost of a trip would be divided among the passengers. An example of a shared-ride/shared-fare system is that of Oklahoma City's Share-a-Fare program, which provides group riding service to elderly and handicapped persons. Eligible passengers pay taxi fares using coupons that are purchased for one-half of the face value; drivers later redeem these coupons for the full amount.

2. *Fixed-route taxicabs.* Shared-ride taxi service could be franchised on transit routes as replacement for regular buses during periods of low demand, such as evening hours and weekends. While following regular routes and schedules, taxicabs could deviate on request to pick up and deliver passengers, perhaps at a small additional fee and with a limit placed on the distance of route deviation.

3. *Taxipooling.* This involves the prearranged hiring of taxicabs by small groups of passengers who travel regularly to common destinations. Taxipooling could be used by commuters as a feeder service to fixed bus routes or for direct trips to the ultimate destination. In terms of service taxipooling is similar to carpooling, but its cost implications might be different.

Barriers to Innovative Taxi Services

Municipal codes often contain provisions that prohibit the shared use of taxis or fixed-route taxi service. Some provisions remove the financial incentive for passengers to use taxis in any other way than on an exclusive-ride basis. If innovative use of taxicabs is to be encouraged, one of the essential requirements would be to amend municipal codes to eliminate existing regulatory impediments.

PRIVATE SECTOR SUPPORT OF PARALLEL TRANSPORTATION

So far we have considered potential improvements in mobility in the context of the publicly provided transportation service. However, public transit and taxis are only the most visible elements in a community's larger mobility system. A broad array of parallel transportation services augment the public transit system. This is what makes it possible in the first place for large segments of a community to remain independent of the public transit system. The parallel services include: pupil transportation sponsored by the school boards; private carpool arrangements entered into by individual commuters; employer-sponsored ridesharing (carpools and vanpools) programs; hotel "courtesy vans" to the airport; and a host of specialized transportation services for elderly, handicapped, and low-income groups operated by social welfare agencies and voluntary organizations.

Could privately sponsored parallel transportation services play an even more expanded role in meeting a community's mobility needs? In the following section we shall focus attention on several distinct approaches.

"Bus Clubs" and Other Cooperative Transportation Arrangements

One example of an innovative approach to parallel transportation is that taken by the Golden Gate Bridge and Transportation District in San Francisco. In 1977 the district was faced with a demand for additional rush-hour service. Instead of purchasing extra buses and running them as usual, the district purchased vans and placed them at the disposal of commuters. Passengers were charged both for operating costs and the cost of vehicle amortization. After a certain period, each commuter pool was urged to purchase its own van and become fully self-supporting. In the first three years of operation the Golden Gate vanpool program has grown to eighty-seven vans, of which fifty-seven have made the transition to private ownership. By imaginatively shifting to a more flexible service, the District was able to fulfill its service obligation to the public at a much lower cost than if it had maintained the traditional posture of transit management and insisted on operating all of its services alone.

Another approach that deserves to be examined is the concept of "bus clubs." The idea was first introduced in Columbia, Maryland, where the homeowner-founded, nonprofit Columbia Commuter Bus Corporation has been providing bus service to downtown Washington, D.C., for more than a decade. It is now practiced also in several suburban communities around Oklahoma City. The residents of these communities have banded together into nonprofit clubs for the purpose of running commuter buses to downtown Oklahoma City. The membership fees cover the local 50-percent share of the cost of the commuter service; federal operating subsidies pay the rest. The club buses are operated under contract to the nonprofit associations by the metropolitan transit agency. Round trips cost from $1.50 to $2.60, depending on the number of passengers in the club bus.

Neighborhood Volunteer Transportation Program

In addition to the daily commute to work, every residential neighborhood generates numerous local trips by those who remain behind: homemakers, elderly people, school children, and visiting friends and relatives. Often these are precisely the groups that have the least access to personal automobiles, either because the family car is being used by the commuting spouse, or because the individuals in question are too young or too old to drive.

Regular bus service is ill suited to serve these daytime travel needs. The buses run on fixed routes centered on the central business district, whereas most of the travelers have destinations outside the central area, be it a regional shopping mall, hospital, dentist's office, community swimming pool, or any number of other community services. To improve the mobility of daytime residents in these neighborhoods, a different kind of transportation service is needed, one that is flexible, responsive, affordable, and self-supporting.

One such approach, introduced in Huntsville and Madison County, Alabama, is a volunteer community transit program, a partnership between neighborhoods and the public sector. Under this approach the neighborhoods, acting through specially organized nonprofit Community Improvement Associations, furnish volunteer drivers, gasoline, and program management (that is, prescheduling of shared-ride trips for shopping, medical, educational, and recreational purposes). The city provides used and reconditioned vans; the county provides preventive maintenance and insurance; and the City Department of Transportation provides overall program management and administration. The cost of vans and insurance is covered by federal funds, since UMTA has determined that these are eligible costs under the block grant.

There are currently fourteen community volunteer vans in operation in Huntsville and the surrounding Madison County, most of them serving elderly and low-income residents who do not own cars. In 1982 these vans carried a total of 33,500 people at a cost of 40 cents per passenger. The city estimates that the program could be placed on a totally unsubsidized, self-supporting basis at a cost of 80 cents per passenger, still 48 percent less than the $1.67 cost of a passenger trip on a city transit bus.

Seeking Greater Community Support
and Involvement

In a growing number of communities, provision of public transportation is being viewed as a joint responsibility of the public and private sectors. Thus, in Oklahoma City, local developers are paying for the cost of trolleys to link the central business district with a newly renovated warehouse district. In Des Moines, Iowa, a private real estate firm and the public transit system have shared the cost of starting bus service to an outlying residential development. In Johnstown, Pennsylvania, a group of merchants situated in a suburban shopping mall pay the local transit system a monthly fee for transit service provided to their mall. In Lexington, Kentucky, a downtown trolley is sponsored by a consortium of local merchants and businesses and is operated by the local transit system. The private sector absorbs one-half of the operating deficit. And in Anapolis, Maryland, downtown restaurants and taverns are underwriting the cost of evening shuttle service from fringe parking lots.

Business involvement is supplemented by grassroots initiatives. Thus, in Lincoln, Nebraska, volunteer "ridesharing agents" organize carpool and vanpool programs in the neighborhoods. In Maricopa County, Arizona, a volunteer-operated transportation system provides transportation to carless persons needing access to medical and social services. In Columbia, Maryland, a homeowners' association operates commuter buses to downtown Washington, D.C. In Des Moines, Iowa, a local homeowners association cooperatively funds public transit service for residents of a housing subdivision. And in Alexandria, Virginia, condominium and tenants' associations in high-rise buildings run a residentially based ridesharing program with the assistance of the city's Ridesharing Service.

In all the above cases, the private sector is assuming a more active role in the solution of local transportation problems because it realizes that government alone can no longer shoulder the full financial burden of the public needs. A new consensus is emerging: that we need to harness a broader spectrum of community resources in addressing common problems.

SEPARATION OF POLICYMAKING
AND OPERATING FUNCTIONS

The increasing diversity of services and service providers is leading to a reappraisal of traditional transit organization. In the past, the functions of sponsoring (planning, financing, arranging) and providing (operating, delivering) transit service were considered inseparable. For example, when a policy decision was made to establish a public transportation program, a public agency was typically set up to finance and administer the program, and it was designated as the sole provider of that service. Public agencies were both the purchasers of service on behalf of the taxpayers and the suppliers of that service. Public transit officials saw themselves both as policymakers and as administrative managers of an operating enterprise.

While this conception of the public sector role is still widely embraced, it is no longer universally accepted. Increasingly, local officials view transportation agencies as policymaking bodies that decide what services are needed, and ensure that those services are delivered by others in the most cost-effective manner. This does not mean that metropolitan transit agencies must abandon all of their operating responsibilities; only that they should not enjoy a monopoly on service provision. Regular services provided by traditional transit agencies are likely to be increasingly supplemented by a range of other, more flexible services, operated by a variety of operators, both public and private.

Even when the transit agencies still regard themselves as operating enterprises, local elected officials no longer see a compelling need for these agencies to remain exclusive service providers for the entire region. They are inclined to view public transit agencies instead as merely one among several potential transportation operators, and they think of themselves as prudent purchasers of service in a competitive market. Thus, the city of Minneapolis, required by law to provide shuttle bus service to a new stadium, considered the Metropolitan Transit Commission, found it too expensive, and contracted for service with a private company, at a savings of $900,000 a year.

In the longer run, we may see a thorough rethinking of the role of regional transit authorities—a rethinking that has already begun in several jurisdictions, notably in Chicago, Newport News, San Diego, San Francisco, and Minneapolis/Saint Paul. In those cities, *arranging* for service and *providing* service have become two distinct roles. One public agency is being used to plan, facilitate, and coordinate public transportation; and another set of agencies, both public and private, is employed to provide and operate transportation service. In the Chicago area, for example, the Regional Transportation Authority (RTA) has been stripped by the Illinois legislature of its operating role and will become only a resource allocation body. Operating functions will be entrusted to three entities: the Chicago Transit Authority (CTA) within the city; a suburban bus board that will take over bus operations in the suburbs; and a regional commuter rail authority. The individual operating agencies will determine their own transit needs and develop services that best respond to those needs. They will set service levels and fares, establish operating policies, and make decisions on how to deliver service (internally or by contract). The RTA will distribute the funds and monitor operations, to make sure that the operating agencies stay within their budgets and recover a defined proportion of operating costs from the farebox.

Another example of a separation of policy and operating roles is the Peninsula Transportation District Commission (Pentran), the public transportation authority serving Newport News and Hampton in southeastern Virginia. The commission sees its function as identifying the region's transportation needs and ensuring that those needs are satisfied in the most efficient and economical manner – that is, of sponsoring rather than supplying services. To this end, the commission coordinates a variety of services and service providers, including employer-based vanpool programs, private commuter buses to employment centers, shared-ride taxi service in low-density areas, and special services for the handicapped operated by social service agencies. The commission retains certain systemwide functions, such as marketing and fare setting; all other functions are carried out by the operating elements, both public and private.

A third example is Westchester County's transportation department, which contracts with sixteen separate private bus companies for service, retaining only fare setting, marketing, and scheduling responsibilities.

As mentioned previously, the new Dallas Area Rapid Transit Authority (DART) will contract with private firms or public agencies to prepare blueprints for the new rail system and to operate the bus and proposed rail systems. DART will thus be able to concentrate on setting general policy, determining annual budgets, and monitoring tax and fare revenue, marketing the system to the public, and responding to the public's needs. Through built-in bonus incentives, fines, and 24-hour cancellation provisions, DART will be able to control transit service.

All four agencies see their principal function as one of managing rather than operating transportation systems: of identifying the region's transportation needs and assuring that those needs are met in the most efficient and economical manner — that is, of arranging or sponsoring rather than supplying transit service.

Minneapolis/Saint Paul has probably taken the most far reaching steps in the direction of sorting out the policymaking and operating responsibilities. A special legislative study commission has concluded that it is inherently wrong for a single agency to both provide transit service and have a policymaking role that gives it the power to freeze out or discourage competition. The study commission has recommended separating the operating and policymaking functions, both of which are presently held by the Metropolitan Transit Commission. The MTC would retain responsibility for day-to-day operation of the public bus system in the central city. A new Regional Transit Authority would be set up to oversee planning, financing, and policymaking, and to serve as an arranger-of-service for the outlying areas. The RTA would purchase service on a competitive-bid basis from interested public and private operators, tailoring it to the needs of individual communities.

RETHINKING TRANSIT

Changing economic, demographic, and fiscal conditions have helped to precipitate a major reappraisal of urban transportation, especially in small- and medium-sized cities. In a growing number of communities, concerned citizens and public officials, faced with the threat of shrinking federal subsidies and mushrooming local budget expenses, are questioning the logic of traditional transportation arrangements and challenging conventional approaches to service delivery.

Out of this reappraisal a new conception of public transportation is emerging. It is a conception built around the principles of choice and competition, of diversity of services and service providers, and of separation of policy and operating responsibilities. The new view recognizes that the urban transportation market is highly fragmented and that it requires not one but many types of service. It acknowledges the fact that large, areawide transit systems are not necessarily the most efficient mechanisms for delivering service. The emerging construct of public transportation is also based on the proposition that government itself need not necessarily provide all the service that is needed, and that assuring adequate mobility should be a cooperative task and a shared responsibility of government and the private sector.

In sum, the stage is set for a searching reexamination of current transportation assumptions. Although it is too early to predict the ultimate outcome, the process that has been set in motion is likely to lead to a fundamental reform of America's public transportation. This may be not only the best way of arresting the present escalation of transit deficits; it may also be the only way of preserving public transit's relevance in America's small- and medium-sized cities.

Chapter 12

GOVERNMENT POLICIES AFFECTING COMPETITION IN PUBLIC TRANSPORTATION

Michael A. Kemp and Ronald F. Kirby

BACKGROUND

Publicly owned urban mass transit systems are currently experiencing serious financial problems. During the 1970s, increases of 20 percent per year (in real terms) in transit operating deficits established trends in public financing that were impossible to sustain. Growing tax limitation movements at all levels of government in the 1980s have begun to slow and even reverse these trends of rapidly increasing public assistance. At the federal level, the Reagan administration has effected significant reductions from the level of assistance projected by the previous administration. And fiscal pressures at the state and local levels have created strong pressures to limit the subsidies provided by these levels of government, too.

The causes of the problems now confronting transit systems go back quite a number of years. The monopoly operating rights of most transit systems, public policies that kept fares unrealistically low, the bias toward large capital expenditures in the federal assistance program, and steady growth in the ownership and use of private automobiles have all contributed to the existing situation.

Monopoly franchises granted to streetcar companies in the early years of the century provided the foundation for the structure of the present transit industry, as described in Chapter 2. The use of a central electric power generator favored monopoly operation in each geographic area to recover installation costs. As buses eventually replaced streetcars, however, the rationale for monopoly franchises disappeared: motorized vehicles operated by several small companies can compete efficiently along the same routes, as is the case in many developing countries. In the United States and most other developed countries, unfortunately, the streetcar monopoly franchises were transferred to bus companies, thus institutionalizing a noncompetitive supply situation.

The monopoly franchises granted to the bus companies typically carried with them requirements that certain service coverage and fare levels be maintained. The companies were allowed monopoly operation on profitable routes theoretically to enable them to subsidize unprofitable routes and service. Potential competitors, such as private taxicab operators, were banned from providing directly competitive shared-ride services so that the bus companies could maintain service on unprofitable routes.

By the early 1960s, however, the bus companies were no longer able to raise sufficient revenues from the profitable routes to subsidize the unprofitable ones. When local regulatory authorities refused to approve the service and fare adjustments the companies needed to maintain a reasonable return on their investment, the companies' response was to defer maintenance of equipment, which gradually became so dilapidated that they could not continue normal operations.

At this time, it was generally believed that an influx of capital support would permit transit systems to survive and that operating costs could be covered by farebox revenues. This assumption provided the initial rationale for federal subsidy to the transit industry, which came in 1964 in the form of a capital assistance program designed to help localities purchase transit equipment and facilities. Cities used this money to buy out the private transit companies and to upgrade their equipment through new capital purchases.

Capital support from the federal government in the 1960s provided mass transit systems with a few years' respite from their financial difficulties, but ridership continued to decline as automobile use increased. The new publicly owned systems incurred steadily increasing operating deficits, in part because of the unwillingness of elected officials to sanction fare increases in pace with the cost increases. Pressure gradually was brought to bear on the federal government for a program of operating assistance to supplement the program of capital support. In 1974, a new section was added to the Urban Mass Transportation Act to provide federal operating assistance funds for up to 50 percent of operating deficits. The Reagan administration is trying to phase out this operating assistance program, arguing that federal aid for operating expenses weakens local management's incentives to keep costs down.

Under a different set of policy decisions, we could now have had urban transit systems characterized by private ownership and competition rather than by public ownership and monopoly operation. Where public officials wished to subsidize certain services, they could have done so through service contracts awarded to select private providers. Because the current structure has evolved over some fifty years, however, persuasive evidence of the benefits of a more competitive system will now be required to stimulate interest in greater private sector involvement.

Rush-hour services are a good example of the potential for more competition and a greater private sector role. Rush-hour commuters are very costly for transit systems to serve, because vehicles and full-time drivers have to be provided on split shifts for a few trips in the morning and early evening. Vanpooling and carpooling programs are promising ways of distributing some of this burden to other services that require no subsidy. The federal government has been promoting these options, and some cities have become actively involved in adopting them. One encouraging case is in the Tidewater Virginia area, described in Chapter 4. Houston recently introduced a similar program. While these are promising approaches, at present they are being pursued in only a handful of cities.

In several cities, private bus companies run high-quality, guaranteed-seat subscription service for rush-hour commuters: some of these have been described in Chapters 6 and 7. These services are predominantly for long-distance trips to and from communities outside the service area of existing transit systems. Private bus companies operate these services profitably, demonstrating that some commuters are willing to pay the full cost of high-quality public transportation. Local regulations often keep the services outside the franchised transit district, however, so they're unable to compete directly with transit buses. Under a more liberal regulatory policy, these private operators could be allowed to supply rush-hour service within the transit district.

Another competitive opportunity lies in the use of companies that employ small vehicles, such as taxicabs and limousines, to operate some of the low-density services on evenings and weekends in place of large buses. Even if such routes have to be subsidized, it may be preferable to contract with these companies rather than to have the central transit authority operate all the services. Again, Tidewater Virginia (Chapter 4) provides an instructive, but unique, example of such an operation.

Several cities throughout the country have examples of competitive, private sector provision of public transportation. By and large, however, provision of public transportation is still dominated by municipal or regional transit authorities protected from competition by government regulatory policies. And even where private sector provision is the rule, as for taxicab services, for example, the regulations often place strict limits on the number of firms allowed to operate, the service types, and the fares charged. If the private sector is to have a greater opportunity to provide public transport services, substantial changes will be required in current administrative and regulatory policies.

EVOLVING PROBLEMS AND
POLICY RESPONSES

Over the next ten to fifteen years, the evolution of metropolitan areas will create gradual changes in the markets for public transportation.[1] Dispersion of residences and jobs will continue, probably at a slower rate than that of the 1960s and 1970s, implying continued decline in the relative importance of suburb-to-downtown commuting, though perhaps not in the absolute numbers of trips. New markets for high-occupancy transport will arise locally in response to a variety of factors—the higher density of new residential construction, the "thickening" of the inner suburbs, the physical and economic difficulties of low-occupancy vehicle use and parking in some dense central areas, and congestion problems in some suburban subcenters. In some places, existing markets will decline because of continued erosion of the economic base of the central city, or because of

1. M. A. Kemp, C. T. Everett, and F. Spielberg, "The Prospects for Public Transportation in U.S. Cities," Project Report 3025-1 (Washington, D.C.: Urban Institute, 1982).

continued substitution of private automobiles for public modes where automobile travel offers relatively large travel time, convenience, or price advantages.

This gradual evolution of the demand structure for urban public transportation could be broadly regarded as "business as usual." In national aggregate it implies no sharp changes in the actual or potential patronage volumes for the more "formal" modes, with probably some growth in ridesharing for commuter travel. There will continue to be a relatively strong demand for scheduled line-haul transit services in the dense corridors of the largest cities. There also will continue to be political pressures for the construction of new line-haul facilities, particularly light rail lines and dedicated busways, in some of the newer, growing cities.

But this "minimal change" scenario on the demand side contrasts sharply with potential problems and constraints on the supply side. We observed earlier that governmental operating assistance for the transit industry increased in real terms throughout much of the 1970s at an annual compound rate of around 20 percent, and at a substantially higher rate in some of the largest cities. But the rate of growth in vehicle miles over the period was only about an eighth as great. It is difficult to believe that this situation can continue for much longer. For financial reasons, if for nothing else, the current situation is virtually certain to change.

In addition to doubts about the continued willingness or ability of society to pay for transit operations on today's scale, there is a growing need for major rehabilitation of the infrastructure of the rail systems in the largest U.S. cities. Dilapidation and deferred maintenance threaten the physical ability to maintain service levels, regardless of the availability of operating funds.

Already, over the last two or three years, rapidly increasing transit deficits have clashed with the willingness of state and local governments to foot the bill. It is ironic that the cities where the benefits of maintaining conventional line-haul services are the greatest—the older, more densely-developed cities of the northeast and midwest regions—are those least able to bear the costs, and it is in Boston, Chicago, New York, and Philadelphia that the financial problems have caused the sharpest and most publicized difficulties.

Two somewhat coincidental factors have added to the concern. Many systems have recently experienced drops in ridership ascribable to relatively large increases in fares, to increasing unemployment in major cities, and to stabilization in the price of gasoline and the unlikelihood of near-term petroleum shortages. Secondly, the Reagan administration has begun to reduce and reshape the federal government's financial support programs by gradually phasing out federal operating assistance and channeling capital assistance into rehabilitation and improvement of existing systems rather than encouraging further starts on new systems or extensions.

The most obvious policy responses to these problems are fare increases to improve the farebox recovery ratio, and supply cutbacks to eliminate the least productive services. The principal drawbacks of both actions are that traffic congestion could increase locally if there is significant diversion of transit patrons to lower-occupancy modes, and that the transit-dependent segment of society may be hurt disproportionately. A second major category of possible responses is that the reduction of government assistance could goad some productivity improvements in the transit industry. And the third broad type of response is a search for alternative, less expensive ways of providing urban public transportation services.

All three major types of response are already in evidence in various parts of the country. After a period of generally declining average fare levels (in real terms), fare increases are now becoming widespread. Service cutbacks have been made in a number of financially ailing systems. Radical changes intended to improve productivity are rare because of the power of transit labor, though in recent years there have been a number of cases of quite large systems facing down the unions over the right to hire part-time operators.

As to finding lower cost substitutes for conventional transit services, there have been a number of recent developments in various parts of the country:

- *Public agencies contracting for services from private operators at a lower cost than if provided by the public transit system.* Specific examples include using private taxicab firms to provide shared-ride demand-responsive services where the demand densities do not warrant fixed-route service (common in California, Michigan, and elsewhere); replacing fixed-route bus services by cab services (as in Norfolk and Phoenix); divesting the operating rights to particularly "unprofitable" fixed routes to private bus operators (as in Boston and London); and contracting with private bus and cab firms to operate peak-hour supplements to transit agency services in order to reduce the degree of supply peaking necessary by the transit agency (so-called "peak load shedding"). In some cases, individual jurisdictions in metropolitan areas (particularly in Kansas City, Minneapolis-St. Paul, and Washington, D.C.) have opted to use private bus companies to provide services in preference to the regional transit authority.

- *Amending the monopoly operating rights of transit authorities to allow competing services, perhaps on a route-by-route bidding basis.* Deregulation of entry to providing public transport or competitive bidding for rights could lead to a revival of jitney services (as in Miami and San Diego), or of private "route associations" such as exist in some New Jersey counties, for the San Juan publico system, and in several South American cities. San Diego, Portland, and Seattle have had limited taxicab entry deregulation in recent years.

- *Passenger groups organizing to charter subscription commuter services.* In response to major 1981 fare increases and service reductions in the Chicago region, long-distance suburban commuters organized to provide subscription services at a price below that offered by the Regional Transit Authority. The number of bus runs grew quite rapidly.

- *Active promotion of ridesharing by public agencies.* Evidence suggests that using public funds for starting and promoting ridesharing schemes may be one of the most cost-effective policies available in many cases. Governments or transit agencies can play a third-party role in the provision of ridesharing vehicles and management (as have Tidewater Transit and the Golden Gate Bridge, Highway, and Transportation District).

- *Vesting the subsidies in the users of the services rather than in the providers.* The social welfare goals for public transport can be achieved by "user-side subsidy" schemes, currently in use in West Virginia, New Jersey, Milwaukee, and elsewhere, whereby identified groups may buy reduced-price tickets, scrip, tokens, or "stamps" usable as cash toward travel on one or more services.

- *Fostering of private sector financing roles.* A number of private-sector groups (particularly various employers, and retail and service interests) have a financial interest in the availability of public transportation to employees and customers. Programs have been devised (transit pass subsidization, ridesharing schemes, joint promotions, and the like) to obtain private financial support for operating costs, and also for capital costs (joint development, value increment taxation, innovative forms of public/private bond financing, and so on).

These examples are probably the harbingers of developments that will be seen increasingly in U.S. cities over the next ten to fifteen years. Primarily spurred by the financial difficulty of maintaining existing services, they will obviously be influenced also by the positive or negative experiences of those communities that are the first to experiment with innovative services, institutional arrangements, and methods.

THE PROSPECTS FOR MORE COMPETITIVE
URBAN PUBLIC TRANSPORTATION SERVICES

The Main Arguments For and Against
More Competition

One characteristic of many of the productivity enhancement or service substitution policies is that they place a greater emphasis on the role of the private sector in financing or operating services than has been customary in recent years. This coincides, of course, with one of the general policy emphases of the Reagan administration, which means that such developments are likely to be encouraged by the federal government for philosophical reasons, at least over the remainder of his term. Measures that would lead to a greater degree of competition in urban public transportation service provision may, however, be completely antithetic to much local policy developed over the last two decades, in which service and fare "integration," interjurisdictional cooperation, and the "coordination" of services have been viewed as important objectives.[2]

Local governments have long exercised a regulatory role with respect to local common-carrier services; over the last twenty years, local, state, and federal governments have all become increasingly involved in providing financial assistance to the transit industry. With this assistance has come further regulation, effected indirectly by the

---

2. Michael Kemp and Carol T. Everett explore in greater detail the prospects for, and practicalities of, increased competition in "Toward Greater Competition in Urban Public Transportation," Project Report 3025–2 (Washington, D.C.: Urban Institute, 1982).

adoption of standards required for the receipt or use of the public funds. For instance, governments have compelled transit systems wishing to receive assistance to offer off-peak reduced fares to the elderly and handicapped, to carry out planning exercises of specified types, and to hold public hearings on certain policy decisions.

In two decades, the transit industry has largely been transformed from a privately owned, publicly regulated status to public owner-ship, and the restraints imposed by formal regulatory commissions have been replaced typically by the legal or political mandates of the various governments that own or subsidize each system. However, restrictions on entry of new providers of both scheduled, line-haul bus services and for-hire, demand-responsive services have been re-tained intact.

Two principal justifications have been given for continuing to restrain competition in this way. First, it is sometimes claimed that urban bus services still have some of the characteristics of a natural monopoly, and in particular, declining cost. But there is little ana-lytical evidence to support that contention. Most statistical studies of the costs of urban bus services in the United States and the United Kingdom show inadequate economies of scale to justify sanctioning a single service provider,[3] and Morlok and Viton's findings on transit wages (Chapter 6) suggest just the opposite.

Second, in defending their current status, transit properties pre-sent the classical argument of protected public utility monopolies: that since they bear relatively unprofitable public service require-ments, imposed upon them by their political masters, they should be protected from potential competitors who need not carry such a bur-den. In other words, internal cross-subsidization of different groups of patrons is deemed by local policymakers to be justifiable for social reasons, and any skimming of the most profitable (or least unprofit-able) market segments by competitors would erode the property's financial position. It would be very easy to undercut the established operator's costs by using unsafe and uninsured vehicles, by hiring nonunion labor, and by serving only limited markets and withdraw-ing from them should the market conditions change unfavorably. The transit property, unable to do any of these things, regards this as "unfair competition."

---

3. R. G. McGillivray, M. A. Kemp, and M. E. Beesley, "Urban Bus Transit Costing," Research Paper 1200-72-1 (Washington, D.C.: Urban Institute, 1980).

Proponents of greater competition argue in response that, first, it is not clear that the entry of new carriers, whose safety standards and financial responsibility could still be controlled by regulation, would necessarily injure the existing carrier financially. Because of a different cost structure, resulting mostly from different labor arrangements, the new entrants might find it most profitable to carry peak-hour riders, for instance, a time when most bus transit systems are losing the most money. Second, it is also not clear that requiring scheduled bus services to serve (and cross-subsidize) thin markets for social welfare reasons is the most cost-effective means by which local policymakers can fulfill their social objectives. Such alternatives as subsidized cab rides or promoting ridesharing may have a lower resource cost and may provide greater net benefits to the users.

An additional argument for entry controls—one heard more commonly in the case of taxicab services than for scheduled bus services—is that "destructive competition" may result from their relaxation. In such a case, the industry as a whole (or a majority of its firms) may be driven by competitive forces to operate at a loss for extended periods of time. However, there is little evidence in theory or practice that existing urban public transportation services (or those which might appear following a relaxation of entry regulations) are threatened by destructive competition.

Fare and service regulation are closely related to entry regulation. The primary reason for prescribing urban public transport fares, historically for the transit industry and up to the present for the privately owned taxicab industry, is to prevent the established carriers from making an "excessive" rate of return by virtue of their protected status. In a more competitive situation, the most compelling argument for regulating fares and service is the difficulty and the time and money cost to the traveler of discriminating between carriers, particularly for unscheduled forms of transportation.[4] This is

---

4. A version of this argument has been developed by Shreiber to justify fare regulation for the cruising taxicab market in New York City. See Chanoch Shreiber, "Economic Reasons for Price and Entry Regulation of Taxicabs," *Journal of Transport Economics and Policy* 9 (1975): 268–79; and idem., "Economic Reasons for Price and Entry Regulation of Taxicabs. A Rejoinder," *Journal of Transport Economics and Policy* 11 (1977): 298–304. Opposing views are presented by Richard B. Coffman in "Economic Reasons for Price and Entry Regulation of Taxicabs. A Comment," *Journal of Transport Economics and Policy* 11 (1977): 288–97; and by David J. Williams in "The Economic Reasons for Price and Entry Regulation of Taxicabs. A Comment," *Journal of Transport Economics and Policy* 14 (1980): 105–12.

a particular case of market failure due to imperfect information dissemination. If the first vehicle to come along offers the consumer an unacceptable fare or service level, it is difficult to judge the expected total cost (that is, waiting time and fare) involved in not taking that first vehicle. If the number of carrier firms is large (such as occurs with taxicabs operated by individual drivers leasing their vehicles, with no strong personal incentive to enhance the corporate identity of a larger firm or association), and if the congregation of vehicles and passengers at specific places or times is relatively rare, then there will be little incentive for the carriers to compete over price and service. Fare "gouging" may be practiced with relative immunity by dishonest drivers.[5] But these anticompetitive conditions would break down for scheduled services, for vehicles hailed by telephone or hired from a rank, or when uniform service and fare levels could be associated with reasonably large fleets of vehicles.

It is difficult to resolve some of the questions raised by the prospect of more competitive urban public transportation because the recent experience is so limited. In North America, there are only isolated examples of competitive services. Reference to earlier periods, particularly to the "jitney craze" years from 1914, is open to the objection that the world has changed substantially since then, particularly as regards the structure of metropolitan areas, the levels of private automobile ownership and use, and the public's disposable income, aspirations, and tastes. Similarly, most of the current-day experience of competitive services comes from third world cities, where economic conditions may differ sharply from those in the United States.

A special case can be made for maintaining public ownership and operation of the fixed-guideway transit modes.[6] It is difficult for technological reasons to conceive of ways in which these services could be operated more competitively, and they show more of the characteristics suitable for a regulated monopoly. This is not to say

---

5. It is for considerations like these that, after reviewing taxicab regulation and recommending the abolition of entry controls, Kirby et al. see some virtue in retaining loose price regulation for cabs. See R. F. Kirby, K. U. Bhatt, M. A. Kemp, R. G. McGillivray, and M. Wohl, *Para-Transit: Neglected Options for Urban Mobility* (Washington, D.C.: Urban Transit, 1975).

6. Commuter rail apart (since commuter rail data are not usually included in the transit industry statistics), these services accounted for roughly 30 percent of the nation's transit patronage in 1980.

that they need necessarily be publicly owned and operated, as Chicago's privately run commuter rail systems show, but in practice they will probably remain so.[7]

The Likely Outcomes of More Competition in Road-Based Services

For conventional scheduled bus services, however, one can think of several ways in which greater competition might be introduced, reflecting a spectrum of possibilities for relaxing entry controls. Similarly, there is a range of extents to which entry to demand-responsive, for-hire markets might be liberalized. Some of the expected characteristics of more competitive market conditions are:

- A larger number of vehicles would provide public transport services, with a greater variety of vehicle types and sizes than is currently customary. On average, the vehicles operating fixed-route services would be smaller than current buses and would operate more frequently.

- The costs of service provision would be lower on average, largely because of a weakening of the power of organized labor and the introduction of more flexible crewing arrangements. Fares to passengers may be higher or lower than at present, depending on the nature and size of any public subsidies to the industry.

- There would be less centralization in the ownership and management of vehicles, with (depending on the nature of the entry deregulation) a larger number of individual owner-drivers.

- Current distinctions between service types would grow more blurred, and the margin between "public" and "private" services would also become more indistinct if entrepreneurial opportunities exist to service private ridesharing arrangements. The traditional functional distinctions between bus enterprises serving different markets—interurban services, charter services, school services, and the like—would tend to break down.

7. A number of observers, however, have recommended transferring the New York City subway system to private ownership. See James B. Ramsey, "Selling the Subways in New York: Wild-Eyed Radicalism or the Only Feasible Solution?" (New York: New York University, C. V. Starr Center for Applied Economics, 1981); and Peter Samuel, "Unload the Subways," *Reason* 14 (1982): 23–32.

- Carriers would probably contract more with specialist firms to perform functions which currently are provided "in-house" in most transit properties; maintenance, scheduling, and public information services are examples.

- The effects on service quality as experienced by the traveling public would be mixed, depending on the extent to which the currently provided services can be economically justified. As a general principle, the wide variance in the financial performance of different bus routes, quite common in most bus systems, would be greatly reduced.

- There is likely to be increased risk of some service disruptions because of bankruptcy or other financial problems, deferred maintenance, and poor management. If a large number of small carriers were to result, enforcement of safety, financial responsibility, and minimum service quality regulations could present problems.

- If increased competition resulted in more smaller vehicles being used to replace existing bus services, the associated road congestion, fuel consumption, and noxious emissions could increase detrimentally in some specific locations.

- There would probably be a greater use of user-side subsidies as a mechanism for any government support.

Local Moves Toward Increased Competition

The uncertainties surrounding these effects will probably preclude any dramatic local policy shifts toward more competitive conditions. A slow process is more likely, whereby the formal or informal barriers to entry continue to be eroded in a gradual way, and new market niches are created for private sector operations and financing. While this process will be driven by a number of factors, chief among them will be the financial crunch facing the transit properties. There may be some isolated deregulation moves for political philosophy or legal reasons: Arizona deregulated all surface transportation in mid-1982, for instance, and Santa Barbara liberalized taxi entry in response to the U.S. Supreme Court's 1982 *City of Boulder* decision.[8]

8. In *Community Communications Co. v. City of Boulder, Colorado* (455 U.S. 40), the court held that municipalities may be deemed to violate antitrust laws in their market regulation activities.

But under most circumstances except for pressing financial threats to the survival of the transit system, the political risks of destroying the existing market infrastructure will be thought to be too great to justify a major reshaping of supply.

There have been several recent examples of changes consistent with a gradual move towards greater competition, and which may become common in coming years:

- The divesting of operating rights on one suburban route to a private company by the Massachusetts Bay Transportation Authority, and the serious consideration currently being given to similar abrogations of monopoly rights for other routes in Boston, St. Louis, and Los Angeles. It should be noted that the authority for the MBTA's action was gained in state legislation passed as part of a package negotiated when the state saved the authority from "bankruptcy" in 1980.

- Suburban jurisdictions opting to buy stage bus services from private operators (as happened in the Kansas City metropolitan area) or to provide them directly (as with Montgomery County, Maryland, in the Washington, D.C., suburbs) in preference to buying more expensive services from the regional authority.

- The rapid growth of rider-initiated subscription bus services for suburban-to-downtown commuting in the Chicago metropolitan area, in response to 1981 fare increases and perceived service deficiencies (see Chapter 3).

- The liberalization of taxicab entry (and in some cases pricing) regulations in Portland (Oregon), San Diego, and Seattle.

Several other gradual steps could be taken in the direction of increased competition. One is to identify those bus routes regarded as chronic lossmakers and are operated only as a public service, and to invite proposals from private contractors to provide services on the routes, either competitively or under an exclusive franchise. Minimal constraints should be specified for such proposals, leaving it open to the bidders to specify the conditions of subsidy and competition under which they would be prepared to operate, the level of service to be provided, and the types of vehicle to be used. This sort of divestiture can benefit the local governments by reducing (or eliminating) the operating assistance requirement for the routes, and it could also improve the financial position of the publicly owned carrier.[9]

A second form of divestiture of especially unprofitable services is so-called "peak-load shedding." This concept assumes that it is uneconomic to design the publicly owned bus system to carry the largest peak-hour loads, particularly given the high marginal labor cost during the peak deriving from typical work rules. Considerable cost savings could accrue from providing less peak-hour service and allowing supplemental carriers into the market, under specific conditions, to help move the peak-hour loads. Some form of bidding and regulatory procedure would need to be developed. Oram has explored the possibilities of using supplemental carriers, and he argues that they can be used in ways which do not necessarily threaten the core system.[10]

Both of these methods have the advantage of being in the interests of the local governments, the transit agency, and the patrons. The only major interest group which stands to lose is transit labor, through possible reductions in the number of existing jobs within the publicly owned system and a dilution of their power over supply. Whether service bidding schemes would be more difficult to implement than, say, the hiring of part-time drivers (for which a number of large systems have successfully negotiated in recent years) is difficult to judge. There is the possibility of such schemes being judged by the courts to contravene Section 13(c) of the federal Urban Mass Transportation Act.

Similarly, a transit property may itself reduce the costs of serving low-density markets by, for instance, subcontracting with taxicab firms to provide feeder or other shared-ride demand-responsive services, or encouraging vanpooling and other ridesharing efforts. The transit system can even enter the market as a third-party provider of vanpooling services, as has been done by Tidewater Transit.

Another form of increased competition implying minimal change to the existing institutions in certain areas would be to encourage separate publicly owned carriers to compete among themselves, prin-

9. A route-by-route bidding system has been developed, with particular reference to major Connecticut cities, by Roger W. Schmenner in *Operating Subsidies for Buses: The Case of Connecticut* (Washington, D.C.: Department of Transportation, Program of University Research, 1974).

10. Richard L. Oram, "Peak-Period Supplements: The Contemporary Economics in the UK and USA," *Progress in Planning* 12 (1979): 81–154.

cipally by fare and service level discrimination. A probable prerequisite for this is that there not be a single metropolitanwide operating agency in existence, for even where a unitary agency is buying services from a number of different carriers rather than operating them directly, it seems politically unlikely that it would purchase parallel services. Such an agency has been created in many cities, and some thought might be given to splitting it up into smaller components.

Other "first step" options can focus on taxicab rather than on transit services. During the 1970s shared-ride taxicab services grew more common, spurred in part by UMTA's de facto determination that shared-ride (but not exclusive-ride) services can qualify under the federal subsidy program. But in most cities, taxicabs are still prohibited from providing shared-ride services. Kirby et al. recommend a substantial relaxation of taxicab entry and service regulations, and outline several possible means of reducing entry controls while minimizing the impact of the inevitable financial loss to the holders of high-valued medallions.[11] Since 1975 there has been some movement in this direction, enough at least to indicate that the liberalization of entry and fare-setting may be politically feasible under favorable circumstances. There has been less movement towards the formal sanctioning of jitney services on specified routes, although an open-entry shared-ride cab system (such as in Washington, D.C.) can effectively provide the same service, particularly if limits are removed on allowable vehicle sizes.

Beyond these relatively modest options, moves towards greater competition are likely to require more decisive and more visible actions by local governments, particularly with regard to opening up routes to competition among the better financial performers. This does not seem to be a likely development in the near term, except under very special circumstances created either by particular local conditions or by extreme financial pressures. In those cities in other parts of the world which appear to have made the most radical regulatory changes, there have been mitigating circumstances to "justify" the moves: in Hong Kong, the 1969 legalization of public light buses simply gave official approval to a system that had existed illegally for some time (cf. the New York City gypsy cabs and Pittsburgh jitneys): in Kuala Lumpur, the Malaysian government permitted the introduction of minibuses in 1975 to add public transport capacity in prepa-

11. Kirby et al., *Para-Transit.*

ration for a proposed area licensing scheme of road pricing (that has yet to be introduced).

SOME BROAD DIRECTIONS FOR FEDERAL POLICY

While urban public transport planning and management decisions are best made at the local level, financial assistance for the services comes in part from higher tiers of government. This is because of such considerations as interjurisdictional tax competition, possible state and national benefits, and economies of scale in tax collection and administration. But a key problem with the provision of funds from the higher tiers is that it can seriously distort the incentives of the local decisionmakers. Difficulties arise because of the categorical structure of the assistance programs, the ways in which the funds are allocated among areas, and the strings attached to the receipt of the monies.

Since federal money is easier to acquire for capital projects than for operations, for instance, this encourages overcapitalization and the premature replacement of capital assets. Dissatisfactions arise over the "fairness" of discretionary and formula allocation procedures. Local decisionmakers feel unduly constrained by such aspects of the federal program as the "Buy America" provision, the requirements to accommodate the elderly and handicapped, the Section 13(c) labor protection clause, and the transaction costs of dealing with the federal bureaucracy. And despite attempts in the federal statutes to protect the interests of unsubsidized private sector carriers, certain provisions of the federal program are seen as unfair competition by taxicab and charter bus interests.

There will not be a single, universal remedy for the likely urban public transport problems of the eighties and nineties. Conventional transit services, the focus of public attention in addressing the urban transportation ills of the sixties and seventies, will probably not be the most economic response to many of this decade's challenges: alleviating localized suburban congestion, increasing the mobility of transportation-disadvantaged groups, and improving transportation fuel efficiency. In many cases, these problems will call for paratransit services tailored closely to the specific demand conditions of the service area. The federal program needs at least to permit, and perhaps to encourage, local decisionmakers to consider a wider range of service forms and carriers than has been customary.

Conditions forecast for the supply side also support changes in the federal assistance program. The projected reduction in the rate of growth of public sector assistance and the burgeoning infrastructure problems of the largest systems make it increasingly important that incentives not exist to overcapitalize or to defer maintenance. Federal, state, and local assistance programs will need to encourage more efficient decisionmaking with respect to capital and operating expenses, service policies, and fare-setting.

A simple and equitable remedy to some of the current problems would be, in general terms, to:

- remove the categorical basis of the assistance program, so that major distinctions are no longer drawn between capital and operating assistance;

- allocate the funds primarily as a matching program, so that federal dollars are used to match and reinforce state and local spending decisions, rather than to drive them; and

- thereby shift a greater responsibility for decisions about investment and operations to the local level.[12]

By comparison with the existing program and some other changes that have been given serious consideration in recent years, this proposal would have several advantages:

- it would eliminate the distortive incentives to overcapitalize and undermaintain;

- it would require no expensive administrative mechanism, and in particular, allocations would not be based on such malleable and difficult-to-audit statistics as vehicle miles; and

- it would improve the ability of local decisionmakers to plan ahead, since the level of federal assistance in future years would be more easily predictable.

In that a distinction would no longer be drawn between federal capital and operating assistance, the proposal can be regarded as a

---

12. Gerald K. Miller and Ronald F. Kirby, "A Matching Procedure for Allocating Public Transportation Assistance," Research Paper 1430-2 (Washington, D.C.: Urban Institute, 1981).

"block grant" urban public transportation scheme. There would no longer be an incentive to "capitalize" maintenance, since the share of federal dollars would not differ between the various uses of the funds. A community's total federal entitlement would be based solely on the total state and local commitments to public transportation. The incentives to opt for capital projects over operating projects, or to keep fares artificially low largely at the expense of higher tiers of government, would be removed.

Under this scheme the current federal Section 3, Section 9, and Section 16(b)(2) programs would be combined into a single funding pool. Local communities could draw assistance from this pool in proportion to the total state and local spending on authorized services. This local revenue base would include all state and local government expenditures on public transportation within the community— whether financed from hypothecated taxes, general revenues, or annualized bond revenues—together possibly with any local private sector expenditures on public transportation services. Both provider-side and user-side subsidies from state and local funds would be counted. Farebox revenues would also be included to ensure that no financial incentives exist for lowering fares.

The federal government would need to define the precise scope of eligible local commitments. This scope should be as wide as possible to permit maximum local flexibility in tailoring services and service providers to the local demand characteristics.[13] So, for instance, along with spending on conventional bus and rail services, one would also count local highway expenditures with a strong public transportation component (for such projects as currently qualify under Sections 142 and 146 of the Federal-aid Highway laws, say), and paratransit services such as demand-responsive and ridesharing modes. The federal payment might be calculated on the previous year's local base, or else it might be aligned to the current year through a system of budget estimates and subsequent adjustments.

Either a single nationwide matching ratio could be determined, or perhaps more realistically, different matching ratios could be applied to different groupings of communities, most likely classified by city size. On the basis of very imprecise calculations of public transportation expenditures in recent years, the overall average federal share of

---

13. Only local governments should be eligible for designation as the ultimate recipients of federal funds, and not regional authorities or transit operating agencies, in order to encourage full consideration of all the service possibilities.

total spending would be around 30 percent if the federal program were to remain at its 1982 level. Adjustments would be made from year to year to reflect slight variations in the ratio of federal appropriations projections and state and local commitments (the historical evidence suggests that such adjustments would be small); more major changes might be necessary to reflect trends in the overall size of the federal program. But the federal funding levels for each city would be reasonably predictable, over, say, a five-year time horizon.

Since a community's share would be based on monetary amounts alone, the auditing task should be significantly simpler and less open to abuse than if allocations were based on such system-descriptive statistics as vehicle miles, passenger counts, or passenger miles. Such measures have been included in the new Section 9 formula, but the necessary data are more difficult to verify independently than are dollar flows. And inclusion of particular factors can create some perverse incentives for grantees: a vehicle-miles factor might encourage the operation of express buses in inappropriate situations.[14] Overall, the total administrative costs of the program (borne both by UMTA and local agencies) should be considerably less than that of the current program.

These suggested revisions to the UMTA assistance program tend to encourage more competition in that localities would have greater freedom of choice in spending their funds. The federal government could also attach standards to the receipt of federal assistance, perhaps along the lines of Senator Hayakawa's 1978 bill to preclude aid to localities without an acceptable measure of open entry for taxicab services. But on balance, using standards of this sort may be unwise. The various strings attached to federal money have often encouraged perverse outcomes, and revision of the program should seek to reduce the number and severity of the standards, not add to them.

If the federal government wished to promote more competition, it would be preferable to underwrite demonstrations of local regulatory revisions that create more competitive outcomes. Experience has shown, however, that such ambitious demonstrations are usually only feasible if the initiative and will to embark on them are sparked at the local level rather than "sold" from the federal level. The fed-

---

14. Michael A. Kemp discusses such effects in "Grant Allocation and the Standardization of Public Transport Service in Dutch Cities," in Jackie Garden and Erik MacKinlay, eds., *Service Levels of Urban Public Transport*, vol. 2, *Report of a Round Table Meeting* (Den Haag, Netherlands: Ministerie van Verkeer en Waterstaat, 1980).

eral government can act as a diffuser of good ideas and offer to stand ready with adequate financial assistance to help (or even indemnify) any local areas willing to try them, but the momentum to tackle the formidable political and logistical problems must be locally generated.

CONCLUSION

The administrative and regulatory environment for mass transportation in the United States is presently not very conducive to greater competition and private sector involvement. Local regulatory practices and federal funding procedures have encouraged government ownership of transit systems and have restricted entry, services, and prices for paratransit services. These practices are so common and have been in place for so long that any changes to encourage more competition will be difficult to accomplish.

Nevertheless, there have been several examples over recent years of increased private sector involvement in urban public transport. Entry and price controls on taxicabs have been relaxed somewhat in San Diego; suburban jurisdictions are contracting with privately operated bus services in Kansas City; rider-initiated subscription bus services have expanded in Chicago; and vanpools and contract taxi services are being operated by the transit agency in Tidewater Virginia. While these examples demonstrate that substantial benefits can be achieved through an expanded private sector role, the administrative and regulatory changes required have not been easy to accomplish.

The federal urban mass transportation program continues to encourage publicly owned, capital-intensive, line-haul transit systems over privately operated services. With the passage of the 1982 Surface Transportation Assistance Act, the prospects for further structural change in the UMTA program are not good for the immediate future. However, since the overall level of federal funding appears to be declining in real terms, the influence of the federal program on local decisionmaking may not be as great as in the past. The level of urban mass transit that can be supported through current and projected levels of federal funding certainly falls far short of the potential demand for service, with the result that pressures for greater unsubsidized private sector involvement may continue to grow.

Dramatic shifts in administrative and regulatory policies to encourage a more competitive environment seem unlikely at present. Gradual reduction of the monopoly rights of transit properties are more possible, however, as local officials seek ways to increase service levels without additional public financing. Growing cities like Dallas and Houston also may be forced to relax restrictions on taxicab and other paratransit services, in order to respond to growing user demand. In most cities, however, substantial benefits will have to be demonstrated for greater competition and private sector involvement to overcome the strong advocates and long history of current administrative and regulatory restrictions.

Chapter 13

IMPLICATIONS OF EFFICIENCY INCENTIVES ON USE OF PRIVATE SECTOR CONTRACTING BY THE PUBLIC TRANSIT INDUSTRY

Anthony U. Simpson

INTRODUCTION AND SUMMARY

This chapter discusses the use of private sector contracting to advance efficiency in public transit in the 1980s. After participating as a principal in over a hundred public/private transit operations during the last fifteen years, I am convinced that long-term success for private sector contractors rests entirely upon their ability to demonstrate that they can help the public sector carry out its mission. Utilizing the private sector is beneficial and feasible:

1. A changing political climate in the 1980s is placing more emphasis on transit efficiency (for example, lower cost per unit of service) and less on effectiveness (for example, route coverage to population). If this is true, then
2. Efficiency can be improved by setting quantitative efficiency objectives for a manager and by providing generous rewards to assure achievement of those objectives. If such incentives are implemented by a transit board, then
3. A fast, simple way for public transit managers to make significant gains in efficiency is to contract appropriate portions of transit operations—such as low-efficiency, high-cost operations that cannot be abandoned—to the private sector.

On the surface, this may seem simplistic. But these concepts, properly executed, can effect substantial improvements in transit efficiency. Yet they have not been widely used.

A key reason for their unpopularity is that transit boards often set policies that directly, albeit unintentionally, create inefficiency. One example is the tendency to serve as many people as possible, even if this means low productivity in suburban areas.

Furthermore, from this chapter's perspective, a key policy question concerns the financial and political rewards paid to transit managers. These rewards are normally set by the transit board based on two principal criteria: the number of employees managed and the base wage rates paid to the drivers. Increases in organizational size or in the salaries of subordinate personnel will normally cause the manager's own salary to be raised at some later date. Thus, transit managers are asked to battle increased costs, yet they tend to accrue most rewards when they lose this fight. In fact, managers who improve efficiency through such tactics as contracting with the private sector, cutting organizational size, or keeping labor costs down can expect a lower reward relative to their peers over a period of time.

When transit boards set such incentives, is it any wonder that for many years transit costs have continually gone up, and that transit service value per dollar (even after adjustments for inflation and cost of living) has steadily declined?

This chapter will develop these issues further and suggest better ways to align managers' incentives with public transit objectives. But first, a detour is necessary to clarify the problem's background and terminology.

CHANGE OF EMPHASIS FROM EFFECTIVENESS TO EFFICIENCY

The words *effective* and *efficient* are the cause of much confusion, because they are casually assumed to be synonymous, whereas they really mean completely different things. Professor G. J. Fielding has defined them, in the context of transit, as follows:

- Effectiveness means *doing the right things*, for example, putting transit service where it will accomplish the goals we set. It means responding to society's goals, such as the reduction of traffic congestion or universal service.

- Efficiency means *doing things right.* It is getting the most performance for the dollar, the lowest cost per service-hour.[1]

These concepts can be combined into sophisticated performance measures, and quantitative comparisons of transit efficiency and effectiveness can be made based on Section 15 of the Urban Mass Transportation Act of 1964 or other data.[2]

During the 1970s, governing boards were primarily influenced by social needs, and thus emphasized the effectiveness of objectives. As a direct consequence of this bias, for example, the miles of route more than *doubled* nationally between 1970 and 1980, whereas the vehicle miles operated increased by only *11 percent.* Service expansion was given priority over increased service on the high productivity routes. In many inner city areas where transit was most efficient, frequency of service was actually reduced so as to extend service into the suburbs.

The present federal administration is attempting to eliminate the operating subsidies that made this emphasis on effectiveness possible. Though the administration's wish may not be fulfilled, it does represent a grassroots trend toward fiscal economy. Public transit advocates can expect a long, hard battle to retain subsidies in the face of competition for public funds from the swelling expenditures for retired persons, national defense, maintenance of public infrastructure including roads and bridges, and advanced medical research implementation. As these competing forces collide in the voting booths, the governing transit bodies will be compelled to get more for the available dollar; they will tend to set more efficiency objectives for transit management.

There will be some resistance to these changes. Many public transit organizations formed in the late 1960s and 1970s on effectiveness objectives will not find it easy to make a quick turnaround to efficiency objectives. There are substantial legal, contractual, and psychological resistance factors that will make any change slow and

1. Gordon J. Fielding, "Changing Objectives for American Transit," July 1982. (Unpublished, University of California at Irvine, UCI–ITS–SP–82–5.)

2. Gordon J. Fielding and S. C. Anderson, "Public Transit Performance Evaluation: Application to Section 15 Data." (Paper presented to the Transportation Research Board, January 1983.)

painful. Many public transit organizations have stabilized. Multi-year labor agreements exist. Comprehensive systems have been established to control all operations and assure effective service. These combine to create an organizational inertia resistant to the use of private sector contracting options.

Nevertheless, private sector contracting offers public transit managers one fast, feasible method to effect some of the changes their governing boards are starting to demand. Contracting can be used, for example, on peak-hour express services and low-patronage routes, where political effectiveness constraints still prevent cutback or abandonment—even though the benefits of such service have become questionable in the light of new efficiency objectives.[3] Private sector contracting is a powerful means to solve some of these dilemmas in a timely manner, but for it to be applied, appropriate public transit management objectives and reward prerequisites must be in place.

MANAGEMENT OBJECTIVES AND REWARDS

Organization theorist Peter Drucker argues that, in order for anything to happen, all of the people involved must see some personal benefit from the action.[4] The transit board perceives increased efficiency, and hence lowered costs, as an obvious benefit because of its sense of public responsibility. The opportunity to increase business is an evident benefit for the private sector. But the methods by which the transit board's objectives can be accomplished are not as clear to the transit managers, nor are the rewards at all obvious. This lack of clear management objectives and rewards warrants careful consideration.

Research into the factors that cause management and employees to reach peak efficiency within organizations has shown that certain elements are almost invariably present:

1. A clear statement of long-range strategic objectives and organizational mission prepared by top management with direct board

---

3. Wendell Cox, "Equity and Efficiency in Urban and Suburban Mobility." (Paper presented at the Annual Conference of the American Public Transit Association, Chicago, Illinois, October 10, 1981.)

4. Peter F. Drucker, *Management: Tasks, Responsibilities, Practices* (New York: Harper and Row, 1973).

participation. Outsiders can help to guide the planning process, but insiders must construct the plan.[5]

2. A negotiated agreement between the board and top management for specific quantitative objectives to be achieved by a specified date. A simple, incomplete example is: "By June 30, 198X, reduce the average systemwide cost per vehicle-mile by 3 percent." Such objectives should leave the methods for their achievement up to management and must not be unilaterally imposed by the board. They must have top management's support, or they will not work.

3. A reward system that ensures convergence between personal benefits and the organization's objectives. This is, perhaps, the greatest deficiency in current management practice, not just in transit, but throughout industry. If employees' work objectives are substantially different from organizational objectives—and they often are, to an astonishing degree—then neither the organization nor the employees can achieve their full potential for success. This principle is obvious and has been reiterated through recorded history. The recent success of Japanese industry has been attributed to its various techniques for making employees feel that they participate in decisions, and that the company's success is their success. But, elsewhere, apathy and inadequate leadership often prevail, ignoring or paying only lip service to this fundamental management principle.

4. Rewards that are negotiated concurrently with the objectives. For example, if a cost reduction of over 3 percent is the objective, then it might further be agreed that "10 percent of the first year's savings and 5 percent of the second year's savings will be an earned incentive to be distributed to the first two levels of management, in proportion to their base salary."

This type of simple management by objectives (MBO) certainly works. Professional managers should, in fact, be prepared to accept a slightly lower base salary with a substantial upside in the MBO portion of their compensation package—for example, 10 to 30 percent—contingent on their performance as measured against a set of quantitative criteria. Rewards should be individually tailored to the desires

5. American Management Associations, "The Management Course for Presidents" course materials, 1984.

and needs of each particular manager. Each manager should be asked what rewards he or she really wants: for some managers, nonfinancial incentives are more important.

MBO can be extended to employees throughout a public or private transit organization, including nonsupervisory personnel and union and non-union employees. Many public transit organizations already have some MBO features. Examples include driver bonuses for safety, on-time attendance, passenger-written commendations, and ratio of service hours to total pay hours. In the private sector, MBO and convergence of corporate and personal objectives can be taken further through employee stock ownership programs, and employees can even vote their shares to elect directors to the board (especially in states that mandate cumulative stock voting rights). Note that this chapter refers to the simple type of MBO, where a brief written understanding is reached about what the subordinate will receive upon attainment of specified objectives by a specified date. I am not endorsing the type of massive MBO structures that some organizations have tried to implement, and which have often collapsed under their own complexity. (MBO and methods for employee participation in company governance are fascinating topics, but further discussion is beyond the scope of this chapter.)

Public transit managers are like senior managers anywhere. They tend to have dominant, self-confident personalities and are comfortable with the opportunity to run a more efficient operation. They are motivated by the ability to effect and control events to achieve specified goals. They sometimes feel uncomfortable with private sector contracting because of their concern over the degree of control they can maintain. They respond well to a fair challenge with a fair reward. Most transit boards, however, set qualitative effectiveness objectives for their managers and do not reward them for success or failure, other than by normal salary adjustments. In fact, where effectiveness objectives prevail, managers' salaries are usually tied to the size of the organization, which creates negative reinforcement for increases in efficiency, such as private sector contracting. Exceptional efficiency performance is not given exceptional reward. Such board policies promote a "don't rock the boat" management style, frustrate energetic managers, and have contributed substantially to the present status of transit inefficiency.

There is concern on some boards that substantial management incentives may expose public transit organizations to criticism. In the private sector, possible stockholder concern over any perceived over-compensation is easily avoided by taking senior management's performance incentives from profits – no profits, no incentives.

In the public sector, senior management's financial incentives should come from a percentage of clearly identifiable savings that they have created – *no savings, no incentives*. The incentive awards need only be a small proportion of total transit cost savings, but will represent major reward and performance reinforcement to the manager. A board should not be alarmed if managers who achieve exceptional results take home big bonuses – for instance, equal to half their annual salary – because the savings realized by the organization will be perhaps ten to a hundred times as great. A transit board is in a safe, even enviable, position when it can be shown that their enlightened management policies have resulted in large cost savings. A declining percent-of-savings formula, or even an overall incentive cap, may be advisable, however, in large transit organizations if really big amounts of money could be distributed as the result of a miscalculation.

Good incentive plans are not easy to develop. All too frequently, the true objectives and the incentives are not properly thought out or aligned. Certainly, cost savings cannot be the only criteria; other factors such as ridership levels must be considered as reflections of the quality and value of a service. Plans must be scrutinized from many angles, and someone must play the devil's advocate to assure that maximizing the incentive will not yield an undesirable result. Moreover, the plan must outline an absolute minimum of criteria, so it is easily understandable. It is usually best to lay out the incentive program as a table or formula, and to make simulations with test numbers in advance to see in what ranges the resulting incentives will fall.

Furthermore, incentive plans in the public sector must lay out a binding legal obligation for payment. Incentives must be explicitly defined using objective, measurable factors to show the basis upon which the incentive is earned. Subjective, discretionary, or retroactive rewards might be misinterpreted as gifts of public funds, which are not normally allowed in a public organization.[6]

---

6. Kenneth R. Smart, Jr., Private communication to Rourke and Woodruff, Attorneys, Santa Ana, California, August 1983.

Of course, these are standard modern management principles; we have all heard them before. But the difference between an organization that excels and one that doesn't is that *the excellent organization takes prompt action, with initiation at the top, that is, by the board.*[7]

PUBLIC TRANSIT MANAGEMENT'S
PRIVATE CONTRACTING OPTION

Some public transit organizations already have some arrangements for contracting with private sector operators. Specialized services for elderly and handicapped persons are sometimes contracted to private bus or taxi operators. Occasionally, an outlying area is served by a private bus company under contract to a public agency. It is generally found that private operators provide these services at about 60 percent of what it would have cost for the public agency to do so. The difference in cost is due primarily to more efficient work rules, lower wages, and lower overhead in the private sector.

Contracting is by no means a panacea for transit efficiency. Rather, it is one of a number of efficiency options available to public transit boards and managers. In general, the transit work suitable for private sector contracting should be relatively independent from main public transit operations, to minimize schedule interfaces and service coordination between portions serviced by separate organizations. Simply creating a credible, competitively priced, private sector option (even if it is not fully exercised) gives management significant leverage to control costs within the organization.

PUBLIC TRANSIT'S CONTROL OF
THE PRIVATE CONTRACTOR

In a public transit organization, financial decisions are tied to budgets—if you spend within your budget, all is usually well. In a private company, on the other hand, budgets are only a planning tool, and a key objective is to come in below budget. The private contractor

7. Thomas J. Peters and Robert H. Waterman, *In Search of Excellence* (New York: Harper and Row, 1982), ch. 5.

has to make a profit to stay in business and to pay for the cost of capital and risk, yet some public transit officials resent a contractor making profits. Such a fundamental difference in attitudes frequently causes misunderstandings between public transit and private companies.

The private operator is motivated by profit, so the contract for services must tie the contractor's potential income to public transit's performance objectives. This seems obvious, so it is surprising that most contract formats do not do this adequately. And even a good contract cannot ensure satisfactory performance from a badly managed private company. Consequently, it is necessary that contracts be awarded on the basis of maximum value for the dollar—that is, contractor competence as well as low cost.[8] Some examples of contract guidelines that can save a public transit organization from subsequent problems, high costs, and embarrassment are:

1. Pricing should include a fixed rate (per month) and a variable rate (per service hour), so that service can be added or deleted without price renegotiation. This avoids the risk that the contractor may make excessive renegotiation demands.
2. The contractor should keep the fares as part of the contract price, so the contractor has an incentive to market service and increase ridership. Moreover, it is the contractor who will suffer if there is poor security of fare receipts.
3. Establishing two separate contracts, one for operations and one for vehicle lease, has major benefits. With this contingency planning by the public transit agency, the operations contractor can be controlled, even terminated and replaced, without loss of vehicle availability for a replacement contractor. It is also best to have the term of the lease contract much longer (for example, five years) than the operations contract. This will minimize the price that has to be charged for vehicle depreciation costs without obligating the transit agency to excessively long operations contracts.

8. San Diego County Department of Public Works, "Request for Proposals for Management and Operation of Public Transportation Services Primary Suburban Bus Service of County Transit System," prepared by Rudy J. Massman, February 1983; San Mateo County Transit District, "Contract Documents and Specifications of the Mobility Impaired Redi-Wheels Program," Bid. No. 104, April 1982; "Martinez/Pleasant Hill (CA) Joint Facilities Authority Request for Proposal," Martinez and Pleasant Hill, California, March 15, 1983.

4. Define measurable performance criteria, such as percentage of missed trips, air conditioning availability, complaint versus praise frequency from independent riders, on-schedule performance, road-call frequency, and so on. Make part of the contractor's compensation an incentive based on the degree of achievement of such criteria. This creates an objective-oriented contract environment that can go a long way towards reinforcing the desired performance.[9] Data on performance should be obtained by random unannounced sampling wherever appropriate, rather than incur the excessive cost of 100 percent data capture.

5. Bids should be evaluated using independent, signed score sheets from each member of the evaluation committee. Score sheets should be prepared with weighted categories, documented in the proposal, such as: price, management quality, performance record, training program, efficiency incentives, safety record, financial stability, accident and general liability insurance (to at least equal the level of the public agency), and references. This insures that an inferior contractor cannot "lowball" a bid.

6. The evaluation should include the contractor's documented internal MBO program. Does it allocate employee rewards on the basis of achieving the contractual obligations and the public transit organization's objectives, or does it emphasize maximizing the contractor's own short-term profits? (If the policies are unwritten, it probably means the company's culture is oriented to short-term profit.)

Public transit agencies are constrained under section 13c of the UMTA Act, and some have further yielded part of their authority to contract with the private sector in order to gain labor concessions.[10] It is naïve to ignore or minimize these issues, but a discussion of the complex ramifications of 13c are beyond the scope of this chapter. A positive view of the legislation, however, shows that section 3e and other legislation creates offsetting and unused authority to contract with the private sector. Moreover, the apparent constraints of 13c can often be overcome by negotiation, planning, and attrition. For a motivated and determined public transit organization, contracting

9. UMTA, "Transit Management Incentive Contracts: Development Guide for Local Transit Agencies," Contract DTUM60-81-C-72091, May 1983. (Unpublished.)

10. N.W. Hamilton and P.R. Hamilton, *Governance of Public Enterprise* (Lexington, Mass.: Lexington Books, 1981), p. 34.

some appropriate operations to the private sector is an available, viable option. This is substantiated by the fact that a number of public transit agencies already do so despite 13c constraints.

CONCLUSIONS AND RECOMMENDATIONS

Although contracting with private operators could make substantial improvements in transit operating efficiency, it is not widely used because it generally goes against transit managers' financial incentives, the transit organization's inertia, and the preference for direct control of all operations. But the grassroots movement for greater efficiency in public organizations appears to be gaining momentum. If the public wants cost reduction through increased transit efficiency, and if the governing board wants to reflect public desires, then the board can quickly achieve these results by negotiating appropriate efficiency objectives and incentives with their top management. Management, in turn, can achieve these efficiency objectives through a variety of approaches, including contracting their least efficient services to private sector operators.

The essential direction and initiating energy must come from the governing boards. Only they have the power to mandate policies that can lead to efficiency improvements for better use of public funds.

Chapter 14

THE PRIVATE CHALLENGE TO PUBLIC TRANSPORTATION

C. Kenneth Orski

INTRODUCTION

Although, historically, the private sector was the principal sponsor, financier, and operator of mass transportation, it largely abandoned this role during the last twenty years. By the early 1970s, virtually every urban transit system and every aspect of urban mass transportation, including construction, financing, and operation, was in government hands.

Under the influence of changing economic and political conditions, the pendulum is now swinging back. Federal dollars have become scarcer, and local budgets have come under a growing strain because of rising demands for services, local tax limitations, and public resistance to new spending initiatives. Efficiency has become an acknowledged goal of government management. Public opinion has come to recognize that there are practical limits to how much money state and local government can devote to local transportation. This realization, in turn, has led to a growing acceptance of the principle that improving urban mobility should be a joint responsibility of the government and private sectors. This conclusion has been reached with varying degrees of reluctance and enthusiasm, but the remarkable thing is that few people dispute the necessity for closer public/ private cooperation.

Business leaders have come to understand that they must, in their own self-interest, assume a more active role in dealing with local transportation problems, lest traffic congestion, decaying infrastructure, inadequate access to jobs, and overburdened transit systems become an obstacle to orderly economic growth. The corporate community realizes that it cannot ignore the health of the communities in which it operates, and that a well functioning transportation system is essential to that vitality. Private developers, no longer able to rely fully on public funding and aware that accessibility is essential to the viability of their real estate ventures, are increasingly prepared to share in the cost of necessary transportation improvements. Private transportation operators sense new opportunities in this changing climate and are moving aggressively to exploit the fast expanding market for customized transportation services.

Local government, for its part, has an equally strong motivation to seek an expanded private sector involvement. By allowing the business community a greater voice in local transportation decisionmaking, public officials increase the likelihood of private sector support. They thus gain an influential ally in their efforts to mobilize public opinion behind new capital improvements. And, by contracting for service with private providers, local government can often improve the efficiency of service delivery and thus lower the cost of public transportation.

In short, there is a growing recognition on the part of both the private and government sectors of a strong interdependence and mutuality of interests in public/private cooperation. The form of this new partnership varies from place to place. In most communities the government sector is likely to retain the principal role. In other places, the private sector may become an important actor. However, no matter how the responsibility should eventually be allocated, one thing already seems certain: because of a stronger private sector role, our communities will be enjoying a wider diversity of services and of service providers, a greater variety of financing arrangements and funding sources, and a more competitive, market-oriented approach to transportation.

FORMS OF PRIVATE SECTOR INVOLVEMENT

Several distinct forms of private sector involvement are emerging in response to the changing fiscal and institutional environment.

Cost-Sharing and Benefit-Sharing of Transportation Investments

First, there is a growing private involvement in the financing of capital facilities, through various forms of cost-sharing and benefit-sharing arrangements.

The practice of cost-sharing, well established in the highway field, is increasingly being applied to the field of transit. Examples include an assessment district in downtown Miami, formed to underwrite a $27 million business contribution toward the cost of Miami's Downtown People Mover; a $12 million private sector contribution toward the rehabilitation of San Francisco's cable cars; and a negotiated agreement by the developers of a large residential complex in Manhattan to underwrite a $30 million rehabilitation of a New York subway station. Another innovative example of cost-sharing is New York City's new zoning code for midtown Manhattan, which provides "floor-to-area ratio" (FAR) bonuses to developers who undertake major transit improvements, such as subway connections to buildings and relocation of sidewalk subway entrances. The development bonuses are expected to generate $15 to $20 million in private funding for station improvements, according to transit authority officials.

The principle of benefit-sharing is also being tested. One example of this technique is the ongoing negotiations in Washington, D.C., between the Metropolitan Transit Authority and local developers, wherein the latter would pay "connection fees" for direct underground links to subway stations. The fees could earn the transit system $30 to $40 million in extra income over the next twenty years, according to one estimate.

Another evidence of interest in cooperative financing comes from Orange County, Florida, which has invited expressions of interest from the private sector to "design, finance, construct and operate" a rail system that would connect the Orlando International Airport to a complex of hotels, tourist attractions, and employment centers and the Orlando central business district. The county's invitation has focused on the lack of federal funds for new rail systems, emphasizing that only the private sector has "the necessary resources to marshall the financing support needed for implementation." Private financing and operation is also being considered in Portland, Oregon, for its second (Westside) light rail line. Both projects are grounded in the belief that local jurisdictions that can combine local government and private funds will have a distinct advantage in competing for federal funds. Both ventures would take advantage of the provisions of recent tax legislation that allow tax-exempt entities such as units of local government to benefit from tax write-offs previously available only to private investors. The vehicle for this would be a lease arrangement: a private consortium would own and operate the rail system and lease it to a local public agency until the indebtedness has been paid off. At the end of the lease the public agency would buy the system from its private owners. The continued viability of this approach depends on the future availability of the tax benefits for tax-exempt property.

Developer Involvement in Highway and Traffic Improvements

As we noted earlier, the use of private funds for highway improvements is not new. For years, local governments have required developers to provide streets and sidewalks within subdivisions. Gradually, as commercial and residential development was extended into newly urbanized areas, the practice of developer contributions was broadened to encompass improvements to highways adjacent to the development sites that were likely to be affected by the traffic generated by the new development. Such contributions often became a condition of subdivision approval or changes in zoning.

In many cases, especially in California and Florida, developer contributions have assumed the form of "development impact fees." Thus, the county of San Diego requires developers to pay a fee as a condition of subdivision approval, which provides for a portion of the local cost of road improvements in a community plan area that includes the subdivision. The city of San Diego requires additional development impact fees "to cover those costs related to the provision of public works facilities, street landscaping and traffic signal installation." The city of Carlsbad, California, recently enacted an ordinance requiring a fee of 3 percent of the construction valuation, to be paid at the time of building permit issuance; the fee is used by the city to pay for street and traffic engineering improvements. The cities of Irvine and Thousand Oaks, California, impose "system development charges" as a way of making developers "buy into" preexisting city infrastructure. The city of Roseville, California, has imposed a one percent surcharge on all new construction in order to raise revenue for traffic engineering improvements necessitated by new development.

The financial participation of property owners in transportation improvements can also be secured through special benefit assessments, wherein property owners are assessed a share of the total cost of a specific improvement, based on the proportionate amount of benefit each owner receives from the improvement. Assessments may be based on front footage, lot area, appraised value of land, or a combination of factors. To finance the improvement, a locality usually issues bonds with the income from the special assessment pledged as security and used to cover the debt service.

Earlier in this century special assessments were used widely, as the principal means of financing a variety of public improvements in residential areas, such as streets, sidewalks, and sewers. Postwar requirements that developers provide basic infrastructure in their subdivisions lessened the traditional dependence on special assessments in residential developments. Instead, emphasis has shifted to the central business districts, where special benefit assessment districts have been extensively utilized in recent years to finance construction of pedestrian malls, for example in Minneapolis, Louisville, Syracuse, Rochester, Fresno, and Madison. More recently, benefit assessment districts have also been employed to finance the maintenance and operation of pedestrian malls, for example, in Denver, Pittsburgh, and Brooklyn (Fulton Street Mall).

A new and inventive form of assessment is being employed by a handful of cities, including Orlando and St. Petersburg, Florida. Under this concept, property owners within a designated improvement district are offered the option of contributing to a "Transportation System Management (TSM) Trust Fund" in lieu of providing a code-required number of parking spaces. The local ordinance in Orlando permits developers to reduce off-street parking by 20 percent; in exchange for that reduction, they must contribute 80 percent of the cost of the foregone parking to the TSM fund. The money thus collected will be used to support the cost of downtown transportation management improvements and the capital and operating costs of the local transit system. Similar approaches are being considered in other jurisdictions.

Development impact fees and assessments are authorized specifically by local statute or in local land-use regulations, and their legal authority is derived from state law. Frequently, however, private sector contributions are determined through ad hoc negotiations between the interested property owners and local officials. Such negotiations often result in agreements stipulating specific off-site transportation improvements to be financed or provided in-kind by the developer to accommodate or mitigate increased traffic levels generated by a proposed development. A wide variety of ad hoc transportation agreements have been negotiated in recent years, as shown by the following examples:

- In Fairfax County, Virginia, a $2.65 per square foot fee will be imposed on bonus development to finance badly needed highway improvements at the intersection of Route 50 and Interstate 66. The site is the location of a future county governmental center and a 620-acre, $460 million complex of offices, hotels, townhouses, and condominiums. The site is expected to become one of the biggest traffic generators in the Washington metropolitan area.

- In the Denver area, a group of private developers and land owners have joined together to form the Joint Southeast Public Improvement Authority, which will undertake a $20 million, privately funded program of highway improvements in order to relieve congestion in the southeast corridor. The authority provides a mechanism for (1) equitably allocating the cost of the program among the developers, (2) an orderly implementation of the planned improvements, without the risk of delays or disagreements over each developer's financial responsibility, and (3) eliminating the need for continuing negotiations between developers and the state government.

- In Orange County, California, the Irvine Company has agreed to provide $60 million in local transportation improvements as part of developing Irvine Center, a 480-acre complex to be located in the triangle formed by the Santa Ana, San Diego, and Laguna freeways. The improvements will include three freeway off-ramps, two parkways, and fourteen projects related to traffic control, including a new interchange and the modification of an existing one at a cost of $12 million. Pacific Mutual Life Insurance Company is working on traffic mitigation measures in the Newport Beach area at a cost in excess of $1.3 million.

- Also in Orange County, a group of developers have agreed to finance the cost of intersection improvements in the cities of

Costa Mesa, Irvine, and Santa Ana in order to relieve traffic congestion generated by new development. The private contributions, in the amount of $1 million, have been paid into a joint TSM fund created for that purpose.

- In northern San Diego County, Shapell Industries, developers of Rancho Carmel, a 1,500-acre mixed-use development expected to cost about $1 billion, have agreed to provide thirty-three separately identified capital infrastructure projects at a total cost of $57.5 million. Included are arterial roads, freeway overpasses and interchanges, park-and-ride facilities, bike trails, and traffic control systems.

- In the Houston area, several large developers, including Friendswood Development Company and Mitchell Energy and Development Corporation, have helped to pay for freeway interchanges and ramps on the Katy Freeway and are helping to finance the cost of other road improvements in the western portion of Harris County.

- In Los Angeles, the MCA Development Company is constructing some $4 million worth of roadway improvements to relieve traffic congestion in the Universal City area.

- In New Jersey, several local governments (for example, the Plainsboro, Parsippany-Troy Hills, and Bridgewater townships) have negotiated agreements calling for private developer funding of highway improvements necessitated by their proposed developments. Elsewhere in the state, Hartz Mountain Industries, major developers at the Meadowlands, have contributed $11 million toward highway improvements and construction of a rail station, designed to accommodate increased traffic generated by its development at Harmon Cove.

- At Tysons Corner in Northern Virginia, a major developer—Tycon Inc., Ltd.—has offered to build at its own expense a $3 million overpass spanning an existing highway in order to provide direct access to its new $100 million office complex.

- The city of Fairfield, California, granted approval for the development of a regional mall after the developer agreed to pay the city an annual fee of 55 cents per square foot for twenty-five years for off-site improvements, including construction of an interchange, street widening, and other traffic improvements.

- In what must be a record of its kind, a group of developers led by the Prudential Company has pledged to invest $80 million in local transportation improvements around the new Hacienda Business Park in Pleasanton, Alameda County. The private funds will be used to construct two new freeway interchanges, widen two freeways (each by two lanes), install a computer-controlled traffic signal system, and provide sound barriers and landscaping.

Obviously, these initiatives are not philanthropic gestures. What these examples illustrate is a new realization on the part of developers that, in an era of tight fiscal constraints on state and local government, helping to finance transportation infrastructure necessary for future growth is in their own best interests.

Will the private sector again assume, on the scale it did in the days of Henry Huntington, Sam Insull, and the Pacific Electric Lines, a role in the financing of new transportation infrastructure? We do not know yet, but there is ample historical precedent and numerous contemporary examples in foreign countries to support this return. Successful public/private arrangements prevailed in the United States at the turn of the century: In Boston, Chicago, and New York City, the municipal governments sold revenue bonds to the public to finance the cost of subway construction, and then leased the completed facilities to private companies for operation, with the debt serviced out of the rental payments. Much of the early suburban development would not have occurred had it not been for heavy private investment in "interurbans" and electric street railways, which opened up land on the urban periphery to development and led to the creation of "streetcar suburbs."

Abroad, private involvement in public infrastructure financing, construction, and operation continues to this very day. In France, a portion of the national network of modern autoroutes has been built with the help of private capital and is being operated by private for-profit "concessionaires." French municipalities award contracts or franchises to private firms to manage, maintain, and operate publicly funded infrastructure, such as water systems. They require the concessionaires to amortize the facilities over the term of the franchise and to pay the initial capital cost to the government.

In Japan, private real estate development companies, such as the Tokyu and Hankyu corporations, still construct and operate suburban commuter rail lines that link their developments to city centers—and manage to return a healthy profit on their investment. The automated guideway transit system in the city of Kobe was built by a consortium that used a combination of public and private financing. The consortium issued stock, roughly half of which was bought by the city of Kobe and the other half by forty-two private Japanese companies, including banks, shipping companies, and construction firms. Stockholders in the system expect no return on their investment until all capital costs have been recovered, and they treat it as an investment in Japan's industrial future. The system is expected to be profitable after ten years of operation and to begin paying dividends after twenty years.

Could similar approaches work in the United States? The question raises some intriguing possibilities for jurisdictions such as Los Angeles, Houston, Dallas, Denver, and Orange County, whose appetite for new infrastructure has outstripped their capacity to raise new revenues.

Privately Managed Transportation Services

The private sector is also assuming a more active role in the provision and management of transportation services. Until recently, this type of involvement was limited to corporate-sponsored employee carpool and vanpool programs. Now, privately sponsored transportation services are also being introduced in residential communities, private resorts, college campuses, suburban office parks, medical centers, and apartment complexes.

In some communities provision of transportation services has become a cooperative undertaking. In Des Moines, Iowa, a private real estate firm and the transit system have shared the cost of implementing bus service to an outlying housing development. A group of merchants in a suburban shopping mall in Johnstown, Pennsylvania, pay a monthly fee for public transit provided to the mall. Downtown restaurants and taverns in Annapolis, Maryland, pay for evening shuttle service from fringe parking lots. And in Oklahoma City, Lexington, Kentucky, Birmingham, Alabama, and Washington, D.C., local businesses are sharing in the cost of running downtown trolleys.

During the last decade and especially in the last several years, there has emerged a new type of growth center, which, because of its size and complexity, defies conventional classification as a "suburban development." Typically, they have sprung up on the periphery of metropolitan areas or in urbanized counties, such as Orange County, California, or Fairfax County, Northern Virginia. Unlike their predecessors of the sixties and early seventies, which were primarily shopping malls, the new growth centers involve a rich mix of activities, including shopping, offices, hotels, recreation and entertainment (restaurants, cinemas, fitness centers), and a variety of professional and service establishments. Many of these "megacenters" range from 4 to 8 million square feet of office space, 2 to 3 million square feet of retail space, and a daytime population of 10,000 to 15,000 people: In other words, they are minicities in their own right.

The archetype of such a megacenter is City Post Oak near Houston, which, with its 16 million square feet of office space, 3.3 million square feet of retail space and a daytime population of 60,000, is called "the tenth largest downtown in America." However, others are not far behind. They include Century City, Warner Center, the El Segundo/Los Angeles International Airport complex, South Coast Plaza, Newport Center, and Irvine Center in California; Denver Technological Center; Greenway Plaza in Houston; Las Colinas near Dallas; Meadowlands in Northern New Jersey; and Tysons Corner in suburban Washington, D.C. Each will ultimately contain at least 10 million square feet of space and a daytime population of 20,000 to 30,000.

One unifying characteristic of these megacenters is that they are seldom adequately served by public transportation. Virtually all access and internal circulation are handled by the private automobile. The prospect for better transit service is dim, both because metropolitan transit agencies have a hard enough time meeting existing commitments, and because these centers cannot be conveniently served by conventional transit. The future traffic impact of these centers is causing much concern to local officials, who realize that the problem cannot be solved through expansion of roadway capacity alone. This situation is stimulating some new and unaccustomed resolve among private developers to join in with local government in search of cooperative transportation solutions.

Transportation Management Associations

One such solution is the privately sponsored, comprehensive "Transportation Management program," offering a mix of services and management actions such as ridesharing programs, shuttle buses to rail stations, commuter club buses, parking management, flexible working hours, transit promotion, local traffic flow improvements, and pedestrian circulation improvements. Privately sponsored transportation management programs are still rare, but interest in them is spreading. The best known examples are those run at Tysons Corner, El Segundo, City Post Oak, The Woodlands near Houston, University Circle, Inc., in Cleveland, and in the Longwood area of Boston (by the Medical Area Service Corporation). Other private transportation management programs are being launched at: the Denver Tech Center; the Hacienda Business Park, Bishop Ranch, Pleasant Hill and South Coast Plaza in California; and in Princeton and the Meadowlands, New Jersey.

Facilitating introduction of these programs are the so-called Transportation Management Associations (TMAs)—nonprofit membership organizations formed by corporate employers, developers, and private institutions to provide transportation services in suburban growth centers and in newly urbanized areas, where public transit is not available or conveniently accessible. TMAs generate their own revenue through voluntary assessments or membership dues, and with these funds support various transportation activities that respond specifically to the needs of their members. Depending on the local requirements, a transportation management association may assume responsibility for running shuttle buses to a nearby commuter rail station, managing a ridesharing program, administering a shared-parking program, coordinating a staggered work hours program, or instituting a program of traffic flow improvements.

More than a dozen TMAs are already in existence. Some are organized around a single activity center: a suburban corporate park or an in-town institutional complex, such as a medical center. Other TMAs are areawide in scope. Some operate their own services; others contract with professional service providers. However, no matter what their form, all transportation management associations share a common philosophy: They pool private resources in the interest of improving public mobility. Some of the better known transportation management associations are:

- Houston: City Post Oak Association, West Houston Association
- Washington, D.C.: Tysons Transportation Association
- Boston: MASCO (Medical Area Service Corporation)

- Cleveland: University Circle, Inc.

- Los Angeles: El Segundo Employers Association

- Hartford, Connecticut: The Rideshare Corporation

- San Francisco: Hacienda Business Park Owners' Association

- Bay Area: Santa Clara County Manufacturing Group.

The Tysons Transportation Association: An Example of a Suburban Transportation Management Association. Twenty-five years ago, Tysons Corner in suburban Northern Virginia, 10 miles west of Washington, D.C., consisted of a small general store and a gas station. Today, with over 10 million square feet of office and commercial space, Tysons Corner is a bustling suburban minicity. It is the home of Washington's largest regional shopping mall, which houses 140 stores and is among the top ten shopping centers in the United States; two corporate office parks that house some of the nation's largest corporations; and a host of hotels, restaurants, banks, and several residential highrise condominiums. Tysons Corner's daytime population is 35,000 workers, who mingle with an estimated 390,000 weekly shoppers.

What it all means is that more than 30,000 cars descend on Tysons Corner each weekday morning, causing gigantic traffic jams twice a day. Adding to this motorist's nightmare are the 60,000 commuter cars that pass through Tysons Corner on their way to other destinations. Despite the intolerable congestion, Tysons Corner is still growing. In the past five years, it has more than doubled its office and retail space, and the forcast is for an additional 6 million square feet of office space by the end of this decade, bringing in 4,000 more people and 3,000 more cars every year.

The traffic situation, and the prospect of even bigger traffic jams ahead, sparked the local business community into action. Supported by county officials, the chief executive officers of forty of the largest companies doing business at Tysons Corner joined with two of Tysons's major developers in 1980 to form a voluntary nonprofit association "to achieve significantly improved traffic conditions" within the area. The association collects annual dues (currently assessed at $6.00 per employee for office tenants and 1.2 cents per interior square foot for building owners), which bring in a total of about $150,000 per year. With this money (plus some advertising revenue), the association sponsors a twin program that consists of a centerwide vanpool program for employees working at Tysons Corner, and a free daytime circulation service for the convenience of employees, residents, and visitors. The association's target is to remove 4,000 to 5,000 cars from the road by 1986, while expanding internal mobility within the center. In addition, the association has been active in catalyzing support for highway improvements designed to take some of the pressure off the local roads, by diverting through traffic onto a new bypass.

The Tysons Transportation Association is run by a board of directors composed of CEOs from the resident companies and the major developers. Sustained top management support has been a key factor behind the association's success. The monthly meetings of the TTA are attended by senior company executives; no replacements are allowed at board meetings. The association has a full-time transportation manager whose salary is paid out of the association's revenues. Board members serve without compensation, donating their time and assistance freely. While participation in the association is voluntary, there is subtle but firm peer pressure on the businesses located at Tysons Corner to join. Presently, about 65 percent of all companies, representing collectively 85 percent of all employees at Tysons Corner, belong to the association.

As the above example shows, transportation management associations are not an alternative to the local political process or to local public agencies. Nor are they study commissions or discussion groups. They are action-oriented alliances of businesses, developers, and civic organizations, with well defined agendas, and with a commitment to tap private initiative and resources to solve community problems.

University Circle, Inc. (Cleveland), and Medical Area Service Corporation (Boston): Two Examples of In-City Transportation Management Associations. University Circle is a 500-acre area in Cleveland, Ohio, in which thirty-five nonprofit institutions maintain their homes. They include Case Institute of Technology, Western Reserve University, the Cleveland Orchestra, the Cleveland Museum of Art, several hospitals, and a host of other educational, cultural and religious institutions. Today, University Circle is Cleveland's second largest activity center (after its central business district), employing some 19,000 people and receiving 15 million annual visitors.

In an effort to bring order to the area and allow all institutions to expand in optimum ways, several of the leading institutions got together in 1957 and sponsored a comprehensive master plan for the area. To cement the cooperative relationship, a nonprofit corporation, University Circle, Inc. (UCI), was formed to manage the entire development on behalf of its resident institutions. Today UCI serves its 39 members as a land bank, helps to coordinate physical planning and development, and initiates and implements construction and environmental projects. UCI also has an Operations Department, responsible for the maintenance of the Circle's parks and landscaped areas, improving internal roads, managing traffic flow, providing internal security, snow removal, and sanitation services, and maintaining liaison with the surrounding neighborhoods.

In the same vein, UCI is also responsible for transportation. It has jurisdiction over 7,200 parking places and manages the parking lots as a shared resource for the common use and enjoyment of its members. It maintains a motor pool of forty vehicles that are available to member institutions. And it operates a thirteen-bus transit system that functions eighteen hours a day, from 6 A.M. to midnight. After 6 P.M., the regular system converts to a "Dial-a-Bus" operation that provides portal-to-portal service to and from all participating institutions in the system. Sixty percent of the cost of operating the UCI bus system is divided, based on ridership, among nineteen participating institutions. The other 40 percent is charged against the parking operation to cover the cost of transporting permit holders from parking lots to their destinations.

Located in southwest Boston, the Longwood Medical Area (LMA) is a grouping of sixteen hospitals, colleges, and other nonprofit institutions that have 35,000 employees and students, all within a one-quarter square mile area. The hospitals further have an annual outpatient population of approximately 600,000 people that visit the area.

To cope with the difficult traffic and transportation problems created by this high concentration of activities, the resident institutions set up a nonprofit organization, MASCO (Medical Area Service Corporation), to provide a wide variety of parking and transportation services and to plan for an orderly accommodation of new growth within LMA.

MASCO acquires, leases, and operates surface parking lots containing 2,200 parking spaces. Because of the intense use of land within the boundaries of the Longwood Medical Area, most of the lots are located as far as 2 miles away (to take advantage of lower lease costs and to lessen congestion around the site), and dedicated shuttle bus service is provided free of charge to selected points within the LMA. The shuttle system carries 2,000 people per day. To reduce operating costs, there is no midday service from 10 A.M. to 3 P.M. If an employee must leave work early, MASCO provides free taxi service from its office. In addition, MASCO runs an internal circulator and a transit shuttle to downtown Boston and commuter rail stations with a combined daily ridership of 2,500.

MASCO also runs a computerized carpool program for employees and students and is considering purchasing its own vehicles to initiate a common vanpool program open to all, without regard to their institutional affiliation. In its role as a private Transportation Management Association, MASCO maintains close contact with city, region, and state planning agencies, lobbies for changes and improvements in traffic systems, and participates in city-wide contingency plans for transit shutdowns and natural disaster emergency access systems.

Downtown Transportation Management

Yet another form of private sector involvement is emerging in the downtowns of our cities. In a score of cities the business community, working through its own organizations, is assuming a growing voice in downtown transportation management and in planning for regional mobility. Examples include the Los Angeles Transportation Task Force, the Denver Partnership, the Greater Hartford Chamber of Commerce, Houston's Regional Mobility Plan and the newly created Central Houston, Inc., Central Atlanta Progress, Inc., the Greater Dallas Chamber of Commerce, and Pittsburgh's Grant Street Cooperative Maintenance Association. All of these groups play a strong role in local transportation decisionmaking. Often, as in the cases of Denver, Dallas, Pittsburgh, and Syracuse, the efforts of the private sector culminate in the creation of a special assessment district, which provides a source of revenue enabling the private sector to undertake independent, entrepreneurial activities. Terms such as "downtown development district," "downtown maintenance district," and "business improvement district" all point to a desire to adapt the concept of the special benefit assessment to a variety of objectives—including the maintenance, operation, and improvement of local transportation services and facilities.

One reason for the growing private involvement is that many aspects of modern transportation management lie outside the jurisdiction of public authorities. Private sector cooperation is required in such matters as staggered work hours, workplace-based ridesharing programs, off-street parking management, employer/merchant subsidies of parking and transit passes, and contract transportation (such as private subscription bus service). The cooperation of the private sector is increasingly viewed as an essential ingredient of any successful transportation management program.

A second rationale for private sector involvement in downtown transportation management lies in the concept of "benefit-based financing." Since developers and property owners, along with downtown merchants and employers, are the chief beneficiaries of improved transportation, there is a good case to be made that the private sector ought to share in the cost of downtown transportation improvements, and that it should have a concommitant right to demand a greater voice in transportation decisionmaking.

Private sector involvement in transportation management—both downtown and in the suburbs—is likely to grow, particularly where it is being actively encouraged by local government, either through public incentives, such as reduced parking requirements or density bonuses, or as a condition of discretionary permits. Such initiatives are multiplying. Thus, Los Angeles, under an ordinance enacted in April 1983, will grant office developers reductions in the code-required number of parking spaces if they elect to institute ridesharing or park-and-ride programs. The ordinance provides for annual city reviews of the developers' transportation management programs and for the withdrawal of the building occupancy permits should the programs fail to be effective. Similar incentives are provided in a number of other cities, either through local ordinances or on an ad hoc negotiated basis. For example, the city of Dallas negotiated with the developers of the suburban Galleria shopping mall a broad package of alternative transportation management actions in exchange for less stringent parking requirements.

Other jurisdictions have made developer involvement in transportation management obligatory. Placer County and Sacramento, California, require employers and developers to design and implement transportation management plans as a condition for the approval of use permits or building permits. In preparing a transportation management plan, the applicant must consider ridesharing assistance, transit pass subsidies, buspool and shuttle bus programs, flexible working hours, bicycle facilities, and other similar measures.

Private Provision of Service

Private enterprise has also become more involved in pursuing opportunities to operate local public transportation services. In some communities, private carriers have been brought in by local government under service contracts or franchise agreements. In other localities, private carriers engage in independent, entrepreneurial activities, providing completely unsubsidized services.

As far back as the 1970s, we began to realize that taxi companies represent an important transportation resource that could be harnessed in the service of public transportation. Today, a score of cities—San Diego, Norfolk, Phoenix, Columbus, Birmingham—are routinely contracting with taxi companies to service low-density areas and low-demand time periods, such as evenings and weekends. This is seen as a way of reducing operating costs and providing more convenient service. In several communities, such as Lexington, Santa Fe, Hammond, and Freeport, the operation of the entire local transit system has been contracted to private firms. Elsewhere, private carriers bring thousands of daily commuters to their jobs without any public subsidies. In Chicago, for example, private "club" buses carry over 5,000 daily commuters from the southern suburbs to the Loop. In New York, 700 private buses bring 100,000 daily commuters into Manhattan every day from destinations in New Jersey, Long Island, and Westchester County. In Los Angeles, fourteen private companies operate 140 buses carrying 6,000 daily riders.

What these examples underscore is that government need not operate all of the services that the public requires, especially when such services can be delivered more effectively and at a lower cost by the private sector. More and more regional transit authorities view themselves not necessarily as suppliers of service but as policymaking bodies that decide what services are needed, and then ensure that these services are delivered in the most cost-effective manner. And that may mean delegating a growing fraction of service delivery to private operators.

Cooperative Transportation

Commuter Clubs. Another manifestation of private sector involvement in local transportation is the growth of cooperative, grassroots initiatives. One example is the commuter "bus clubs" that have sprung up in the suburbs of several metropolitan areas, notably Chicago, Los Angeles, San Francisco, Washington, D.C., and Oklahoma City. The residents of these communities have banded together into nonprofit clubs for the purpose of running commuter buses to downtown destinations. The idea was first introduced in Columbia, Maryland, a residential community located about 25 miles north of Washington, D.C., where the homeowner-founded, nonprofit Columbia Commuter Bus Corporation has grown from two buses in 1971 to a fleet of eighteen. These buses carry nearly 900 residents of Columbia to downtown Washington every weekday, and the corporation has an operating budget of nearly $1 million. In the case of Oklahoma City, membership fees cover 50 percent of the service's costs, and the federal operating subsidy pays the other half. The service is operated by the metropolitan transit agency under contract to the clubs. In other cases, the participants cover the full expense of leasing a bus and driver from a private operator.

Neighborhood-Based Programs. Another approach utilizes a partnership between neighborhoods and government, through volunteer community transit programs. It was first used in Huntsville and Madison County, Alabama, where the local nonprofit Community Improvement associations provide program management (such as prescheduling shared-ride trips), gasoline, and volunteer drivers. Reconditioned used vans are furnished by the city government, preventive maintenance and insurance by the county, and overall administration by the city Department of Transportation. Federal funds (eligible under UMTA block grant) cover the cost of the vans and of insurance. Fourteen community volunteer vans currently operate in Huntsville and Madison County, serving mostly elderly and low-income residents without automobiles. These vans provided mobility to 33,500 people in 1982, at a cost of 40 cents per passenger. According to city estimates, the program could be run on a self-supporting, unsubsidized basis at an increased cost of only 40 cents per passenger.

Neighborhoods such as these have only recently come to be considered as potential providers of municipal services by financially strapped local governments. The arrangements vary widely. Sometimes neighborhood organizations simply enlist volunteers or part-time workers. A next step is a formal "co-production" agreement, in which neighborhood residents, as volunteers or as paid workers, carry out part of a municipal task. Finally, some neighborhoods sign contracts to take over municipal services in their entirety. In Louisville, for example, a neighborhood organization that was engaged in housing rehabilitation obtained a city contract to build sidewalks. Jacksonville, Florida, has commissioned neighborhood groups to manage local social service centers for senior citizens. In Kansas City, neighborhood groups perform building code inspections under contract to the city. In Baltimore, San Diego, and Columbus, Ohio, they do park maintenance. In Essex County, New Jersey, they manage services for the elderly. And the city of Philadelphia enters into formal service-sharing agreements with neighborhoods for vacant lot maintenance, securing deserted buildings, and pothole filling.

While formal neighborhood-run transportation services have not yet been established, several neighborhood-level programs do already exist. Others are under consideration, in addition to the pioneering effort at Huntsville.

Homeowners Associations. A third potential approach to the cooperative provision of transportation service is through homeowners' associations, of which there are estimated to be some 20,000. For many years, homeowners' associations have been used as a means of maintaining and improving common facilities such as streets, neighborhood parks, and swimming pools. Homeowners' associations have more recently been assuring—generally through contracts with private commercial service companies—selected services, such as street maintenance, upkeep of recreational facilities, refuse collection, snow plowing, and security patrols. A few associations even provide emergency medical and fire protection, day care, and in-home elderly care. Currently, there are only a few examples of homeowners' associations providing transportation services, but interest in this approach is growing. In Lincoln, Nebraska, volunteer "ridesharing agents" organize carpool programs in the neighborhoods. In Des Moines, Iowa, a local homeowners' association cooperatively funds public transit service for residents of a housing development. And in Alexandria, Virginia, condominium and tenants associations run a residentially based ridesharing program with the assistance from the city's Ridesharing Service.

Mobility Clubs. Finally, there are a few instances of "mobility clubs," organized primarily to serve the needs of elderly persons. Using parttime, nonprofessional drivers such as college students, retired persons, and homemakers, these clubs provide highly personalized transportation/escort service to their members. Drivers use their own vehicles, are paid modest rates, and are employed only on an as-needed basis. The clubs can thus keep operating costs very low. The Point-to-Point Club in Ardmore, Pennsylvania, provides service at only $8.00 per hour. Each club member also pays a $10.00 annual membership fee. The combination of fares and membership fees covers over 85 percent of the operating costs of the club.

MOTIVATION FOR PRIVATE
SECTOR INVOLVEMENT

While the phenomenon of private sector involvement in urban transportation can no longer be ignored, the motivation behind it is still poorly understood. Some transit officials, having observed a trend of rising business interest in local transportation, have concluded that private contributions could become a new source of transit operating assistance, replacing a portion of any lost federal subsidy. This thinking shows a serious misreading of private sector motivation. The business community does not generally regard public transit as a valid object of corporate philanthropy, to be supported by charitable contributions. (There are some exceptions: San Francisco businesses raised $12 million toward the cost of rehabilitating the famed cable cars; Seattle merchants assessed themselves over $1 million to help finance a vintage trolley line along Seattle's historic waterfront.) Thus, the American Public Transit Association's efforts to rouse business support through its "Transit Means Business" campaign has fallen largely on deaf ears, and local efforts to raise special business assessments to support transit—such as San Francisco's proposed Transit Maintenance District—have for the most part been unsuccessful.

The most solid and enduring basis for private sector involvement lies in the concept of enlightened self-interest. Business executives must be convinced that their participation in local transportation activities will result in a positive gain. This is not to say that corporate leaders will weigh the benefits of their participation in narrow dollars-and-cents terms. On the contrary, their motivations often may be quite diffuse. It may be a desire to attract and retain a work-force, to improve employee productivity and morale, to avoid the cost of building additional parking facilities, to facilitate access and reduce congestion around company facilities, to enhance the value of sunk investment in real estate, or even to improve the general business climate in the community. But, however indirect, the element of self-interest must be there in order to sustain long-term support.

Conclusion

Ten years ago, virtually every aspect of urban transportation—from planning to financing, operation, and service delivery—was considered to be the exclusive domain and responsibility of government. Today, for reasons that partly have to do with fiscal stress, but partly also with changing attitudes, urban transportation has come to be viewed increasingly as a *shared* responsibility of the private and public sectors.

Because this perception is still so new, there is no commonly agreed upon definition of public/private partnership. Instead, the concept of partnership means different things to different people. To a private transportation carrier, for example, partnership means an opportunity to participate more actively in the provision of public transportation services. To an investment banker, partnership means joint public/private ventures in the financing of transportation equipment and infrastructure. To a land developer, partnership means sharing with the public sector the costs and benefits of combined land use/transportation development. And to a businessman, employer, or merchant, partnership means participating actively in the solution of downtown or suburban transportation problems and obtaining a greater voice in local transportation decisionmaking. To a public official, the phrase "public/private partnership" is increasingly becoming all of the above. But whatever forms this partnership may locally assume, one thing seems certain: Greater private sector involvement will mean economically healthier, more diverse, and responsive transportation for tomorrow's urban America.

SELECTED BIBLIOGRAPHY

Altshuler, Alan. *The Urban Transportation System: Politics and Policy Innovation.* Cambridge, Mass.: MIT Press, 1979.

American Public Transit Association (APTA). *Transit Fact Book.* Washington, D.C.: American Public Transit Association, various yearly issues.

Anderson, Shirley C. "The Effect of Government Ownership and Subsidy on Performance: Evidence from the Bus Transit Industry." *Transportation Research-A* 17 (1983): 191–200.

_____ . "The Effect of Operating Subsidy and Transit Tax Financing on Performance in the Bus Transit Industry, 1975–81." *Proceedings of the Transportation Research Forum 1983*, 24 (in press).

Arthur Anderson and Company. "Bus Route Costing for Planning Purposes." Transport and Road Research Laboratory Supplementary Report, 108UC. 1974.

Baumol, William J.; John C. Panzar; and Robert D. Willig. *Contestable Markets and the Theory of Industry Structure.* Chicago, Ill.: Rand McNally, 1982.

Beesley, M. E. *Urban Transport: Studies in Economic Policy.* London: Butterworths, 1973.

Belovin, Barbara; Emily Griske; Tom Hauser; and Kurt Richwerger. "Commuter Vans and Surface Transportation in Manhattan." New York City: New School for Social Research, December 1982.

Cervero, R. "Transit Cross-Subsidies." *Transportation Quarterly* 36 (1982): 377–89.

Cherwony, Walter. "Cost Centers: A New Approach to Transit Performance." *Transit Journal* (Fall 1977).

_____ ; Greg Gleichman; and Ben Porter. "Bus Route Costing Procedures." *Interim Report No. 1: A Review.* Report No. UMTA-IT-09-9014-81-1. Washington, D.C.: U.S. Department of Transportation, Urban Mass Transportation Administration, 1981.

_____, and Subhash R. Mundle. "Peak-Base Cost Allocation Models." *Transportation Research Record* 663 (1978).

Chicago Transit Authority Historical Data. Chicago: Chicago Transit Authority, various dates.

Clarke, Geoffrey; Gary Grobman; and Douglas Jacobs. "Provision of Express Bus Service in New York City." Harvard University, John F. Kennedy School of Government, May 1982.

Coffman, Richard B. "Economic Reasons for Price and Entry Regulation of Taxicabs. A Comment." *Journal of Transport Economics and Policy* 11 (1977): 288-97.

Condit, Carl W. *Chicago 1930-70: Building, Planning, and Urban Technology.* Chicago: University of Chicago Press, 1974.

Cook, B. L., and E. Lounsberry. "3,000 in Suburbs Stranded in SEPTA Strike." *Philadelphia Inquirer*, 3 June 1982.

Cox, Wendell. "Deficit Control Through Service Contracting." *Transitions* (Autumn 1983): 21-30.

_____. "Contracting for Public Transportation Services: Public-Private Partnership at Work." Presentation to the Eastern Regional Meeting of the American Bus Association, Hershey, Pennsylvania, March 21, 1983.

Davis, Frank W.; John Beeson; and Frederick Wegmann. "The Knoxville Transportation Brokerage Project." Three-volume report #UMTA-TN-06-0006-78-1/2/3 for the Urban Mass Transportation Administration. Washington, D.C., November 1978.

A Directory of Special Transportation Services for Senior Citizens and Handicapped Persons in: Cook, DuPage, Kane, Lake, McHenry, and Will Counties. Prepared by the Regional Transportation Authority. Washington, D.C.: Urban Mass Transportation Administration, February 1981.

Eckert, Ross D., and George W. Hilton. "The Jitneys." *Journal of Law and Economics* 15 (1972): 293-325.

Feldman, Paul. "Why It Is Difficult to Change Regulation." *Urban Transportation Economics: Special Report* 181. Washington, D.C.: Transportation Research Board, 1978, pp. 121-23.

First Annual Report of Board of Supervising Engineers Chicago Traction. Covering period ended January 31, 1908. Chicago: The Board, 1908.

Fowler, Norman. "UK Deregulates the Bus Industry." *Urban Transportation Abroad* 4, no. 1 (1981): 1, 3.

Gambaccini, Louis J. "Economic Regulation of Urban Public Transportation: An Operator's Perspective." *Urban Transportation Economics: Special Report* 181. Washington, D.C.: Transportation Research Board, 1978.

Gitz, Nina C. *Another Way to Go? Private Commuter Buses in the Chicago Area.* Chicago, IL: The Metropolitan Housing and Planning Council, August 1982.

Goldsack, P. J. "Transit Subsidies: Road to Inefficiency or to Benefits for Users?" *Mass Transit* 10 (November 1983): 12-13.

Herzenberg, Anne Y. "Who Should Run Boston's Buses?" M.S. thesis, Massachusetts Institute of Technology, Department of Civil Engineering, 1982.

Hibbs, John. *Transit Without Politics . . . ?* London: Institute of Economic Affairs, 1982.

Hilton, George W. *Federal Transit Subsidies.* Washington, D.C.: American Enterprise Institute, 1974.

Ho, Louise. "Contract Management and Service Contracting in Public Transit." M.S. thesis, Massachusetts Institute of Technology, Department of Civil Engineering, 1981.

Illinois Transportation Funding 1984-1988 Recommendations of the Illinois Transportation Study Commission to the 83rd General Assembly. Springfield, Ill.: Illinois Transportation Study Commission, 1983.

Illinois Transportation Funding 1984-1988 Recommendations of the Illinois Transportation Study Commission to the 83rd General Assembly. Technical Appendix of the Commission Report to the 83rd General Assembly. Springfield, Ill.: Illinois Transportation Study Commission, 1983.

International Union of Public Transport. *UITP Handbook of Urban Transport*, vol. 1. Brussels, Belgium: UITP, 1975.

Kahn, Alfred E. *The Economics of Regulation*, vol. 1. New York: John Wiley, 1970.

Kemp, Michael A. "Grant Allocation and the Standardization of Public Transport Service in Dutch Cities." In Jackie Garden and Erik MacKinlay, eds., *Service Levels of Urban Public Transport.* Vol. 2, *Report of a Round Table Meeting.* Den Haag, Netherlands: Ministerie van Verkeer en Waterstaat, 1980.

_____, and Melvyn D. Cheslow. "Transportation." In William Gorham and Nathan Glazer, eds., *The Urban Predicament.* Washington, D.C.: The Urban Institute, 1976.

_____, and Carol T. Everett. "Toward Greater Competition in Urban Public Transportation." Project Report 3025-2. Washington, D.C.: The Urban Institute, 1982.

_____, Carol T. Everett; and Frank Spielberg. "The Prospects for Public Transportation in U.S. Cities." Project Report 3025-1. Washington, D.C.: The Urban Institute, 1982.

Kirby, Ronald F. "Innovations in the Regulation and Operation of Taxicabs." *Transportation* 10 (1981): 61-86.

_____. "Targeting Money Effectively: User-Side Transportation Subsidies." *Journal of Contemporary Studies* 4 (1981): 45-52.

_____; Kiran U. Bhatt; Michael A. Kemp; Robert G. McGillivray; and Martin Wohl. *Para-Transit: Neglected Options for Urban Mobility.* Washington, D.C.: The Urban Institute, 1975.

Kolderie, Ted. "Many Providers, Many Producers: A New View of the Public Service Industry." Minneapolis: University of Minnesota, Hubert H. Humphrey Institute, 1982.

_____ . *Public Services Redesign Project.* Minneapolis: University of Minnesota, Humphrey Institute, 1983.

_____ . "Rethinking Public Service Delivery." *Public Management* 64 (October 1982): 6-9.

Landau, Martin; Donald Chisholm; and Melvin M. Webber. *Redundancy in Public Transit. Vol. I: On the Idea of an Integrated Transit System.* Berkeley: University of California, Institute of Urban and Regional Development, 1980.

Lave, Charles A. "Dealing with the Transit Deficit." *Journal of Contemporary Studies* 4, no. 2 (Spring 1981): 53-60.

_____ . "Forecasting the Financial Effects of Work Rule Changes." *Transportation Quarterly* 37, no. 3 (July 1983): 453-73.

Levinson, Harold M. "Unionism, Concentration, and Wage Changes: Toward a Unified Theory." *Industrial and Labor Relations Review* 20 (1967): 198-205.

Levinson, Herbert S. "Peak–Off-Peak Revenue and Cost Allocation Model." *Transportation Research Record* 662 (1978).

_____ . "Urban Travel Characteristics." In Wolfgang S. Homburger, ed., *Transportation and Traffic Engineering Handbook.* Englewood Cliffs, N.J.: Prentice-Hall, 1982.

_____ , and Paul E. Conrad. "How to Allocate Bus Route Costs." *Transit Journal* (Fall 1979).

Lind, Alan R. *Chicago Surface Lines.* Park Forest: Transport History Press, 1974.

_____ . *Chicago Surface Lines*, 3rd ed. Park Forest: Transport History Press, 1979.

McClenahan, J.W.; D. Nicholls; M. Elms; and P.H. Bly. "Two Methods for Estimating the Crew Costs of Bus Service." *Transport and Road Research Laboratory Supplementary Report* 364 (1978).

McGillivray, Robert G.; Michael A. Kemp; and Michael E. Beesley. "Urban Bus Transit Costing." Working Paper 1200-72-1. Washington, D.C.: The Urban Institute, September 1980.

Maher, Philip, and David Hackney. "Transit Nightmares Fade as Area Gears for Close." *Crain's Chicago Business*, vol. 4, no. 22, Week of June 1-7, 1981.

Masters, Stanley H. "An Interindustry Analysis of Wages and Plant Size." *Review of Economics and Statistics* 51 (1969): 341-45.

Mayer, Harold M., and Richard C. Wade. *Chicago: Growth of a Metropolis.* Chicago: University of Chicago Press, 1969.

Meyer, John R.; John F. Kain; and Martin Wohl. *The Urban Transportation Problem.* Cambridge, Mass.: Harvard University Press, 1981.

Meyer, John R., and Jose A. Gomez-Ibanez. *Autos, Transit and Cities.* Cambridge, Mass.: Harvard University Press, 1981.

Miller, Gerald K., and Ronald F. Kirby. "A Matching Procedure for Allocating Public Transportation Assistance." Research Paper 1430-2. Washington, D.C.: The Urban Institute, 1981.

Morgan, R. Travers & Partners. *Costing of Bus Operations: An Interim Report of the Bradford Bus Study.* Prepared for the West Yorkshire Passenger Transport Executive. 1974.

Morlok, Edward K. "Innovation in Urban Transportation: A Case Study." Final Report to UMTA, project no. PA-11-0022-3. NTIS No. PB 82-201005. U.S. Department of Transportation, 1980.

_____, P. A. Viton, et al. "Self-Sustaining Public Transportation Services." Final Report UMTA-PA-11-0017-80-2. Philadelphia: University of Pennsylvania, Civil and Urban Engineering Department, November 1979.

_____, and Stephen E. Krouk. "Variations in Driver Wage Rates and Opportunities for Transport Cost Reduction." *Proceedings, Transportation Research Forum* 24 (1983): 108-15.

_____; Walter M. Kulash; and Hugo L. Vandersypen. "Effect of Reduced Fare Plans for the Elderly on Transit System Routes." Report 93-P-75058/5-01 to UMTA, Northwestern University, 1971.

Morlok, O. A. "Attitudes and Mode Choice Behavior for Work Trips of Chicago Suburbanites." M.S. thesis, Loyola University, Urban Studies Program, 1974.

Moving People: An Introduction to Public Transportation. Prepared by the University of Illinois at Chicago Circle, School of Urban Sciences. Washington, D.C.: Urban Mass Transportation Administration, January 1980.

Moving People: The Case for Public Transportation. Prepared by the University of Illinois at Chicago Circle, School of Urban Sciences. Washington, D.C.: Urban Mass Transportation Administration, 1980.

New York City Department of City Planning. "Bus Franchise Review Criteria: Final Report." (n.d.)

New York City Department of Transportation. "Better Integration of Transportation Modes Project." Final Report. New York: NYCDT, 1977.

New York State Department of Transportation, Transit Division. "1982 Report on Transit Operating Performance in New York State." Albany, N.Y., 1982.

Newman, D. A., and M. Holoszyc. "Evaluation of the Rochester, New York Community Transit Service Demonstration." Prepared for UMTA under contract DOT-TSC-1416 by Systan Inc. of Los Altos, California, 1980.

Oram, Richard L. "Peak-Period Supplements: The Contemporary Economics of Urban Bus Transport in the U.K. and the U.S.A." In D. Diamond and J. B. McLoughlin, eds., *Progress in Planning* 12 (1979): 81-154.

Philips, I., and J. W. Rat. "The Effectiveness and Benefits of Financial Support for Public Transport." Paper presented at the 45th International Congress of the International Union of Public Transport, Rio de Janeiro, Brazil, 1983.

Pickerell, Don H. "The Causes of Rising Transit Operating Deficits." UMTA report MA-11-0037. Washington, D.C., July 1983.

Pucher, John; Anders Markstedt; and Ira Hirshman. "Impacts of Subsidies on the Costs of Urban Public Transport." *Journal of Transport Economics and Policy* 17, no. 2 (1983): 155-76.

Purchase of Service Agreement Between Regional Transportation Authority and Chicago and North Western Transportation Company July 1, 1979–June 30, 1983. Chicago: Regional Transportation Authority, October 1980.

Ramsey, James B. "Selling the Subways in New York: Wild-Eyed Radicalism or the Only Feasible Solution?" New York: New York University, C. V. Starr Center for Applied Economics, 1981.

Regional Transportation Authority: Future Financing, Structure, and Operations. Chicago: The Metropolitan Housing and Planning Council. December 1980.

Reilly, John M. "Transit Costs During Peak and Off-Peak Hours." *Transportation Research Record* 625 (1977).

Report and Recommendations to the Eightieth General Assembly. Springfield, Ill.: State of Illinois Legislative Advisory Committee to the Regional Transportation Authority, March 1977.

Richards, Martin G. *The Role of Buses in Urban Transport.* London: Institution of Civil Engineers, forthcoming.

Roth, Gabriel, and George G. Wynne. *Free Enterprise Urban Transportation.* Learning from Abroad Series, no. 5. Washington, D.C.: Council for International Urban Liaison, 1982.

Samuel, Peter. "Unload the Subways." *Reason* 14, no. 1 (1982): 23–32.

Schmenner, Roger W. *Operating Subsidies for Buses: The Case of Connecticut.* Washington, D.C.: U.S. Department of Transportation, Program of University Research, 1974.

Schroeder, Werner W. *Metropolitan Transit Research Study.* Chicago: Chicago Transit Board, 1954.

Shreiber, Chanoch. "Economic Reasons for Price and Entry Regulation of Taxicabs." *Journal of Transport Economics and Policy* 9 (1975): 268–79.

_____ . "Economic Reasons for Price and Entry Regulation of Taxicabs: A Rejoinder." *Journal of Transport Economics and Policy* 11 (1977): 298–304.

Sosslau, Arthur B. *Home to Work Trips and Travel.* 1977 Nationwide Personal Transportation Study, Report 4. Washington, D.C.: Federal Highway Administration, Highway Statistics Division, December 1980.

Southern California Association of Governments. *Commuter and Express Bus Service in the SCAG Region: A Policy Analysis of Public and Private Operations.* U.S. Department of Transportation, Office of Technology Sharing, 1982.

Systems Surveillance and Operations Planning Divisions, in cooperation with Transportation Operations Committee. *CTA Strike Impacts.* Chicago Area Transportation Study. Chicago, March 1980.

Teal, Roger; Mary Berglund; and Terry Nemer. "Urban Transportation Deregulation in Arizona." *Transportation Research Record* (in press).

Teal, Roger, and Genevieve Giuliano. "Increasing the Role of the Private Sector in Commuter Bus Service Provision." Built Environment 8 (1983): 172–83.

Tecson, Joseph A. "The Regional Transportation Authority in Northeastern Illinois." *Chicago Bar Record*, May-June 1975 and July-August 1975.

Tramco Incorporated. *A Study to Develop Policy Recommendations Designed to Upgrade Intercity Bus Service in Massachusetts.* Prepared for the Executive Office of Transportation and Construction, Massachusetts Department of Transportation. Cambridge, Mass.: Tramco Inc., April 1980.

Transportation Research Board. "Transit Operating Subsidies." *Transportation Research Record* 573. Washington, D.C.: Transportation Research Board, 1976.

Tri-State Regional Planning Commission. "Interim Technical Reports 4594-1206, 2126, 2127: Public Transportation Equipment, 1975." New York: Tri-State Regional Planning Commission, 1976.

Tunbridge, R. J., and R. L. Jackson. "The Economics of Stage Carriage Operation by Private Bus and Coach Companies." Laboratory Report 952. Crowthorne, England: Transportation and Road Research Laboratory, 1980.

Twentieth Annual Report of Board of Supervising Engineers Chicago Traction. Covering period ended January 31, 1927. Chicago: The Board, 1927.

U.K. Transport and Road Research Laboratory. *Symposium on the Costing of Bus Operations.* Supplementary Report 180UC. Crowthorne, England: U.K. Department of the Environment, Transport and Road Research Laboratory, 1975.

U.S. Bureau of Labor Statistics. *Handbook of Labor Statistics.* Washington, D.C.: Government Printing Office, 1977.

U.S. Department of Transportation. *National Transportation Report.* Washington, D.C.: Government Printing Office, 1975.

U.S. Department of Transportation. *Taxicab Innovations: Services and Regulations.* Washington, D.C.: Government Printing Office, 1980.

U.S. Department of Transportation. Urban Mass Transportation Administration. *Second Section-15 Annual Report.* 1982.

Valente, Paula. "Final Report: Public Transportation Management Project." Washington, D.C.: Internation City Management Association, 1983. (Unpublished.)

Viton, P. A. "Eliciting Transit Services." *Journal of Regional Science* 22 (1982): 57-71.

_____. "On Competition and Redundancy in Urban Transportation." Berkeley: University of California, Institute of Urban and Regional Development, 1980.

_____. "The Possibility of Profitable Bus Service." *Journal of Transport Economics and Policy* 14 (1979): 295-314.

_____. *Redundancy in Public Transit. Vol. II: The Profits of Competition in Public Transit.* Berkeley: University of California, Institute of Urban and Regional Development, 1980.

_____. "A Translog Cost Function for Urban Bus Transit." *Journal of Industrial Economics* 29 (1981): 287-304.

_____ ; E. K. Morlok; et al. "The Feasibility and Desirability of Privately-Provided Transit Services." Final Report of UMTA, project no. PA-11-0027. Philadelphia: University of Pennsylvania, Civil Engineering Department and Regional Science Department.

Wallis, Ian P. "Private Bus Operations in Urban Areas—Their Economics and Role." *Traffic Engineering and Control* 21, no. 12 (1980): 605-10.

Walder, Jay H. "Commuter Van Service on Staten Island." M.S. thesis, Harvard University, John F. Kennedy School of Government, April 1983.

Walters, A. A. "Costs and Scale of Bus Services." Staff Working Paper 325. Washington, D.C.: The World Bank, 1979.

Webster, F. V. "The Importance of Cost Minimisation in Public Transport Operations." TRRL Supplementary Report 766. Crowthorne, England: Transport and Road Research Laboratory, 1983.

Williams, David J. "The Economic Reasons for Price and Entry Regulation of Taxicabs. A Comment." *Journal of Transport Economics and Policy* 14 (1980): 105-12.

Womack, James P., and Alan Altshuler. "An Examination of the Transit Funding Process at the Local Level." Washington, D.C.: Urban Mass Transportation Administration, 1979.

INDEX

ACCESS, 207–8
Adelaide, Australia, 223 (Fig.)
Ad hoc transportation negotiations, 316–18
Administration, public v. private ownership and, 224
Advertising, 262
Africa, 186, 229
Airlines, 122
Airport Limousine Company, 91
Airports, concentration of taxi service at, 189–92 *passim*
Alameda–Contra Costa Transit System, 243
Albany, New York, 145 (table), 246
Alexandria, Virginia, 271, 329
Allstate Insurance, 51, 68
Amalgamated Transit Union, 48
Amalgamated Transit Union, Local Division 1177, 96
Amalgamated Association of Street Railway Employees, 39
American Electric Railway Association, 38, 42
American Public Transit Association, 330
Amtrak, 122
Anderson, Shirley C., 238
Annapolis, Maryland, 271, 319

Ann Arbor Transportation Authority, 195–96
Annual Housing Survey (1980), 257
Antelope Valley Bus, Inc., 158–60, 168–69
Ardmore, Pennsylvania, 330
Argentina, 186
Argentine Ministry of Public Works and Services, 218
Arizona, 289
Arnett Cab, 194–95
Asia, 186, 226, 229
Association of Suburban Railroads, 59
Atlanta, Georgia, 183, 185 (table), 186, 187 (table), 189–90, 191
Atlanta Chamber of Commerce, 190
Atlantic City, New Jersey, 37, 132, 148
Austin, Texas, 201–2, 209, 211
Australia, 221–25, 226, 236 & table
Automated guideway transit system, 319
Automobiles. *See also* Carpools; Courtesy cars
    alternatives to, 105, 106 (table), 117, 128–30, 161, 169
    and commuter preferences, 257–58, 281
    cost-effectiveness of, xx–xxi

as feeder to rapid transit, 249
impact of, on urbanization, 43–44
operating cost of, 140 (table), 141
relief of congestion from, 322–23
restriction of, as common carrier, 41
supplanting of public transit by,
    46–47
use of, as common carrier, 36–37
use of, v. transit fares, 261

Baltimore, Maryland, 329
Bangkok, Thailand, 226, 227
Bangkok Mass Transit Authority, 227
Baumol, William J., 247
Baxter Laboratories, 68
Bay City, Michigan, 38
Belfast, 218–20
Benefit assessments, 315
Benefit-sharing, 313
Binghampton County Transit, 145
    (table)
Birmingham, Alabama, 319, 327
Birney, Charles O., 42
Birney car, 42, 43
Bishop Ranch, 321
Black taxis, 218–20
Blue Cab Company, 70–71
Board of Estimates, NYC, 124–25
Boards, transit
    and management incentives, 300
    negotiation of efficiency objectives
        by, 309
    rewarding of efficiency by, 302–6
Bombay, India, 226
Boston, Massachusetts, 1, 32, 40, 43,
    45, 47, 132n
    bus service in, 135 (table), 137 (Fig.)
    commuter buses in, 153–58 passim,
        154 (table), 170, 173, 174, 176,
        177
    commuter rail in, 138 (table), 139
        (Fig.)
    contract services in, 282
    cooperative financing in, 318
    fiscal crisis in, 281
    labor costs in, 243
    modification of monopoly in, 290
    taxi service in, 185 (table), 187
        (table)
Boyd, Hayden, 44
Bradford, England, 250

Bridgewater, New Jersey, 317
Brisbane, Australia, 223 (Fig.)
Brokerages and taxi services, 202,
    206–8, 211. See also Paratransit
    brokerage program
Bronx, New York, 126, 139, 140
    (table)
Brooklyn, New York, 104, 315
Brower, Abraham, 32
Buenos Aires, Argentina, 216, 217–18,
    229, 230–31
Buffalo, New York, 39
Bureau of Franchises, NYC, 102,
    105–6, 124
Burlington Northern, 136, 146 (table)
Buses. See also Express buses; Fixed-
    route service; Microbuses; Mini-
    buses; Regular-route commuter
    buses
    alternatives to, 106 (table), 219–20
    community sponsorship of, 271
    as competition for streetcars, 36, 38,
        42
    in competitive market, 215, 285,
        286, 288–89
    cooperative management of, 319
    cost-effectiveness of, 228–29
    costs of, 144, 145 (table), 147, 234
        (table), 259–60
        v. combination of inputs, 244–45
        v. degree of competitiveness,
            240–41
        labor input as factor in, 242
            (table), 242–43
        v. mode of ownership, 220–26,
            236 (table), 236–39 passim,
            237 (table)
    and economies of scale, 246, 247
    efficiency of, v. organizational scale,
        226–27
    and management efficiency, 261–62
    monopoly control of, 278
    as natural monopoly, 285
    peaking patterns for, 247, 250
    private commuter, 51. See also
        Buspools; Commuter bus clubs
    private management of, 324
    private operation of, 327
    prospects for privatization of,
        151–52
    regulation of, by route associations,
        231

and relaxation of entry restrictions, 290-91, 292, 297
service characteristics of, 133-34, 135 (table), 137 (Fig.)
and service redesign, 260, 262-65
subsidization of, 47
technical innovations in, 45
use of, v. urbanization patterns, 45, 46
Bus lines
cartelization of, 40-41
consolidation of, 55
contracting of, 61
incorporation of, into regional transit, 60
regulation of vanpools as, 105-6
Buspools, 169. *See also* Commuter bus clubs
areas served by, 154 (table)
cost-effectiveness of, 171, 172 (table 7-4), 173
definition of, 153, 155
market for, 174
and peak-hour service, 83, 279
service characteristics of, 158-62
and service redesign, 263, 264
Buyout of commuter rail service, 64. *See also* Public ownership

Cable cars, 33-34, 313, 330
Cairo, Egypt, 192
Calcutta, India
competitive transit in, 215
public v. private ownership in, 225-26
route associations of, 230, 231
Calcutta State Transport Corporation, 226
California, 209-10, 211, 265, 282. *See also* under city names
California Public Utility Commission, 159
Capital costs
and commuter bus efficiency, 171, 173
federal subsidies for, 278, 282
and operating costs, 146
and peaking patterns, 249
public v. private ownership and, 221, 224, 225 (table)
public/private underwriting of, 313-14

and streetcar decline, 39
and trend toward privatization, xx-xxi
and vehicle size, 228-29
Capitol District Transportation Authority, 145 (table)
Caracas, Venezuela, 216
Carlsbad, California, 314
Carpools
community-based, 271, 329
corporate sponsorship of, 155
integration of, into ridersharing program, 167
and peak-hour levels, 83, 279
private management of, 325
and service redesign, 263, 264
Case Institute of Technology, 323
Census Bureau, documentation of demographic shifts by, 256-59 *passim*
Central Atlanta Progress, Inc., 325
Central Houston, Inc., 325
Century City, California, 320
CETA, 169
Checker and Yellow Taxi Companies of Chicago, 65
Cherwony, Walter, 250
Chesapeake, Virginia, 79, 80 (table), 87-89, 264
Chicago, Illinois, 1, 18, 32, 34, 37, 43, 47
bus service in, 135 (table), 137 (Fig.)
commuter buses in, 173, 327, 328
commuter rail service in, 136, 138 (table), 139 (Fig.), 145-46, 146 (table), 288
competitiveness of markets in, 241
cooperative financing in, 318
diversification of transit in, 49-77
fiscal crisis in, 281
operational units in, 226
peaking patterns in, 250
relaxation of entry restrictions in, 290, 297
role of transit agency in, 272, 273
subscription buses in, 283
taxi service in, 185 (table), 187 (table), 209
Chicago and North Western Railway Company, 59, 251
incorporation of, into regional transit system, 126-27

operating costs of, 145–46, 146 (table)
patronage on, 142 & table
profitability of, 125 (table), 127–28, 133, 147
regulation of, 127
service characteristics of, 126–27
service quality of, 136, 138 (table), 139 (Fig.), 140 (table), 141–42, 142 (table), 143
"Chicago Commuter Computer," 69
Chicago Motor Coach Company, 55
Chicago Park District, 54
Chicago Rapid Transit Company, 56
Chicago Surface Lines, 55, 56, 59
Chicago Transit Authority, 26, 46, 50, 61, 126–27. See also Regional Transportation Authority, Chicago
financial crisis of, 51, 59
formation of, 56–57
inflexibility of, 19, 58
operating costs of, 145 (table)
operational functions of, 273
strike against, 74, 77
Cincinnati, Ohio, 261
Cities, demographic trends in, xix–xx. See also Suburbanization; Urbanization; under name of specific city
City of Boulder, 289
City Post Oak, 320, 321
City Post Oak Association, 321
Civil War, 32
Cleveland, Ohio, 135 (table), 137 (Fig.), 236 (table)
Cleveland Museum of Art, 323
Cleveland Orchestra, 323
Cleveland Railway, 42
Colectivos. See Microbuses
Columbia, Maryland, 269, 271, 328
Columbia Commuter Bus Corporation, 269, 328
Columbus, Ohio, 327, 329
COMBUS, 159
Community Improvement Associations, 270, 328
Community Transit, 243
Commuter bus clubs, 51, 66–68, 75, 76, 77, 269, 283, 327, 328. See also Buspools; Subscription bus service
Commuter Bus Lines, Inc., 158–61, 168–69

Commuter bus services
cost-effectiveness of, 170–73
decline of, 170
market for, 173–74
and public transit monopoly, 177–78
regulatory obstacles to, 176–77
service characteristics of, 156–59
types of
subsidized, 154 (table), 155
unsubsidized, 152–53, 154 (table), 155
Commuter club service, 106–7
Commuter rail
buyout of, 64
as competition for commuter buses, 156, 157
in competitive market, 241
contracting for services of, 61
cooperative funding of, 313–14
cost of, 125 (table), 144–46, 146 (table), 234 (table)
financial crisis of, 51, 52
incorporation of, into regional transit, 59–60, 126–27
as natural monopoly, 287–88
patronage of, 142 & table
private financing of, 318–19
profitability of, 125 (table), 127–28, 133, 147
regulation of, 127
rehabilitation of, 281
service characteristics of, 126–27
service quality of, 136, 138 (table), 139 (Fig.), 140 (table), 141–42, 142 (table), 143
Commuting, impact of suburbanization on, 256–58, 280–81
Competition
bankruptcy from, 56
in contract services, 209–12
as determinant of costs, 240–41
deterrence of, through subsidies, 23–24
effects of, 288–89
and federal subsidies, 296–97
implementation of, 289–93
and innovation, 54, 73–74
in low-density service, 280, 291
merits v. demerits of, 284–88
in peak-hour service, 279, 286, 291

regulatory restrictions on, 279, 280, 297–98
reinvigoration of public transit through, 25–29
role of, in service redesign, 265–67
in successful public transit, 215–29 *passim*
in taxi market, 184, 191–92, 209–12
Congestion, traffic
in competitive market, 289
developer-financed remedies for, 316–17
impact of vanpools on, 116–18
relief of, through private initiatives, 322–23
Congress, 4. *See also* Urban Mass Transportation Act
cartelization of motor carriers by, 40–41
creation of subsidies by, 47–48
Connecticut, 146
commuter buses in, 172 (tables)
contract services in, 239, 240
vanpools in, 174
Connection fees, 313
Consolidation v. decentralization, 73–75. *See also* Coordination of services
Contract carriers
regulating safety of, 115
regulation of vanpools as, 105, 106–7
Contract services, 327
as alternative to fixed-route service, 87–89
commuter buses as, 155
in competitive market, 289
control of, 92–95, 306–9
cost of, 175
cost reductions from, 14–16, 237 & table, 282–83
degree of competitiveness in, 209–12, 239, 240
demand-responsive, 84–85
economies of scale in, 208–9
efficiency of, 299–302, 306–9
for elderly/handicapped clients, 85–87
financial impetus for, 80, 82 (Fig), 83

implementation of, 16–17
for low-density areas, 280
and monopolization of subsidies, 177
productivity of, 209
promotion of, 89–90
reaction of interest groups to, 95–99
in regional transit, 61–62
regular-route buses as, 162–66, 168–69
reinvigoration of public transit through, 25–28 *passim*
relaxation of entry to, 290–91
restriction of, in labor contracts, 178
role of taxis as, 182, 193–212
and service redesign, 265–67
solicitation of, 90–92
specification of performance in, 250–52
subscription buses as, 166–68
success of taxis as, 213
unreliability in, 63–64
Contra-flow lanes, 117
Cook, B. L., 243
Cook-DuPage Transportation Company, 70
Cooperation
in contracted taxi services, 209–11
in transit financing, 313–19
Coordination of services
through brokerages, 206
v. decentralization, 73–75
by market pressures, 55
by monopolistic enterprise, 6
and public ownership, 49–50
and regional transportation concept, 59–60
as responsibility of transit agencies, 272–74
by route associations, 229–31
suppression of diversity by, 18–19
Corporate Enterprise (Argentina), 217
Corporations, transit sponsorship by, 51, 68, 75, 76, 77, 155, 169, 271, 283–84
Costa Mesa, California, 317
Cost of Living Adjustment (COLA), 51
Costs. *See also* Capital costs; Labor costs
as argument for privatization, 122

of automobile operation, 140
(table), 141
of buses, 144, 145 (table), 147
of buspools, 160, 161-62
and combinations of inputs, 244,
282-84
of commuter rail, 125 (table),
144-46, 146 (table)
competition as factor in, 240-41,
288
of contract services, 14-16,
195-211 *passim*, 265-66
and degree of competition, 209-11
and differentiation of services, 201,
203
distortion of, by subsidies, 1-2
of elderly/handicapped services,
86 (table), 86-87, 92 (table)
of express buses, 108-14 *passim*,
125 (table), 144, 145 (table), 147
of fixed-route service, 80, 82 (Fig.),
83, 88 (table), 92 (table)
hidden, of consolidation, 73
labor input as factor in, 241-44
and management efficiency, 261-62
v. mode of ownership, 220-26,
235-40
of parallel transportation, 269, 270,
271
of production, 7-8
recovery of, 55, 56
of regular-route buses, 158, 163,
165, 168-69
of ridesharing, 88 (table), 92 (table)
scale economies as determinant of,
245-47
and service contract provisions, 175
and service redesign, 262-65
v. size of operating unit, 226-28
of standardization, 62-63
of subscription services, 66-67,
167-68, 169
of taxi deregulation, 191-92
upward trend in, 7-10, 12, 234-35,
259-60
variation of, with peaking patterns,
247-50
v. vehicle size, 228-29
Cost-sharing, 313
County Connection Transit, 243
Coupons, taxi, 205-6

Courtesy cars, 71-72
Courts (federal and state) and contract
services, 96
Cream-skimming, 2, 9, 10, 101,
107-8, 123, 147-48, 285
Cross-subsidization, 5
as incentive to competition, 36
and social objectives, 285, 286
of streetcar routes, 34, 36

Dallas, Texas
infrastructure of, 319
private transportation management
in, 325, 326
relaxation of entry restrictions in,
298
taxi service in, 185 (table), 209
Dallas Area Rapid Transit Authority
contracting of services by, 265-66
as policymaking body, 273-74
DART (San Diego), 198-99
Davis, —, 57
Davis, Frank, 18
Decentralization
and bankruptcy, 56
in competitive market, 288
v. consolidation, 73-75
and coordination, 55
and economic development, xix-xx
economies of, 246-47
and federal subsidies, 293-97
impact of, on transit patterns,
52-53
and innovation, 54, 66-72
in marketplace decisions, 20
public ownership as alternative to,
56-58
public v. private ownership and, 53,
66-72, 75-76
and transit finance, 76-77
and trend toward privatization, xxi
Decision-making, decentralized, 20
Deep Creek, Virginia, 87, 88 (table),
92, 93 (table)
Demand-responsive service, contracting of taxis for, 194-96, 198
Denver, Colorado, 34, 39
developer funding in, 315, 316
downtown transportation management in, 325
infrastructure of, 319

Denver Partnership, 325
Denver Technological Center, 320, 321
Department of Transportation, mandating of special services by, 200
Deregulation
  defects of, 252
  of entry, 283
  gradualism in, 289–93
  of taxis, 181–83
    case studies in, 188–90
    cost of, 191–92
    effects of, 190–93
    inadequacies of, 212–13
    justification for, 184, 186
    opposition to, 186, 188
Des Moines, Iowa, 45
  cooperative financing in, 319
  parallel transportation in, 271
  ridersharing in, 329
Detroit, Michigan, 15–16
Developers
  involvement of, in cooperative financing, 313
  involvement of, in transit improvements, 314–19
  responsibility of, for transit, 69
  role of, in transportation management, 326–27
  transit sponsorship by, 271
Development, economic
  and transit patronage, 3
  and trend toward privatization, xxi
  and urban decentralization, xix–xx
Development impact fees, 314–15
Dewey, Michael, 17
Dial-a-Bus, 324
Dial-a-ride services, 14, 15, 83, 86, 194–95
Disabled, the
  cost of services for, 86 (table), 86–87, 92 (table)
  and social services transportation, 69
  special services for, 264, 267
  taxi service for, 85–87, 195, 197, 200–207
Domenico Bus Company, 102
Downtown People Mover, 313
Downtown transportation management, 325–27
Draper, L. P., 36

Drucker, Peter, 302
Duplication of service, innovation from, 73–74

Echols, James C., 14, 15, 17, 197
Economies of scale, 226–29
  and consolidation, 33–34, 73
  in contract services, 208–9
  as factor in cost, 245–47
  and monopolistic enterprise, 5–6, 285
Elderly, the
  cost of services for, 86 (table), 86–87, 92 (table) ,
  special services for, 267, 270, 328, 330
  taxi service for, 85–87, 195, 197, 200–207
Elderly and Handicapped Advisory Committee (Tidewater, Virginia), 85, 87
Electric power generation as regulated industry, 35
Elevated lines, 42
El Segundo, California, 155, 169, 321
El Segundo Employers Association, 322
El Segundo/Los Angeles International Airport complex, 320
Employees, rewarding efficiency of, 302–4. *See also* Labor costs; Labor unions
Empresas. See Route associations
Entry opportunities
  competitive impact of, 25–28 *passim*
  in deregulated taxi market, 188–91 *passim*
  deregulation of, 283
  and economies of scale, 246–47
  effect of subsidies on, 130, 132
  justification of restrictions on, 285–86
  and potential profitability, 129–32
  regulatory obstacles to, 176
  relaxing restrictions on, 22–25, 288–93, 297, 298
  and route associations, 230
Erie Canal, 32
Essex County, New Jersey, 329
Everett, Washington, 38

Express buses. *See also* Regular-route
  commuter buses
  commuter service of, 102
  in competitive market, 241
  conditions for profitability of,
    128-32
  deficits of, 101, 108-9, 110 (table)
    route-by-route, 109, 111 (table),
      111-12, 112 (table), 113 (table)
  impact of vanpools on, 105, 106
    (table), 114, 117, 118, 119
  operating costs of, 125 (table), 144,
    145 (table), 147
  privatization of, 2, 20
  profitability of, 125 & table,
    132-33, 147
  regulation of, 124-25
  service quality of, 133-34, 135
    (table), 136, 137 (Fig.), 139, 140
    (table), 141
  services offered by, 123-24, 126
  subsidization of, 155
  use of contra-flow lanes by, 117
Express Transit District (ETD), 23-24

Factor substitution, 244-45, 282-84
Fageol, 45
Fairfax County, Virginia, 316, 320
Fairfield, California, 317
Fares
  bus, 135 (table), 136, 137 (Fig.),
    221, 222, 226, 227, 231, 261, 265
  buspool, 160, 161
  collection of, by contractors, 307
  commuter rail, 51, 126, 127, 136,
    138 (table), 139 (Fig.), 140
    (table), 141, 142 & table
  in competitive market, 55, 188-92
    passim, 216, 219, 221, 226, 241,
    246-47, 288
  corporate subsidies for, 155
  cross-subsidization of routes with, 5
  decline in, 11, 12
  for elderly/handicapped services,
    85-86
  express bus, 102, 109, 124-25, 129,
    130 & table, 135 (table), 136, 137
    (Fig.), 139, 140 (table)
  ferry, 104
  jitney, 37
  and profitability, 129, 130, 132
  under public ownership, 221, 226

  recovery of costs through, 56, 278,
    282
  recovery of deficits through, 261
  regular-route commuter bus,
    157-58, 169
  regulation of, 34-35, 102, 124-25,
    127, 177, 285, 286-87
  and service redesign, 265
  shared, 88, 89, 267
  streetcar, 34-35, 39
  subscription bus, 167, 169
  subsidization of, 1-2, 4, 23-24,
    148, 174, 222, 226
  subway, 139, 140 (table)
  taxi, 88, 89, 188-92 *passim*, 219,
    220, 230, 286-87
  under contract, 199, 201, 202,
    205, 206, 207
Federal Electric Railways Commission,
  39-40
Feeder service
  contracting of taxis for, 198-99
  to rapid transit, 249
Ferry Building, 36
Fielding, G. J., 300-301
Fifth Avenue Coach Company, 42
Fixed-route service. *See also* Buses
  contracting of, 91, 265, 282-83
  costs of, 80, 82 (Fig.), 83, 88
    (table), 92 (table)
  and low population density, 79-80
  phase-out of, 260
  prevalence of, 121
  privatization of, 89, 148-49
  restructuring of, 255-56
  and suburban commuters, 256-57
  substitutes for, 87-89, 98-99,
    263-64, 265, 268, 270, 282
Fort Worth, Texas, 185 (table)
Fragmentation. *See* Decentralization
France, 318
Franchises
  authorization of monopolies
    through, 277-78
  for express buses, 124
  for infrastructure management, 318
  regulation of fare structure by,
    34-35
  regulation of taxis through, 183-84,
    185 (table)
  service-at-cost, 40
  unification of service under, 34

Freeport, 327
Fresno, California, 190, 315
Friendswood Development Company, 317

Gary, Indiana, 45
Gasoline tax, exemption of vanpools from, 174
G. D. Searle, 68
General Accounting Office, 260
General Finance Corporation, 51
General Motors, 45
Giuliano, Genevieve, 124n., 132n.
Golden Gate Bridge, Highway, and Transportation District
express buses of, 172 (table 7-3)
operation of subscription buses for, 166-68
ridesharing program of, 283
subsidization of commuter buses by, 174
vanpool program of, 269
vehicle specifications of, 175
Grand Central Terminal, 32
Grand Rapids, Michigan, 34
Grant Street Cooperative Maintenance Association, 325
Grava, Sigurd, 216, 220
Great Depression, 43
Greater Dallas Chamber of Commerce, 325
Greater Hartford Chamber of Commerce, 325
Great Society, 11
Greenway Plaza, 320
Greyhound commuter buses, 167

Hacienda Business Park, 318, 321
Hacienda Business Park Owners' Association, 322
Hammond, Indiana, 237 (table), 327
Hampton, Virginia, 273
Hankyu corporation, 318
Harmon Cove, New Jersey, 317
Harris County, Texas, 317
Hartford, Connecticut, 132n., 154 (table), 155, 174
Hartz Mountain Industries, 317
Hayakawa, S. I., 296
Herzenberg, Anne Y., 243
Hibbs, John, 17
Hilton, George W., 3

Hirshman, Ira, 238
Ho, Louise, 239
Hobart, Tasmania, 223 (Fig.)
Homeowners associations, 329
Hong Kong, 215, 230, 292
Honolulu, Hawaii, 185 (table), 187 (table)
Hopkins, Minnesota, 205
Horsecar lines, 32-33, 34
Hotels, concentration of taxi service at, 189-90
Housing Act (1961), 47
Houston, Texas, 132n
commuter buses in, 154 (table), 155, 162-66, 170-71, 172 (table 7-3), 174, 175
developer funding in, 317
infrastructure of, 319
peak-hour service in, 279
relaxation of entry restrictions in, 298
taxi service in, 209, 211
Houston Metropolitan Transportation Authority, 178
administrative costs of, 175
contracting of taxi service by, 206-7
operation of regular-route buses by, 162-66, 172 (table 7-3)
Hughes Aircraft, 155, 169
Huntsville, Alabama, 270, 328

Illinois Central Gulf commuter rail, 136
Illinois Commerce Commission, 59, 127
Illinois Constitutional Conventions (1870 and 1970), 57
Illinois Department of Environmental Resources, 68-69
Illinois Department of Transportation, 69
Illinois state legislature, 273
and transit subsidies, 50-51, 64-65
Incentive contracts, 266-67
India, 227
Indianapolis, Indiana, 188
Infrastructure, private financing of, 314-19
Innovation
agents of, 26-27
and competition, 73-74

and decentralization, 54
and operating costs, 146
Insurance coverage
for taxis, 219
for vanpool operators, 114, 115
International City Management
Association (ICMA), 13, 260
International Taxicab Association,
190-91
Interstate Commerce Commission, 40,
61
Investment, public/private partnership
in, 61, 313-19 *passim*
Ireland. *See* Northern Ireland
Irvine, California, 314, 317
Irvine Center, 316, 320
Irvine Company, 316
Istanbul, Turkey, 230

Jacksonville, Florida, 329
Jamaica Bus Lines, 145 (table)
Japan, 303, 318-19
Jeepneys, 215
Jitneys, 132, 184, 190, 231, 283, 287,
292
anticompetitive discrimination
against, 23-24
as competition for streetcars, 36-38
and cream-skimming, 148
suppression of, 37-38, 41-42
Job security, 96
Johnson, Christine M., 6, 17, 19,
127n., 192
Johnstown, Pennsylvania, 271, 319
Joint Southeast Public Improvement
Authority, 316
*The Journey to Work in the United
States: 1975,* 256

Kansas City, Missouri
contract services in, 283
neighborhood programs in, 329
relaxation of entry restrictions in,
290, 297
taxi service in, 185 (table), 187
(table)
Kemp, Michael A., 11, 210
Kempsville, Virginia, 89
Kinshasa, Zaire, 226-27
Kirby, Ronald F., 11, 292
on contract services, 210
on response to transit deficits, 193
Kobe, Japan, 319

Kolderie, Ted, 13, 20
Krouk, Stephen E., 147
Kuala Lumpur, Malaysia, 192, 215,
292-93

Labor costs
for buspools, 160, 161-62
and commuter bus efficiency,
170-71
and efficiency, 261-62
as factor in overall costs, 144, 147,
241-44
and peaking patterns, 249
and public subsidies, 8, 51
public v. private operation and, 151
public v. private ownership and, 221,
224, 225 (table), 226
of regular-route bus service, 158,
163
and streetcar decline, 39
and trend toward privatization,
xx-xxi
and vehicle size, 228
and wage increases, 238n
Labor unions
accommodation of, to private contracting, 96, 98
and federally subsidized programs,
47, 48
impact of competitive markets on,
288
limitation of contract services by,
163
monitoring of contract services by,
95, 96
monopoly position of, 74, 178
opposition of, to private contracting,
96, 98, 99
and peak-service costs, 259
power of, under public ownership,
58
and relaxation of entry restrictions,
291
and shift to private workforce, 267
and transit reorganization, 149
and wage inflation, 243, 244
Lag, regulatory, 176-77
Lake Geneva, Wisconsin, 127
La Plata, Argentina, 218
Las Colinas, 320
Late-night service, contracting of taxis
for, 195-96
Latin America, 186, 229, 283

Lave, Charles A., 235, 249
Levinson, Harold M., 243
Levinson, Herbert S., 247
Lexington, Kentucky
  cooperative financing in, 319
  contract services in, 327
  parallel transportation in, 271
Liberty Lines, 145 (table)
Licenses, taxi, 188–89, 190
Lincoln, Nebraska, 271, 329
London, England, 23, 33, 226, 282
Long Island, New York, 104
Long Island commuter rail, 145–46
Longwood Medical Area, 324–25
Los Angeles, California, 36, 42
  anticompetitive transit subsidies in,
    23–24
  bus clubs in, 328
  bus service in, 327
  contract services in, 266
  developer funding in, 317
  downtown transportation manage-
    ment in, 326
  infrastructure of, 319
  modification of monopoly in, 290
  public v. private ownership in, 236
    (table)
  taxi service in, 185 (table), 187
    (table)
Los Angeles County, California, commuter buses in, 153, 154 (table)
  155, 158–61, 168–69, 172
  (table 7-3), 173, 174, 178
Los Angeles Transportation Task
  Force, 325
Louisville, Kentucky, 315, 329
Lounsberry, E., 243
Low-density service
  competition in, 280, 291
  contracting of, 14–15, 87–90, 98,
    194–95, 265, 302
  cost of, 9, 259–60
  and cream-skimming, 147–48
  and fixed routes, 79–80
  privatization of, 2
  subsidization of, 4

Madison, Wisconsin, 315
Madison County, Alabama, 270, 328
Maintenance
  in buspools, 160
  privatization of, 3, 16
  public v. private ownership and, 224

quality of, 143
  standardization of, 62, 63
Management
  adopting of efficiency objectives by,
    309
  disincentives to efficiency of, 300
  effect of subsidies on, 8–9
  efficiency of, 261-62
  innovation by, 27
  rewarding efficiency of, 302-6
  and tradition of monopolies, 177–78
Manhattan and Bronx Surface Transit
  Operating Authority, 145 (table)
Manhattan Island, 32, 42
  cooperative financing on, 313
  express buses on, 102, 123, 124,
    126, 139, 141
  subway service on, 139, 141
  vanpool service on, 104–5, 107,
    114, 116-18, 119
Manila, The Philippines, 215, 227, 230
Maricopa County, Arizona, 271
Marin County, California, 166
Market system, coordination by, 55.
  See also Competition; Deregula-
  tion; Privatization
Markstedt, Anders, 238
Marshall Field, 71
Martin and Voorhees Associates of
  London and Hong Kong, 239
Massachusetts Bay Transportation
  Authority, 290
Massachusetts Department of Public
  Utilities, 156
Masters, Stanley H., 243
Maxi-Ride, 97, 99–100, 197
MCA Development Company, 317
Meadowlands, New Jersey, 317, 320,
  321
Medicaid, 85, 90
Medical Area Service Corporation,
  321, 324–25
Medicars, 70
Megacenters, 319–25
Melbourne, Australia, 223 (Fig.), 236
  (table)
Memphis Area Transit Authority, 199
Memphis Transportation Company,
  199
Merchants, transit sponsorship by,
  71–72, 75, 76, 271, 283–84
Metrolift, 207
Metro Mobility System, 201, 202-3

Metropolitan Boston Transit
Authority, 157
Metropolitan Housing and Planning
Council of Chicago, 66–68
Metropolitan Planning Organization,
Chicago, 68–69
Metropolitan Suburban Bus Authority,
145 (table)
Metropolitan Transit Authority, 313
Metropolitan Transit Commission,
272, 274
Mexico City, 216
Miami, Florida
cooperative financing in, 313
modification of monopoly in, 283
taxi service in, 185 (table), 187
(table)
Michigan, 282
Microbuses, 216, 217–18
Military Circle Mall, 89
Milwaukee, Wisconsin, 283
Milwaukee County, Wisconsin, 204–5
Milwaukee Road commuter rail, 52,
136, 145, 146 (table)
Minibuses, 96, 98
in competitive transit market, 215,
216, 226, 227, 292–93
cost-effectiveness of, 228, 229
driver costs of, 242 (table)
Minneapolis, Minnesota
contract services in, 283
developer funding in, 315
role of transit agency in, 272, 274
taxi service in, 201, 202–3, 209, 211
Minority neighborhoods, taxi service
for, 189–90
Mitchell Energy and Development
Corporation, 317
Mobility clubs, 330
Monopolies. *See also* Public ownership
alternatives to, 19
and consolidation, 74
and coordination of services, 6, 19
defects of, 21–22, 29
and economies of scale, 5–6,
245–47
and federal regulation, 40–41
federal subsidies for, 47, 48
as impediment to commuter buses,
177–78
as impediment to market entry, 132
institutionalization of, in public
transit, 277–78

justification for, 285, 286–87
and labor costs, 242
modification of, 283, 290
operation of electric streetcars
under, 34–38
prevalence of, 121
private, 17, 239
public v. private, 57
regulated, 252
unresponsiveness of, to changing
conditions, 31
Montgomery County, Maryland, 290
Montgomery Ward, 68
Monthly evaluation report, 92, 93
(table), 94 (table)
Moon Valley Dial-A-Ride, 195
Morlok, Edward K., 10, 129, 147,
148, 244–45, 250, 285
Motor Carrier Act (1935), 40–41
Motorola, 51, 68
Multiple-class services, 19–20, 24–25,
29, 122

Nairobi, Kenya, 216
Napa County, California, 166
National Bus Company, 23
Neighborhood-based programs, 270,
271, 328–29
Newburg, New York, 38
Newcastle, Australia, 222
New Jersey
commuter buses in, 170, 174
developer funding in, 317
express bus service through, 102
modification of monopoly in, 283
user-side subsidies in, 283
Newman, D. A., 243
New Orleans, Louisiana, 32, 39
Newport Beach, California, 316
Newport Center, 320
Newport News, Virginia, 154 (table),
158, 161–62, 174, 176, 272, 273
New School for Social Research, 105,
117
New South Wales, Australia, 222,
223 (Fig.)
New York and Harlem Railroad, 32
New York Bus Service
operating costs of, 144, 145 (table)
service characteristics of, 126
service quality of, 133–34, 135
(table), 136, 137 (Fig.), 139, 140
(table), 141

New York City, 1, 2, 20, 32, 33, 34, 39, 42–43, 47
  bus service in, 135 (table), 137 (Fig.), 144, 145 (table), 327
  commuter buses in, 170, 173, 174
  commuter rail in, 138 (table), 139 (Fig.)
  competitiveness of market in, 240–41, 292
  cooperative financing in, 313, 318
  fiscal crisis in, 281
  operational unit in, 226
  public v. private ownership in, 236 (table), 239
  taxi service in, 185 (table), 187 (table)
  transit subsidies in, 130, 132
New York City Transit Authority
  bus service of, 239
  express bus deficits of, 107–14
  operating costs of, 145 (table)
  operation of express buses by, 102, 124, 125 (table), 125n., 126
New York state, 146
New York State Department of Transportation
  regulation of contract carriers by, 106
  regulation of public safety by, 115
New York Transportation Law, 105
Night Ride (Ann Arbor), 196
Norfolk, Virginia, 85, 91, 92
  commuter buses in, 154 (table), 158, 161–62, 174, 176
  contract services in, 282
  demographic characteristics of, 79, 80 (table)
  taxi service in, 197, 327
Northern Ireland, 216, 218–20
Northwestern Commuter Railroad, 64

Ocean View, Virginia, 92, 94 (table)
Office des Transports en Commun du Zaire, 226–27
"Off-the-shelf" equipment, 63, 228
Oklahoma City
  bus clubs in, 328
  cooperative financing in, 319
  parallel transportation in, 269, 271
  shared-ride taxis in, 267
Omnibus, horsedrawn, 32
Operations analysis, 95
Oram, Richard L., 176, 291

Orange County, California
  developer funding in, 316–17
  infrastructure of, 319
  megacenters of, 320
Orange County, Florida, 313–14
Orlando, Florida, 315
Orlando International Airport, 313
Orski, C. Kenneth, 29

Pacific Mutual Life Insurance Company, 316
Panic of 1907, 43
Panzar, John C., 247
Paradise Hills, California, 198
Paradise Valley, Arizona, 195
Parallel transportation, private underwriting of, 268–71
Paratransit brokerage program, 51–52, 60
  rejection of, 65
  vehicle standards of, 62–63
Paratransit companies, 70–71
Paratransit services. *See* Contract services
Park-and-ride service
  corporate sponsorship of, 169
  cost-effectiveness of, 172 (table 7-3)
  private management of, 326
Parking
  developer responsibility for, 315
  free, 41
  private management of, 324–25
Parsippany-Troy Hills, New Jersey, 317
Patronage
  bus, 42, 44, 45
  buspool, 159, 161
  commuter rail, 142 & table
  in competitive market, 25, 26, 29
  decline in, 3
  for elderly/handicapped services, 86 (table), 86–87
  evaluation of, 93
  expansion of, 13, 18–20
  impact of wartime on, 45
  rapid transit, 42, 43
  regular-route bus service, 156, 157–58
  streetcar, 38, 39, 42–45 *passim*
  subscription bus, 169
  taxi, 65, 181, 195, 196, 201, 202, 206, 219

trolley coach, 44
vanpool, 104–5, 117
Peak-hour service
  combination of inputs in, 244–45
  competition in, 279, 286, 291
  contracting for, 282–83, 302
  cost-effectiveness of, 170–73
  costs of, 9–10, 247–50, 259
  and cream-skimming, 147
  feeder service for, 198, 199
  operation of vanpools during,
    116–18
  potential profitability of, 128–29,
    130 (table), 131 (Fig.)
  privatization of, 2, 10, 83
  regulation of, 176
  restructuring of, 263–64
  and ridesharing, 167
Pelham express buses, 125 (table)
Penalties and service costs, 175
Peninsula Transportation District
    Commission, 15, 26
  as policymaking body, 273
  service redesign by, 264–65
Penn Central commuter rail, 136, 145,
    146 (table)
Pennsylvania, 146
Performance incentives, 27
Performance standards, 175, 308
Permits
  contract carrier, 106–7
  regulation of vanpool safety
    through, 115
  for use of contra-flow lanes, 117
Perth, Australia, 223 (Fig.)
Philadelphia, Pennsylvania, 1, 32, 43,
    45, 47, 133
  bus service in, 135 (table), 137
    (Fig.), 145 (table)
  commuter rail in, 136, 138 (table),
    139 (Fig.)
  fiscal crisis in, 281
  labor costs in, 241–42, 243
  neighborhood programs in, 329
  taxi service in, 209
Philips, I., 238n.
Phoenix, Arizona, 27, 44
  contract services in, 265, 282
  taxi service in, 194–95, 209, 211,
    327
Phoenix Transit, 14–15, 194, 195, 265
Pickerell, Don H., 12

Pierce, Neal, 186
Pikarsky, Milton, 6, 17, 19, 127n., 192
Pittsburgh, Pennsylvania, 39
  competitive market in, 292
  developer funding in, 315
  downtown transportation manage-
    ment in, 325
  taxi service in, 207–8, 209, 211
Placer County, California, 326–27
Plainsboro, New Jersey, 317
Pleasant Hill, California, 321
Pleasanton, California, 318
Point-to-Point Club, 330
Police, ticketing of vans by, 107
Polk, Sol, 72
Polk Brothers, 71–72
Poor, the
  contracted taxi service for, 200, 205
  special services for, 69, 270
  subsidized fares for, 4, 261
Portland, Oregon
  cooperative financing in, 313–14
  modification of monopoly in, 283
  relaxation of entry restrictions in,
    290
  taxi service in, 188–89
Portsmouth, Virginia, 79, 80 (table),
    87, 88, 89, 91
Predatory competition and public
    subsidies, 132
"President's Conference Committee"
    streetcar, 43, 45
Princeton, New Jersey, 321
Private sector. See also Corporations;
    Developers; Merchants
  involvement of, in public transit
    forms of, 313–30
    motivation of, 330–31
  partnership of, with public sector,
    311–12, 331
  public suspicion of, 57
  response of, to entry relaxation,
    22–23
Privatization. See also Contract
    services
  autonomy v. regulation in, 252–53
  choice of vehicle under, 229
  conditions for profitability of,
    128–32
  contract approach to, 250–52
  cost-effectiveness of, 143–47
  and cream-skimming, 10, 147–48

and decentralization, 53, 66–72, 75–76
easing restrictions on, 22–25
and economic development, xx–xxi
efficiency of, v. organizational scale, 226–28
expanding patronage through, 13, 18–20
of fixed-route service, 148–49
increasing efficiency through, 13, 14–17
modification of public transit by, xxi–xxii, 2–3
in parallel transportation, 268–71
profitability of, 132–33
and provider/producer distinction, 13
relative efficiency of, v. public ownership, 220–26, 235–40
as response to fiscal crisis, 233–34
service quality offered under, 133–43 *passim*
and subsidies, 151–52
viability of, as transit alternative, 121–23
Production, rising costs of, 7–8
Productivity of contract services, 209
Profitability analysis, 128–32
Project Mobility, 211
Providence, Rhode Island, 34, 39
Provider associations
and consolidation, 55
and political decision-making, 52
Prudential Company, 318
Public ownership, 47. *See also* Monopolies
as alternative to decentralization, 56–58
choice of vehicle under, 229
and coordination, 49–50
and decentralization, 53, 69–70, 75–76
efficiency of, v. organizational scale, 226–27
and entry restrictions, 285–86
of fixed-guideway transit, 287–88
inflexibility of, 58
justification for, 122–23
relative efficiency of, v. privatization, 220–26, 235–40
role of, in rapid transit, 59–61, 64–65

Public safety
in competitive market, 285, 289
and taxis, 219
and vanpool operators, 114–16
Public sector, partnership of, with private sector, 311–12, 331. *See also* Public ownership; Regional transit authorities; Transit agencies
Public transit. *See also* under specific mode (e.g., Buses)
competitive reinvigoration of, 25–29
decline of, 3, 46–48
declining productivity of, 259–60
and demographic shifts, 256–59
diversification in, 274–75
and economic development, xx–xxi
expanding patronage of, 13, 18–20
financial crisis of, 1–2
government intervention in, 4–12
and management efficiency, 261–62
modification of, by privatization, xxi–xxii, 2–3
policymaking/operating functions in, 272–74
private contracting in, 13, 14–17
response of, to entry relaxation, 23–24
service redesign of, 260, 262–65
and urbanization patterns, 44–46
Public Transit in Small Cities and Counties, 260
Pucher, John, 238

Queens, New York, 104, 123
Queensland, Australia, 222
Queens/Steinway express buses, 125 (table)

Railroads
cartelization of, 40
as regulated industry, 35
Railways. *See* Commuter rail; Rapid transit; Streetcars, electric
Rancho Carmel, 317
Rapid transit
cost of, 234 (table)
peaking patterns for, 247, 249
subsidies for, 47
suitability of, v. urban demographics, 42–43
Rat, J. W., 238n.

Reading Company commuter rail, 136, 145, 146 (table)
Reagan administration
  sympathy of, for competitive markets, 284
  and transit subsidies, 48, 277, 279, 280, 282
Red Arrow Lines, 133
Redfield, Commerce Secretary –, 39
Red-tape in contract services, 62
Regional Mobility Plan (Houston), 325
Regional transit authorities, 17, 47.
  See also under specific name
  as coordinators, 50
  innovation by, 26–27
  labor costs of, 243
  noncompetitive contracting by, 239
  policymaking/operating functions of, 272–74
Regional Transportation Authority, Chicago, 251, 283
  and competition from commuter buses, 66–68
  and competition from private para-transit companies, 71
  contracting for services by, 61–62
  financial crisis of, 51, 64–65
  incorporation of commuter rail by, 126–27
  maintenance standards of, 62, 63
  as policymaking body, 273
  public/private partnership under, 59–65 passim
  role of, as facilitator, 75–76, 77
  and suburbanization, 51–52, 59–60
  takeovers by, 52, 64
  and unreliable providers, 63–64
  and vanpooling, 68–69
  vehicle standards of, 62–63
Regular-route commuter buses. See also Express buses
  areas served by, 154 (table), 155
  competitive impact of, 165–66
  contracting for, 162–66, 168–69
  cost-effectiveness of, 170–71, 172 (table 7-3)
  decline of, 170
  definition of, 152–53
  market for, 174
  service characteristics of, 156–58, 163, 165, 168–69
  subsidization of, 154 (table), 155

Regulation
  of buspools, 159
  of commuter rail, 127
  and competitive markets, 241, 279, 280, 297–98
  of express buses, 102
  of fares, 34–35, 102, 124–25, 127, 177, 285, 286–87
  as obstacle to commuter bus service, 176–77
  and privatization, 252–53
  of public safety, 114–16
  rationale for, 4–6
  and ridesharing, 268
  of streetcars, 34–35
  and subsidies, 284–85
  of taxis, 219, 286–87
    justification for, 183–84
  and technical innovation, 54
  of vanpools, 105–7, 118–19
Request for Proposal, 84–85, 91, 99–100
Residential density and commuter services, 67. See also Low-density service
Revenues
  from commuter rail, 125 (table)
  from contracted taxis, 195
  decline in, 10–11
  from express bus service, 109–14 passim, 125 (table)
  from fixed-route service, 80, 82 (Fig.), 83
  from regular-route bus service, 164 (table)
Richards, Martin G., 239
Richmond, Virginia, 34
The Rideshare Corporation, 322
Ridesharing, 15. See also Buspools; Carpools; Vanpools
  as alternative to fixed-route service, 87–89, 278
  community-based, 271, 329
  in competitive transit market, 216–20 passim
  contracts for, 90–91, 99–100
  corporate-sponsored, 51, 169
  cost of, 88 (table), 92 (table)
  cost reduction through, 282, 283
  evaluation of, 92, 94 (table), 95
  implementation of, 96–97
  multi-service, 167

private management of, 326
and private paratransit service, 70
public promotion of, 283
and relaxation of entry restrictions, 291, 292
and service redesign, 263, 264
and transit strike, 52
use of taxis for, 84–85, 87–89, 194–208 *passim*
Ridesharing agents, 271, 329
Risk in public/private partnership, 61, 212
Riverdale express buses, 125 (table)
Riverside County, California, 155
Rochester, New York, 243, 315
Rock Island commuter rail, 52, 136
Rosenbloom, Sandra, 17
Roseville, California, 314–15
Roth, Gabriel, 6
Route associations, 283
coordination of transit by, 229–31
operation of microbuses by, 218
organizational structure of, 230–31
Routes. *See also* Fixed-route service; Regular-route commuter buses
cross-subsidization of, 5, 34, 36
flexibility of, in jitney service, 36–37
flexibility of, in subscription services, 67, 68
R. Travers Morgan Pty. Ltd., 222
Rush-hour service. *See* Peak-hour service

Sacramento, California, 326–27
Safety Car. *See* Birney car
St. Joseph, Missouri, 34
St. Louis, Missouri, 33–34, 39, 290
St. Paul, Minnesota, 39
contract services in, 283
role of transit agency in, 272, 274
taxi service in, 201, 202–3, 211
St. Petersburg, Florida, 315
Sales tax, financing of transit agency by, 162, 163
Salt Lake City, Utah, 44
San Antonio, Texas, 44, 201, 209, 211
San Diego, California
contract services in, 265
developer funding in, 314
modification of monopoly in, 283
neighborhood programs in, 329

relaxation of entry restrictions in, 290, 297
role of transit agency in, 272
taxi service in, 190, 191, 198–99, 211, 327
San Diego Cab Owners' Cooperative Association, 198
San Diego County, California, 317
San Diego Transit System
operation of taxi feeder service by, 198–99
wage levels of, 238n.
San Francisco, California, 33, 36, 37, 40, 46, 330
bus clubs in, 328
commuter rail in, 138 (table)
cooperative financing in, 313
role of transit agency in, 272
San Francisco Bay Area, 130
commuter buses in, 154 (table), 166–68, 170–71, 172 (table 7-3)
labor costs in, 243
parallel transportation in, 269
San Jose, California, 44
San Juan, Puerto Rico, 228, 283
Santa Ana, California, 317
Santa Barbara, California, 289
Santa Clara County Manufacturing Group, 322
Santa Clarita Valley, 168, 266
Santa Fe, New Mexico, 205–6, 327
Schuylkill Valley Lines, 243
Sea-Tac airport, 189
Seattle, Washington, 40, 46, 330
modification of monopoly in, 283
relaxation of entry restrictions in, 290
taxi service in, 189, 191
Self-supporting transit systems
and anticompetitive subsidies, 23–24
diversification of services through, 18, 20
Shapell Industries, 317
Share-a-Fare, 267
Sherman Anti-Trust Act, 57
Shoup, Donald C., 41
Shrauner, Rachel, 16
Shuttle buses, 325
Simpson, Anthony U., 27, 251
Singapore, 192, 215
Smyth v. *Ames*, 35

Snyder, –, 57
Social service transportation, 69–70,
  71, 77, 206–8
Sonoma County, California, 166
South Coast Plaza, 320, 321
Southeast Asia, 239
Southeastern Michigan Transportation
  Authority (SEMTA), 15–16, 17,
  26
Southeastern Pennsylvania Transporta-
  tion Authority, 145 (table)
Southern California Rapid Transit
  District (SCRTD), 23–24
Special interests, reaction of, to
  private contracting, 95–99
Special services. *See also* Social service
  transportation
  cost of, 86 (table), 86–87, 92 (table)
  privatization of, 2
  use of taxis for, 85–87, 200–203
Spokane, Washington, 190
Sprague, Frank J., 34
Staten Island, New York
  express bus service on, 108–14, 124
  map of, 103 (Fig.)
  mass transit on, 102, 104
  operation of vanpools on, 101,
  104–7, 114, 118
Staten Island Ferry, 102, 104
Staten Island Rapid Transit, 104
State regulatory commissions and
  entry restrictions, 176
Steam dummies, 33
Steam engine, stationary, 31, 33
Stone & Webster Utility group, 42
Streetcars, electric, 31
  consolidation of service by, 55
  cooperative financing of, 318
  cost of, 234 (table)
  decline of, 38–40, 43
  monopoly operation of, 34–38,
  277–78
  technical innovations in, 42, 43
  use of, v. urbanization patterns,
  45–46
Strikes
  effect of, on transit patterns, 52
  response to, by decentralized transit,
  74
Subscription bus service. *See also*
  Commuter bus clubs
  areas served by, 154 (table), 155

contracting of, 166–68
cost-effectiveness of, 170–71, 172
  (table 7-4)
definition of, 153
market for, 174
rights of, to dormant routes, 159
service characteristics of, 166–68,
  169
subsidization of, 154 (table), 155
vehicle specifications for, 175
Subsidies. *See also* Cross-subsidization; User-side subsidies
allocation of, 179
for capital costs, 278, 282
competition for, 301
for contracted taxis, 195–208
  passim, 212
as deterrent to competition, 23–24
effect of, on entry opportunities,
  130, 132
for fares, 1–2, 4, 23–24, 148, 174,
  222, 226
federal programs for, 47–48
for fixed-route service, 80, 83
growth in, 6–11
impact of, on costs, 1–2, 238 & n.,
  239
inevitability of, in public transit, 122
legislation of, 50–51
masking of market erosion by, 258
monopoly of, 177
for operating costs, 278–79, 281,
  282
operation of commuter buses with,
  154 (table), 155, 162–69
phase-out of, 260, 277, 279–82
  passim
as political instrument, 4
politics of, 12–13
and privatization, 151–52
pro-labor union bias of, 178
reform of, 293–97
and regulation, 284–85
as restriction on commuter buses,
  173–74
and transit objectives, 301
Suburbanization
  impact of, on commuting patterns,
  256–58, 280–81
  impact of, on transit patterns, 44,
  46, 51–52, 53
  and regional transit concept, 59–60

and transit costs, 259–60
and transit patronage, 3
Suburbs
  cost of service to, 9
  expansion of service to, 10–11
  subscription service to, 66–67
Subways, 217, 218
  cooperative financing of, 313, 318
  patronage of, 42, 43
  rehabilitation of, 313
  service quality of, 139, 140 (table),
    141
Suffolk, Virginia, 79, 80 (table)
Sunday Dial-A-Ride (Phoenix),
  194–95
Supreme Court, U.S., and deregulation, 289
Surface Transportation Assistance Act
  (1982), 297
Sydney, Australia, 222, 223 (Fig.)
Syracuse, New York, 315, 325

Tariffs, railroad, 35
Taxation
  dedicated v. nonearmarked, 238
  financing of public transit by, 76, 77
Taxi and Limousine Commission,
  NYC, 105 n. 4
Taxicab companies, impact of contract
  services on, 96–98, 99
Taxi-owner associations, regulatory
  function of, 219
Taxipooling, 268
Taxis
  as alternative to fixed routes, 87–89
  as competition for buses, 278
  in competitive transit market, 216,
    218–20
  contracting of, 62, 64, 65, 90–91,
    99–100, 265, 327
  and cream-skimming, 147–48
  deregulation of, 283
    case studies in, 188–90
    effects of, 190–93
    inadequacies in, 212–13
    justification for, 184, 186
    opposition to, 186, 188
  driver costs of, 242 (table)
  efficiency of, v. organizational scale,
    228
  financial crisis of, 65

fixed-route, 268, 282
patronage of, 181, 195, 196, 201,
  202, 206, 219
percapita, 183, 185 (table)
prevalence of, v. economic activity,
  184, 186, 187 (table)
as public transit vehicle, 14, 15, 19
regulation of, 286–87
  rationale for, 183–84
  by route associations, 229, 230
and relaxation of entry restrictions,
  289–92 *passim*, 297, 298
role of, as contract service, 182,
  193–212
role of, in deregulated market,
  181–83
and service redesign, 263, 264
shared-ride, 84–85, 87–89, 194–208
  passim, 216, 218–20, 263, 264,
  267–68, 278, 282, 291, 292
and suburbanization, 52
success of, as contract service, 213
use of, for elderly/handicapped
  services, 85–87
Taxi Study Committee, TTDC, 90–91
Teal, Roger, 124n., 132n., 209–10
Telephone service as regulated
  industry, 35
Texas Department of Health and
  Mental Retardation, 201
Thousand Oaks, California, 314
Tidewater Transportation District
  Commission, 14, 15, 26, 279, 280,
  291, 297
  allocation of services by, 80
  commuter services of, 83
  contracting of taxis by, 197
  contracting procedures for, 90–92,
    99–100
  demographic characteristics of,
    79–80, 80 (table)
  elderly/handicapped services of,
    85–87
  finances of, 80, 82 (Fig.), 83
  implementation of contract services
    by, 95–99
  investigation of demand-responsive
    service by, 84–85
  map of, 81 (Fig.)
  monitoring of contracts by, 92–95
  promotion of contract services by,
    89–90

ridesharing services of, 87–89, 283
service redesign by, 264–65
Tokyu corporation, 318
Tower Mall, 88
Traffic Bureau, NYC Department of
Transportation, 117
Tramways, 217, 218
Transbus, 8
Transfers
city-wide, 34
in competitive environment, 55, 56
and coordination, 73
and feeder service, 198, 199
unpopularity of, 74
Transit agencies. *See also* Boards,
transit; Employees; Management;
under specific name
administrative costs of, 175
as brokers, 264
as commuter bus sponsor, 155
as competition for private commuter
buses, 173–74
contracting of regular-route bus
service by, 162–66
contracting of subscription buses by,
166–68
control of contracts by, 306–9
efficiency objectives of, 301–2, 309
and entry of commuter bus service,
176
funding of, 238
labor costs of, 243
as partner in parallel transportation,
269, 271
partnership of, with taxi companies,
193–212 *passim*
policymaking/operating functions
of, 272–74
rights of, to dormant routes, 159
specification of services by, in
contracts, 250–52
social objectives of, 301–2
"Transit Means Business" campaign,
330
Transport Act (1980), 22–23
Transportation Act (1920), 40
Transportation funding agencies, 155
Transportation Management Associations, 320–25
Transportation System Management
Trust Fund, 315

Transportation Systems Center, 204
Transportes de Buenos Aires, 218
Transport of New Jersey, 145 (table)
Trenton, New Jersey, 139 (Fig.)
Trolleybuses, 218
Trolley coaches, 42, 44, 45, 46
Trolleys
community sponsorship of, 271
cooperative management of, 319
rehabilitation of, 330
Truck lines, cartelization of, 40–41
Trucks as competition for railroads, 35
Tycon Inc., Ltd., 317
Tysons Corner, Virginia, 317, 320,
321
Tysons Transportation Association,
321, 322–23

U.K. Transport and Road Research
Laboratory, 221
United Kingdom
bus service in, 285
operational unit in, 227
public v. private ownership in, 221,
236 & table
relaxation of entry restrictions in,
22–23
transit regulation in, 4–5
University Circle, Inc., 321, 322,
323–24
Urbanization. *See also*
Suburbanization
and the automobile, 43–44
impact of, on transit patterns,
44–46
and transit innovation, 32–34
Urban Mass Transportation Act
(1964), 47, 163, 178, 301
and contract authorization, 308–9
funding of operations through, 279
and work rules, 291
Urban Mass Transportation Administration (UMTA), 4, 7, 8, 243, 250
and contracted taxi services,
195–96, 199, 200, 207, 208, 210,
212
and neighborhood-based transit,
270, 328
on paratransit brokerage program,
62–63
revision of subsidies from, 293–96

and ridesharing, 292
study of taxi service by, 188
and user-side subsidies, 204-6
Urban Mass Transportation Assistance Program, 47-48
User charges
funding of public transit through, 76
for highways, 41
User-side subsidies, 11, 77, 148, 204-6, 261, 264, 283, 289

Vanpools, 51, 68-69, 75-76, 77, 169, 291, 297
as alternative to fixed-route service, 89
community-based, 270, 271, 328
as competition for buspools, 160-61, 162
as competition for commuter buses, 174
competitive impact of, 105, 106 (table), 118, 119
concern of city officials over, 101-2
contracting of, 91
corporate sponsorship of, 155
cost-effectiveness of, 172 (table 7-4)
cost of, 92 (table)
evaluation of, 92, 94 (table), 95
integration of, into ridesharing program, 167
patronage of, 104-5, 117
and peak-hour levels, 83, 116-18, 279
private management of, 322-23
reaction of interest groups to, 99
regulation of, 105-7, 118-19
relief of express bus deficits by, 114
safety of, 114-16
and service redesign, 263, 264
transition of, to private ownership, 269
Vans
driver cost of, 242 (table)
lift-equipped, 194, 195, 200, 201, 207
use of, v. urbanization patterns, 46
Van stops, 118
Vehicles
for buspools, 160, 161-62
and commuter bus efficiency, 171, 173
efficiency v. size of, 228-29, 242 & table
leasing of, to contractors, 307
prices of, 8
public v. private fleets of, 224, 226
for regular-route bus service, 165
and service costs, 175
standardization of, 62-63
Ventura County, California, 155, 169, 175
Veterans Cab, 196, 199
VIATRANS, 201
Victoria, Australia, 222, 223 (Fig.)
Village of Schaumburg, Illinois, 51, 69
Virginia, 172 (table 7-4)
Virginia Beach, Virginia, 79, 80 (table), 84, 85, 89
Virginia General Assembly, 97
Visible permiture, 115
Viton, Philip A., 10, 129, 148, 244-45, 252, 285

Wages. *See* Labor costs
Walder, Jay H., 125n.
Walters, A. A., 220
Warner Center, 320
Washington, D.C., 34
bus clubs in, 328
bus service in, 228-29
contract services in, 283
cooperative financing in, 313, 319
open entry in, 292
parallel transportation in, 269, 271
route association of, 230
taxi service in, 183, 185 (table), 186, 187 (table)
Washington Post, 186
Wassell, Martin, 4-5
Watt, James, 31
West Bengal, India, 226
Westchester County, New York, 273
Western Reserve University, 323
West Houston Association, 321
West Virginia, 283
Wilcox, Delos F., 40
Willig, Robert D., 247
Wilson, Labor Secretary –, 39
The Woodlands, 321
Worcester, Massachusetts, 239, 240

World War I, 31, 35, 38–39, 40
World War II, 45, 256

Yellow Cab, 201, 207
Yellow Cab of Chesapeake, 91
Yolo County, California, 155, 237
    (table)

Zaire, 186
Zenith, 68
Zoning
    and developer-sponsored transit
        improvements, 313
    regulation of transit through, 69

ABOUT THE EDITOR

Charles A. Lave, Professor of Economics at the University of California, Irvine, received his B. A. in political science and physics from Reed College and his Ph. D. in economics from Stanford University. He has been Visiting Scholar at the Center for Transportation Studies, MIT (1981–82); Visiting Scholar at the Joint Center for Urban Studies, Harvard University and MIT (1981–82); Visiting Scholar at the School of Education, Stanford University (1973); Visiting Associate Professor of Economics, Hampshire College (1972); Chairman of the Economics Department, University of California, Irvine (1978–1983).

Dr. Lave is consultant to several transit evaluation and planning institutions and has received grants from the U.S. Department of Transportation, the U.S. Department of Energy, the California Committee on Appropriate Technology, The National Institutes of Mental Health, the Federal Energy Administration, the Federal Energy Research and Development Administration, and the Rockwell Foundation.

He is the author or editor of several books including *Energy and Auto-Type Choice, An Introduction to Models in the Social Sciences* (with James G. March), and *Education and Cognitive Development* (with D. Sharp and M. Cole). His articles have appeared in a variety of popular publications, including *Atlantic Monthly, Newsweek, New York Times, Wall Street Journal*, and *CoEvolution Quarterly*. And in a variety of scholarly publications: *Traffic Quarterly, Transportation Research, Transportation Research Record, Journal of Transportation, Urban Review, Policy Analysis, Review of Economics and Statistics, Science, Technology Review, Journal of Contemporary Studies, Journal of Economic Literature, Energy Use Management, Parking, Economics of Education Review, American Anthropological Review, Current Anthropology, and Human Organization.*

ABOUT THE AUTHORS

James C. Echols is Executive Director of the Tidewater Transportation District Commission in Norfolk, Virginia. He received his B.S. in civil engineering at Virginia Polytechnic Institute and State University, a Bureau of Highway Traffic Certificate at Yale University, and has studied urban transportation at the Carnegie-Mellon University.

Mr. Echols has been District Traffic Engineer, Virginia Department of Highways (1959–63); Urban Transportation Planning Engineer, U.S. Bureau of Public Roads (1963–66); Chief of Transportation Systems Planning and Special Project Divisions, and Assistant Director for Program Development with the Metropolitan Washington Council of Governments (1966–72); and Deputy Director in charge of the technical program of the Northern Virginia Transportation Commission (1972–74).

Genevieve Giuliano received her B.A. from the University of California at Berkeley and her Ph.D. in social science (transportation) from the University of California at Irvine. She is currently Associate Research Specialist and Assistant to the Director at the Institute of Transportation Studies (ITS) at U.C. Irvine. Dr. Giuliano has conducted research on a variety of transit-related topics and has taught at U.C. Los Angeles and U.C. Irvine.

A contributor to the volume, *The Technological Woman*, her studies have appeared in several journals including *Transportation Research, Built Environment, Traffic Quarterly* and *Transportation Research Record.*

George W. Hilton is Professor of Economics at the University of California, Los Angeles. He holds an A.B. from Dartmouth College and a Ph.D. from the University of Chicago. He was chairman of President Lyndon B. Johnson's Task Force on Transportation Policy in 1964, a consultant on transportation deregulation to the Council of Economic Advisors under the Nixon administration in 1970 and a member of the Task Force on Railroad Productivity in 1973.

He is the author of *Amtrak: The National Railroad Passenger Corporation, Federal Transit Subsidies, Monon Route, The Cable Car in America, The Electric Interurban Railways in America* (with J. Due), *The Great Lakes Car Ferries, The Ma and Pa: A History of the Maryland and Pennsylvania Railroad, The Northeast Railroad Problem, The Night Boat, The Staten Island Ferry, The Transportation Act of 1958*, and *The Truck System.*

Christine M. Johnson received her B.A., her M.A. in urban planning and policy, and her Ph.D. in public policy analysis from the University of Illinois, Chicago Circle. Currently Director of Research at the American Public Works Association (APWA), Dr. Johnson has been Assistant Director of Research at the APWA (1982); Director of Marketing, Checker Taxi Company (1981–82); Adjunct Lecturer, University of Illinois at Chicago Circle (1980-present); Director of Transportation Operations Analysis, a division of the Chicago Area Transportation Study (1980–81); Chief Regional Systems Analyst at Chicago Area Transportation Study (1979–80); Assistant Professor of Urban Sciences, University of Illinois at Chicago Circle (1979); Visiting Lecturer, University of Tennessee (Fall 1978); and Lecturer and Research Associate, University of Illinois at Chicago Circle (1975–78).

A consultant to both private and public organizations on the assessment of transportation issues, she is the author of *Financial Analysis of the Chicago Taxi Industry* (with D. Thacher), *Moving People: An Introduction to Public Transportation, Ride-Sharing and Park and Ride* (with A. Sen and S. Soot), *Van Pooling* (with A. Sen), and other studies. Her articles have appeared in such publications as *Com-*

mentary on Urban Economic Development, Paratransit, Transportation Research, Transportation Forum, and *Transportation Research Board.*

Michael A. Kemp, a graduate of the University of London, is a Senior Associate with Charles River Associates. From 1970 to 1984 he was with the Transportation Studies Program of the Urban Institute. His major interests lie in evaluating the impacts of public transport service, regulatory, and financing policies. In 1981–82, he directed a study of the future economic structure of urban public transportation for the U.S. Department of Transportation, on which the chapter in this book draws. He has consulted on public policy analysis in Canada, the Netherlands, Puerto Rico, Saudi Arabia, Turkey, and the United Kingdom.

Prior to joining the Urban Institute, Mr. Kemp specialized in survey research and economic analysis for public policy purposes with consultant firms in London. He is coauthor of *Paratransit: Neglected Options for Public Policy* and *The Urban Predicament*, and author of many study reports and papers in the professional literature.

Ronald F. Kirby received his B.A. and Ph.D. in applied mathematics from the University of Adelaide in South Australia. He joined the Urban Institute in 1971 and has been Director of Transportation Studies since 1975. He is also the Director of the Institute's Productivity and Economic Development Center, of which the Transportation Studies Program is a part.

Dr. Kirby's research interests focus on regulatory, investment, and pricing strategies for urban transportation. He has been extensively involved in the administrative and implementation aspects of policy innovations. He recently directed the institutional and policy elements of the Metropolitan Manila Urban Transportation Strategy and Planning Project in the Philippines. He has also consulted in Australia, Egypt, and Puerto Rico.

Chairman of the Transportation Research Board's Paratransit Committee since 1980 and former Chairman (1974–76) of the Transportation Science Section of the Operations Research Society of America (ORSA), Dr. Kirby is the author or coauthor of *Paratransit: Neglected Options for Urban Mobility, The Reagan Experiment*, and numerous research papers.

Edward K. Morlok is UPS Foundation Professor of Transportation and Chairman of the Graduate Group in Transportation at the University of Pennsylvania. He has been Associate and Assistant Professor of Civil Engineering and Assistant Director of The Transportation Center at Northwestern University. Dr. Morlok received his B.E. in mechanical engineering and Certificate in Transportation (transportation economics and management) from Yale University, and his Ph.D. from Northwestern University.

Dr. Morlok has been an advisor to the National Transportation Policy Study Commission and the Congressional Sub-Committee on Land Transportation, and has been a consultant to the National Research Council, the American Society of Civil Engineers, and various transportation companies and shippers. He has been President of the Transportation Research Forum and serves on the Transportation Research Board, in addition to other international research organizations. Dr. Morlok received the Von Humboldt Foundation U.S. Senior Scientist Award in 1980–1981 for his contributions to transportation research.

The author of *Introduction to Transportation Engineering and Planning* and *An Analysis of Transport Technology and Network Structure*, Dr. Morlok has authored more than sixty papers and articles appearing in such publications as *Highway Research Record, Transportation Engineering Journal, Transportation Planning and Technology*, and *Transportation Research*.

C. Kenneth Orski is President of Urban Mobility, a professional corporation offering consulting services in the field of urban transportation. The Corporation works with local government and private sector clients interested in addressing transportation concerns through public/private cooperation.

Mr. Orski is former Associate Administrator of the Urban Mass Transportation Administration (1974–78), Vice President of the German Marshall Fund (1978–82) and Director of Urban Affairs and Transportation at the Organization for Economic Cooperation and Development (1967–74).

A graduate of Harvard College and Harvard Law School, Mr. Orski has had 18 years of professional involvement in urban affairs and transportation that includes writing, lecturing and public policy consulting.

He has authored numerous articles dealing with urban transportation, including a recent chapter on transportation in *Meeting Human Needs: Toward a New Public Philosophy.*

Milton Pikarsky is currently Distinguished Professor of Civil Engineering at the City College of New York. He has been director of Transportation Research at I.I.T. Research Institute, Research Professor at the Illinois Institute of Technology, and Adjunct Professor at the University of Illinois at Chicago. He received his B.S. from City College of New York and his M.S. from the Illinois Institute of Technology. He has been Chairman of the Regional Transportation Authority in Illinois (1975–78); Chairman of Chicago Transit Authority (1973–75); Commissioner of Public Works, Chicago (1964–73); Engineer of Public Works, Chicago (1960–63); Consulting Engineer, Plumb, Tuckett and Pikarsky (1956–59); and Designer and Field Engineer, New York Central Railroad (1946–56).

The recipient of a number of civil works awards, including the Townsend Harris Medal and the James Laurie Prize, Mr. Pikarsky has been a member of the Executive Committee of the U.S. Department of Transportation's Advisory Council and the Federal Energy Administration's Transportation Advisory Committee, a member of the National Academy of Engineering, and a Fellow of the American Association for the Advancement of Science. He is the author of *Chicago Public Works: A History, Urban Transportation Policy Management*, and papers for numerous journals.

Sandra Rosenbloom is Professor of Community and Regional Planning at the University of Texas at Austin, and has been studying the development of paratransit services, and particularly the taxi industry for a number of years. She is currently involved in a study of the potential for privatization of municipal services in rapid growth and Sun Belt communities.

Dr. Rosenbloom received her A.B., M.P.A. in urban planning, and Ph.D. in political science from the University of California at Los Angeles. She is Chair of the Paratransit Committee of the Transportation Research Board and Associate Editor of the journal *Transportation* as well as a member of the editorial boards of the journal *Specialized Transportation Planning and Practice* and the *Journal of Planning Education and Research.*

Her articles on paratransit development and the travel needs of the elderly and handicapped have been published in the *Journal of the American Planning Association*, the *Journal of Contemporary Studies*, the *Policy Studies Journal, Traffic Quarterly*, and the *Transportation Research Record.*

Gabriel J. Roth, civil engineer and transport economist, received his B. Sc. in engineering from Imperial College in London and his M.A. in economics from the University of Cambridge. He is currently serving in the Economic Development Institute of the World Bank, where he is writing about the role of the private sector in providing public services in the less developed countries. His earlier work for the Bank involved transport pricing, planning and deregulation in many countries, including Korea, Malaysia, and Singapore; Bangladesh, India, and Pakistan; Kenya and Nigeria; Colombia and Venezuela; Cyprus and Turkey.

Prior to joining the World Bank in 1967, Mr. Roth worked in consultancy as a Research Officer at the University of Cambridge, and as Rees Jeffreys Fellow at the Road Research Laboratory. He is the author of *Paying for Parking, Paying for Roads, A Self-Financing Road System, Free Enterprise Urban Transportation* (with George Wynne), and many articles for professional journals.

Anthony U. Simpson received his B.A. and M.A. in engineering sciences from Cambridge University, his M.S. in mechanical engineering from the University of Southern California, and his Ph.D. in chemical engineering from the University of Colorado, Boulder. In addition to serving as Chairman of DAVE Systems, Inc., Dr. Simpson is Lecturer at the University of California, Irvine. He has been involved in transportation projects for one hundred communities ranging from large bus and rail systems to small city transportation.

Before joining DAVE Systems in 1971, Dr. Simpson was Program Manager for Ground Transportation, Garrett Corporation, in Los Angeles, California, where he was responsible for the design and manufacture of transportation equipment, mass transportation vehicles, and high speed trains.

His published works include numerous papers, reports, and articles on various facets of transportation, management, computer sciences, and engineering.

Roger F. Teal, Assistant Professor of Civil Engineering at the University of California, Irvine, received his B.S. in civil engineering from the Massachusetts Institute of Technology, his M.S. in civil engineering from the University of California, Berkeley, and his Ph.D. in political science from Tufts University.

Dr. Teal's recent publications include *Private Sector Options for Commuter Transportation, Shared Ride Taxi Services as Community Public Transit, Taxi-Based Special Transit Services*, and *Urban Transportation Deregulation in Arizona.* His articles have appeared in *Transportation, Built Environment, Current Issues in Transportation Policy, Policy Studies Journal, Transportation Research Record*, and other journals.

Philip A. Viton is Associate Professor of City and Regional Planning at The Ohio State University. He has been Assistant Professor at the University of Pennsylvania and Visiting Assistant Professor at the Institute of Urban and Regional Development at the University of California at Berkeley. Philip Viton received his B.A. from Brown University and his Ph.D. in economics at U.C. Berkeley.

Dr. Viton has been economic consultant to many public and private groups and provided expert testimony on behalf of the U.S. Department of Justice in the Eastern Airlines–National Airlines merger discussions conducted in 1979. Dr. Viton has written papers which have appeared in the *Antitrust Bulletin*, the *Bell Journal of Economics, Economics Letters, International Journal of Transport Economics, Journal of Industrial Economics, Journal of Regional Science, Journal of Transport Economics and Policy, Transportation Research*, and the *University of Pennsylvania Law Review.* He is the co-author of *The Full Costs of Urban Transport, The BART Experience: What Have We Learned?, Self-Sustaining Public Transportation*, and *The Effect of Budgetary Constraints on Transit System Performance.*

Jay H. Walder received his B.S. from the State University of New York at Binghamton and his M.A. in public policy from the J.F.K. School of Government at Harvard University. Mr. Walder is currently Assistant Director, Capital Program Administration for the New York State Metropolitan Transportation Authority.

Mr. Walder has been Associate for the New York City Office of Management and Budget, Economic Assistant to the U.S. Office of Management and Budget, and Research Assistant to the U.S. Council on Wage and Price Stability under the Carter Administration. Mr. Walder's contribution to this book is based on his master's thesis, *Commuter Van Service on Staten Island*, written prior to and independently of his affiliation with MTA. It does not indicate a position of the MTA in relation to this issue.